The Spirituality of Western Christendom. II

THE ROOTS OF THE MODERN CHRISTIAN TRADITION

The Spirituality of Western Christendom, II

THE ROOTS
OF THE MODERN
CHRISTIAN TRADITION

Introduction by Jean Leclercq
Edited by E. Rozanne Elder

CISTERCIAN PUBLICATIONS, INC.
Kalamazoo, Michigan 49008
1984

Published for
The Medieval Institute &
The Institute of Cistercian Studies,
Western Michigan University

Available in Britain and Europe from
A. R. Mowbray & Co. Ltd.
St Thomas House — Becket Street
Oxford OX 1 1SJ

The work of Cistercian Publications is made possible
in part by support from Western Michigan University.

Library of Congress Cataloguing in Publication Data
Main entry under title:
The Spirituality of Western Christendom, II.
  (Cistercian studies series ; 55)
  Includes bibliographical references.
  1. Spirituality — History — Addresses, essays,
lectures.   I. Elder, E. Rozanne (Ellen Rozanne),
1940-   . II. Series.
BV4490.S74   248.2'094   82-4227
ISBN 0-87907-855-3   AACR2

Typeset by Edgecombe/Printer and Superior Typesetting,
Kalamazoo, Michigan

Printed in the United States of America.

With great affection and respect
we dedicate this volume to

BRENDA KAY LANCASTER

22 July 1957 - 14 January 1982

and

FRANCIS RIPLEY EDGECOMBE

15 June 1910 - 24 May 1983

TABLE OF CONTENTS

INTRODUCTION

I. THE ROOTS OF MODERNITY

In 1975 a first workshop was held on the subject of *The Spirituality of Western Christendom*,[1] covering its most ancient historical period and the first centuries of the Middle Ages. Six years later we discussed the further development of this evolution. This was the 'Ruysbroek year', the sixth centenary of the death of the great Jan van Ruysbroek. Several towns in the Lowlands sponsored conferences which shed new light on his work. The present year, 1982, is for Europe a year of congresses on the spirituality of the fourteenth and fifteenth centuries — especially in the germanic language areas on Ludovico Barbo and on the Italian Renaissance in Padua. It is also the year in which we celebrate the fifth centenary of the death of St Teresa of Avila. We may properly say, then, that the workshop of Kalamazoo fits in quite naturally with contemporary research in the field of spirituality and is most aptly entitled *The Roots of Modern Christian Spirituality in the West*.

And in fact, recent studies converge to show that the transitional period between one great era and another is precisely the century which is, so to speak, the pivot between the two workshops at Kalamazoo, the thirteenth century. Before then, the major influence came from the cloister, those of traditional monks and of regular canons. And after the thirteenth century the 'modern' age began. When we use this word 'modern' we usually mean 'contemporary'; we say something is 'modern' when it is contemporaneous with our generation. With the passage of time, however, historians observe that 'new' times — times which are 'modern' because they are nearer to the present

— have emerged in the course of that century during which all the mutations of society which were already in germ became widespread, were defined, and confirmed. The tradition of antiquity and of the earlier Middle Ages is the fertile soil, the seed bed, so to speak, of this new vitality within Christendom. But the roots thrust deep into geological strata and convey ancient values to highly differentiated mentalities and to varied social groups.

The chronological space to be bridged in this second workshop was considerable. It was not possible to say everything about each age — no more than it was at the first. A choice had to be made. For each period 'representative' men, and women, were elected. They were not necessarily the most famous. Rancé, for example, does not have a very great importance for general history and Catherine de Bar is only beginning to be known. But in the paradoxical field of spirituality what counts most is not outward success, the surface flap which a person creates in his time. No, what counts is depth. As Joseph Hall wrote, 'an obscure nameless monk' can well be at the origin of texts pregnant with spiritual experience and having vast and lasting influence.

Once again, we notice that the fourteenth and the fifteenth centuries are rich in such people, either famous or obscure. In the sixteenth century, we are discovering in Teresa of Avila — in spite of her strong markings by the culture of her native land — certain elements which she has in common with the Reformation. The seventeenth century was one of rare balance. The very different spiritual persons of that age were able to bring about a living synthesis — more exactly, a symbiosis — of the legacy of the Bible and the Fathers with the heritages of the monastic middle ages, the *devotio moderna* — modern devotion — Humanism, and the Renaissance. On the continent, even more than in England, we notice the confluence of currents from the Lowlands, the Empire, Italy, and Spain. For this reason there are some today who wonder whether we should still use such simple categories as 'Reformation' and 'Counter

Reformation."[3] This does not suggest that we throw everything into the melting pot. It merely recognizes that many of the deep realities of persons and societies are common to every man or woman of a single christian period.

This is why it was important to get down to the historical truth of, for example, Rancé or Puritanism, to get over and beyond the deformations produced by the nineteenth century. Over-simplified and over-drawn images live long and linger on as caricatures. Even today — even worse, I was going to say — the *Vie de Rancé* which Chateaubriand wrote at the height of romanticism, in the full fervour of his conversion, is still being re-edited. Chateaubriand wrote his life as a penance given him by his confessor. We should remark in passing that this was not an altogether new idea: already in the thirteenth century, Jean de Journy had written a romance by order of his confessor.[4] But a biography is not supposed to be a romance. Yet, intense experiences are always a temptation for those who write literature and the recent penitential death of Rancé inspired a beautiful chapter in the book *Sept morts d'amour*.[5]

Just as the tormented life of this passionate reformer fed the imagery of Catholics among the romantics, so the ardent pietism of Gottfried Arnold, Spencer, and A. M. Francke at the beginning of the eighteenth century was destined to leave its mark, as Peter Erb has shown, on Kant, Goethe, Schilling, Hegel, Novalis, Schleiermacher, and Kirkegaard. This whole period of the late *Aufklärung* and the nineteenth century offers a wide field for new research along the lines given by the dense book written by Cornelio Fabro on prayer in modern thought.[6] To the philosophers already mentioned by Peter Erb, he adds Franz Baeden, Feuerbach and others. But this 'modern' period lies beyond the medieval scope.

On the other hand, the patristic and medieval roots of the 'modern' age which extends from the late Middle Ages to the seventeenth century are certain. An outstanding example is given in the richly documented studies of Ernst Benz on the sources of inspiration of what he calls the 'protestant Thebaide.'

The desert models, the solitary life as known through the Fathers of the desert — especially Macarius — and medieval eremitism had great influence on the German and Pennsylvania pietists.[7] Of its heritage from the past, each period and tradition made its choice, passed over or stressed one or another doctrine. But the reserve of experiences and sources produced by the Middle Ages or handed on by them assures continuity and, often, concordance. Arnold, for example, was careful not to be at odds with Tauler. It happened that the same texts were diversely interpreted, but the experiences behind these interpretations were identical. Their lasting and universal value lies in the fact that they were deep and inexpressible other than in the language of poetry. Literature which tried to express or at least to suggest these experiences was always clothed in something of the mysterious nature of the single reality which inspired them: love.

II. SPIRITUALITY AND SOCIETY

The purpose of an Introduction is not to summarize the texts to follow — the delight of discovering them must be left to the reader — nor even to judge them, for this is the right of the experts in each subject. But we can at least try to see what it is that creates a certain coherence between the different authors studied. In the present case we find several common factors.

The first thing that strikes us is that each witness dealt with in this book has been studied not as an isolated case but in connection with the social context of his time and his country. At the beginning of the period examined here a series of social changes occurred throughout Christendom. Does this suggest that we should develop a 'sociology of spirituality'? It has been said that the only point on which sociologists agree is the difficulty of defining sociology. There can be no question of drawing up statistics and computerizing the mysterious experiences in which the traditions under consideration are rooted. But we are obliged to notice certain general facts. First, spirituality is never something purely individual: a person receives the grace of God only within a given group or society and partly by its mediation. Then, every personal christian experience, though connected with a definite group, has by its very nature a universal echo far beyond the individual himself and his milieu. His experience always echoes the immense call which God, the maker of all humankind, addresses to all men that they may come back to him. Christian experience is never to be reduced to or explained by social, economic, political, or ideological pressures. For indeed, it constantly brings into play two mysteriously spontaneous facts: a freedom of the unpredictable choices which men are capable of making, especially within the experience of a genius or a saint, neither of whom can ever be programmed beforehand; and secondly, a grace which further liberates freedom from personal or collective conditionings.

Within the bounds so set for the interpretation of the facts, the works collected here show that a social phenomenon did exist. It is twofold, or to be more exact, it shows itself in two ways, the second being a consequence of the first which is of a more general nature. This first manifestation of a social phenomenon is difficult to express adequately: what happened was that spiritual experience, though still rooted in past tradition, stretched out to a wider and more varied milieu. But, we may ask, what is this new milieu? It would be facile simply to say that spirituality passed from the hands of monks and clerics to those of the laity. There had always been *viri spirituales* and *mulieres sanctae* in various milieux. St Gregory the Great often mentions the men of God, *viri Dei*, taught directly by the Holy Spirit, among those who had no clerical learning.

Yet, slowly, and especially from the thirteenth century onward, new centres of spiritual life developed and multiplied: we may say broadly that they spread from men and women in the cloister to men and women outside the cloister. Perhaps the best word for describing these new centres is the latin word *illiterati*. This does not mean that the people were illiterate, unlettered, but merely that they did not share the traditional culture of clerics, monks, and nuns, and this is seen first of all in the fact that they no longer wrote in the language of theologians, but in the vernaculars which had until then been used only for writing about profane subjects. And once spiritual men and women started writing in living languages they did so beautifully and often produced classics.

The anonymous author of the *Ancren Riwle* began this transfer of cultural and institutional forms by saying that the three sisters for whom he was writing belonged to the religious 'order of St James', because this apostle says that 'pure and stainless religion is to visit the sick . . .'[8] Thus crept onto the spiritual scene what Joseph Hall calls 'the devout Christian', those men and women who, according to Francis de Sales, lived a 'devout life' in the world and whom Arnold called good 'parishioners'; 'mystical union', experiential knowledge of God came within everyone's reach. Bérulle could be read by others than priests.

The wonderful thing is that this transfer came about with no discontinuity with the older social groups and institutions which guaranteed their permanency. Traditional monasticism was still very much alive, as is shown, for example, by recent works on Cluny.[9] In particular, behind all this new spirituality we often find the Carthusians, not so much as authors of original texts, but as copyists, translators, and especially readers. If we may so say, they were a little 'consumer society' of the ideas produced by others, and they beamed out the light and warmth they had thus accumulated. Practically the only way they taught was by the example of their prayerful solitude, and in this way they sent out a secret appeal which was heard by many a man and woman. One of the best-sellers of the whole of the late Middle Ages and again in the sixteenth century was the *Letter to the Brothers of Mont-Dieu*, the 'Golden Letter' written for the Carthusians by a Benedictine who had become a Cistercian.[10]

This hidden role played by the Carthusians supports the thesis that in the history of spirituality what counts most, what has *real* importance, is not what enjoys immediate success on a superficial level, but what wells up from the depths: the mystery of the living God within often obscure and anonymous men and women of prayer. There is no doubt about it, the history of spirituality is a discipline unto itself. In this field, as in others, a possible illusion lies in wait for historians who study masterworks whch enjoyed popularity in their day, neglecting the manuscript tradition which witnesses to the diffusion and real influence of other texts.

Consequently, the Carthusians, the hermits, the recluses, the solitaries of every kind, men and women who lived with God and in God are the only efficient mainstays of this new spirituality. This did not become a mass spirituality, but it was no longer a spirituality reserved for an elite. And as the heart of the radiating spirituality, the contemplative life continued to beat as the model and major quickener.

The most spectacular manifestation of the sociological transfer of spirituality — and this follows from what we have just said — is the transformation of an almost entirely male monopoly to an ever-increasing minority, sometimes even a majority, role for women. This phenomenon is all the more remarkable in that it had to overcome prejudices shared even by women themselves. In the *Ancren Riwle*, a recluse admits in confession that 'by right, she is weak': *debilis de iure*. And she hastens to add: 'my sin is more grave than that of a man?[11] But in spite of all this, more and more women got a new hand: St Teresa of Avila is just one example. But they showed no feminist aggressiveness. Quite the contrary, they kept close, often intimate, ties with monks, priests, confessors, secretaries, translators, and 'counsellors' who were sometimes married men like Don Francisco de Salcedo in whom Teresa of Avila confided. Moreover, counselling and spiritual help was often mutual. The best word for describing all these spiritual ties is neither spiritual fatherhood nor motherhood nor even spiritual direction, a word coined in a later period, but friendship. Already in the thirteenth century Beatrice of Tienen had received from another mystic, Ida of Nivelles, the light and encouragement she needed.[12] In these relationships of spiritual friendship, one person does not so much obey another as both are open to the Spirit of God. In the seventeenth century the Visitation nuns had such an experience, and Francis de Sales, learning from them, analyzed and formulated its theoretical content.

There were many consequences of this double transfer of spirituality both outside the cloister and to an increasing number of women. We have already seen one of them — the use of the vernacular. Another is the importance of handbooks made up of relatively short texts, easy to read and containing a summary of spiritual teaching on some subject, for example, *The Letter to the Brothers of Mont-Dieu*, St. Bonaventure's *Journey of the Soul to God* and, of course, St. Augustine's *Confessions*. A third consequence is the increasingly greater part played by images. Those conjured up by the imagination gradually became the object of special, sometimes quite explicit, teaching as, for example, with Gerard Groote, who wrote a whole treatise on them. Drawings were also made and as soon as it was possible these were printed so people could look at them. This iconography was accessible to those who did know how to read, even in the vernacular, and it was put to the service of the imagination. The imagined world of Hadewich of Antwerp, for example her visual, auditive, gustative and tactile perceptions, her representations of light, water, space and all the realities of life and death, everything that served *minne*, love, is being studied in our day.[13] There remains still an immense field to be researched.

One major consequence of this sociological transfer of spirituality was the rise of a permanent tension between two ways of knowing, and this again is not easy to express in simple categories. But to what we might call the *translatio spiritualitatis* corresponds a new form of the *translatio studii*. The alternatives may be expressed in terms like 'mystic', 'affective', 'platonic', 'Augustinian' on the one hand, and on the other, 'scholastic', 'speculative', 'Aristotelian'. But it is always the same old dilemma — already very acute in the twelfth century — between the cloister and the school. Oxbridge versus the hermitage: it would be worth having a special workshop on this, for it is a permanent problem. In the periods studied in this book, as in earlier periods, there was conflict only rarely. There was even collaboration between those who thought and those who lived the mystical life. The whole claustral tradition from Cassian to the Cistercians and the Victorines of the twelfth century continued constantly, but it gained richness from the influence of Pseudo-Denys and the new insights given by the psychological analysis of the christian experience. For, in the end, the proper field of 'spirituality' is experience. And the personal element of the encounter with God explains the place held in mystical literature by aesthetics: beautiful style, abundance of metaphors, musicality. Even Rancé, a musicologist assures us, was sensitive to musical quality. And indeed it is true that the experience of God can only be evoked by poetry, a language which everyone understands.

Lastly, a factor common to almost all the texts studied here is their authors' reforming tendency, at work not only in their lifetime but even in later ages. For example, Henri de Lubac has shown in a recent book that the reform of Joachim of Fiore still persists today.[14] This reforming tendency wended its way often without causing division. With Catherine of Siena and so many others of every tradition it is seen as a dispute within institutions. But the specific role of spirituality seems to be to keep alive the seeds of dissatisfaction in the face of any sort of compromise between the spiritual and the powers of Church or society. Spirituality fans the aspiration for something better. Without provoking an evasion of reality, it stimulates an attitude of rejection of anything mediocre. It refuses any sort of establishment. In this way, without shattering religious societies, spirituality endeavors to broaden them, to stretch their bounds, to bring them ever more into keeping with the unbounded limits of God, who is infinite.

III.

THE SPECIFICITY OF CHRISTIAN SPIRITUALITY

Without the slightest doubt, Jesus Christ is at the centre of everything experienced and expressed by the authors studied here. There can be a centre only if there is a circumference. But in this case — wonderful because divine — the circumference is nowhere: union with Christ opens up to everyone who experiences and receives this grace what has been called, in recent times, the mystical body and a universal solidarity which knows no bounds. The centre is not self, even a purified, pacified, unified self. Christ is the centre. We are to reach out from him who is the true centre of our renewed existence.

What an exhilarating outlook! And yet, among the witnesses who speak from experience, the present-day reader finds it difficult not to notice a sort of depressive tendency. This is so when we read the Lives — either biographical or autobiographical — of many great spiritual men and women. And the same is true when we look at many of their works, which nearly always have a biological element in them. All these men and women seem to be obsessed with the sense of human weakness, with the gravity of the presence of evil in the world and even in religious society. There are many excuses for all this — famines, wars, the Great Schism, the Black Death and many other calamities which brought about suffering inflicted by human beings on other human beings. It is easy to understand why people sought and found a refuge in the cross of Christ. But is not the contemplation of his resurrection and his glory even more than meditation on his Passion, also a compensation, perhaps even an explanation? There lies, we must admit, one of the limits of spirituality at the end of the Middle Ages. So much stress was laid on the *kenosis* of the Son of God in his dying that it was more frequently mentioned than the spirit of his resurrection. It was not so much that his glorification and the Holy Spirit were either left out or forgotten, but simply that they were not often mentioned and they were rarely explicitly called to mind except by the Pietists and the Puritans.

To that may be added another element which may seem to us to be a limitation, and perhaps it was, objectively speaking. Still, let us not forget that we are considering persons whom God managed to save and to sanctify in a specific society by means of his own choosing. The wonderful thing is indeed that in so many journeys towards God, human beings worked out their spiritual growth without the psychological aids which, humanly speaking, would have been of such help to them. The developments are slow and tormented, but they come about solely under the workings of grace. This is something which baffles us, but the history of souls proves time and time again that it really does happen. Sometimes the counsellors themselves have been led astray. Often the only guide is God above: he brings the soul out of any pathological state, protecting it from harm though not from suffering. He heals, but his love does not always lead along the way of security. But it is by means of this 'test' which, from a human point of view, could well have been dispensed with, that God acts, fashions an instrument, prepares a witness. He makes use of many sufferings similar to and sharing in those of Christ on the cross. It is not always easy to discern clearly between the psychological and the spiritual, the 'psychic' and the 'pneumatic'. But God's way always leads to peace. Historians would like to pierce this darkness, this dark cloud they are unable to explain in the mystery of the relation between a human person and God. But what they notice in these extreme cases — the alleviation of deep suffering by immense joy — at least enlightens them as to what happens to those who seek God, those whom God seeks, and those who finally find him. This accounts for the unlimited variations of the *Brautmystik*.

In biographical and autobiographical witnesses, conscious or unconscious choices rouse our curiosity and stir up our critical sense, but also warn us to be wary of our so-called 'scientific' methods. Spiritual experience and holiness are objects of knowledge which cannot be reduced to the methods of investigation of either the exact sciences or the 'human' sciences, those which are based only on human methods without regard for an element which eludes their grasp: grace. When we have made every effort to penetrate the 'psychology of the mystics', we are finally forced to subside in the presence of this element, which slips through our fingers, which undoubtedly exists even though we are unable to grasp it. It must not be forgotten that all this concerns a union, a unifying love. This unity is won, this peace is grasped at the cost of inner combat — sometimes even an outer one — against evil and sometimes against the Evil One. Happily for us such battles were not spared these witnesses of God who tell us and teach us how, over and beyond such tensions, temptations, and inner divisions, we ourselves can attain peace.

This is probably true too of outward divisions, those existing between religious groups, between Churches, between the Churches and the Pietist movements. Beyond doctrinal and institutional considerations, the sufferings occasioned by these oppositions and the prayers which spontaneously surged up are surely of greater worth, of greater strength, than any controversy or political conflict. What a few have suffered in their identical search by various paths for an identical union with God, surely compensates for the objective disorder which unfortunately the historian cannot but notice. In parallel with often increasingly deep theological polemic and dissensions of all kinds, common, or at least closely related, spiritual experiences have brought about progress in an area which transcends divisions: the area of the existential approach to God, of participation in his love through Christ and his Spirit. Unceasing conversion to God, directed along the same lines in all men and women, seems to be the common reality of every spiritual movement.

At the core of so many variations in time and space, unanimous tradition has been constantly conserved: the liturgy handed down from antiquity, fashioned by the Middle Ages and admirably transmitted by *The Book of Common Prayer*, has always maintained a balance between, on the one hand, faith in the mysteries of God and, on the other, devotional prayers which have sometimes been quite legitimately linked with them. And the unfailingly constant source of all this is the Word of God, revealed once and for all. Variously understood, its fundamental truth triumphs over all interpretations. The Word of God survives them all. In every generation, in every tradition, the Bible read, meditated on, studied, and prayed in a lifegiving way has always been the springboard for the experience of union with God and with all who drink at this same source.

So, in conclusion, it is not beside the point to stress another aspect of the timeliness of the studies presented here: they all attest to the specificity of christian spiritual experience. It has long been — and still is — tempting to compare the 'self-emptiness' mentioned by Suso, Eckhart and Ruysbroek with the 'inner emptiness' created by certain techniques of Hinduism and Buddhism.[15] Rudolf Otto and Aldous Huxley succumbed to temptation and identified the two 'emptinesses' as being the same. R. C. Zaehner reacted strongly, especially in the second case, and a recent study has proved the solidness of his reaction.[16] Perfectly acquainted with eastern and western religious traditions, he admitted that similarities exist between certain things said by, for example, Eckhart and Sankara, but he insisted that this does not entail identity of experiences. It is, however, another matter for the Islamic and Christian traditions: by the fact that both are theist, the Rhineland mystics and certain Sufi mystics are sometimes very near one another and far removed from the monism of the Hindus. This singularity of the Christian experience is confirmed in *The Cloud of Unknowing*, in Teresa of Avila, John of the Cross, Ignatius of Loyola, and Francis de Sales.[17] Zaehner borrowed much from Ruysbroek, especially from his *Spiritual Espousals*. And recently Hans Küng,[18] quoting Jaspers, noted in the same vein that all religions are not seeking the same realities.[19]

The difference between the Christian mystics and those of Hinduism and Buddhism lie on various levels: first, that of the emptiness experience. 'Emptiness is the prelude to Holiness', but it may be dangerous, if 'it is the Gospel's clean-swept house which is open to seven more devils'.[20] Everything depends on the presence which fills the emptiness. It is not enough merely to liberate self from everything and go no further. For Eckhart and the Christian mystics, 'Liberation is a lower stage; it is the emptying-out process which begins deification, belonging to a very primitive, but necessary, time in God's coming to man, but it is a time of "clearing out" before God actually gets there'.[21] So too, there is a difference on the level of the presence: Buddhist 'nothingness' or emptiness is a psychological state of unity with the Self. Eckhart's nothingness is a state of unity with another in God.[22] Consequently, there is a difference in the peace thus obtained: the peace Christians seek is not to remain at rest in the self, since it is not union with God, but a rest in which man contemplates himself in his own eternity.[23] It may be a true rest, but it is a rest without the grace of God. Ruysbroek had grasped that this peace is not the peace of God but another peace which anyone could have if he knew the proper technique of ridding himself of distractions, images and leaving the higher power free . . . . There are two types of peace then: peace in the Self without God's grace, and peace in God through his love and grace'.[24]

Newell comments:

> It is significant that Ruysbroek, without knowing anything of yoga and the techniques of the East employed to bring about this state of bliss (peace) in isolation by the self, knew that it could be done by one's own power — i.e. without grace, if one but knew the technique.[25]

To conclude,

> If a mysticism does not end in prayer and love, it is not Christian . . . [26] in a religion where one must obey the Book, as in Judaism, Christianity and Islam, it is a case of conform one's experience to the experiences of the Book or get out.[27]

For Christian mystics, the Book is obviously the Gospel. Or, more exactly, it is Christ himself, who contains and reveals everything we need to know to come to union with the Father in the Spirit.

Thus, from all the studies assembled in this volume there stands out the evidence of a real continuity and fidelity. There were developments, progressions and continuations which were sometimes parallel, sometimes divergent, but always stemming from the same traditional roots, watered and quickened by a single source, the word of God.

JEAN LECLERCQ

Clervaux

NOTES

1. Papers were published under this title in 1977.

2. Jean Boulet, *Thérèse d'Avila et Martin Luther: deux grandes figures du siècle de Charles Quint*, in *Carmel*, 10 (1982) p. X.

3. Jean Delumeau, *Catholicism Between Luther and Voltaire: A New View of the Counter-Reformation* (London: Burns and Oates; Philadelphia; The Westminster Press, 1977).

4. Jean-Charles Payem, 'La peinture aux XIIe et XIIIe siècles', in *Revue des sciences philosophiques et théologiques*, 61 (1977) p. 424.

5. Gilbert Prouteau, *Sept morts d'amour* (Paris: Hachette, 1981) 189-221.

6. Cornelio Fabro, *La preghiera nel pensiero maderno* (Rome: Edizioni Storia e Letteratura, 1979).

7. Ernst Benz, 'Le littérature du Désert chez les Evangeliques allemands et les Piétistes de Pennsylvanie', in *Irénikon*, 51 (1978) 336-57.

8. *The Ancren Riwle*, p. 7.

9. *Cluny in Lombardia. Atti del Convegno Storico celebretivo del IX Centenario della fondazione del priorato cluniacense di Pontida (22-25 aprile 1977)*. (Centro storico benedettino italiano, n.d.).

10. Volker Honemann, *Die 'Epistola ad fratres de Monte Dei' des Wilhelm von Saint-Thierry. Lateinische Überlieferung und mittelalterliche Übersetzungen; Münchenen Texte und Utersuchungen zur deutschen Literatur des Mittelalters*, 61, (Zürich-München: Artemis Verlag, 1978).

11. *The Ancren Riwle*, p. 121.

12. L. Reypens, ed., *Die Autobiografie van De Z. Beatriis van Tienen O. Cist.*, (Antwerp, 1964) 54.

13. J. Reynaert, *De Bields van Hadewich* (Lanoo: Tielt-Buson, 1981).

14. H. de Lubac, *La posterité spirituelle de Joachim de Flore, II. De Saint-Simon à nos jours* (Paris 1981).

15. This is attested to, for example, by the publications mentioned in a recent number of *14th Century English Mystics Newsletter*, vol. VIII, Nr. 1 (March 1982), where are pointed out connections between *The Cloud and* Vedanta (p. 2), *Zen and Meister Eckhart* (p. 34), *Europe and Asia 600-1000* (p. 6). And we may also recall the reinterpretation according to Zen of *The Cherubinic Wander* of Angelus Silesius, a German mystic of the seventeenth century, in *The Book of Angelus Silesius*, translated, drawn and calligraphed by Frederick Franck, author of *The Zen of Seeing* (New York, 1976).

16. William Lloyd Newell, *Struggle and Submission: R. C. Zaehner on Mysticism*, foreword by Gregory Baum (Washington, D.C.: University Press of America, 1981).

17. Newell, 237-254, 291-2 etc....

18. Hans Küng, *On Being a Christian* (London: Collins, 1977) 101-103, quoted in Newell, p. 63.

19. See Newell, p. 15.

20. *Ibid.*, p. 230.

21. *Ibid.*, p. 238.

22. See *Ibid.*, p. 51.

23. *Ibid.*, p. 225.

24. *Ibid.*, p. 279.

25. *Ibid.*, p. 224.

26. *Ibid.*, p. 226.

27. *Ibid.*, p. 278.

APOCALYPTIC TRADITIONS AND SPIRITUAL IDENTITY IN THIRTEENTH-CENTURY RELIGIOUS LIFE

Religious movements of the thirteenth century, both orthodox and heterodox, sought support for their sense of group identity from many sources, not least from apocalyptic and millenarian expectations.

Apocalypticism (or apocalyptic eschatology): a revealed message about the structure and meaning of history and its approaching end. The movement involves pessimism about the present, a sense of impending crisis, and the conviction of the proximate judgement of evil and the vindication of the just.

Millenarianism: the belief that salvation is collective, terrestrial, imminent, total, and miraculous.

THIS PAPER GROWS out of a question that has long intrigued me: what were millenarian and apocalyptic ideas used for in the Middle Ages? One influential school of interpretation has concentrated upon the disruptive and at times revolutionary aspects of millenarian traditions, but this approach gives only part of the story.[1] The expectation of the imminent end of the present historical age, which is roughly what I mean by apocalypticism, whether or not it entailed hopes for a coming more perfect situation on earth, which is what I mean by millenarianism, was as often a rallying-cry for the defense of the established order as it was a form of revolutionary ideology.[2] The more one investigates the complex history of the use of these ideas within particular social and historical situations, the less any single stereotype of function seems to hold up. I would argue that there is a pressing need for a more inclusive and nuanced model of how such traditions were put to use during the medieval period.[3]

The question of what apocalyptic and millenarian ideas were used for cannot be separated from the question of who disseminated them. The evidence suggests that the most important and effective innovations in apocalyptic ideas were usually not the products of semi-educated renegades from the margins of clerisy,[4] but were produced by the establishment intelligentsia of the day, bishops and priests in good standing, university professors, and even educated laymen.

In the production of apocalyptic texts in the late medieval era one salient fact cannot be missed. From 1200 onward, they came to be more and more the special concern of the members of the religious orders. These religious made use of apocalyptic traditions not only for the customary purposes of admonition, consolation, education, denigration and inspiration, but also for the magnification and frequently the purification of the orders to which they belonged. The majority of apocalyptic authors between AD 600 and 1200 had been benedictine monks, but it is hard to find many authors before Joachim of Fiore who gave monasticism a special apocalyptic significance. Though after 1200 we can find cases of laymen such as Arnald of Villanova and Cola di Rienzo, monks such as some fourteenth-century members of the English community of Bury St Edmunds, and secular clergy such as William of St Amour and a number of Hussite propagandists among the important apocalypticists, the great majority of the key authors of the later Middle Ages belonged to the religious orders. The involvement of the orders with apocalyptic ideas, and especially their use for the enhancement of a particular order's consciousness of its historical importance has long been known. The difficulties that such senses of special destiny led to, especially for the unity of the respective orders and their serviceability to the Church universal, have also undergone considerable investigation. In our own time the research of Marjorie E. Reeves has uncovered a wealth of new material on these aspects of apocalypticism amply set forth in the second part of her *Prophecy in the Later Middle Ages*.[5] The purpose of this paper is not to uncover new material, but to reflect on the significance of this marriage of apocalyptic hopes and the identity of particular religious groups for the spirituality of the later Middle Ages.

Joachim of Fiore (*c*. 1135-1202) was the originator of hopes for the *viri spirituales*,[6] the coming holy men of the apocalyptic crisis of history. The notion grew out of his long concern with the historical meaning of monasticism. From the time of his conversion, Joachim's career can be seen as a search for the most perfect form of the monastic life.[7] In one of his early works, the *On the Life of St Benedict and the Divine Office*, written about 1186, the abbot applied his method of concordances, or exact historical parallels between events in different ages, not only to the text of scripture but also to Gregory the Great's account of the Father of western monasticism and to the monastic office described in the *Regula Benedicti*. A concordance between the Patriarch Isaac and his descendents and the various religious orders in the history of the Church gives pride of place to Joseph. 'This very chaste young man points to the order of monks begun by St Benedict which, as I have said, is special to the Holy Spirit.'[8] Just as benedictine monasticism succeeded the less perfect western forms, the cistercian reform, represented in Joseph's liberation from prison, succeeded the cluniac period when monasticism was imprisoned in worldly concerns.[9] Cîteaux, in the person of St Bernard, marked the second stage of monastic advance, a stage that was the foreshadowing of a more perfect realization of monasticism yet to come in the *ecclesia contemplantium*.[10] The Cistercians of the present are criticized for not living up to their ideals;[11] they must yield to a soon-to-come stage of monasticism when two orders that Joachim finds figured in Enoch and Elijah will preach and suffer at the critical time of the transition to the third *status* of history.[12]

Joachim's three major works, as well as his shorter treatises, most of which date in their finished form to the 1190s after his full withdrawal to San Giovanni da Fiore,[13] return again and again to the theme of the future significance of the religious life. In these writings the abbot distinguished between two orders to come at the imminent time of crisis of the second *status* and the monasticized *ecclesia contemplantium* that would dominate in the final third *status* of history, the time of the Holy Spirit. The two orders were announced as a black-clad order of preachers and an order of contemplative hermits. Various scriptural figures and symbols were seen as prefiguring the two.[14] Joachim emphasized the suffering that they would undergo for their opposition to the Antichrist and his followers. Despite his own activities as the founder of the florensian order,[15] there is no evidence that the abbot ever identified his group with either the coming preachers or the hermits.

Our best evidence for Joachim's beliefs regarding the role of monasticism in the purified Church of the third *status* is to be found in the famous diagram of the *Liber figurarum* known as the *Dispositio novi ordinis pertinens ad tercium statum ad instar superne Ierusalem*, which following a suggestion of Joseph Ratzinger,[16] could be translated as 'The Arrangement of the New People of God in the Third State after the Model of the Heavenly Jerusalem.'[17] This remarkable utopian vision distinguishes seven oratories or religious communities arranged in the form of a cross on a predella, each with an identifying animal, patron saint, and part of the body, as well as respective rule of life. Around the central oratory containing '. . . the Spiritual Father who will govern all and whose direction all will obey'[18] are grouped oratories of the virgin contemplatives, the holy doctors, the ascetics, and the elderly brothers—a hierarchical monastic society. At some distance from these (the specification of actual distances and details of the common life argue that Joachim's *figura* is not to be taken in a purely ideal sense) are found the oratory for the priests and clerics who wish to lead a chaste common life and the oratory of the married with their children. Dress code, sexual regulations, and educational and economic rules distinguish this monasticized vision of a communistic lay order. All the oratories function under the leadership of the Spiritual Father who may well be seen as the monastic pope of the coming perfect state of the Church.[19]

What is presented in this *figura* is more detailed than, but not essentially different from, discussions of the orders and mansions of the third *status* to be found elsewhere in Joachim.[20] What is important to realize is that for the abbot of Fiore the Church was to be thoroughly monasticized in the coming *status*. Just as the third *status* had found its *germinatio* in St Benedict,[21] it was to achieve *consummatio* in the coming monastic Church. For Joachim the meaning of history was essentially tied to the development of the forms of religious life of which monasticism was the most perfect. The church of Joachim's own time, the Church of the second *status* in which the order of the clerics predominated, was to be raised to a higher level in which its various institutions would all be brought under the transforming influence of monasticism. Perhaps the best way to understand this transition is to reflect on the relation of letter to spirit in medieval exegesis – after all, Joachim's third *status* was to be an era of spiritual understanding. The letter is not destroyed by the spiritual interpretation, but is rather brought to a level of fulfillment totally beyond the ken of one who grasps only the literal sense. Joachim never denied that the institutions of the second *status* would continue into the third; he did believe that they would function there in a way that could not be imagined by those still caught in the toils of the present. I have argued elsewhere that this was the root of the clash between Joachim and his followers and the authority of the late medieval church.[22]

There is an interesting paradox involved in Joachim's view of the history of religious states of life. The abbot's concentration on monasticism, the purest but still developing form of religion, was in many ways reactionary. The benedictine centuries were over by 1190; the new forms of religious life that had proliferated in the twelfth century were soon to reach their culmination in the creation of the mendicant orders. The monasticized world of the *Dispositio novi ordinis* could not be taken over directly to serve the identity of the religious groups of the later Middle Ages. The two orders of *viri spirituales* needed some adjustment before they could be easily applied to new contexts. Fortunately, Joachim's remarks on the two orders were characteristically ambiguous and thus allowed for modifications and adaptations to quite diverse groups.[23] It was not the monks who were to profit from this monastic theorist, but a host of other forms of religious life. As Marjorie Reeves has put it: 'Joachimism was a doctrine for religious orders.'[24]

Nothing did more to build Joachim's subsequent fame as a prophet than the applicability of his hopes for the coming *viri spirituales* to the two great orders of mendicants that burst on the scene soon after his death. Although primarily known as a prophet of the Antichrist in the first third of the thirteenth century, the fame of his predictions of coming religious orders came to be more and more widespread. Even Thomas Aquinas had to admit that the abbot's predictions had sometimes proven to be true, though he claimed that this was only by human conjecture.[25] Joachim's dissatisfaction with the religious of his time and his hopes for imminent more holy forms of life mirrored the aspirations of the people of the later Middle Ages.[26] Because he was so good a witness to these strivings he could not help but be taken for a prophet.

The full history of the use of these potent new apocalyptic images — the coming *viri spirituales* and the *nova dispositio* of a perfect church — is complex and lasts well into the seventeenth century. In order to illustrate some of the dynamics of this element of apocalyptic piety in the later Middle Ages I have chosen to present a brief triptych sketching three forms of its use in the years between 1240 and 1320. These three panels have been chosen to illustrate three types of application that might also be vindicated *mutatis mutandis* in later centuries.

The large central panel of the triptych is the history of the involvement of the Franciscans with apocalyptic ideas of a Joachite variety.[27] This interest began about 1240 and continued for centuries, though we shall follow the story only down to the suppression of the Spirituals by Pope John XXII in the 1320s. The panel contains a spectrum of applications of apocalyptic ideas in the service of franciscan identity ranging from those quite close to the characteristically conservative forms found in the right panel (that of the dominican appropriation of Joachite apocalyptic) to those virtually indistinguishable from the radical sectarian use of apocalyptic found in the Apostolic Brethren illustrated in the left panel.

There is much that we do not know about the origins of franciscan interest in Joachim's apocalyptic beliefs.[28] A key problem concerns the milieu in which the most important of the works pseudonymously ascribed to Joachim, the *Commentary on Jeremiah*, was produced, sometime in the early 1240s. The traditional notion that this text was a franciscan product has been challenged by Marjorie Reeves, who finds the paradoxical attitude it adopts towards the cistercian order — on the one hand criticism for its involvement in Joachim's condemnation by the Fourth Lateran Council,[29] and on the other hopes for a major role for the Cistercians in the coming *status*[30] — an argument for its production among Joachim's followers in florensian and cistercian circles in southern Italy.[31] In any case, the two orders of *viri spirituales* of the coming time of crisis are of great importance in this treatise. Some texts seem to make their identification with the Franciscans and Dominicans explicit, as when we are told: 'Spiritually, Peter signifies the order of Preachers, James their lay brothers, and John the other order of the Minors made a little lower than the angels themselves because it is the final order . . . .'[32] The significance of this work, as F. Simoni has put it, is that it represents: '. . . the point of contact between a trinitarian vision of history and an historical-providential interpretation of the new orders.'[33]

Whether or not the *Commentary on Jeremiah* is franciscan in origin, it is certain that groups of friars had begun the study of Joachim in the 1240s. Beginning perhaps from the priory at Naples,[34] this interest fanned out to many houses in the order under the leadership of Hugh of Digne and John of Parma. Despite the valuable evidence given by Salimbene (not written down until almost forty years after the events), we still lack key details of the teaching of the earliest franciscan Joachites, but we do know that emphasis on the apocalyptic significance of the two mendicant orders was an important part of their beliefs.[35]

In 1247 the Joachite John of Parma was elected Minister General.[36] In order to understand the importance of his generalate, it is necessary to consider the situation of the Franciscans at the time. Just over forty years earlier, Francis had begun to attract followers to his way of life. The tensions between the charismatic example of the poverty of Francis, his desire to follow the naked Christ, and his abhorrence of the moneybag of Judas,[37] and the physical necessity of organizing and providing for a large body of followers had surfaced even in the saint's lifetime. His final message to his brethren, the Testament of 1226, was a ringing call not to abandon the practice of poverty and the literal observance of the Rule under any circumstances: 'I absolutely order all my brothers, clerics and laymen, on obedience, that they shall not put glosses on the Rule or on these words saying: This is how they are to be understood.'[38] But the first papal glosses began with the Bull *Quo elongati* of 1230, and under the generalate of Brother Elias (1232-39) the tensions between absolute poverty and modest security, simplicity and learning, lay and clerical ideals, and humility and papal privilege became painfully evident.[39] Elias was deposed, ostensibly on the grounds of autocracy and luxury of life. The next few Generals, though not offending against poverty in their manner of life, embarked on large-scale building programs, furthered the administrative rationalization of the order, and encouraged papal approval of modifications in the practice of poverty. What is clear is that by the time of John of Parma's election strong elements within the order felt that these accommodations had gone far enough.

The new General, though fully supporting the clerical and academic interpretation of the Rule, suspended the recent papal bulls of accommodation and made the practice of poverty the center of his concern. John also made abundant use of Joachite apocalyptic ideas to understand the historical significance of the Franciscans. Though our evidence is partial, there is reason to believe that it was he who was primarily responsible for the dissemination, if not the creation, of the three classical themes of franciscan Joachitism.[40] The first of these was the identification of the Franciscans and Dominicans as the two orders of *viri spirituales* predicted by Joachim, but more familiar in the form found in the *Commentary on Jeremiah*. John may not have been the first Franciscan to make this identification, but the evidence of the Joint Encyclical he issued with the dominican Master Humbert of Romans in 1255 shows that he made ample use of it even in authoritative documents.[41] The second element was the specification of poverty of life as the unique mark of the *viri spirituales*. Perfect contemplation, not poverty, had been the hallmark of Joachim's higher order of *spirituales*;[42] the stress on poverty, while present in the *Commentary on Jeremiah*, still did not play an essential role.[43] We have no direct evidence that it was John who made poverty the apocalyptic sign *par excellence*, but he was the spokesman for those favoring the maintenance in practice of the strictest poverty and he was in an unrivalled position to encourage the apocalyptic interpretation of *paupertas vitae*. Given the strength of his apocalyptic views, and the status he achieved in the later Spiritual party's version of the franciscan myth, it is difficult to think that he did not play some role in this narrowing of Joachim's original program.[44] Finally, if we can believe the late testimony of Ubertino of Casale, John was the first recorded witness to the identification of St Francis with the Angel of the Sixth Seal of Apocalypse 7:2,[45] thus indicating belief that with the Poor Man of Assisi the final decisive age of history had begun.[46]

It would be a grave mistake to see John of Parma as some kind of sectarian leader attempting to divide the order or pitting the order against the Church. Everything that we know about his personality and ideas indicates that although he was profoundly dedicated to poverty, he was an able administrator, moderate in action, well-respected by the curia, and dedicated to the unity of the order.[47] As a part of his aim '. . . to foster the order's popularity and to restore and maintain its good name,'[48] John turned to a distinctive franciscan apocalyptic that concentrated on only the first part of Joachim's double message about the future of the religous life. Although he saw the Franciscans as the *viri spirituales* founded by the saint whose life had marked the beginning of the time of crisis, we have no evidence that John tried to identify the historical franciscan order with the *nova disposito* of the age to come. The point, as we shall see, is a crucial one.

Not all Joachites in the order were as cautious. A young friend of John of Parma's, Gerard of Borgo San Donnino, who had been sent to Paris to study theology, in 1254 issued an *Introduction to the Eternal Gospel*. The text has perished, but we have a good idea of its contents from the proceedings of the Papal Commission of Anagni (1255) which condemned it.[49] Gerard's work was intended as a guide to his edition of the 'Eternal Gospel', that is, the major writings of Joachim, which he saw as superseding the New Testament in the third *status* about to dawn in the year 1260. (Such a crude interpretation did no justice to the subtlety of relation of the second and third *status* in the thought of Joachim.) Gerard gave a key role to the franciscan order in his radical Joachite program. Francis was identified with the Angel of the Sixth Seal,[50] and as a part of his literal reading of the third *status* Gerard appears to have viewed the Franciscans not only as the highest present form of the religious life but also as the mode of life that would be triumphant in the perfect *status* to come.[51] As Marjorie Reeves has observed:

> Gerard picked out, not the prophecies of the two new orders which would effect the transition from the sixth age to the seventh, but the concept of the final order which would embody the life of the third *status* and might be claimed to supersede all others. In so doing he was probably making a claim for the Franciscans which had not been explicitly voiced before.[52]

This insight is a crucial one and can be further extended. The subsequent history of the use of Joachite apocalyptic in the franciscan order, as well as a comparison with the right- and left-hand panels of our triptych, suggests that the use of the apocalyptic *topos* of the *viri spirituales*, that is, the identification of any religious order as the bearers of unique meaning in the imminent crisis of history, could generally be incorporated into the life of the Church universal, but that the claim that an existing religious group possessed the seeds or the form of a more perfect Church to come was radically unacceptable to medieval Christendom.

The secular Masters at Paris, many of them foes of the mendicants, delighted in the ammunition provided by Gerard's *Introduction*. In the midst of the *contretemps* Gerard was condemned and imprisoned. John of Parma, the foremost Joachite, now tainted by his follower's excesses, stepped down from his position at the wishes of the pope in 1257. Such was the respect in which he was held that he was asked to name his own successor, and he chose the youthful Paris theologian, John of Fidanza, better known as Bonaventure. Recent scholarship has emphasized the continuity between the generalships of John and of Bonaventure.[53] As Rosalind Brooke put it:

> Both had to deal with the same problems caused by over-indulgent and over-zealous friars within, and by attacks of the seculars without. St. Bonaventure was more successful: he was not handicapped by a weakness for Joachite prophecies, and he was more constructive in thought and action; but they had, on most essentials, the same mental outlook.[54]

I would agree with this evaluation with the exception of the observation on the role of Joachite prophecies, because a close reading of Bonaventure's *Collations on the Hexaemeron* shows that like John of Parma he too was ready to make use of Joachite notions, though with notable modifications that grew out of his awareness of the dangers of the more radical side of the Joachite vision.[55]

As early as the time of the writing of the *Major Life* in 1261,

Bonaventure identified Francis with the Angel of the Sixth Seal.[56] This formed the basis for the new moderate Joachite theology of history in the *Collations* that were delivered to the Paris community in the spring of 1273. In this work the Seraphic Doctor makes use of the Joachite theory of exegesis,[57] as well as Joachim's pattern of the double seven ages of the Old and New Testaments,[58] in order to show that the Church now exists in the apocalyptic crisis of the Sixth Age. The chief sign of the mounting evil of this Age is the adulteration of christian truth with false philosophy; the positive sign of the coming Seventh Age of peace and contemplation is the appearance of Francis.[59] In *Collations* XX-XXII, dealing with hierarchical order in the Church, Bonaventure shows how well aware he was of the dangers of identifying any existing religious order with the spiritual form of life in the coming age. *Collation* XXII 20-23 sketches an ascending hierarchy of contemplative orders consisting of the 'supplicants' corresponding to the angelic thrones and exemplified by the monks and regular canons; the 'speculators' corresponding to the Cherubim, who are the Dominicans and Franciscans; and 'the third order of those intent on God according to the mode of elevation', that corresponds to the Seraphim. He goes on to say:

> It is the Seraphic order to which Francis seemed to belong.
> . . . The Church will reach its consummation in these men.
> But what this future order will be, or now is, is not an easy
> thing to know. . . . He [Bonaventure] said that the appearance of the Seraph to St. Francis, which was both expressive and impressed, showed that this order would correspond to him, but would nonetheless reach this through tribulations.[60]

Bonaventure's Christocentric theology put him in radical opposition to any claim of a coming age that would negate the New Testament;[61] he also effected a significant modification of the apocalyptic pattern found in John of Parma and revived by the later Spirituals. St Francis, as the initiator of the order of contemplatives who would triumph in the final age, remained a key apocalyptic figure for him; but the franciscan order itself was clearly distinguished from this coming order of contemplative *virtuosi*.[62] Insofar as the Franciscans try to live up to the model that Francis left them, and insofar as they war against the mounting evils of the crisis of history, they are indeed a part of the apocalyptic struggle; but neither the order itself nor the practice of poverty *per se* is assigned the same kind of unique apocalyptic meaning it has in the later Spirituals.

The subsequent history of the struggle over poverty after the death of Bonaventure shows that the Seraphic Doctor's solution was unacceptable to the Spirituals. Despite the pronounced influence that elements of his theology of history had upon some of the Spiritual Party that developed in Provence, Tuscany, Umbria, and the Marches about 1280, a hallmark of these rigorists was their identification of the Franciscans with the hoped-for spiritual men and their lifting up of poverty as the essential proof of this status. A brief review of the positions of three major thinkers will show how this apocalyptic pattern was responsible for the radicalism that eventually forced some of the Spirituals into a position that broke the unity of the order and provoked condemnation by the papacy.

In the evolution of the full-fledged Spiritual program (which we can date from about 1280 to 1325), the distinction between the two aspects of Joachim's view of the future of the religious life began to vanish. The *viri spirituales* and the *nova dispositio* began to merge. At the same time, apocalyptic ideology became less and less helpful for the self-understanding of the *whole* order, as John of Parma and Bonaventure, each in his own way, had intended it, and more and more a rallying-cry for the select few against the majority and eventually for that select few against both the order and the full weight of papal authority, now perceived as the Antichrist.

All the genius of the redoubtable Peter Olivi (*c.* 1248-98) could do nothing to halt this inexorable movement. The provençal Master of Theology was as committed to the practice of poverty as John of Parma and Bonaventure had been, but his emphasis on the *usus pauper* found little support among the majority of the order. Olivi's use of elements of Joachite apocalyptic was more detailed than that of his predecessors, but it does not appear to have been different in intent. His desire was to vindicate the apocalyptic identity of the whole franciscan order and thus to restore it to the model set down by Francis. Nevertheless, there were distinctive elements in the way Olivi set out his program and these were to pave the way for the excesses of his followers.

In his *Commentary on Revelation* Olivi, dividing the history of the Church into the customary seven periods, saw an overlap in his own age between the Fifth Time, that of the laxity of the carnal Church, and the Sixth, the time of the spiritual Church begun with St Francis, the Angel of the Sixth Seal.[63] His view of the apocalyptic importance of Francis emphasized the normative character of the Rule and Testament of the founder as the unchangeable foundation for the practice of the order. Francis '. . . has in his hand, that is, in the fullness of work and full possession and power, the open book of the Gospel of Christ, as is evident from the rule which he kept and wrote down, and also from the evangelical way of life that he founded.'[64] Poverty, along with missionary activity, were the keys to this evangelical way of life. The danger that Olivi dreaded was the coming attack on the evangelical life by a false pope, the *Antichristus mysticus* who would sum up in his person the wickedness of the carnal church of the Fifth Time.[65]

Olivi made use of both aspects of the Joachite program for the future of the religious life.[66] He spoke of the two witnesses of Apocalypse 11 as two poor preaching orders who would withstand the Antichrist,[67] and he also looked forward to '. . . an evangelical order, who, like rational man made to the image of God, would subdue the beasts and the entire earth and would rule over the fishes and birds, that is, all the orders formed in the Fifth Time.'[68] Such texts indicate that he identified the final order of the perfected church with the Franciscans, as does his assertion that authority would be taken from the clergy and given to the *ordo evangelicus* in the Third Age.[69] This was undoubtedly an important factor in the condemnation of his work.

The carnal and spiritual churches were seen by Olivi as two tendencies within the concrete historical Church of his day. He nowhere identified the carnal church with the roman curia, nor did he claim that any living pope, even Boniface VIII with his suspicious accession to the See of Peter and opposition to the Spirituals, was the Mystical Antichrist.[70] But when a pope did mount a direct attack on the franciscan rule and the poverty it enjoined, even the most moderate of the Spirituals would find it hard to resist viewing Olivi's *ecclesia carnalis* as realized in John XXII and the Roman Church and the *ecclesia spiritualis* as being the purified church of the true followers of Francis and their lay adherents. Like Joachim, events were to prove Olivi a better prophet than he had realized.

Two other important witnesses can be used as signposts on the Spirituals' road to sectarianism. Both were influenced by Olivi, both were intimately involved in the events leading to the condemnation of the Spiritual Party in the period 1317 to 1320, and both were notably more direct in their attacks on the Roman Church than Olivi had been.

The tension between obedience to the papacy and obedience to the apocalyptic significance of poverty was bound to prove more and more intolerable as the power of the majority, or Conventual Party, grew and the papacy came to side increasingly with its viewpoint. The brief pontificate of Celestine V had provided a deceptive realization of the hopes of the Spirituals that was soon dashed by the accession of Boniface VIII. The situation grew worse under his successors and reached a culmination under John XXII. Ubertino of Casale (*c.* 1259– *c.* 1330), a leader of the Spirituals in Tuscany, wrote his *The Tree of the Crucified Life of Jesus* in 1305. The apocalyptic pattern found in Olivi received a detailed expansion in the fifth book of this lengthy treatise that Gordon Leff has termed 'a complete Franciscanizing of the Apocalypse'.[71] Ubertino seemed unaware of any distinction between the function of the Franciscans as opponents of the Antichrist in the current crisis of history and their role as the model of life in the coming more perfect state of the church.[72] Even more significant is the fact that for him the Mystical Antichrist opposing the practice of franciscan poverty was no longer an enemy to come, but identified with the two most recent popes — Boniface VIII as his open appearance and Benedict XI as his more dangerous hypocritical manifestation.[73] Confrontation with the papacy had now become direct.

Angelo of Clareno, a leader of the Spirituals in the Marches of Ancona, had been imprisoned for his beliefs before being allowed to go off on mission to Armenia. Returning under Celestine V, Angelo and his band received permission from the pope to withdraw obedience from their Conventual superiors and to associate themselves with Celestine's own benedictine reform group as the 'Poor Hermits of Celestine'.[74] They continued to observe the Rule and Testament of Francis, however, and this may be taken as a sign that they considered themselves the true heirs of the poor man of Assisi. It may seem surprising that the Conventual and Spiritual parties had not attempted to settle their differences by splitting into two orders at an earlier stage of the quarrel, but this is an indication that both sides had agreed on the important premise that they were fighting for the whole soul of the order, the entire inheritance of Francis, and not just a remnant of it. Angelo's willingness to accept a separation can be viewed as a dangerous precedent, a writing-off of the majority of the order as unredeemable, the beginnings of a new 'sectarian' mentality.[75]

Angelo's major apocalyptic work, *The History of the Seven Tribulations of the Order of Minors*, was composed in the 1320s after the tragedy of the Spirituals' defeat had run its course. It is dangerous to use the *History* in straightforward fashion as unbiased evidence for details of the struggle between the Spirituals and the Conventuals, but it is a priceless document for the self-understanding of the rigorists. Like the Gospels in relation to the historical Jesus, it presents us primarily with the kerygma to which true believers were expected to adhere. In this work, as in the statements found in inquisitorial records of the trials of the Spirituals and in the pamphlets of their successors, the Fraticelli groups,[76] the sectarian mentality into which franciscan use of apocalyptic and millenarian ideas had been forced is evident.[77] Yet even in their darkest moments of alienation from the Church around them, the Spirituals and their successors were sectarians of a special kind. They did not totally abjure the papal church of the current era, but looked forward instead to a coming holy pope, a *pastor angelicus*, who would ally with them to defeat the papal Antichrist.[78]

So much space has been devoted to the examination of the central panel of our triptych that little remains for treating the respective wings. Fortunately, the two sides are so like the edges of the center scene that they can be summarized in brief fashion.

It might seem that the reputation for sobriety, scholarship, and reasonableness of the dominican order would have preserved it from any taint of Joachite apocalyptic speculation. Such is not the case, however, though the incidence among the Dominicans is minor in comparison with the Franciscans. What is significant, however, is that dominican use of Joachite apocalyptic was kept within narrow confines where it was occasionally helpful in heightening the order's sense of its providential role but where it would offer no threat to the structures of the Church universal.[79] It cannot be claimed that apocalyptic thought was in any way central to the identity of the dominican order as such, but it is instructive that some Dominicans apparently found it useful.

A popular story repeated by dominican chroniclers relates how, when the sons of Dominic first encountered the Florensians, they were greeted with processions and hailed as one of the groups of *viri spirituales* predicted by the abbot of Fiore.[80] Whether this incident actually took place, the figure of Humbert of Romans, the fifth Master of the Order (1254-63), shows that identification with the *viri spirituales* could be fostered in the highest circles of Dominicans. Humbert, a noted theologian and preacher whose administrative and liturgical decrees were of great moment in the history of the order, combined with John of Parma to issue a joint Encyclical, *Salvator seculi*, to both groups of mendicants in 1255 during the crisis of the attack of the Paris Masters. According to this important document:

> In the last days of the End of the world, as we believe without doubt, he [the Savior of the World] raised up our two orders in the ministry of salvation, calling many to himself and enriching them with celestial gifts through which they are effectively able to work salvation by word and by example not only for themselves but for others. . . . They are the two shining stars that according to the Sibylline prophecy have the appearance of the four animals and in the last days will cry out in the name of the Lord in the way of humility and voluntary poverty.[81]

That this acceptance of the ideology of the *viri spirituales* by Humbert was not merely due to the influence of John of Parma is shown by the Dominican's use of another Joachite theme for the enhancement of his order in the *Legenda* he wrote.[82]

Thomas Aquinas's opposition to Joachite speculation by no means extended to all his followers. John Quidort, a Paris Master active from about 1280 to 1306, was among the most prominent successors of Thomas. His popular *Treatise on the Antichrist*, written before 1300, is on the whole a moderate work, but he does look forward in Joachite fashion to two coming orders that will help the Church in the time of final crisis.[83] John's separation of the present-day Dominicans and Franciscans from the more perfect orders to come suggests a transposition of Joachite themes similar to that of Bonaventure.

Other dominican authors, such as the historian Francesco Pipini of the early fourteenth century,[84] also showed an interest in the two orders of Spiritual men; but some of the most fervent dominican apocalypticists, such as one Brother Arnold, active around 1250, and Robert d'Uzès, in the 1290s, show no interest in the apocalyptic significance of their order and little contact with Joachite traditions.[85] There is only one text from the first century of dominican life that moves towards a more radical appropriation of Joachite apocalyptic.

The vision ascribed to a spanish hermit named John was apparently produced in dominican circles in the 1290s and was soon incorporated by Dietrich of Apolda into his *Acts of St Dominic*.[86] According to the text, one day at nones in the year 1216, a six-winged seraph with the face of Christ and surrounded by the faces of everyone of note in the Old and New Testaments and the history of the Church appeared to the hermit. The seraph image descended to earth in the form of a chariot and was led through the world by Francis and Dominic by means of a cord and a chain. Then the image (obviously the Church) underwent severe attacks first from a dragon who was easily defeated and then from the Beast of the Abyss who briefly overthrew it. At last the Beast was defeated by Francis and Dominic and the intervention of Christ so that: 'The wheels were repaired, and Francis's cord and Dominic's chain were inseparably threaded into them. Their splendor shown forth sevenfold.'[87] The details of the vision and its partial exegesis make it clear that the second attack on the church, that of the Antichrist, was to be caused by the covetousness of the religious and the avarice of prelates and would involve divisions among all the ranks of christian society. Because the author looked forward to some form of millennial state of the church on earth in which Francis and Dominic would exercise a preponderant role, this 'Vision of John' seems to unite the activity of the mendicants before and after the defeat of the Antichrist and thus come within striking distance of some of the more radical Franciscan views.[88]

Some years after the Franciscans and Dominicans began to make use of apocalyptic and millenarian ideas from the Joachite tradition, another group stressing the evangelical way of life and strict poverty got its start in northern Italy. About 1260 an illiterate layman from Parma, Gerard Segarelli, through his preaching began the formation of a new religious group. The 'Apostolic Brethren', as they were called, may have appropriated Joachim's prophecies about coming *viri spirituales* to themselves from the beginning. Surely, their appearance at the time of the famous Joachite date for the initiation of the third *status* is suggestive.[89]

The ecclesiastical situation that confronted the Apostolic Brethren was one far more hostile than that which the earliest mendicants had faced. The strictures of Fourth Lateran Council against the approval of new religious orders created considerable difficulties for all new movements, even those, like the Carmelites, which eventually won ecclesiastical approbation. The Apostolic Brethren, viewed as dangerous competition by the mendicants, experienced problems from the start; but despite the condemnations of Honorius IV and Nicholas IV, they continued to grow. Debate continues about the social significance of the movement, which one marxist historian has seen as a prototype of the peasant rebellions widespread in the following century.[90]

Segarelli was imprisoned and executed in 1300. At this time the dynamic Fra Dolcino, the son of a priest from Novara, took over the leadership of the Brethren. We are fortunate to have paraphrases of some of Dolcino's letters to his followers reported in the treatise that Bernard Gui, the noted inquisitor, penned on the sect.[91] These give us direct insight into the apocalyptic identity of the movement, at least in the final days of its flourishing.

Dolcino's message to his brethren involved a radical apocalypticism that was an original adaptation of strands in the Joachite tradition. It was Joachim who first interpreted the seven churches of Asia Minor, addressed at the beginning of the Apocalypse, as the Seven Ages of the history of the Church, a pattern known to some dominican commentators as early as 1235.[92] Dolcino expanded on this to create a schema of Church history involving the gradual perfection of forms of religious life.

> . . . the Angel of Ephesus was St Benedict and the congregation of monks was his Church. The Angel of Pergamum

was Pope St Silvester and the clerics were his Church. The Angel of Sardis was St Francis and the Friars Minor; the Angel of Laodicea St Dominic and the order of Preachers. The Angel of Smyrna was Brother Gerard of Parma whom they killed; the Angel of Thyatria was Brother Dolcino, himself of the Diocese of Novara. The Angel of Philadelphia is the coming Holy Pope. These three final Churches form the 'Apostolic Congregation' sent forth in the last days.[93]

Like the contemporary franciscan Spirituals, poverty of life was the central identifying mark of the Apostolic Brethren; but Dolcino's program was far more revolutionary than that of his contemporaries Ubertino and Angelo. For him the Roman Church was the 'Great Whore of Babylon' to which his followers no longer owed any obedience at all. All spiritual power had now passed to the Brethren,[94] and there was no hope of salvation for anyone outside the confines of the group. Dolcino announced that the secular clergy, the religious, and the prelates of the Church '. . . will soon be slaughtered and destroyed. Those who are left will be converted to his sect and united to him. Then he and his will prevail over all . . . .'[95] Dolcino looked forward to a Last World Emperor who would undertake the bloody purge of the corrupt Church, and the final years of the history of the sect show that the Brethren were not above taking arms in defense of their views against the forces of the established christian order.[96]

There is no space here to pursue the many questions raised by the story of the Apostolic Brethren. They are used in this context primarily for comparative purposes — as an example of a group certainly suspect and probably apocalyptic from the start. By Dolcino's time at least, we find in them a classic example of the use of apocalypticism to highlight a sense of separation from and opposition to the body of the Church universal.

What does the history of the groups surveyed here have to tell us about the relation between apocalypticism and the spiritual identity of religious groups in the thirteenth century? I would suggest that the evidence presented points to one important reason why apocalyptic ideas proved useful to thirteenth-century religious groups: they provided a new kind of warrant for *diversitas ordinum*.

The studies of Giles Constable and others on the debates over the legitimacy of diversity in the religious life during the twelfth century indicate that even those who came to recognize the need for some legitimate diversity of form had difficulties dealing with the notion.[97] This anxiety was heightened in the thirteenth century, especially in the wake of the new situation created by the Fourth Lateran Council, which seems to have been prepared to admit past diversity, but put a definite clamp on greater diversity in the future.

In this restrictive atmosphere new religious groups, even the Franciscans whose approbation was not quite yet firm, were in an anomalous position. They could scarcely turn to the traditional hierarchical models of validation of forms of the religious life. Hierarchy by definition is a-temporal, and innovation in the religious life could find nothing for its support in that which has nothing to do with time. But diversity could be defended on historical grounds by incorporating innovation in the religious life within the perspective of a renewed sense of God's creative action in history. This form of warrant was implicitly present in traditional apocalypticism, but it required the new apocalyptic theology of history created by Joachim of Fiore with its melioristic and terrestrial hopes for a coming third *status* of the Holy Spirit and for the role of the *viri spirituales* in the preparation and consummation of that *status* to make it a concrete possibility. The man and the needs of the times were matched. One of the ways open to new forms of the religious life for validating their own identity and significance was by an appeal to the apocalyptic future. Joachim provided a prophetic myth perfectly tailored to this purpose.

Apocalypticism, because of its ability to incorporate change and innovation into the teleological christian scheme of history, has often served such purposes. Any institution, office, or group that can be seen as having a significant role to play in the final and most decisive moments of history obviously demands both respect and support as an essential structure of society. This *a posteriori* function, that is, one that attempts to make sense of some new development in the light of its future providential meaning, can be seen at work in many of the most important creations of medieval apocalyptic literature, from the figure of the Last World Emperor to that of the *pastor angelicus*, the Angelic Pope of the last days. I would submit that it is also of significance for our understanding of the special bond between apocalypticism and the new religious orders and groups in the later Middle Ages.

Monastic reforms found their sense of identity in the proclamation of a return to the sources, the restoration of the purity of Benedict's *Rule*, or even the renewal of the eremitical life of the Desert Fathers. Both the Franciscans and the Dominicans used elements of this appeal, which Michael Hill has called 'revolution by tradition.'[98] Dominic based his way of life on the Augustinian Rule; Francis, in more daring fashion, but one fully in harmony with many twelfth-century religious movements, appealed to the literal observance of the Gospel, the 'Evangelical Rule.'[99] But every form of recognized religious life was in some way evangelical by definition, and the novelty of the mendicant practices could not be gainsaid. Something more was needed.

It was not only the novelty of the mendicants that demanded this, but also their consciousness of competition. Various reform movements within Benedictinism had been at odds during the previous century; the tensions between monks and canons had also been evident. The necessity of justifying new forms of religious life and their claims to the *cura animarum* in the face of conservative obstinacy had led to such noted historical defenses of the new orders as that found in book one of Anselm of Havelberg's *Dialogues*.[100] The inherent competition among the older orders was exacerbated by the rise of the immensely successful mendicants in the first quarter of the thirteenth century. Opposition between the mendicants and the secular clergy was even more overt, since the urban context of the friars' labors made the conflict of interests more intense here. No new religious groups in the medieval church ever had greater need to achieve a clear sense of identity and mission.

I do not suggest that the apocalyptic element, the sense of a unique role in the imminent crisis of history, was more than one of the instruments in achieving and strengthening identity in the midst of competition. This is patently true in the case of the Dominicans, where apocalyptic appeals were used only sporadically and in moderate fashion. It is even true in the case of the Franciscans, where apocalyptic re-enforcement played a large role, though never an all-embracing one. But the power of the appeal to validation from the future was real for the new religious movements of evangelical character in the thirteenth century. This is especially evident in the case of the Apostolic Brethren, who turned immediately to apocalyptic and millenarian ideas to achieve their sense of identity and appear to have given them a much more central role than either of the accepted orders of mendicants. The success of their apocalyptic sectarianism can be gauged by the fact that long after the defeat and death of Dolcino in 1307, the Inquisition continued to turn up true believers in the church of the Brethren.[101] The case of the Apostolic Brethren, as well as that of the radical adherents of the Spiritual Party among the Franciscans, show us that the use of apocalypticism had inherent dangers. Apocalypticism could be used as a means for individuals to achieve identity as a special group, but because the apocalyptic frame of mind always implies a measure of moral and historical dualism, the belief in the impending final clash between good and evil in the world, in the midst of misunderstanding, repression or persecution, it can easily become an identity conceived in terms of separation and radical opposition.

Apocalyptic ideas have important functions not only for the religious order or group considered in itself, but also for the group as it functions within a universal Church. The study of the dynamics of this type of relation is scarcely past its infancy.

Since Ernst Troeltsch's *The Social Teaching of the Christian Churches*, some authors have tried to make use of the ideal-type of the sect to understand the role of the orders in medieval religious life.[102] More recently, M. Hill's *The Religious Order* briefly surveys the main lines of the history of medieval religious orders to demonstrate that an order is not a pure sect, but a 'sect within a Church', with a dynamic of its own based upon its situation and its membership composed primarily of religious *virtuosi* in the Weberian sense.[103] This seems to me a step forward, as does Hill's recognition that monastic reforms and new orders have generally found their identity in an appeal to tradition: the re-instatement of the primitive ideal.[104] Unfortunately, his failure to recognize a form of authority based on validation from the future, apocalyptic validation, leads him to misunderstand the full dynamics of the history of many religious orders, especially after 1200.[105]

There is real need for an expansion of the current models of the role of religious groups and orders within the framework of the medieval church and the role of apocalyptic thought as an important element in this broader picture has thus far not received the theoretical consideration it deserves. On the basis of the thirteenth-century evidence presented here, the observation seems to hold that the apocalyptic identity of any particular group was compatible with integration into the life of the Church universal insofar as this identity centered on a special role for the group in the imminent crisis of the persecution of the Antichrist. The Church could accept, perhaps even welcome, *viri spirituales* who were to lead the fight against the Final Enemy. But insofar as any historical group claimed to enshrine an order or way of life that was apocalyptically superior to the present state of the *ecclesia*, one that was a foretaste of a better age to come, or one that surpassed all degrees of past holiness, tension and opposition soon became evident. Any religious order, any group within an order, or any new movement of piety that came to see itself as the incipient realization of the millennium had already set foot on the perilous slope toward sectarianism, whatever its intentions may have been.

BERNARD McGINN

The Divinity School
The University of Chicago

DEVOTIO MODERNA ATQUE ANTIQUA: THE MODERN DEVOTION AND CARTHUSIAN SPIRITUALITY

The Devotio Moderna, *a religious reform movement that flourished in the Netherlands and in Germany throughout the fifteenth and well into the sixteenth century, originated with Geert Groote of Deventer (1340-1384). His followers, dedicated both to the contemplative and active life, founded communities of the 'Brothers of the Common Life' and the 'Sisters of the Common Life'. Groote was also instrumental in establishing at Windesheim a monastery which soon grew into the Windesheim Congregation of Augustinian Canons Regular, the best known member of which is Thomas à Kempis (1380-1471).*

The Carthusian order was founded in 1084 by Bruno of Cologne at the Grand Chartreuse near Grenoble, France. The Carthusians combined cenobitic (community) life with eremetic (solitary) life. They have never been a large Order, but recent scholarship has pointed out the strong influence of the Carthusians on monastic as well as on ecclesiastic reforms throughout the later middle ages.

MEDIEVALISTS HAVE on occasion displayed a certain fondness for natural images in characterizing the late Middle Ages. For example, the fifteenth century in particular has been described as the 'waning' as well as the 'harvest' of the Middle Ages. More recently, it has been referred to by yet another image — that of the 'turning tide'.[1] All this seems to imply a foregone conclusion: 'the old has passed away, behold, all things have become new' — or are about to become new. Modernity is replacing antiquity, innovation is supplanting tradition. There is, in fact, nothing wrong in applying those images to human history provided we remember that harvest is followed by seed-time, that the waning moon also waxes, and that the tide that turns inevitably returns. In his *Myth of the Eternal Return*, Mircea Eliade has analyzed a corresponding

27

cyclical pattern in the history of religion. *Homo religiosus* has always believed in the necessity of a regular periodic return to the origins, the primordial beginnings, so that the fragile fabric of man and society, worn and torn by time and corruption, may be renewed and its original form restored.

Jürgen Moltmann, in an essay entitled 'Turning to the Future' (*Umkehr zur Zukunft*), finds that the 'Myth of Eternal Return' also dominates the religion and theology of early and medieval Christianity as well as the various movements for social and political renewal in western history.[2] We speak of the Renaissance and the Reformation, of revolution, revival, renewal, and restoration. As the prefix 're-' indicates, all of those movements did not seek discovery of a *novum* but rather the recovery of an *antiquum*: the 'paradise lost', the 'golden age', the original natural state of man, or the initial order of things. The Protestant Reformation wished to recover the golden age of primitive Christianity; the humanists called for a 'return to the sources'; and Copernicus, who is credited with revolutionizing our view of the cosmos, meant by revolution the return of a stellar system to its initial constellation. One is tempted to conclude that nothing is as conservative and reactionary as is the idea of the revolution of history to its point of departure.

In this context, innovation appears as renewal rather than as *novum*. It does not constitute a break with tradition but rather tradition's revitalization and continuation. One could say that tradition, in order to stay alive, demands innovation while the latter depends upon tradition for its authenticity and legitimacy. A case in point is the *devotio moderna*, a religious movement of the fifteenth century that began in the Netherlands and quickly spread into Germany. The very name *modern* which the modern devotionalists applied to themselves seems to suggest that in this movement we are indeed confronted with a *novum*, which is, in large part, discontinuous with medieval tradition. The majority of studies which have appeared during the past decades make that claim in one way or another.[3] The modern devotion is seen as a radical break with medieval monasticism, and the Reformation in Germany is indeed itself regarded as the product of the *devotio moderna*.[4] The movement has been credited with widespread reform of public education and, through its own schools and teaching, with having influenced nearly every humanist of the fifteenth and sixteenth centuries.[5] Furthermore, the modernity of the modern devotion is seen in its primarily lay membership, its democratic organization, its individualism and tolerance, its alienation from the Church, its rejection of external forms of religious practices, and its members' lack of vows and monastic rule.[6]

In a more recent and extensive study of the *devotio moderna*, R. R. Post has raised serious questions about these suppositions.[7] Without going into details, let me briefly summarize Post's conclusions.[8] The movement counted among its foundations two communities without vows (the Brothers and Sisters of the Common Life) and, in addition, a monastic foundation (the Windesheim Congregation of Augustinian Canons Regular). The recognized founder of the modern devotion, Geert Groote, was fully in sympathy with the monastic state and extolled it as being the most perfect way of salvation. 'To enter the monastery is to choose the highest state of life and that which pleases God the most', he asserted in one of his letters. Such an attitude does not suggest any basis for a radical break with medieval monasticism. From the very beginning, in all the places where the Brothers of the Common Life settled, they devoted their care to the pupils of the city schools. Some they admitted to their hostels and there prepared them for the monastic life and the priesthood. Apart from providing them with room and board and helping them with their studies by going over the lessons which these boys received in the city schools, the brothers emphasized their spiritual formation and religious training. Until the end of the fifteenth century this was the limit of the Brothers' work as teachers. Since with very few exceptions they did not attend universities, they were completely outside the academic world and not qualified to teach in schools. Hence the influence of the Brothers on the development of humanism was negligible.

Still less can the Brothers of the Common Life be considered to have fostered the Reformation. Again, with few exceptions, they opposed the new doctrine everywhere and as a result, their houses ceased to exist in many German cities. According to most extant sources, the membership of each brother house consisted of priests, unordained clerics and at most two or three lay brothers, the *familiares*, who carried out the menial tasks of cooking, cleaning, and tailoring. If one adds the fact that the modern devotion included the many monasteries of the Windesheim Congregation, the term 'lay movement' is hardly an appropriate description. Finally, no substantial basis exists for the claim that the modern devotion alienated itself from the Church, and even less for the argument that its emphasis on inner devotion represented an outburst of modern individualism. On the contrary, there is overwhelming evidence that the movement continued throughout to be faithful to the Church in its emphasis on the importance of the Mass, daily vigils, and breviary prayer, as well as in its obedience to the hierarchy. In short, the *devotio moderna* seems to demonstrate, if anything, continuity rather than a break with tradition.

The movement originated under the impact of Geert Groote of Deventer (1340-84) who gathered followers dedicated both to the contemplative and active life. This led to the foundation of the community of the 'Brothers of the Common Life' and its counterpart, the 'Sisters of the Common Life'. Upon Groote's advice, his successors established — in addition to existing brotherhouses and sisterhouses — a monastery at Windesheim which soon grew into a congregation that included four new monasteries and was later to become the famous Windesheim Congregation of Augustinian Canons Regular. All these communities practised what they called 'inner devotion', from which they derived their name. To study what the modern devotionalists meant by 'inner devotion', how they put it into practice, and how they related the practice of devotion to the life of the community seems essential to a valid assessment of the extent to which the *devotio moderna* must be seen as either a return to or a turning away from medieval spirituality.

I.

Geert Groote emerged as the founding father of the *Devotio Moderna* during the last decade of his life (1374-84). Following a conversion he resigned the two benefices he had held at Utrecht and Aachen, donated his paternal house in Deventer to the city as a hospice for poor women, and, in 1374, entered the Carthusian monastery at Monnikhuizen near Arnhem where his friend Henry of Calcar was then prior and where he stayed for the next three years. It is curious that very few studies even mention this period in Groote's life, let alone assign any significance to it. Yet it was at Monnikhuizen, within the context of a monastic order that claimed *Cartusia nunquam reformata quia nunquam deformata*, that Groote developed his basic concepts of the spiritual life. It seems most unlikely that the formation of his spirituality remained untouched by this encounter with the monastic tradition of devotion. Thomas à Kempis, the later Windesheim Canon, describes Groote's life at Monnikhuizen:

> Dressing in a long coarse garment of hair-cloth, totally abstaining from the use of meat and other lawful things, and passing a considerable portion of his nights in vigils and prayer, he forced his feeble body into complete subservience to the spirit.[9]

During the first period of his stay in Monnikhuizen Groote formulated his thinking under the title *Conclusa et Proposita*, a summary of how he intended to order his life thenceforth. In the opening paragraph he declared his purpose:

> I intend to order my life for the glory, honor, and service of God and the salvation of my soul; to prefer no temporal good either of the body, or of honor, or of fortune, or of knowledge to my soul's salvation.[10]

He resolved to desire a benefice never again, to possess only essentials, and to be content with what is in accordance with participation in community life. He renounced all profit which he might acquire from learning and proposed to abandon all manner of scholarship. He did not wish to obtain any academic degree in medicine, law, or theology. He resolved not to devote himself to any field of study or to write any book to enhance his reputation. He wished to avoid all public debates and any dispute with private individuals. He even refused to continue his studies in Roman Law and in medicine. He rejected scholasticism, its conclusions as well as its method. Indeed, he rejected every branch of academic learning as non-essential.[11]

What emerges in these resolutions is an attitude characteristic of the *devotio moderna* and one deeply rooted in the monastic tradition: the *contemptus mundi*, the contempt for the world. Indeed, Groote's *Conclusa* echo to a large extent the *Meditations* of Guigo I, fifth Prior of the Carthusian charterhouse, a book which had been widely copied and distributed and with which Groote no doubt became familiar at Monnikhuizen. Guigo wrote:

> Lack of interior vision, that is, of God . . . causes you to go outside your interior, in fact you cannot abide within yourself as in seeming darkness, and you spend your time admiring the exterior forms of bodies or the opinions of men. To gain an interior vision of God and to receive his benefits one must deny the world and himself.[12]

Guigo continues:

> The way to God is easy because one goes by disburdening. But it would be hard were one to go by taking on burdens. So, disburden yourself to the point where, having left all things, you deny yourself . . . Wean yourself henceforth from those forms of bodies, . . learn to live without them, learn to live and rejoice in God.[13]

For Groote, the choice of this way of life depends upon man's knowledge of himself and upon his consciousness of the presence of the Spirit within him. Groote saw a correlation between interiority (the *locus* where God speaks to man) and piety (man's zeal for the glory of God). Both these notions make up the concept of devotion, and Groote considered both interior devotion and exterior works necessary components of the virtue of religion. He writes:

> By the virtue of religion, man is inclined to consecrate himself to the service of God, in order to honor him in an appropriate way. The work and interior exercises of religion are an intimate devotion, interiority and submission to the will of God. Exterior works and exercises consist in adoration and the offering of oneself.[14]

This devotion manifests itself in a fervent desire for union with God and the salvation of the soul. The way to God is a life of struggle, of contempt for the world, and of self-denial. In order to attain the goal, one must imitate the humanity of Christ, especially the passion of Christ, the *passio Christi*. By *imitatio Christi* Groote meant a desire to share in Christ's passion and cross through meditation, prayer, and humble self-dispossession: '*Crux Christi in ruminatione passionis fabricanda est*.'[15] Imitation is an actualization of the model that one wants to become perfected in one's life. Groote called it the very door to an authentic spiritual life and urged 'that we should contemplate frequently on the passion of our Lord Jesus Christ.'[16]

Despite his emphasis on interiority and conscious inner devotion, Groote did not reject what he called 'exterior works and exercises which consist in adoration and the offering of oneself.'[17] Indeed, to external actions and bodily gestures he assigned considerable significance as symbols of inward devotion. Commenting in the *Conclusa* on one's actions during Mass, Groote wrote:

> Our bowing ourselves at these words [the Gospel], and the bodily posture of reverence are symbols of the reverence of our minds ... Moreover, the outward observance is a

means to induce inward reverence, but it is vain if one answers not to the other.[18]

And again:

A bent posture does admirably befit devotion of mind, for the motions of spirit do bear relation to the posture of the body.

These statements again resemble a similar opinion in Guigo's *Meditations:*

The greatest utility of bodies is in their use as signs. For from them are made many signs necessary for our salvation, . . . nor do men know the movements of one another's souls but by sensible signs.[19]

K. C. DeBeer in his study on Groote provides a list of the books which Groote had copied and of the authors to whom he constantly referred.[20] The list includes nearly the whole of medieval devotional literature, but notably the works of Cassian, Gregory I, and St Bernard. Clearly, Groote's spirituality sprang from the past and in no way can it be called revolutionary. It certainly shows the influence of the Carthusians.

Equally traditional in their spirituality were Groote's two immediate disciples, Florens Radewijns and Geert Zerbolt van Zutphen. Florens Radewijns (1350-1400) was, with Groote, the co-founder of the Brothers of the Common Life and the rector of the brotherhouse in Deventer from Groote's death until his own — that is, from 1384 to 1400. Apart from a few letters and various *Notabilia Verba,* two of his works have been preserved; these are referred to by their first words, namely *Multum valet* and *Omnes inquit artes.*[21]

The former work, *Multum valet,* is a devotional treatise that examines the goals of the spiritual life: purity of heart and love of God. Florens described two ways of attaining these goals. The first is the *via purgativa,* the practice of virtue through spiritual reading, meditation, and prayer. All three are discussed in detail with special emphasis on meditation and the subjects for meditation.[22]

The second way is the *via illuminativa*, the luminous way, which consists of reflection on the benefits received from God. Once again Florens emphasized meditation and suggested texts concerning the *passio Christi* for every day of the week.[23] The classic third way, the *via unitiva*, is not mentioned at all by Florens. This is the way of perfection that is to culminate in union with God. In ignoring this aspect of traditional spiriuality, Florens Radewijns reveals a certain anti-mystical attitude or at least a disinterest in mysticism which was also characteristic to some extent of Groote.[24] Florens instead tended towards the severely-ascetic, the practical-didactic, and the affective aspects of devotion. He strongly disapproved of purely theological learning, speculative mysticism, and, especially, scholasticism, all of which he thought hindered devotion and distracted one from the eradication of faults. He made no distinction between real and specious learning, but only between *studium devotum et morale* on the one hand and *studium intellectuale* on the other. All scholastic learning was therefore suspect and the Brothers were not permitted any such study. To make sure that they did not engage in it surreptitiously, the Brothers could enter the house library only through the librarian's rooms.[25]

Florens' second work, *Omnes inquit artes*, is essentially a collection of texts from Scripture and from devotional writings linked together in such a way as to form a logical whole.[26] The first part closely resembles Florens' first treatise, *Multum valet*, with an exposition of the chief virtues to be practised — love of God and love of neighbour. Among the Brothers the latter must find expression in brotherly harmony, in giving and accepting fraternal reproof, and in obedience, which means above all renouncing one's own will. The aids toward attaining these virtues are again study (spiritual reading), meditation, and prayer as well as manual work which must also be accompanied by prayer and meditation.[27] The second part of the work deals with the subject matter of meditation: the passion of Christ, the Four Last Things, our sins, and the benefits received from

God. Florens selected his texts from among the numerous authors who were frequently quoted in the late Middle Ages and who were considered authorities. A great deal of monastic literature — i.e., writings by and for monks — is included in the selection, but the one author who is quoted above all others is John Cassian, whose writings were held in the highest esteem throughout the Middle Ages and who provides the theoretical basis for Florens' asceticism. As much as a third of the entire text of *Omnes inquit artes* is derived from Cassian. For a number of themes only or mainly texts from Cassian are introduced, as in, for example, the nature of perfection, the struggle between flesh and spirit, vices in particular and in general, brotherly harmony, obedience, prayer, and spiritual direction. Thus the spirituality of Florens Radewijns is completely determined by the monastic tradition in general and by Cassian's fund of ideas in particular.[28]

Geert Zerbolt of Zutphen was perhaps the most successful and most important author the Brothers ever produced, although he — unlike Groote and Radewijns — had no academic training and only lived to be thirty-one years of age. He was one of the first Brothers to enter the brotherhouse in Deventer, where he assisted Florens, the rector, in difficult matters. He wrote two important spiritual treatises, *De reformatione virium animae* and *De spiritualibus ascensionibus*.[29] Both had a wide circulation and greatly influenced later spiritual writers, including — if only indirectly — Ignatius of Loyola. Their contents resemble Florens' two treatises, but the major themes were treated in different ways.

Zerbolt began with the concrete situation of sinful man who must through self-examination become conscious of his sin and of the necessity of conversion. In the very first chapter of his *De spiritualibus ascensionibus* Zerbolt described how man is inclined by nature to turn upwards to God:

> I know, O man, that you are desirous of going upward and that you long earnestly to be lifted up, for you are a creature reasonable and noble, endowed with a certain great-

ness of mind, wherefore you seek lofty heights and ascend thereto by reason of a desire that is of your nature.[30]

However, the spiritual ascent is blocked by man's depravity and degeneration as experienced in original sin, concupiscence, and mortal sin. Zerbolt continued:

From this it comes that now these powers and afflictions are inclined in a direction far removed from that to which God ordained them being prone to evil and going headlong to the desire of that which is unlawful . . . the will has become crooked, does often choose the worst part and loves carnal things, making light of things spiritual and heavenly.[31]

Zerbolt then proceeded from the decline of the soul's powers to their restoration by contrasting the threefold deprivation of the soul to a threefold ascension: conversion, ordered love, and sanctification of the soul's faculties. The means of ascending from one level to the other are self-knowledge, repentance, combat of sins, mortification, and the practice of humility and obedience.[32] This framework of levels of ascent displays, according to Zerbolt, an order and pattern which is revealed and exhibited in the *vita Christi* which therefore becomes our model. Christ is the only model to be followed and imitated; *imitatio Christi* is at the very center of Zerbolt's spirituality. Imitation of Christ is realized in three different steps or ascents.[33] The first imitation is based on an appreciation of Christ's humanity and of the beauty of this humanity. The second imitation is found in the discovery of the divinity in Christ, which demands both devotion and love and fear and reverence. The third ascent in our imitation of Christ is union with God. Zerbolt wrote:

A man does begin to be in a certain manner and spirit with God, to pass outside himself, to perceive the very truth and to be made united with God and to cleave to him.[34]

To achieve one's ascents in the imitation of Christ, Zerbolt prescribed four exercises: *lectio* (spiritual reading), *meditatio*, *oratio*, (prayer), and *contemplatio*, all of them centered on the passion of Christ.[35] He explained meditation as follows:

By meditation is meant the process in which you diligently turn over in your heart whatsoever you have read or heard, earnestly ruminating the same and thereby enkindling your affections in some particular manner or enlightening your understanding.[36]

The material for meditation listed by Zerbolt included besides the passion of Christ the Four Last Things — death, judgment, heaven, and hell.[37]

Zerbolt's description of the spiritual ascent to God resembles another Carthusian classic, the *Scala claustralium* of Guigo II, the ninth prior of Chartreuse, written in the form of a letter to a friend.[38] Its content concerns the four steps of the ladder that stretches from earth to heaven, and the four steps are *lectio, meditatio, oratio*, and *contemplatio*.[39]

Guigo's purpose was not merely to enumerate the various steps in the spiritual formation of monks but to show their necessary order and inter-relatedness. Spiritual reading is the foundation that prepares one for meditation, meditation prepares for prayer and prayer for contemplation. Reading without prayer, Guigo insisted, is arid, meditation without reading is erroneous; prayer without meditation is tepid, and meditation without prayer is fruitless. Contemplation without prayer is rare or miraculous.[40]

Giles Constable has shown that Guigo's steps were well-known by later spiritual writers, and that the *Scala claustralium* had become a favorite by the late Middle Ages.[41] Its influence on Zerbolt's thought is unmistakable. Not only do his four steps in achieving one's ascent in the imitation of Christ — *lectio, meditatio, oratio*, and *contemplatio* — exactly parallel the four steps of Guigo, but Zerbolt, like Guigo, insisted on their inter-relatedness. Meditation follows from spiritual reading but is quite distinct from it, and meditation, in turn, is distinct from prayer but not separate from it insofar as true prayer cannot be achieved without meditation.[42] Zerbolt, unlike Groote and Radewijns, also emphasized the fourth step, contemplation, as the highest step attainable here on earth and treated the way that leads to it, though the state of contemplation was not itself described in his work.

It seems, then, that the ideas of the founding fathers of the *devotio moderna* on the nature and meaning of devotion and the spiritual life were entirely traditional and closely similar to those of their favorite authors: Cassian, Gregory I, St Bernard, Guigo I, and Guigo II of Chartreuse. To see the modern devotion as a radical departure from the medieval concept is therefore totally unfounded and misleading. But what about the way these ideas were put into practice? Is it not true that the religious communities that were founded for this purpose — the Brothers and the Sisters of the Common Life — constituted a departure from tradition and, therefore, a radical innovation? My contention is that they did not, all outward appearances to the contrary. A comparison, however brief, of the *Consuetudines* (Customary) of the brotherhouses at Deventer and Zwolle with the Carthusian *Consuetudines* compiled by Guigo I will substantiate and confirm this contention.

II.

It is essential to remember, first of all, that the modern devotionalist's movement included, in addition to the establishments of many houses of the Brothers and the Sisters of the Common Life, the foundations of and subsequent alliance with the various monasteries that ultimately comprise the Windesheim Congregation of Augustinian Canons as well as the numerous convents of nuns that formed part of the Franciscan 'tertiaries', the third order of Franciscans. The widespread conversion and integration of brotherhouses and sisterhouses into canonical Augustinian chapters and tertiary Franciscan convents, is certainly indicative of the traditionalism of the modern devotionalist movement during its period of confrontation with Humanism and the Protestant Reformation. This traditionalism became apparent in the initial constitutions of the brotherhouses at Deventer and Zwolle which, without any essential modifications, were adopted and followed by all the subsequent establishments of the movement throughout the Low Counties and Germany.[43]

The 'Original Constitution of the Brothers of the Common Life' at Deventer, edited and published by A. Hyma, demonstrates the close association with, and the practical implementation of, the ideals of the Modern Devotionalist Movement — i.e. the revival of the medieval devotionalist tradition.[44] It is curious how the Brethren absorbed so much monastic and, in particular, Carthusian discipline in their attempt to reform the Church. The rigorous discipline of Windesheim is predictable. The brethren were, after all, a monastic body engaged in the reform of monasticism itself. Quite naturally they borrowed Carthusian discipline as it suited their aims. Much more noteworthy is the development of a style of life and discipline in a 'secular' institution which, in many respects, paralleled the externals of Carthusian life. A comparison of the 'Original Constitution of the Brethren of the Common Life' at Deventer with the *'Consuetudines Guigonis'* or the customs of Guigo will allow for some examples.[45] Although the Brethren's Constitution was not compiled until 1413, the practice of its precepts had been in use since the days of Radewijns and Zerbolt. Thus, the indirect influence of Groote can be assumed. The *Consuetudines* had also been a fact of Carthusian Life before Guigo collected and compiled them about 1128. So both documents represent a pre-existent style of life inspired by spiritual motivations.

The Brethren lived 'in the world' in a very real sense, in the cities, but, as the scriptures demand (John 15:18-19), they were not part of the world. Part of their stated purpose, in the introduction of the Constitution, was the imitation of the example of the 'primitive' Church.[46] Their apostolate was geared to service in the secular sphere as copyists, operators of student hostels, preachers, and teachers. But throughout the Constitution there are admonishments to the effect that in no way should the apostolate draw one away from the spiritual life. The Carthusians, on the other hand, were not 'in the world' in the same sense as were the Brethren, their apostolate being within the bounds of the cloister. Given the diverse nature of the two institutions, the similarities in their respective customs are remarkable. In the ninth chapter of the Brethren's Constitution there occurs a phrase which is often repeated thereafter in the document: *in camera sua.*[47] Also, in Chapter 37, we read: '*Sicut piscis ex aqua eductus statim moritur ita monachus perit, si foras cellam suam tardare voluerit.*'[48] This emphasis on the cell as a place crucial to one's spiritual life, as water is to fish, was certainly a Carthusian tradition. The Carthusian cell was indeed a very special place where one spent the bulk of his monastic life. The monk's cell was the physical focal point in his search for God. Guigo's *Consuetudines* delineate the function, property, and purpose of the cell.[49] The monk is exhorted never 'to make excuses for leaving his cell, at other than the appointed times, for he should consider it as necessary to his health and life as water is to fishes . . .'[50] It is obvious that the stress which the Brethren placed on the cell's importance to their spiritual well-being had its roots in the Carthusian customs.

The second chapter of the Constitution proposes topics for meditation with which the Brethren were to occupy themselves — i.e., sin, death, judgment, and hell. However, lest the brothers despair over such matters, they are also advised to meditate on the mercy of God, on hope, heaven, divine benefits, and the life and Passion of Christ. These topics of meditation are further ordered by the day and church season.[51] A Carthusian parallel is best seen in the work of the twelfth-century Carthusian, Adam de Dryburgh, entitled the 'Quadripartite Exercise of the Cell', which deals in part with topics and degrees of meditation.[52] For Adam, there were eight degrees or kinds of meditation, the second being penitential and the third being hopeful.

> The inhabitant of the cell is to turn over in bitterness of spirit all his bygone days and years, his sins of thought and deed, his carnal inclinations and human frailty; then he is to consider the awfulness of the Creator, of death, and to

picture to himself the general resurrection and last judgment . . . Nevertheless, there should be wrought in the
monk a certain illumination of mind, whereby he can pass
to the third manner of meditations, which is to consider the
sweetness of the divine clemency in the Father of Mercies,
. . . and the love of the Son in his Passion and in His gift of
His Body and Blood for our food and drink. This consideration is to do away with fear lest it degenerate to
despair. . . .[53]

There is nearly a one-to-one correspondence of favored subjects of meditation between the Carthusians and the Brethren.
The formulaic prescription for daily practice of meditation appears to be in keeping with the regimen of Carthusian life as
well as with that of the Brethren, as described in the *Consuetudines* and the 'Constitution.'

Manual labor was an essential part of the Carthusian vocation
as it was of the Brethren's. The Brethren's Constitution states
that man's nature is such that it cannot bear constant study
or prayer and that labor is required to occupy part of one's
time.[54] Guigo relied on the teachings of Cassian and St Gregory's Homilies and Morals to express the same notion. Manual
labor, therefore, was undertaken as a means of relaxing the
mind from constant study and contemplation. Yet for both the
Brethren and the Carthusians, there was a greater significance
to manual labor than merely as a sort of 'spiritual therapy.' The
copying of books in which both groups were employed provided a source of income to both, but even this was not their
primary concern. The ultimate reason and goal for the production of books by either group was the dissemination of the
Word of God. In his *Consuetudines* Guigo wrote:

> Books . . . we wish to keep very carefully as the everlasting
> food of our souls, and most industriously to be made, so
> that since we cannot do so by the mouth, we may preach
> the word of God with our hands.[55]

The prior continues:

> For so many books that we write, it seems to us that we
> make so many publishers of the truth, hoping for reward

from the Lord for all those who by them shall be corrected
from error, or advanced in Catholic truth. . . .[56]

The Brethren shared the same purpose, love, and care for books
as the Carthusians did, as evident in their Constitution.[57] They
produced books not only for income but for reform. They also
had an advantage which their Carthusian mentors did not —
i.e., the advantage of accessibility to the whole Church.

Many more parallels exist between the respective customs
of the Carthusian and the Brethren. In fact, the entire meticulous approach for materially ordering the life of the community
to spiritual ends was common to both groups. The examples
given above were not mere coincidence. Diverse as their institutions were, the Brethren resembled the Carthusians in many
respects.

III.

CONCLUSION

My purpose has been to emphasize the importance of Geert
Groote's encounter with monastic spirituality for the movement which he founded, the *devotio moderna*. Both the devotional literature and language of Groote, Florens Radewijns,
and Geert Zerbolt, and the ordering and structures of the communities they founded reveal a highly traditional monastic
style. Jean Leclercq has clearly demonstrated the existence of
a distinctive and identifiable monastic language and experience,
large elements of which had been set down as early as Gregory
the Great and given shape during the Carolingian revival.[58]
The monastic style flowered in the work of the spiritual writers
of the twelfth century who exercised widespread appeal, as
Giles Constable has shown, in the fourteenth and fifteenth
centuries.[59] The devotional writings of the Modern Devotionalists drew directly upon this monastic/meditative tradition —
with particular emphasis on the *Vita Christi*, especially the
scene of the Passion: "I have sinned gravely, my conscience is
disturbed but not confounded, because I shall remember the
wounds of the Lord."[60]

An essential aspect of this literature is a clearly prescribed set of responses in its hearers and readers. The basic rubric is *imitatio* — an external imitation of the deeds and gestures of the narrative and an internal imitation of appropriate attitudes, emotions, and self-awareness. Both modes of imitation are inter-related. As we have seen, external gestures both represent and shape internal attitudes. The appropriate responses to the literature are clearly and extensively spelled out: obedience, self-denial, suffering, humility, and self contempt.[61] A second important aspect linking the Modern Devotio with the monastic tradition is the inter-relationship between devotion and the ordering of the community. The primary contact between monks and their tradition was an aural contact. As Jean Le-clercq has pointed out, devotional reading, whether private or public, entailed an aural experience; the *lectio divina* was an 'acoustical reading', which fully engaged one's physical, emotional, and intellectual activities.[62]

Both the customs of Guigo and the Constitution of the Brethren are quite clear about what may be called a code of behavior. This code has two parts: external actions and gestures (obedience, silence, service), and internal attitudes (humility, self-denial, hatred of self, and love of others). This two-part code, moreover, is based upon the capacity of the members to respond to the language and example of models of authority and to imitate them in attitude and deed. This interplay between christological imagery and monastic order is evident in an early sermon by John Staupitz, an Augustinian contemporary of Martin Luther:

> In the first place, we should follow the life of Jesus Christ which is our instruction; if we have the example of the apostles and other saints, this [the life of Jesus Christ] ought to be examined most carefully . . . Christ, the living son of God, is foremost among the brothers and therefore he is the rule and norm of the brothers.[63]

What we see here is the striking identity of devotional literature and the constituted order and social structure of monastic groups. Devotional and constitutional literature share a common vocabulary precisely because the use of religious language is embedded in the very structure of the community.[64]

The institutions of the *Devotio Moderna* are no exception to this generality. Indeed, they serve as a late medieval example of the continuing traditional monastic spirituality. This also explains why the Modern Devotion resisted the Reformation and why the latter must be understood as a radical break with the monastic tradition.

The devotion of the Modern Devotionalists, then, was modern only in the manner in which they put it into practice outside the cloister. In their effort to stem the tide of relaxation of discipline the Devotionalists brought a most necessary renewal to a wide area. They may indeed have propagated the *contemptus mundi* over too wide a field, as R. R. Post suggests,[65] permeating religious life with a pessimism against which the optimism of the Renaissance and the evangelical freedom of the Reformation reacted.

OTTO GRÜNDLER

The Medieval Institute
Western Michigan University

THE CLOUD OF UNKNOWING AND
MYSTICA THEOLOGIA

The Cloud of Unknowing is an anonymous fourteenth-century book written for someone about to enter a solitary form of monastic life. It treats elements of spiritual growth — sin, humility, grace, charity — and the ordering of human faculties — imagination, reason, and will — to God. Steeped in the western tradition of mystical theology, the unknown author of the Cloud distilled and made his own that rich tradition.

No Middle English work of spiritual doctrine has received more comment or met more enthusiasm than the anonymous *Cloud of Unknowing.* The work was composed in an East Midlands dialect in the last quarter of the fourteenth century, probably by a Carthusian monk.[1] The doctrine of *The Cloud* is highly distilled, or, as pseudo-Dionysius says mystical theology should be, *minimam . . . et rursus concisum . . . et brevium dictionum.*[2] Perhaps it is the distilled quality of *The Cloud*'s teaching which has made it susceptible to diverse interpretations. Among the most persistent of these is one which would relate *The Cloud* to eastern mysticisms. Several decades ago, for example, Aldous Huxley praised *The Cloud* for its 'pure Vedantic spirit' which transcends the narrow confines of a 'Christo-centric' dogmatism.[3] Today, *The Cloud*'s teaching is perceived to be similar to the practices of Zen Buddhism. Compatible with both of these is the interpretation which discovers in *The Cloud* fashionable psychological techniques, such as 'centering'.

However appealing such interpretations may be, however uncluttered *The Cloud*'s teaching may seem, and even though the author chooses not to display his authorities, *The Cloud* is full of medieval, Latin learning. We intend to show in this study that *The Cloud of Unknowing* is, according to a traditional and precise generic definition, a work of 'mystical theology', and to explore the implications of this definition for an understanding of the work.

To begin, we should remember that the author of *The Cloud* composed a small corpus of closely related works. He made an English translation, entitled *Deonise Hid Diuinite*, of pseudo-Dionysius' *De mystica theologia*, based upon a conflation of Johannes Sarracenus' Latin rendering and Thomas Gallus' paraphrases. He also adapted and translated into English parts of Richard of St Victor's *Benjamin minor (De duodecim patriarchis)* giving his work the title *A Tretyse of þe Stodye of Wysdome þat Men Clepen Beniamyn*.[4] The author's major works are *The Cloud* and its later companion piece, *The Book of Privy Counselling*, both probably addressed to the same person. Finally, the author of *The Cloud* composed three other small works, *A Pistle of Preir*, *A Pistle of Discrecioun of Stirings*, and *A Tretis of Discresyon of Spirites*.[5] In these works, the author applies the general teaching of *The Cloud* to particular matters of the spiritual life.

As their editor notes, four of these works, *The Cloud*, *The Book of Privy Counselling*, *A Pistle of Preir*, and *Pistle of Discrecioun of Stirings* 'are written in the form of letters', at times achieving a 'noticeably personal, and even intimate' tone.[6] This fact is significant. Medieval spiritual writers, especially in the more eremitic orders such as the Cistercians and Carthusians,[7] were fond of the epistolary genre. Their exemplar, of course, was Paul. One should also remark that pseudo-Dionysius, the presumed disciple of Paul, composed a series of letters, and cast his *De mystica theologia* in epistolary form (*Compresbytero Timotheo, Dionysius presbyter salutem*).[8]

Furthermore, ancient rhetorical theory suggested the appropriateness of an epistolary style for spiritual teaching. Cicero distinguished a less adorned style, particularly suited for philosophic discourse, from the more abundant style suited for public forensic persuasion. Cicero designated the plainer, personal style *sermo* in contrast to the more adorned, public *oratio*. It was Seneca, however, who most clearly defined the 'idea' of the *sermo* style, and developed its characteristic form, the personal letter to a like-minded friend. For many centuries his *Epistulae ad Lucilium* were the model for the genre. Throughout the Middle Ages, admiring christian writers called Seneca 'our Seneca', 'the moral Seneca', a 'doctor of souls'. Seneca's favoring of the personal epistle was consistent with his Stoic beliefs, which recommended more the cultivation of an interior, private virtue than an outward, public one.

Indeed, the ends of the epistolary style, as taught and practised by Seneca, were easily accommodated to the purposes of christian, especially monastic, spiritual writers. The major themes of Seneca's letters — self-knowledge, reason's governance of the passions, conformity to the divine will, the joys of solitude and fruitful leisure — are commonplaces of monastic literature. Precisely because it urged man to a spiritual governing of himself, Seneca's rhetoric made sparing use of the figures of sound, regretably necessary when one wished to move a crowd swayed by every passion. Figures of thought were more appropriate to a form designed to communicate mind to mind. The primary purpose of the epistolary style, Seneca taught, is, on the one hand, to reveal candidly the soul of the writer, and on the other, to effect self-knowledge in the reader. The intimate style of the epistle, directed to a well-known, individual recipient, allowed for another important effect. By means of such personal communication, the writer could provide diagnosis and therapy for the exact condition of the recipient's soul, preventing or curing any spiritual illness caused by disordered passions, and establishing the soul's healthy condition of harmony.[9] In his *Epistola ad fratres de Monte Dei*, William of St Thierry directly borrowed this theme from Seneca's letters.[10] The author of *The Book of Privy Counselling*, in turn borrowing a metaphor from Augustine and William of St Thierry,[11] likewise claims a therapeutic effect for his own doctrine:

> Take good gracyous God as he is, plat & pleyn as a plastre, & legge it to þi seek self as þou arte. Or, ȝif I oþer-wise schal sey, bere up þi seek self as þou arte & fonde for to

touche bi desire good gracious God as he is, þe touching of
whom is eendeless helþe by witnes of þe womman in þe
gospel: Si tetigero vel fimbriam vestimenti eius, salvo ero.
'If I touche but þe hemme of his cloþing, I shall be saa[f]!'
Miche more schalt þou þan be maad hole of þi seeknes for
þis heiȝe heuenly touching of his own beyng, him owne
self. Step up þan stifly & taast of þat triacle.[12]

Since the epistolary, *sermo* style and the notion of its effects
were assimilated and transformed by christian fathers such as
Tertullian, Jerome, Augustine, and Gregory, and by medieval
monastic writers, we need not argue that the author of *The
Cloud* was directly influenced by Seneca. Walsh, interestingly,
remarks the close resemblance between the intent of William
of St Thierry's *Epistola aurea* and that of *The Cloud*.[13] Whatever his reading among the ancients, the author of *The Cloud*
knew the purpose and customary usage of the epistolary form.
The Cloud's form instructs the reader that he should pay close
attention to the one for whom the work was specifically intended, and to the recipient's particular spiritual condition as
diagnosed by the author. But even if *The Cloud* was not immediately addressed to a general audience, a larger audience was
not deprived of its teaching. Having described its arduous
material production, Jean Leclercq says of the monastic spiritual letter:

> a letter was a gift whose value was appreciated because
> everyone knew just how much it entailed. Even personal
> letters therefore are almost always somewhat public in
> quality. It is generally taken for granted that the letter's
> contents will fall under the eyes, or reach the ears, of sev-
> eral others and that the receiver will take pains to see that it
> is available. This explains how it can happen that the writer
> will tell his correspondent things that both already know.
> ... The writer of a letter took great pains with it because he
> knew it would be brought to the attention of a more or less
> extensive audience.[14]

The spiritual epistle, then, at once conceals and reveals.
Accordingly, *The Book of Privy Counselling*, as its title sug-

gests, is addressed to the particular spiritual condition of a personal friend. At the same time, the author is aware that his writing will find a larger audience:

> Goostly freende in God, as touching þin inward ocupacioun as me þink þee disposid, I speke at þis tyme in specyal to þi-self, & not to alle þoo þat þis writyng scholen here in general. For ȝif I schuld write vnto alle, þan I must write þing þat were acordyng to alle generaly. Bot siþ I at þis tyme shal write vnto þee in special, þerfore I write none oþer þing bot soche as me þink þat is moste speedful & acording to þin disposicion only. If eny oþer be so disposid as þou arte, to whom þis writing may profite as vnto þee, in so moche þe betir, for I am wel apaied. Neuerþeles, at þis tyme, þin owne inward disposicion is only by it-self, as I may conceiue it, þe poynte & þe prik of my beholdyng (p. 135).[15]

The author directs *The Cloud* in the same manner. In the prologue to the work, the author enjoins its recipient to keep the writing to himself, unless he should find another who would be 'a parfite folower of Criste, not only in actyue leuyng, bot in þe souereinnest pointe of contemplatife leuing.' He further charges his reader, under the authority of charity, to make sure that any other readers read it 'al ouer,' lest any of them fall into error by heeding 'o mater & not anoþer.' The work must be kept not only from carnal and ignorant men, but also from 'corious lettred' men who take pride in their over-subtle speculations (prol., pp. 1-2).

In *The Cloud*'s first chapter the author specifies the spiritual state of his intended reader. He tells his 'goostly freende in God' that there are 'foure degrees & fourmes of Cristen mens leuyng ... Comoun, Special, Singuler, & Parfite.' The first three begin and end in this life; the last (like the virtue of charity, we might add) begins in this life 'bot it schal euer laste wiþ-outen eende in þe blis of heuen.' Having specified these four degrees of christian living, the author tells his reader something he already knows, that he has already passed through the common form of life, wherein he was called to God through the divine love which 'made þee & wrouȝt þee when þou were nouȝt, & siþen bouȝt þee wiþ þe prise of his precious blood when þou were loste in Adam.' Pulled by the leash of God's longing for his soul, the reader has also passed through the special form of christian living, wherein he had become a servant of God's special servants. He has now entered into a solitary, singular form of living, wherein he will learn to ascend through love 'towardes þat state & degree of leuyng þat is parfite' (1, pp. 14-15).

What do these degrees signify? First of all, I think, they refer to outward christian vocations, determined by vows of the will. In this manner *The Cloud*'s fifteenth-century Latin translator, the Carthusian Richard Methley, understood them. Methley says that in this passage, the common degree signifies the state of the ordinary layman, the special degree that of a professed cleric or religious, and the singular degree that of a solitary, that is, a hermit or anchorite. Methley adds that in modern times, the terms 'hermit' or 'anchorite' usually refer to a Carthusian monk.[16] According to this understanding, the recipient of *The Cloud* has for some time been a professed religious, and has newly entered solitude, either by receiving permission from his superior to live the life of a hermit, or more likely by having taken up a new vocation in the 'wilderness' of the Charterhouse.[17] Perhaps this was the occasion of the epistle addressed to him. In any case, we need not accept Methley's interpretation as definitive to admit its general likelihood.

The author of *The Cloud* knows that a habit does not an interior perfection make, that outward professions are but signs and instruments of an inward progress. Actually, only three degrees of living are visible; the last degree, perfection and the anticipation of eternity, takes place within and by means of a singular form of life. In this passage, the author carefully indicates the inner graces corresponding to outward vocations. In the common form of christian life, one enters the general economy of christian salvation as explained by scriptural exegetes. Man, in his creation, was made for God. Through participation in Adam's human nature he shares in the Fall. Likewise, through the common christian sacrament of baptism, he participates in the life of the new Adam and shares in Christ's redemption. The divine acts of creation and redemption benefit all men. By a special act of love, God calls some men to serve him and his people in a particular way. Finally, a few, like the recipient of *The Cloud*, are called to be alone with God in a solitary state where nothing distracts. In this state one is more readily disposed to seek the highest perfection, to be, as it were, hidden with Christ in God.

Throughout *The Cloud*, the author speaks of a threefold order of interior perfection which corresponds with the three outward degrees of christian living delineated in the first chapter. The author of *The Cloud* derived his notion of a threefold spiritual order from a number of Latin works which by the fourteenth century constituted a fairly well-defined corpus of 'mystical theology' This corpus crystallized around the synthesis of Augustine and pseudo-Dionysius accomplished, in large part, by the Victorine writers in the twelfth century.[18] Within the corpus of mystical theology, the works of pseudo-Dionysius, thought to have apostolic authority, held pride of place. His *De mystica theologia* defined the genre for writers of the late Middle Ages. Virtually as important, I believe, are Thomas Gallus' (*Vercellensis*, †1246) paraphrases of pseudo-Dionysius. It was he who established the standard, affective interpretation of pseudo-Dionysius' mystical union.[19] Included also within the corpus were works by Hugh of St Victor, notably his commentary on pseudo-Dionysius' *Celestial Hierarchy*, and the *Benjamin minor* and *Benjamin major* (*De arca mystica*) of Richard of St Victor. The corpus included two important later works. In his *Mystica theologia* (*Viae Syon lugent*), the Carthusian Hugh of Balma (fl. 1300) carried the priority of affection over understanding to its extreme, teaching that affective union with God required neither a preceding nor concomitant act of the intellect. Hugh hardened the distinction between mystical and scholastic theology, which had become traditional, and which perdured into modern times. He also is a primary source for the threefold purgative, illuminative, and unitive ways.[20]

In the middle of the fourteenth century, the Franciscan Rudolph of Biberach (†1362) defined and codified the basic canon of mystical theology. Rudolph's *De septem itineribus aeternitatis* is a convenient mystical encyclopaedia. Throughout, Rudolph generously excerpts works of Origen, Augustine, Gregory, the twelfth-century *Liber de spiritu et anima* falsely attributed to Augustine, Bernard, Hugh and Richard of St Victor, Thomas Gallus, and the Dionysian commentaries of Robert Grosseteste. He disposes the excerpts of these authors according to a threefold order of sensible, intellectual, and affective, mystical theology.[21] Especially in gathering germane texts from the wide-ranging works of earlier fathers, and accommodating them to well-known classifications among later writers, Rudolph's work was useful for anyone seeking authorities on points of mystical theology. Both Hugh of Balma's and Rudolph of Biberach's works circulated under the name of Bonaventure. This is not surprising, since Hugh's *Mystica theologia* and Rudolph of Biberach's *De septem itineribus* show clear signs of Bonaventure's influence. It is just to say that Bonaventure, in his *Itinerarium mentis in Deum* and other works, perfected the synthesis of Augustine and pseudo-Dionysius begun by the Victorines. In a chain of remarkable analogies, he unified the various threefold orders advanced by previous authors.

Two further points concerning the late medieval corpus of mystical theology should be made. First, since the later writers quote or allude to the same texts of the same earlier writers, it is difficult to determine exactly the source of their citations. Secondly, in the late Middle Ages Carthusian and Franciscan authors were generally the leading proponents of pseudo-Dionysius' mystical theology, interpreted affectively and always assimilated to the theology of Augustine. And Carthusian and Franciscan writers shared a particular point of interpretation: an emphasis upon the mediating role, within the spiritual ascent, of meditation on Christ's passion. Although pseudo-Dionysius stated that Christ was the head of every hierarchy and the mediator between spiritual and material worlds, such an emphasis upon Christ's passion cannot be found in his works. The *De contemplatione* of the Carthusian monk Guigo du Pont (†1297) is a typical example of late medieval mystical theology. Recently, James Walsh has argued for the influence of this work upon the author of *The Cloud*. Certainly, Guigo's particular variation of the threefold ascent — 'purification by means of contrition, union with Christ by means of meditation on his life and passion, and contemplation of the Divine Majesty' by means of affective aspiration[22] — is close to the teaching of *The Cloud*, as we shall see.

The preceding catalogue of authors and titles, although not exhaustive, is none the less meant to be restrictive. The author of *The Cloud*'s reading was within this library. From it he acquired his precise definition of mystical theology in relation to other kinds of theology. The *locus classicus* of what came to be called the three modes of theology[23] is pseudo-Dionysius' *De mystica theologia*. Of pseudo-Dionysius the author of *The Cloud* says:

> & trewly, who-so wil loke Denis bookes, he schal fynde þat his wordes wilen cleerly aferme al þat I have seyde or schal sey, fro þe beginnyng of þis tretis to þe ende (70, p. 125).

In chapter three of *De mystica theologia*, pseudo-Dionysius classifies the various works he has written. His *Symbolica theologia*[24] (not extant), Dionysius says, praises (I quote *The Cloud* author's translation)

> alle þe names þat ben applied vnto God from þees sensible þinges — as which ben þe godliche fourmes, which ben þe godliche figures ... & what oþer sensible formes þat on any maner in Holy Scripture ben applied vnto God.[25]

In another work, 'þe booke of *Goddes Names* it is affermyngliche set & preised how þat he is namyd Good, how Beyng, how Liif, how Wisdome, & how Vertewe, & what oþer þat þei be of þe vnderstonable namynges (*intelligibilis . . . nominationis*) of God? Commentators generally understood that pseudo-Dionysius' two other major works, 'þe *Ierarchies of Heuen* & . . . þe *Ierarchies of þis Fiȝtyng Chirche*', exemplified these two modes of theology, sensible and intelligible. The first shows how the angelic orders, the immaterial 'liȝtes of goodness', burst forth out of God, and the second how God's goodness is manifest in the sacraments of the visible world.[26]

These two kinds of theology differ from a third — mystical theology — in a fundamental way. Whereas the first two affirm God by assigning to him names derived from the properties of creatures, mystical theology denies all of these names, and entering 'þe derknes þat is aboven mynde [*in caliginem quae est super mentem*]',[27] ascends to the creator himself. Within the context of these modes of theology — sensible or symbolic, intelligible, and mystical — medieval writers understood Dionysius' famous injunction to forsake

> þi bodely wittes (as heryng, seyng, smelling, taastyng, & touching), and also þi goostly wittes, þe whiche ben clepid þin vnderstondable worchings; and alle þoo þinges, þe whiche mowe be knowen wiþ any of the fyue bodely wittes without-forþe; and alle þoo þinges, þe whiche mow be knowen by þi goostly wittes wiþinne-forþ; and . . . rise . . . in a manner þat is þou woste neuer how, to be onid with hym þat is abouen alle substaunces and al manner knowyng.[28]

The Cloud author's rendering of this passage is faithful enough, but his paraphrase expansion of the single terms *sensibilia et intelligibilia* ('knowen . . . without-forþe; knowen . . . wiþinne-forþ') reveals the influence of later interpreters, namely, Richard of St Victor and Bonaventure.[29] In these texts from pseudo-Dionysius' *De mystica theologia*, one may discern the seeds of a threefold analogy among modes of being (sensible, intelligible, divine), modes of apprehension (imaginative, intellectual, above mind), and modes of theology (symbolic, intelligible, mystical). These analogies were amplified by the writers to whom we have alluded. What the apprehension

above mind is, Dionysius does not expressly say. The author of
The Cloud, however, in a sentence which he inserts in his translation, says that it is 'wiþ affecyon' that one rises 'abouen
mynde.'[30] In so doing, he states his agreement with Thomas
Gallus, Bonaventure, Hugh of Balma, and a long line of commentators.

The analogy between modes of apprehension and modes of
theology becomes clearer by reference to works of Richard of
St Victor, whose *Benjamin minor* the author of *The Cloud*
translated in part. In the *Benjamin major*, Richard generally
distinguishes three kinds of contemplation. One, founded in
the imagination, perceives God in sensible things. Another,
founded in the reason, discerns God in intelligible things. The
highest, founded in the power (*intelligentia*) above reason, sees
God in invisible, incomprehensible things (*intellectibilibus*).[31]
This hierarchy is expressed allegorically in the *Benjamin minor*.
In Richard's allegory, Leah, who signifies the imagination
which brings the information of the senses to the soul, is replaced by the fairer Rachel, who signifies the abstract knowledge of reason. In turn, Rachel must herself die in giving birth
to her favored son, Benjamin. The author of *The Cloud* translates:

> For whi in what tyme þat a soule is rauished abouen him-
> self by habundaunce of desires & a greet multytude of loue,
> so þat it is enflawmyd with þe liȝt of þe Godheed, sekerly
> þan dyȝeþ al mans reson . . . so þat it be fulfillid in þee þat
> is wretyn in þe psalme: 'Ibi Beniamyn adolescentulus in
> mentis excessu.' Þat is: 'Þere is Beniamyn, þe ȝonge childe,
> in rauesching of mynde.'[32]

Before coming to such a rapture of the mind, Richard says, we
must 'þorow þe grace of God lyȝtenyng oure reson' come 'to
þe parfite knowyng of our selfe and of God,' insofar as it is possible in this life. One must not presume 'to knowe þe vnseable
þinges of þe spirit of God' before he knows 'þe vnseable
þinges of his owne spirit.'[33] The strands we have been following are woven together tightly by Bonaventure in the *Itinera-*

rium. Through symbolic theology we rightly use those sensible things outside of us; through the theology proper to our rational capacity we rightly use those intelligible things within us; finally, through mystical theology we are rapt *ad supermentales excessus,* to those divine things above us.[34]

These texts suffice to indicate that the work of mystical theology presupposes previous exercise of the imagination and reason. If the intended reader of *The Cloud* is a beginner,[35] he is so in the sense of the initiate who is prepared finally to enter the hidden mysteries of God.

The threefold order we have sketched informs many chapters of *The Cloud of Unknowing.* The author introduces it into his treatment of Martha and Mary, who according to traditional exegesis signify the active and contemplative lives. The author of *The Cloud* notes that Holy Church customarily speaks of only two lives. Nevertheless, the active and contemplative lives should be divided once more, since there is an intermediate life wherein the active flows into the contemplative. In the usual medieval way, the author seeks the justification for his new division in the text he is expounding. Martha and Mary may be considered singly and apart, or together as sisters. In the intermediate life 'is contemplatyue liif & actyue liif couplid to-geders in goostly sibreden & maad sistres', like Martha and Mary (21, p. 53). The active life, then, consists 'in good & onest bodily werkes of mercy & of charite.' The intermediate life 'liggeþ in good goostly meditacions of a mans owne wrechidnes, þe Passion of Criste, & of þe ioyes of heuen' (21, p. 53). The contemplative life, finally, 'hangeþ in þis derk cloude of vnknowyng, wiþ many a priue loue put to God by him-self' (21, p. 54). The author's terms mark the specific psychological character of each of the three lives. The first is concerned with 'bodily' things, the second with the just exercise of the discursive reason in good meditations, and the third with the work of the affections which reach beyond knowledge.

An earlier division of active and contemplative lives into four turns out to be, like this one, threefold. Both the active life and

the contemplative life may be divided into higher and lower
parts. However, the higher part of the active life and the lower
part of the contemplative life are in fact the same (8, pp. 29-33).
Again, the active life is said to consist of 'bodily werkes'. The
intermediate life, as stated above, consists of 'goostly meditacions, & besy beholding' of Christ's passion and of 'þe wonderful ʒiftes, kyndnes, & werkes of God in alle his creatures' (8,
pp. 31-32), or in other terms, of the *liber scripturae* and *liber
creaturae*. The contemplative life, which *The Cloud* properly
concerns, consists of 'a louyng steryng & a blind beholdyng
vnto þe nakid beyng of God him-self only' (8, p. 32).

In the same chapter, the analogy between states of life and
powers of the soul is explicit:

> In þe lower partye of actiue liif a man is wiþ-outen him-
> self & bineeþ him-self. In þe hiʒer party of actyue liif & þe
> lower party of contemplatiue liif, a man is wiþinne himself
> & euen wiþ himself. Bot in þe hiʒer partie of contemplatiue
> liif, a man is abouen him-self & vnder his God. Abouen
> him-self he is, for whi he purposeþ him to wynne þeder bi
> grace, wheþer he may not come bi kynde; that is to sey, to
> be knit to God in spirite, & in oneheed of loue & acordaunce
> of wile (8, p. 32).

A man is outside and beneath himself when he relies on the
senses, which he shares with other animals beneath him in the
order of creation. He is within and 'euen' with himself when
he exercises what defines his specific human nature, the reason.
He is above himself when through the affection of the will he
dilates to embrace God. Then he is 'vnder his God'. I think
this latter phrase refers to a famous teaching of Augustine, repeated by William of St Thierry, the author of *De spiritu et
anima*, and others, stating that nothing, not even the angels, in-
tervenes between God and the mind (*mens*), that highest and
innermost part of human nature superior both to other animals
and to other parts of the soul.[36]

Presently we shall comment upon the author of *The Cloud*'s
use of the term 'mind'. For now we shall note that man's discursive reasoning, by exercise of which he is 'euen' with him-

self, can never, according to the author of *The Cloud*, attain to
that which is purely spiritual. This is so because as long as the
soul dwells in a mortal body,

> euermore is þe scharpness of oure vnderstanding in behold-
> ing of alle goostly þinges, bot most specialy of God, mede-
> lid wiþ sum maner of fantasie; for þe whiche oure werk
> schuld be vnclene (8, p. 33).

Therefore the author says, only 'loue may reche to God in þis
liif, but not knowing'. On this point the author consciously
parts way with Richard of St Victor and adheres more closely
to the affective teaching of Thomas Gallus and Hugh of Balma.
For not only does Richard teach a completely spiritual cognition in the soul's highest power, which he calls *intelligentia*, but
he also posits a contemplation 'formed in the reason according
to reason', wherein the rational soul, 'far removed from every
function of imagination, directs its attention toward those
things alone which the imagination does not know but which
the mind gathers from reasoning or understands by means of
reason'.[37] Developments of the thirteenth century intervene
between Richard and the author of *The Cloud* here. The latter
accepts the scholastic adage that there is nothing in the understanding which was not first in the senses. Consequently, all
reasoning and meditation, however abstract, is rooted in sensibility, and one cannot attain God, who is pure spirit, by means
of it. For this reason, the author of *The Cloud* associates meditation closely with the 'bodily' active life. The immediate
source for the author's teaching is probably Hugh of Balma,
who sharply distinguished scholastic theology, the abstract con-
ceptions of which are always more or less remotely rooted in
sense, from mystical theology, in which the affection of the will
frees the soul from all attachment to the senses.[38]

The threefold order of the spiritual life finds a fit object in
Christ who, having a sensible nature, rational soul, and a divine
person, unites created and divine natures. Once more returning
to the commonplace of Martha and Mary (16-17, pp. 44-48),
the author of *The Cloud* points out that when Christ visited

their house, while Mary was engaged in contemplation Martha was busy preparing food for Christ's flesh. Martha's business was good; it corresponds to the work of the active life. However, the work of Mary, who sat attentively at Christ's feet, was better. In fact, in terms of the threefold comparison good, better, best, it was the best. For Mary did not heed, as would one in the intermediate life, the 'preciouste' of Christ's 'blessid body', or 'þe swete voyce & þe wordes of his Manheed'. Rather she beheld 'þe souvereynest wisdom of his Godheed lappid in þe derk words of his Manheed'. By means of a 'swete prive & a lysty loue' Mary penetrated Christ's human words, which stood as a 'cloude of unknowing bitwix hir & hir God' (17, p. 47).

In the light of this passage, to rise from meditation to contemplation is to rise from Christ's humanity into his divinity, which is as much concealed as revealed by the humanity. The author's terms, 'the obscure human words that envelop the divine wisdom', are taken from the tradition of exegesis. Usually such terms refer to the allegorical sense, by which one discerns the light of the spirit through the obscurity of the letter. The allegorical sense, however, corresponds more to the author of *The Cloud*'s meditation. Mary's hearing of Christ's words is anagogic, in the sense rather singularly defined by Hugh of Balma. Hugh conflated the exegetical term 'anagogy' with the Dionysian use of the term to mean 'a rising, an ascent', and in turn interpreted the latter as an affective aspiration. Each word in the Old and New Testament, and each creature in the world, referred to the 'point of love' (*ad punctum amoris*), is an occasion for union with God, Hugh says.[39] The author of *The Cloud* develops his practice of the single-word prayer in relation to this notion of anagogy. Those in the active and meditative lives, the beginners and the proficient, cannot pray without having first heard or read the 'mirour' of God's word (35, pp. 71-72). However, the prayers of contemplatives, the author says, echoing Hugh of Balma directly, 'risen euermore sodenly vnto God, wiþ-outen any meenes or any premeditacion in special comyng before, or going þer-wiþ' (37, p. 74). For contemplatives, a single word can be a syllabic instrument upon which to affix an affective 'stering', 'a scharp darte of longing loue' that pierces the cloud of unknowing (6, p. 36):

> Þerfore, what tyme þat þou purposest þee to þis werk . . . lift þan up þin herte vnto God wiþ a meek steryng of loue . . . & ʒif þee list have þis entent lappid & foulden in o worde, for þou schuldest have betir hold þer-apon, take þee bot a litel worde of o silable . . . & fasten þis worde to þin herte, so þat it neuer go þens for þing þat bifalleþ (7, p. 28; see also 26-40, pp. 72-79.)

On the one hand, to accommodate human souls God 'envelops' ('lappid', 17, p. 47) his unitive wisdom darkly in the glass of the many words of Scripture. On the other hand, man returns to the source of wisdom by enfolding ('lappid & foulden', 7, p. 28) his dispersed powers in an undivided act of love.

In *The Book of Privy Counselling* the author relates the person of Christ to the active and contemplative lives in a similar way. He does so by means of a scriptural interpretation which he borrows from the *Liber de spiritu et anima*, and which is also amply developed in Rudolph of Biberach's *De septem itineribus aeternitatis*.[40] In John 10:9-10, Christ says: 'I am the door. If anyone enters by me he shall be safe, and shall go in and out, and shall find pastures. He who does not enter through the door but climbs up another way is a thief and a robber.' In order to be saved, the author of *The Cloud* says, all must enter through the door of Christ's humanity, by meditating on his passion and sorrowing for the sins which caused it. Whoever does not enter the spiritual life through this door, preferring to humble meditation on the passion 'þe corious fantastic worchyng in his wilde wantoun wittis', is a thief and will not be saved. 'Faire meditations' on the passion are the truest, the only way through which a sinner may enter the spiritual life (p. 158). One must stand patiently at this door until 'þe grete rust of his boistous bodelynes be in grete party rubbid awei' (p. 161). Then he may be drawn within to Christ's divinity, to perfection and a 'more special worching of grace.' If so drawn, one must enter, leaving

off consideration of Christ's humanity and passion in order to
penetrate his divinity. The author opines that if there were no
greater perfection available to men in this life than 'beholdyng
& louing' Christ's humanity, Christ would not have ascended
before the world ended and withdrawn his bodily presence
from 'his specyal louers in erþe'. As he asked his disciples then to
forego his bodily presence, so now he asks his special friends to
forego their 'corious meditacions & queinte sotyl wittes' in
order to taste the love of God (pp. 170-71). Presumably, those
who forego such meditations will become, like the recipient of
The Cloud, singular friends of God.

From the texts I have cited, it should be clear that the author
of *The Cloud* does not slight the soul's sensible, imaginative,
and rational powers, or the highest object of their attention and
devotion, the humanity of Christ. Moreover, the degrees of
active and contemplative living, and the corresponding hierarchy of the soul's powers, must be understood not only in relation to the person of Christ, but also in relation to the redemptive work of Christ accomplished through sanctifying grace.
This relation is manifest in chapters sixty-two through sixty-
seven of *The Cloud*, where the author, in part following Richard of St Victor, discusses the faculties of the soul and their
perfection.

The author of *The Cloud* says that the 'mynde conteneþ &
comprehendeþ in it-self' four major powers: 'reson & wille . . .
ymaginacion & sensualite' (63, p. 115). The first two are independent and spiritual. The last two are dependent and bodily,
and serve the former. By nature, imagination, through which
the images of sensible things enter the soul, should serve reason.
It works properly when it is disciplined by 'þe liʒt of grace in
þe reson', as it is when it serves the meditation of spiritual things
such as 'þe Passion & þe kyndenes of oure Lorde God' (65, pp.
117-18). Correspondingly, sensuality, or the appetite for necessary sensible things, should be governed by the spiritual appetite of the will (66, pp. 118-19). As a result of the Fall, however, this created order has been disturbed. The lower faculties

have become insubordinate, and the mind's single focus is scattered. Undisciplined by reason, the imagination never ceases 'to portray dyuerse vnordeynd ymages of bodely creatures', turning the mind's attention downwards towards them (65, p. 117). Unable to govern easily the unruly imagination, the reason, which before the Fall was able naturally to discern good from evil, the good, better, best, can now do so only when illumined by grace (64, p. 116). Likewise, the rebellious sensual appetite thirsts after sensible things in an unrestrained, unmeasured way (66, p. 117). The will, which before the Fall was never deceived in its choice of the highest good, and by nature took delight in created things according to their relative measure of goodness, can now resist the lusts of the flesh only if anointed by grace (64, pp. 116-17).

In sum, man was made upright, (Ecclesiastes 7:30), pointed towards the heavens. Through the Fall he has become 'crokid', like the beasts bent towards the earth, towards sensible things (61, p. 113). The mystical doctrine of *The Cloud*, which urges man to rise above himself towards the heavens, teaches the final perfection, through grace, of the restoration of man's original rectitude, justice and integrity. The central teaching of the work is the regathering of the mind's dispersed powers into a single aspiration towards the highest good, God. The author of *The Cloud* summarizes his discussion of the soul's powers by arranging them according to his threefold order:

> euer whan þe mynde is ocupied wiþ any bodely þing . . .
> þou arte bineþe þi-self . . . & with-outen þi soule. & euer
> whan þou felist þi mynde ocupied wiþ þe sotil condicions
> of þe myʒtes of þi soule & þeire worchynges in goostly
> þinges . . . þat þou miʒtest by þis werke lerne to know þi-
> self . . . þou arte wiþ-inne þi-self & euen wiþ þi-self. Bot
> euer when þou felist þi mynde ocupyed wiþ no maner of
> þyng þat is bodely or goostly, bot only wiþ þe self sub-
> staunce of God, as it is & may be in þe preof of þe werk of
> þis book; þen þou arte abouen þi-self & vnder þi God . . .
> for whi þou atteynest to come þedir by grace wheþer þou
> mayst not come by kynde: þat is to sey, to be onyd to God

in spirit & in loue & in acordaunce of wille (67, pp. 119-20).

The author's use of the term 'mynde' in these texts deserves comment. Many of the authors whom we have cited used the term *mens* to designate the highest part or power of the soul.[41] It seems of no little significance, however, that the author's use of the term 'mynde' wholly agrees with Augustine's extended definition of *mens* in *De Trinitate*. The author of *The Cloud* says that 'mynde', the 'souereynest pointe of þe spirit' (37, p. 74) which comprehends all of the soul's powers, 'is soche a miȝte in it-self þat properly to speke & in maner it worcheþ not it-self . . . bot ȝif soche a comprehencion be a werke' (63, p. 115). This notion is identical with that of Augustine, for whom the term *mens* signifies the undivided, spiritual essence of the soul, embracing its powers of loving and knowing.[42] These powers are indistinct and simultaneous in the mind, since the mind knows and loves itself in an act identical with its very substance.[43] Whereas the mind is turned fixedly to the unchangeable truth, a rational power, deputed to govern inferior, temporal things, issues from it. This rational power does not depart from the mind in such a way as to sever its unity, but rather is related to mind as a helpmeet. Thus, just as Adam and Eve are embraced in one flesh, so the reason and the rational appetite are embraced in the one spiritual nature of the mind.[44] Finally, we should note that the *acies mentis*, as Augustine often calls it,[45] is nearly synonymous with the spiritual memory, which recollects the diverse powers of the soul in unity.[46]

There is no reason to doubt that the author of *The Cloud* read Augustine's *De Trinitate* immediately. However, Augustine's teaching concerning *mens* was echoed faithfully, if formulated more rigidly, in the handy *compendium*, *De spiritu et anima*.[47] Indeed, certain formulae of this text are especially close to those of *The Cloud*, for example, the terms of the relation between reason (*ratio*) and mind (*mens*).[48] Moreover, the author of *De spiritu et anima* speaks of the mind's capacity to sink below, retreat within, and rise above itself, to ascend from outward and lower things to its own level, and from thence

above itself to God.[49] As a result of the Fall, the powers of the
mind, 'manifold in duty but simple in essence,'[50] were scattered
among the delights of the earth.[51] Thus, the mind must now
'collect itself within itself' by rejecting the images and phan-
tasms of earthly things, and by coming to a certain forgetting
of itself (*quodam modo in oblivionem sui veniat*).[52] This last
phrase anticipates our author's 'cloude of forȝeting.'

Augustine's definition of *mens* illumines *The Cloud*'s central
teaching, the recovery of the created soul's essential unity. This
unity can only be accomplished in the soul's highest, undiffer-
entiated power, the 'mynde,' where there is no distinction
among being, knowing, and loving. The single word prayer is
efficacious precisely because it gathers 'al þe myȝt . . . all þe
wittis of þe spirit' in a single act (38, p. 75). Reason must be
transcended not because it is inherently perverse or conducive
to vanity. These it cannot be when illumined by grace. Rather,
reason must be transcended because by nature it is discursive,
and therefore, unlike mind, is not directly 'vnder God.'

We are now able to define narrowly the teaching of *The
Cloud*. According to a traditional scheme of the genera of
theology, *The Cloud* is a work of mystical theology, teaching
one to rise above himself and all other creatures, after, however,
he has learned to love God in sensible and intelligible revelations, and after he has exercised his sensible faculties in good
works, and his reason in meditation. Having accomplished a
certain perfection in these lower faculties, one may reach out
with affection towards that which human understanding cannot grasp.

In mystical theology, however, considerations of before and
after are inappropriate. Such considerations are the work of
the sequential, discursive reason, that faculty which at once distinguishes man from what is beneath him and from God, who
is above him. The author of *The Cloud* addresses this matter
in chapter four, where he lays the philosophic foundation for
his mystical, affective practice.

The contemplative work, in which one perceives in his will

nothing except 'a nakid entent vnto God' (3, pp. 16-17), rein-
tegrates the soul's powers dispersed and scattered through the
Fall. Elsewhere the author of *The Cloud* says that prayer is
nothing else 'bot a deuoute entent directe vnto God' (39, p.
77), and that the substance of all perfection is nothing else 'bot
a good & an acordyng wil vnto God' (49, p. 92). Once again,
the author's teaching is nowise unique. Cassian in the *Conlationes*, the guidebook of the Latin eremitic tradition, speaks of
the monk's intention and prayer in metaphors similar to those
of *The Cloud*;[53] the notion of a rectified will as the means to
perfection was a commonplace of Latin theological literature.[54]
Rudolph of Biberach's *De septem itineribus* gives a comprehensive account of the way in which the *recta intentio* of the will
is transformed into an *intentio . . . immediata, simplificata, &
Deificata*, that is, into perfect union.[55] The forming of a 'nakid
entent', the author of *The Cloud* says, is the shortest work imag-
inable to man. It is no longer or shorter than an atom, the small-
est and indivisible unit of time. It is so short that it is nearly
inconceivable. The author identifies these atoms of time with
each stirring and desiring of the soul's principal faculty, the
will:

> so many willinges or desiringes — & no mo ne no fewer —
> may be & aren in one oure in þe wille, as aren athomus in
> one oure. & ȝif þou were reformid bi grace to þe first state
> of mans soule, as it was bifore sinne, þan þou schuldest
> euer-more, bi help of þat grace, be lorde of þat stering or
> of þoo sterynges; so þat none ȝede forby, bot alle þei
> schulde streche in-to þe souerein desirable & into þe heiȝest
> wilnable þing, þe whiche is God (4, p. 18).

All of the soul's faculties are ordered to the will, each desire of
which must be directed immediately towards God. If the faculties are dispersed in things beneath, or even equal with, itself,
the soul's desires will not reach their destined mark. The reason,
naturally discursive, cannot be the source of the soul's unity.
Besides, the end which should order the soul's acts, God, is 'incomprehensible to alle create knowable miȝt' (4, p. 18). Only
the 'blynde stering of loue' (4, p. 22), which outruns the objects

presented to it by the understanding, can reach out to touch God. The author makes clear that human consciousness, by the necessity of human nature and as a result of sin, can never be free of images (10, pp. 35-37). However, the naked intent for the highest good never rests in or consents to the limited goods these images present, but continually pushes beyond them. The acts of the soul, then, must be united and directed towards God in what the author of *The Cloud* calls, interchangeably, 'naked intents', 'flaming darts', 'blind stirrings'. Such single, momentary acts of desire, even though they can have no ground in sensible images or rational concepts, are none the less, if not diverted, sure of their mark, because of the will's intrinsic ordering to God. As the author says, the human soul, by virtue of being created in his image and likeness, is measured by and proportioned to God (4, p. 18). Hence, the soul's desire is necessarily directed to the source of its created goodness.

The intrinsic proportion between God and the soul is the proportion between eternity and time. The source for the author of *The Cloud*'s conception is Augustine, this time the *Confessiones*. Augustine contrasts eternity with time by stating that whereas in eternity everything is present simultaneously, and nothing moves into the past, time is characterized exactly by a great number of movements flowing into the past.[56] And yet, after scrutinizing the division of time into past, present, and future, Augustine concludes that even for the human soul nothing exists except the present. The past has already ceased to exist, and the future does not yet exist. Any being they have derives only from the present memory or present desire of the soul. If this is so, how does time, which exists only in the present, differ from eternity, which is always present? Augustine distinguishes the two in terms of the being they possess, or more precisely, in terms of the being which one lacks:

> if the present is time only because it moves into the past, how can we say that even the present is, since the reason that it is is that it will not be? Thus, we can say truly that time is, only because it tends not to be.[57]

The creature is in time by virtue of being created: in making the heavens and the earth God made time, Augustine says, and there was no time before God made time.[58] The creature is in time because its wholly dependent, contingent being is always on the verge of the nothingness from which it was created. The precariousness of the creature's being, and its total dependence upon the being of God, is indicated by the fact that the creature's existence is measured out in the briefest moments. The present, in which the creature exists, is a moment so short that it cannot be divided into the most minute parts, and it passes so quickly from the future into the past that it has no extended duration.[59]

Augustine's reflections provide the sufficient reason for *The Cloud*'s practice. If created existence is only a moment, an atom, the duration of a single desire, then a single intention, a simple dart of love, a monosyllabic prayer wraps in itself the creature's whole existence. Such an undivided act pierces the cloud of unknowing and reaches the source of the soul's momentary, created being. This being is not dispersed into non-being as long as the soul does not dwell on the past or entertain created images of future happiness (10, pp. 35-37). Proper use of the indivisible atoms of time is a foretaste of the truly indivisible present, eternity.

In *The Book of Privy Counselling* the author likewise conceives the relation between creator and creature, although in somewhat more scholastic terms. Most affective mystics, like Bonaventure, follow pseudo-Dionysius in asserting that the highest name of God is Goodness. In *The Book of Privy Counselling*, however, the author follows the usual doctrine of the schools, saying that the highest name of God is 'IS' (p. 143). The proportion between God's being and the creature's is the same as that between eternity and time. As the indivisible atom of time is an image of eternity, so our 'nakid beyng', the indivisible source of our diverse acts, is an image of God's self-subsistent being. By a 'nakid beholdyng' and 'nakid blynde felyng' of our being in 'þe first poynte' of the spirit, we are led ineluctably to the being of God (p. 143, *et passim*). For the being of God is the source of our being; he is in us as our cause and as our being. In a sense, our undivided act of being and his being are the same, although whereas he is the cause of his own being, we are not the cause of ours, and are dependent on his (p. 136). When we worship God with the undivided substance of our being, we thereby worship him with himself:

> for þat þou arte þou hast of him & he it is. & þof al þou had-
> dest a biginnyng in þi substancyal creacion, þe whiche was
> sumtyme nouʒt, ʒit haþ þi being ben euer-more in hym
> wiþ-outyn beginning & euir schal be wiþ-outyn ending, as
> him-self is. & þerfore oft I crie, & euer upon one: 'Do wor-
> schip to þi God with þi substance' (p. 144).

In both *The Cloud of Unknowing* and *The Book of Privy Counselling* the reader is instructed to unite himself with the eternal source of his fleeting existence by means of single, con-centrated acts of the spirit that bear his whole being. Doing so, he will imitate Christ, who made a total sacrifice of himself for God and for all men through a single 'comon entent' (*Book of Privy Counselling*, p. 142).

If *The Cloud*'s teaching concerning the redemption of time through affective aspirations is consoling, it also seems discour-aging. What does one do about all of those past atoms of his existence which were not integrated and were dispersed into nothingness? The author foresees this anxiety in chapter four of *The Cloud*. These seemingly lost moments are redeemable through the mingling, by means of a renewed intent, of one's life with the life of Christ. One shares Christ's life through love, since love makes all things common. As God, Christ is the crea-tor and giver of time. As man, who came in the fullness of time, he is the preserver of all the time bestowed upon creatures. As God and man together, he will be the future judge of man's use of time. United to him, one is as well united to Mary, who was full of grace at every moment, and lost no time. Likewise, he is united to the angels, who having made the one instantaneous choice offered them, are confirmed in grace and can never more lose time. Finally, he is united 'with all þe seintes in heuen & in erþe, þat by þe grace of Ihesu kepen tyme ful iustly in vertewe of loue' (4, 21). In other words, through participation in the body of Christ, one is united to the single, eternal intention of Christ, and to the intention of all those confirmed in his grace, an intention which redeems and restores past acts. 'For' as the author of *The Cloud* states, 'Crist is oure hede, & we ben þe lymes, if we be in charite' (25, pp. 60-61). By the same means, when one constantly renews the unified act of his mind, he offers to God not only the fullness of his own being, but the plenitude of all created being.

The Cloud of Unknowing presents a rich, coherent doctrine firmly rooted in theological tradition. Surely this tradition was not a closed book to *The Cloud*'s intended reader. Why then does the author of *The Cloud* conceal his learning, and why did he write in the vernacular? I suspect he does both for two related reasons. First, by writing in the vernacular, the author of *The Cloud* would not likely draw the attention of 'corious lettred or lewed men' not so spiritually advanced as they think themselves to be. For such men, the author often repeats, knowledge serves only to puff up. The author knows the kind of books such men read and write:

> somtyme men þouȝt it meekness to sey noȝt of þeire owne hedes, bot ȝif þei afermid it by Scripture & doctours wordes; & now it is turnid into corioustee & schewyng of kunnyng. To þee it nediþ not, & perfore I do it nouȝt. For who-so haþ eren, lat him here (70, p. 125).

Secondly, the author hoped his reader would assimilate *The Cloud*'s teaching to his personal substance, as the author, clearly, had digested the teaching of others. And what better way to express one's own naked being than in the mother tongue? For, as Dante says, one's native tongue is intimately near his mind, and inasmuch as it was the language of his parents' conversation, it is, in a sense, the cause of his being in time.[60]

KENT EMERY, JR.

The University of Dallas

THE CONTINENTAL WOMEN MYSTICS
OF THE MIDDLE AGES: AN ASSESSMENT

In the study of medieval theology and, more latterly, spirituality, the outstanding figures have long been the theologians, monks, and friars whose writings have preserved their thought and tradition. Less attention has been given to various women who lived in cloisters, anchorholds, and 'in the world'. Deprived by social custom of the education open to men, women often depended on clergy as counsellors and secretaries. Frequently conscious of their educational inferiority to male contemporaries, they were further limited by prevalent opinions that women could not lead the contemplative life and, regardless of their vocation, should not enter into secular or ecclesiastical affairs. Their Lives and works reveal a great deal about their personalities, religious experiences, and strivings for justice, mortality, and peace in the medieval world.

THE GREAT CONTINENTAL WOMEN MYSTICS of the Middle Ages are the subject of this study: Hildegard of Bingen and Elizabeth of Schönau in the twelfth century, which witnessed clashes between Emperor and Pope, constant warfare, an apocalyptic *Zeitgeist*, and the waning of benedictine monasticism; the *mulieres sanctae* of the Low Countries, notably Mary of Oignies, Lutgarde of Aywières, Juliana of Cornillon, Beatrice of Nazareth, and Hadewyjch of Antwerp, the Helfta mystics Mechthild of Hackeborn, Mechthild of Magdeburg, Gertrude the Great, Marguerite d'Oingt, and finally Angela of Foligno, during the thirteenth century, which saw the rise of the Cistercian, Franciscan, and Dominican orders, the *Frauenfrage* and *Frauenbewegung* phenomena, the beguine and beghard movements, the *cura monialium*, and the chivalric and courtly love milieux coalescing with the Bernardine *Brautmystik*; and finally, the Dominican nuns in Bavaria and Switzerland, notably Margaret and Christine Ebner and Elsbeth Stagel, Birgitta of Sweden, and Catherine of Siena in the fourteenth century, with its continuation of the laxity and worldliness which plagued the Church and cried out for reform, the Black Death, the *Gottesfreunde* and *devotio moderna* movements, and power struggles between temporal and ecclesiastical forces which culminated in the Great Western Schism.

When we consider the direct contribution of women to the society and culture of the Middle Ages, we are, according to Lucia of the Incarnation, 'struck by the fact that, whenever she left her vast kingdom of silence and revealed her genius in a more outstanding way, it was almost always in the religious sphere; and here her contribution bears more characteristically that of a charismatic vocation than in the case of a man. She does not speak on her own account, but as an instrument: in this way, again, profoundly true to her nature. But in so doing, each time she reveals her unmistakable individuality.'[1]

The continental women mystics represented all social classes, secular life styles, and religious vocations, and their revelations ranged from prophecy to autobiographical accounts of their mystical experiences to treatises on the contemplative life. Yet, despite their idiosyncratic responses to their milieux and the *via mystica*, an assessment of their lives and writings reveals several notable similarities.

First, they all professed their reluctance to record their ecstatic experiences, which were unsought, usually because they felt unworthy to be the recipients of such graces. This might represent the modesty topos, but should more fairly be attributed to genuine humility, a lack of education ranging from illiteracy with Catherine of Siena to an inadequate knowledge of theology and Latin, or the prevalent ecclesiastical view that women could not be contemplatives and therefore should remain silent. This attitude is epitomized by John Gerson's attack on St Birgitta at the Council of Constance, with its basic tenet: 'All words and works of women must be held suspect.'[2] Another

impediment was the ever-present danger of fraudulent visionary experience, which necessitated a great level of discernment
of spirits and stirrings on the part of the mystic and her spiritual
director:

> It is well known that the Church views with great reserve
> the visions and revelations even of highly virtuous persons.
> Besides the possibility of fraud and delusions (which may
> be diabolical), there is also the strong possibility that, if
> the manifestation comes from God, the visionary's account
> of it may be impaired by error or exaggerations arising
> from preconceived ideas.[3]

There is ample evidence of the women mystics' awareness of
and scrupulous attention to this danger. Yet, because the mystic
is a human vessel for transmitting visions, her mental, emotional,
imaginative, and spiritual capacities necessarily enter into shaping those visions. There was the added fear of being accused
of sorcery or heresy, particularly in view of growing semi-
religious movements in the later thirteenth and fourteenth centuries, such as the beguines and beghards, which, while predom-
inantly orthodox, sometimes transgressed the periphery of orthodoxy and lapsed into schism, as with Bloemardine of Brussels,
Margaret Porete, the heresiarch Waldensians, and the Brothers
and Sisters of the Free Spirit.

The mystic's reluctance and self-doubt were overcome either
by a divine dictum or strong encouragement from her spiritual
director, compelling her to make known her revelations for the
edification and guidance of her even-christians. Mechthild of
Magdeburg's responses to this situation are typical:

> I cannot write nor do I wish to write — but see this book
> with the eyes of my soul and hear it with the ears of my
> eternal spirit and feel in every part of my body the power
> of the Holy Spirit.[4]

> Ah! Lord God! Who has written this book? I in my weak-
> ness have written it, because I dared not hide the gift that is
> in it. Ah! Lord! What shall this book be called to Thy
> Glory? It shall be called The Flowing Light of My God-
> head into all hearts which dwell therein without falseness.[5]

After receiving God's command to write, Mechthild says:

> Then went I, poor trembling wretch that I was, in humble shame to my confessor and told him all this and asked for guidance. He said I should go joyfully forward; God Who had called me would look after me. Then he commanded me to do that for which I often weep for shame when my unworthiness stands clear before my eyes, namely, that I, a poor despised little woman, should write this book out of God's heart and mouth. This book therefore has come lovingly from God and is not drawn from human senses.[6]

Responding to incredulous queries from her confessor, Mechthild states:

> You are surprised at the masculine way in which this book is written? I wonder why that surprises you. But it grieves me to the heart that I, a sinful woman, had so to write.[7]

And again:

> Ah, Lord, were I a learned man, a priest, in whom thou hadst made manifest this power, thou would'st see him honored. But how can they believe that on such unworthy ground thou hast raised a golden house?[8]

Fortunately, this conviction of inadequacy did not deter the mystic from recording her experiences. One indeed senses the spirit of the popular *Schwester Katrei* exemplum, which, in all of its variants, concerns how a simple woman triumphed over her confessor, a learned theologian.[9]

Secondly, all of the women mystics were under learned directors and confessors, who provided the necessary spiritual counsel and guidance, and, at the same time, educated the mystic in theology, liturgical and scriptural lore, and church doctrine. This *magister*/pupil relationship is seen with Hildegard of Bingen and the monks Vollmar and Gilbert of Gembloux; Elizabeth of Schönau, Abbot Hidelin, and her brother Eckbert; Mary of Oignes and Jacques de Vitry; Christine of Stommeln and Friar Gerard von Griesen and other friars from Cologne; Christine of St Trond and the Dominican Thomas of Cantimpré; Mechthild of Magdeburg and Henry of Halle, a pupil of Albert the Great; Elsbeth Stagel and Henry Suso;

Margaret Ebner and Henry of Nördlingen; Angela of Foligno and the Franciscan Fra Arnaldo; Birgitta of Sweden and Master Matthias of Linköping Cathedral, Peter of Skänninge, the Cistercian Peter of Alvastra, and Alphonse of Pecha, Bishop of Jaén; Catherine of Siena and Raymond of Capua; Dorothea of Prussia and John of Marianwerder; and Catherine of Genoa and Dom Cattaneo Marabotto. One must also recall that the Cistercians, Franciscans, and Dominicans were specifically charged with and executed the spiritual care of convents, beguinages, and individual recluses in the thirteenth, fourteenth, and fifteenth centuries.

Nowhere is the close relationship between the spiritual director and the mystic more clearly delineated than in Alphonse of Pecha's *Epistola solitarii ad reges* (1379), defending the divine source and validity of Birgitta's visions, and John Gerson's *De probatione spirituum* (1415), disparaging Birgitta and all women contemplatives, but at the same time carefully limning the role of the spiritual director.[10]

The third similarity concerns the mystic's education. As a corollary of the visionary's 'unlettered state', a term usually implying an ignorance of Latin, revelations were written and/or dictated to an amanuensis in the vernacular and subsequently translated into Latin, usually by the secretary. In most instances, the same person served as spiritual director and scribe, giving an added sanction to the work. Hagiographers and possibly spiritual directors 'stressed inspiration rather than learning, divine assistance in place of formal schooling, "inner light" instead of reason. Such a source of knowledge or information immediately assigns to writings *dictante Spiritu Sancto*, an authority that defies criticism.'[11] In most cases, they were not far from the mark, as the educational level of women in the Middle Ages varied greatly according to country — Germany had a stronger tradition than England in this regard — and vocation. Only Juliana of Cornillon and Gertrude were well versed in Latin, although Birgitta of Sweden gained a reasonable command of the language after going to Rome. Despite the growing demand for devotional and spiritual works in the vernacular by religious and lay audiences, Latin was still considered the only suitable medium for such writings.[12] Latin's preferred position is brought home forcefully by the anonymous Perugian *libellus*, impugning Birgitta's claim that Christ had dictated the Rule of St Saviour and an angel, the *Sermo Angelicus*, in Birgitta's mother tongue, Swedish. This attitude indicates the entirely irrational but very widely-held belief of the times that God and his angels and saints would not make use of any vernacular tongues, a belief which is reflected in the questions which the inquisitors put to St Joan of Arc about whether St Catherine and St Margaret spoke to her in French.[13]

This transmission process raises the question of scribal emendations and editorial license. Several of the mystics — notably Hildegard of Bingen, Angela of Foligno, and Birgitta of Sweden proofed their dictation and often reproved the scribe for failing to convey accurately the ineffability of their visions, or for departing from what had been dictated. Just as Margery Kempe's *Book* has been credited to her second scribe, a good portion of Elizabeth of Schönau's revelations were felt to be unduly influenced by her brother and scribe, Eckbert. The manuscript tradition of Mechthild of Magdeburg's *Das fliessende Licht von Gottheit* is complicated by its original transcription into Low German, its translation into Latin by her secretary Henry of Halle, and its subsequent retranslation into High German by Henry of Nördlingen, working from a Low German original no longer extant. Mechthild of Hackeborn's *Liber Specialis Gratiae* was compiled by Gertrude the Great, while only Book II of Gertrude's *Legatus* was actually written by her, the remainder being accomplished by the Helfta nuns. Alphonse of Pecha reordered and revised to some extent Birgitta's *Revelations*, and John of Marianwerder was responsible for the final editions of Dorothea of Montau's three works. Both the Italian and Latin versions of Catherine of Siena's *Dialogue* show scribal intervention; and the final form of Catherine of Genoa's *Treatise on Purgation and Purgatory* and *Spiri-*

tual Dialogue were entirely the posthumous product of Dom Cattaneo Marabotto, Ernesto Vernazza, and others among her disciples.

The original integrity of a mystic's writings was further challenged by its retranslation from Latin into its native or another vernacular. This is the problem raised, for example, by the numerous translations of Latin Continental works into Middle English, such as Elizabeth of Schönau's *Visiones*,[14] Mechthild of Hackeborn's *Liber Spiritualis Gratiae (The Booke of Gostlye Grace)*,[15] Birgitta's *Revelations*,[16] Catherine of Siena's *Dialogue (The Orcherd of Syon)*,[17] Margaret Porete's suspect *Mirror of Simple Souls*,[18] and the *Vitae* of the three Low Countries mystics, Elizabeth of Spalbeek, Christina Mirabilis, and Mary of Oignies.[19] Additional textual problems occurred through the incorporation of portions of continental mystical writings into Middle English devotional compilations and meditational works, as demonstrated by Birgitta's revelations concerning prophecy, the spiritual life, and the lives of Christ and Mary.[20] Often, as Norman Blake has shown, later vernacular versions of mystical texts adapted their originals to de-emphasize mystical content and stress devotional material, indicating a more popular audience.[21]

According to F. P. Pickering, a similar situation prevailed in Germany, with innumerable manuscripts containing the literature of the German mystics, not only codices dating from the fourteenth century with the complete works of one writer or selections from works of a group of mystics, but also fifteenth-century miscellanies of mystical and devotional texts, epigonic in composition, often omitting the name of the mystic author, and exemplifying a spirit of *docta ignorantia*. The contents of these compendia can be called *zerschriebene*, i.e., simplified and popularized for the devotional reading of a large part of the population.[22] Much remains to be done on these compendia, which have been largely ignored by scholars.

The fourth point concerns the mystics' attitude toward suffering and penance. The *via mystica* necessarily imposed on both men and women mystics a *modus vivendi* of penance, grief for sins, mortifications, self-abnegation, and an intensified prayer life, with concomitant physical and spiritual suffering. The goals of self-knowledge and knowledge of God which leads to love were not easily attained, and, indeed, 'the fire of infused contemplation must first sear both sense and spirit until a soul is purged and purified.'[23] Several of the women mystics experienced a serious 'conversion illness', as did Mechthild of Magdeburg, or, as it is often pointed out, suffered poor health, as did Elizabeth of Schönau, Mechthild of Hackeborn, Angela of Foligno, Catherine of Siena, and Catherine of Genoa. In fact, considerations about the mysticism of women often state or imply 'that their more delicate bodies and minds were especially sensitive and susceptible to hysteria and the like.'[24] Speaking of the high incidence of mystical life at Engelthal, Rufus Jones writes: 'Few things are more contagious than the type of holiness, and one would expect that a saintly woman like Christine Ebner would become the quickening exemplar for a large number of persons in her environment.'[25] Concerning Margaret Ebner, Oskar Pfister states: 'She was strongly emotional and sentimental, a victim of lifelong illness and plainly enough psychopathic.'[26] Among some critics there is a consensus that some forms of constitutional instability and lack of intellectual strength and structure 'are favorable to genius and to the making of the prophet type of person.'[27] These and similar opinions employ a *reductio ad absurdum* logic that women who have visions are usually ill, or vice versa, denying the mystical life to their healthier but by no means less holy sisters.

All too often, modern psychoanalytical approaches to the medieval *mulieres sanctae* somehow ignore or fail to understand the dimensions, demands, and context of their mystical experiences. One would wish that Baron Friedrich von Hügel[28] or Fr Benedict Groeschel,[29] with their balanced and sympathetic assessment of Catherine of Genoa's 'basically healthy personality', had wielded more influence on scholars, and thus precluded such judgments and categorizations as 'hysterical', 'pathological', 'suppressed', 'repressed', and 'psychotic'. For, as Kenneth Wapnick has shown, while pathological states lead to disintegration of the personality, mysticism does the very opposite.[30]

The mystics considered suffering, both physical and spiritual, as a sign of divine grace, 'a grave, but kindly teacher of immortal secrets',[31] an essential concomitant of the progressive spiritual life. And the spiritual pain of desolation, despair, loneliness, and spiritual dryness was far worse than any physical affliction. Accordingly, suffering was creative, positive, and utilitarian in its end of purification not only of the mystic's soul, but, even more, the sinful souls of others, living and in Purgatory. Such expiation and atonement became a topos in the writings of the women mystics. This concept of the redemptive power of suffering, reinforced by and sharing in Christ's exemplar sacrifice, and combined with the purging of self-love and the corresponding increase of charity, was the keystone to achieving mystical union with God. As the soul was purified and strengthened by grace, in Catherine of Siena's words, it 'no longer merely suffers with patience, but eagerly longs to suffer for the glory and praise of His name . . . [so that] suffering is a delight, and pleasure is wearisome'.[32] The highest form of suffering—and one welcomed joyfully by the women mystics—was the stigmata, which was granted to Mary of Oignies, Ida of Louvain, Christine of Stommeln, Gertrude of Oosten, Gertrude the Great, and Catherine of Siena. In the latter two instances, the stigmata were invisible, at the mystic's request, reflecting the mystic's characteristic dislike of being singular or attracting unusual attention. As further justification of suffering, these women realized that their sins and imperfections not only affected themselves, but their whole communities, just as their expiatory acts benefited the community and the Mystical Body of Christ. One final comment: Austere asceticism and penitential practices which may seem excessive to modern man were an accepted part of medieval spiritual life, and yet many of the women mystics practised and urged moderation in the area of self-imposed penances.

The fifth likeness is found in the content and stylistic features of women's mystical writings. The revelations are autobiographical accounts of visions, auditions, and other mystical experiences, which, at the same time, are treatises on the life of prayer and contemplation, as, for example, Beatrice of Nazareth's *Seven Ways (or Degrees) of Love*, Gertrude the Great's *Spiritual Exercises*, and Angela of Foligno's *Memoriale* account of the thirty steps to perfection. Another component of these works is denunciatory reproach of the immorality and laxity in the Church and secular spheres. In the cases of Hildegard, Elizabeth of Schönau, Mary of Oignies, Lutgarde of Aywières, and Birgitta of Sweden, these cries for reform were cast as divine prophecies with judgmental sanctions, and a strong sense of apocalyptic urgency. Hildegard, Elizabeth of Schönau, the Helfta nuns, Birgitta, Angela of Foligno and Catherine of Siena also wrote numerous letters of admonition, spiritual guidance, theological disquisition, and consolation which complement and often illuminate their mystical works, as does the extensive correspondence of the *Gottesfreunde* circle, and, in particular, that between Margaret Ebner and Henry of Nördlingen and Elsbeth Stagel and Henry Suso. Legends of the mystics' lives were yet another avenue for promulgating their teaching and example. Some of the more famous of this hagiographic subgenre are the lives of Mary of Oignies, Christine the Admirable, Elizabeth of Spalbeek, Birgitta, Catherine of Siena, and the *Vitae Sororum* of the Dominican nuns at Adelhausen, Töss, Engelthal, Katharinental, Unterlinden, and Ötenbach.[393]

In general, although the visions are received, as Hildegard of Bingen states, 'with the eyes and ears of the soul', the visionary language of the women mystics is far more imaginative, colorful, sensuous, and descriptive than that of their male counterparts, with much use of symbol, allegory, and similitude. This is evident in Hildegard's *Columba aspexit*, with its cascade of images from the Song of Songs and the Apocalypse, and the thirty-five manuscript illuminations of thirteen visions from her *Scivias*, executed under her direction; the opulence and pageantry of the celestial court described by the two Mechthilds; Mechthild of Magdeburg's 'Ghostly Cloister'; Gertrude the Great's Tree of Love; and Catherine of Siena's Bridge of Christ and graphic depiction of the Passion and Crucifixion of Christ. Teresa Halligan notes:

> Such psycho-physical phenomena, merely accidental concomitants to the highest reaches of the interior life, might be considered the artistic expressions and creative results of the mystic's intuition of God's presence in her soul. It is only in terms of a language of the spiritual senses, applicable by analogy, that the mystic can reconstruct what is essentially intellectual and non-corporeal.[34]

Quite often the women visionaries adopted the rhetorical strategy of colloquy between God and the mystic's soul, the latter speaking in the third person, or between personified aspects of the soul, or between the soul and Love, in the interests of distancing themselves from and, at the same time, communicating the immediacy, truth, and didactic import of their visions. Dialogue is primary in the writings of Elizabeth of Schönau speaking with the Angel of the Lord, Hadewyjch, the Helfta nuns, Catherine of Siena, Margaret Porete's *Mirror for Simple Souls*, and Catherine of Genoa's *Spiritual Dialogue*. The added element of psychomachia is employed to delineate the spiritual struggle within the soul, an element especially apparent in Hildegard's *Liber Vitae Meritorum* and her *Ordo Virtutum*, which has been called the earliest known morality play.[35] Personification in semi-dramatic settings is widely used, but nowhere more effectively than by Mechthild of Magdeburg. And not a few of this group of mystics were skilled poets, among them Hildegard, Hadewyjch, and Mechthild of Magdeburg.

In the works of the women visionaries, one notes the prevalence of the *Brautmystik* — the love affair between Christ and the soul, leading to espousal and marriage, inspired by Bernard of Clairvaux's sermons on the Song of Songs, and Richard of

St Victor's *Four Degrees of Passionate Love*, and amplified with incursions from the chivalric and courtly love milieux. This is another aspect of the women mystics which has come under sharp critical attack, usually based on instances of excess (and there were such instances), and resulting in such caustic phrases as 'morbidly exaggerated sensibility.' One representative example of the latter is Rufus Jones' appraisal of Mechthild of Magdeburg: 'There is a large element of pathology in the story, far too much reproduction of the experiences reported in the Song of Solomon, and unwholesome dialogues of love intimacies which mark this type of amorous, romantic, cloistered mysticism.'[36] Yet the basic *Brautmystik* similitude is one of the most universally used means of describing the ineffability of divine Love, nor was its usage limited to women ecstatics. Speaking of the inadequacy of language to communicate the mystical heights, Odo Egres notes in his study of Mechthild of Magdeburg:

> It must be stressed that words and images, when used as metaphors, will never completely express a mystical experience in all its dimensions. Even a mental and emotional comprehension of linguistic metaphors is still far from comprehension of the experience itself. Yet there is no other, more reliable way to the mystical experience of an individual or to the mystical heritage of a certain time period than the linguistic study of those images used by a mystic touched with grace, and intended to make the spiritually attuned reader understand or at least surmise what a blissfully overburdened soul wants to say.[37]

Fortunately, several competent studies on the language of the mystics are now available, which should encourage further research in this important area.[38]

The central spiritual foci for all of the women mystics were Christ Crucified, the Blessed Virgin, the Trinity, the Eucharist, and divine Love. A number of works show a correlation with liturgical feasts and other aspects of the *Opus Dei*, inclusivism in the form of cosmic visions, Trinitarian exemplarism, love of the Infant Jesus, and devotion to the Sacred Heart, the latter particularly with Lutgarde and her *consorores*, the Helfta nuns, and Catherine of Siena. While there are elements of Hell, Purgatory, and diabolic temptations, the major emphasis is on Love. Furthermore, all of this corpus is marked by doctrinal orthodoxy and an unwavering support and reverence for the Church and sacraments. Yet despite their holy lives and endeavors, the majority of the women mystics were not formally canonized, but they were eventually included in the roman martyrology.

All of the women ecstatics evinced a forceful social consciousness and the capacity to lead the mixed life of action and contemplation. In his seminal article, 'Social Responsibility and the Late Medieval Mystics'[39] Ray C. Petry countered the charges of selfish isolation, quietism, and social irresponsibility on the part of the mystics by illustrating how they, in actuality, sought to achieve a christian equilibrium between contemplative worship of God and active service to humanity. Pointing to Ramon Llull, Eckhart, Suso, and Tauler, Petry clearly showed that, despite the primacy accorded to contemplation, these great mystics were vitally involved in secular and ecclesiastical affairs, following 'the Pauline and Augustinian notion of an ongoing presence or indwelling of God within the soul, by virtue of which God operates through the instrument of a human person.'[40] Similarly, in the spirit of *Imitatio Christi*, the women mystics applied 'the contemplative way opened through Christ to the active way pursued with Christ,'[41] and achieved this *Wirkeinheit* or working union with God as a result of *libertas cordis* — the true liberty of spirit, found only in the highest reaches of the mystical life.[42] Their vocation was not to escape from the world but to reform it,[43] and, while enriching the *depositum fidei* with their contemplative prayer, to respond actively to the needs of their fellow Christians, as a correlative of their spiritual progress. Kenneth Wapnick comments on the integral and integrating nature of this return:

> The mystic now no longer finds his involvement with the world to be abhorrent, but, in fact, seems to welcome the opportunity to move in the social world he had abandoned.

This seeming paradox becomes understandable when one considers it was not the world the mystic was renouncing, but merely his attachments and needs relating to it, which precluded the development of his personal asocial experience. Once he was able to abandon these dependent, social needs, and felt freed of the social world, he experienced the freedom to live within society in conjunction with his inner strivings, rather than experiencing society's customs and institutions as obstacles to his self-fulfillment.[44]

William Ernest Hocking, among others, sees the mystic's return to social action as the end-product of the *via mystica*, the ultimate extension of his love for God, and God's love for him.[45]

Speaking to Catherine of Siena, and reflecting the mystical dictum that love cannot be idle, God said:

I have set you as workers in your own and your neighbors' souls and in the mystic body of Holy Church. In yourselves you must work at virtue. . . . Every virtue and every sin is realized and intensified through your neighbor. Therefore, I want you to serve your neighbor, and in this way share the fruits of your own vineyard.[46]

Similarly, Christ advised Gertrude the Great:

I do not find my pleasure merely in the interior exercise of contemplation, but also in various exterior and useful works which are directed to my honor. . . . Furthermore, it is by manual works that men find occasion to practice charity, patience, humility, and other virtues.[47]

There is a further consideration regarding this aspect of the mystical life. As pointed out by Katherine Dyckman and Patrick Carroll, the mystics were ecumenical in the most profound sense: reconciling and uniting people everywhere and so extending Christ through the *oikumene* — the whole world. And they were prophetic in the most profound sense:

All these holy people are holy not just because they pray or write eloquently about . . . prayer, but because their prayer leads them to respond to Christ in the given historical cultural moment. All of them respond in a unique way to unique situations in which they find the Lord calling to

his people. But all respond outside themselves in service.
Each mystic becomes a prophet. . . . The beauty of God's
love and God's activity in the world are profoundly realized; the invitation to celebrate this beauty is equally intense. This intensity is coupled with the deepening desire
to mend what is unfinished in this broken world, at least in
that part that touches and calls to us. . . . Justice is the
prophet's goal. Prayer in some form will always become a
critique of ideologies, putting into question what is, in the
presence of a vision of what might be, a vision of justice.[48]

All of the women mystics were ardent prophet-reformers,
many campaigning strenuously against heretics like the Cathars
and Free Spirit adherents, and all sharing a special animus toward the amorality and worldliness of the Church. A representative example of their anticlerical stance, which frequently resulted in persecution and calumniation by ecclesiasts, is Mechthild of Magdeburg's diatribe against evil priests:

> Alas! O crown of Holy Church, how dim art thou become!
> Thy precious stones have fallen [the rulers and holy doc-
> tors] because thou dost wound and injure holy Christian
> Faith. Thy gold is dimmed in the filth of evil desires; thou
> art become poor, thou hast no true love, thy purity is
> burned up in the consuming fire of greed; thy humility is
> sunk in the swamp of thy flesh; thy truth is brought to
> nought by the lies of this world; the flowers of all the vir-
> tues have fallen from thee. Alas! for the fallen crown of the
> priesthood! . . . If any one is ignorant of the way to Hell,
> let him look at the depraved priesthood . . . hastening with-
> out let to the nether regions.[49]

Hildegard, Birgitta, and Catherine of Siena worked for societal
and church reform with prophecies, counseling, letters, sermons, and apostolic missions to spiritual and secular leaders.
Catherine also played a significant role in the reform of the
Dominican Order, and her influence in this regard continues to
the present day.[50]

Many of these women, as mystic social activists, were closely
associated with the dispossessed, the poor, the sick, and the in-
curably ill, as seen in Hildegard's medical treatises and work in

the convent infirmary, and in the heroic nursing of lepers and plague victims by Catherine of Siena, Angela of Foligno, and Catherine of Genoa. Those who chose the beguine vocation necessarily led the mixed life, since they had to support themselves, but were particularly devoted to humanitarian and charitable works. Combining the Mary-Martha lifestyles, those in cloister performed a wide variety of conventual tasks, such as serving as abbess, training novices, working in the scriptorium and library, participating in the office and other observances of their Rule, gardening, and menial household chores. In addition to leading exemplary lives, the women mystics taught, counseled, and gave spiritual guidance unceasingly, and especially those who were surrounded by circles of lay and religious followers and whose spirituality was often translated into social and ecclesial reform. One thinks immediately of Catherine of Siena's *bella brigata* of *Caterinati*, Angela of Foligno as Mistress of Theologians to her spiritual sons, and Catherine of Genoa's and Ettore Vernazza's Oratory of Divine Love, devoted to church reform through spiritual reform of the individual and care of the poor. As a part of their teaching charge, the women mystics wrote their revelations, prophecies and treatises on the *via mystica* as theodicies, for the inspiration and direction of all their neighbors. In so doing, they refuted the charge that mysticism did not lead to any activity in theological thought or produce a religious reformation. Moreover, their 'enquiries into the nature of the soul and its relation to God . . . are full of speculative interest, and have played no small part in paving the way towards a more rational interpretation of the position of man with regard to faith, to merit, to retribution, and to the other great questions of dogma.'[51]

The influence of the women visionaries is seen in several areas. In the case of the English mystics, many of the major works were written for women religious, such as the *Ancrene Riwle*, the Wooing Group, Thomas of Hale's *Love Rune*, Ælred of Rievaulx's *Letter to His Sister*, Richard Rolle's *Form of Living*, and Book I of Walter Hilton's *Scale of Perfection*.

Although we do not have a similar amount of evidence-con-cerning the continental women mystics as audience, we do know that Eckhart, Tauler, and Suso preached and wrote in the vernacular, at least in part, for an audience of mystically-inclined women and religious. In this regard, Ernest McDon-nell writes:

> A sound basis for religious prose literature in the vernacular could be found only when regular and semi-religious wom-en's communities without Latin clerical education but with the need for devotional writings and theological instruction adopted a permanent and ordered form, thus opening up the possibility of appropriating Latin theological-mystical material. These conditions were found in groups affiliated with mendicant orders, especially the Dominicans in the Low Countries and Germany, as borne out by nunnery catalogues. We must assume that such a popular religious literature existed in southern France and Italy, where the feminine religious movement sought direction from the Dominicans and Franciscans.[52]

As we noted above, the writings of the mystics in the vernac-ular were also demanded and read by an increasingly literate laity. And through translation and dissemination, the works of the continental women mystics enjoyed great popularity throughout Europe and in England, where there apparently was a growing interest in these visionaries.[53] Undoubtedly the *Index of Middle English Prose*, currently under way in North America, the British Isles, and Europe, will uncover further manuscript evidence concerning the transmission, translation, and popularity of the works of these continental mystics. This and similar inventories of vernacular manuscripts will help to establish patterns of influence, confluence, and what Ruth Dean has termed the 'dynamics of diffusion' of manuscripts belonging to the several traditions of feminine mysticism.[54]

Much has been written on the contribution of the English mystics to the development of the English language,[55] and James Franklin imputes a similar importance of the German mystic for the historical development of the German language.

By word coining, word combinations, translations of Latin terms, and extension of word meanings, the mystics expanded the capacity of German for use as a philosophical and literary language.[56]

Above all, these great women mystics manifested an important moral and spiritual presence in their own ages, the full influence and consequences of which cannot be measured.

With regard to more specific influences, Hildegard of Bingen's prophecies were not only heeded by the leading personages of her time, but were seized upon by Jacob van Maerlaent (c. 1235-1300) and the moral-didactic school of Flemish poetry, by Lodewijch van Velthem in his continuation of the *Spieghel Historiael*, by the Cistercian monks at Villers, and by other prelates and laymen in the Low Countries.[57] Her *Scivias* served as the model for Elizabeth of Schönau's *Liber Viarum Dei*. It is interesting to note that she is receiving growing recognition from modern scholars as one of the most significant poets and musicians of the twelfth century, a medieval Sor Juana.[58] Elizabeth of Schönau promoted the liturgical feast of the Assumption of the Blessed Virgin Mary, and wrote the official legend of St Ursula and the 11,000 virgin martyrs of Cologne, one of the favorite hagiographic legends of the Middle Ages. Mary of Oignies, Juliana of Cornillon, and Eve of St Martin promoted the feast of Corpus Christi, established at Liège in 1246, while Lutgarde of Aywières and the Helfta mystics promoted the cult of the Sacred Heart, to be sanctioned by the Church in 1673, following the revelations of St Margaret Mary Alacoque. According to Stephen Axters, Beatrice of Nazareth's *Seven Ways (or Degrees) of Love* is important for the history of Low Countries' spirituality, especially in its delineation of theopathic soul states,[59] while Hadewyjch's influence is manifest in the writings of Ruysbroeck. Mechthild of Magdeburg's *Flowing Light of the Godhead* was widely distributed among the *Gottesfreunde* groups in Bavaria and Switzerland, even reaching the eremitic Waldschwestern near Einsiedeln, and may have affected Eckhart's thought on the mutual craving between the soul and God.[60] The impact of Mechthild of Hackeborn's *Revelations* is evident in England in the *Speculum Devotorum*, the devotion of the the *Hundred Pater Nosters*, and the *Myroure of Oure Ladye*, all associated with Syon Abbey and the Carthusians.[61] Both of the Helfta Mechthilds have been considered as the inspiration for Dante's Matelda in *Purgatorio* 18 and 31. Henry of Nördlingen's correspondence with Margaret Ebner and other contemporary mystics represents the first collection of letters in the German language, while Elsbeth Stagel at Töss was as central to Henry Suso's life as Clare was to Francis of Assisi, encouraging him to write his *vita*, collecting his letters to his spiritual daughters, and translating some of his works into German. Angela of Foligno's guidance of her disciple-priests bore rich fruit in Ubertino da Casale, whose *Arbor Vitae Crucifixae Jesu* contains a glowing encomium to his *pia mater*. Birgitta's Order of St Saviour flourished throughout the Middle Ages, and still exists under her original rule at Syon Abbey, South Brent, Devon, as well as in an active branch established by Sr Maria Elizabeth Hesselblad (d. 1957). For her life and works, the Roman Church proclaimed Catherine of Siena as Patroness of Italy, with Francis of Assisi, in 1939, and in 1970 she and Teresa of Avila became the first women Doctors of the Church. Catherine of Genoa's greatest historical contribution was to inspire the founding of the Oratory of Divine Love, which later merged with the Theatines and became a vital force for church reform.

The ongoing impact of the continental women mystics is attested to in the lives and writings of St Ignatius Loyola, Venerable Augustine Baker and his disciple Dame Gertrude More, St Francis de Sales, St Alphonse Liguori, Madame Acarie, Archbishop Fénelon, Bousset, Fr Isaac Hecker, and Cardinal Newman—to name only a few.

With the current renascence of interest in Western mysticism, medieval and modern, it is hoped that scholars will address themselves to much-needed critical editions, translations, and balanced assessments of the works of this extraordinary group of women, so that their message of hope and divine Love may be heard in our own age and beyond.

Valerie M. Lagorio

The University of Iowa

ST TERESA AND THE SPIRITUALITY
OF SIXTEENTH-CENTURY SPAIN

Teresa of Avila (1515-1582) entered the Carmelite monastery of her native town at twenty-one. A serious illness interrupted an initial fervent period, and led to fourteen years of lukewarmness. Undergoing an intense conversion in 1554, she once more began experiencing contemplative prayer. This led her to consult many of the theologians of her day and ultimately to become a teacher and writer on prayer and the mystical life. At the age of forty-seven, she set out to found new, small communities of contemplative Carmelites. With great vigor and unflagging good humor she traveled up and down Spain organizing and directing these communities, seventeen of which she founded before her death. Her works include letters, an autobiography, The Way of Perfection, The Interior Castle, Meditations on the Song of Songs, Foundations, Spiritual Testimonies, Constitutions, *and others.*

A SUBSTANTIAL PART of the teaching of St Teresa (1515-1582) comes to us in the form of narrative, with its storylike character of life itself, with its tensions and surprises, its shocks and achievements, its revelations of authentic and inauthentic life. Her narrative is the account of her own life which she used as the backdrop for a further account, a testimony to the mercy of God, persistent and inexhaustible, as it reaches out to the misery of each man and woman and waits for the hour to give.

As Teresa's story begins to unfold, we can note that books play a decisive role in the early development of this future saint. In her childhood she enjoyed reading, with her brother, the lives of the saints, becoming so deeply inspired by them that even though a child she already felt a strong desire to die and go to heaven so as to enjoy more quickly the wonderful things she read were there.[1] Later, when in her upper teens, while staying at the home of a devout uncle, Don Pedro de Cepeda who, though a layman, was both caught up in a spiritual movement spreading through Spain and moved to dedicate himself to the life of prayer, she was invited to read to him from his many spiritual books. Though she did not care at the time for the books she was asked to read, one of them, *The Letters of St Jerome*, unexpectedly touched her soul and pushed her to a decision she was trying to avoid: to leave the world and enter a monastery of Carmelite nuns.[2]

At another time, after her profession of religious vows, when because of illness she was again staying at her uncle's home, she received from him another quite different book to read, Francisco de Osuna's *Third Spiritual Alphabet*. From this book she learned for the first time about interior prayer, especially the prayer of recollection, and began to practise what Osuna advised, only to receive almost from the start the experience of passive prayer, what she called in a specialized vocabulary of the time the prayer of quiet and the prayer of union.[3]

Shortly afterward she underwent intense physical suffering as a result of some unsound remedies used by a quack in Becedas. Brought to the point of death, she subsequently suffered a paralysis for three years. In these painful times, Teresa found strength from a renowned classic she had read by St Gregory the Great; it was his *Moralia*, a commentary on Job.[4] From the story of Job, she learned patience and acceptance. 'Since we receive good things from the hand of the Lord, why do we not suffer the evil things?'

Her long illness brought an end to her initially happy experience with prayer; after her cure she went through many years of floundering as though lost at sea and going nowhere. One day, after some fourteen years of these troubles, a conversion took place while she was reading about St Augustine's conversion in his *Confessions*.[5] His narrative evoked so strong a response in her that it seemed the very grace the Lord had given to Augustine was now being given to her. Fortified by this she began to devote more of her time to being with Jesus Christ and loving him. Now, indeed, a whole new life began for Teresa.

'The life lived up to this point was mine,' she says; the one she lived from that point on 'is the one God lived in me.'[6]

In this new life, Teresa began to receive an inundation of spiritual delight and sweetness, often without being able to avoid it. While in her experiences of union with God, she felt much certitude; later, 'after a little distraction', as she says, she began to doubt and then to fear.[7]

These doubts and fears were due in large measure to the religious climate of Spain in her day. The spiritual books she read and benefited by were the product of a vast movement of religious reform and renewal being cultivated mainly through the efforts of Cardinal Cisneros who, in addition to being a Franciscan, became the confessor of Queen Isabella, archbishop of Toledo, primate of Spain, the supreme inquisitor, and the founder of the University of Alcalá. Initiated before the Council of Trent, this Spanish Catholic reform movement coincided with the first half of Teresa's life[8] and affected not only religious and clergy but laity as well, since one of its points of emphasis was the call to christian perfection of all the baptized. Newly-founded printing presses at Alcalá, Montserrat, and Sevilla provided people with abundant literature on prayer and the interior life. There were translations from the Fathers, from the Italian, Flemish, and German schools, from Erasmus, the scholastics, Protestants, and humanists. Much cross-fertilization of ideas from these various schools, traditions, and movements took place. From the Netherlands, where Christianity had developed a strong pietist strain, came the tendency to emphasize mental prayer and inwardness and to react against outward devotional practices, forms, and ceremonies; there came also what is called the Modern Devotion with its systematization of mental prayer. From Florence, the heart of Italy, came Savonarola as a reformer and a spiritual writer with an apocalyptic interest in visions and revelations. This whole push for spiritual reform set in motion an illuminist movement that blossomed into excellent forms of spirituality, but also distorted ones.

The *alumbrados*, members of this movement, urged the interior life. Some placed the highest emphasis on recollection, a method of turning inward and allowing oneself to be influenced by the divine action. The teachers of recollection were more often from the religious orders and worked to develop a method of the interior life and mental prayer that would help individuals along a path to union with God.[9] Francisco De Osuna, a Franciscan friar, gave this movement a definitive expression in his book *The Third Spiritual Alphabet*, the book, as we said, that launched Teresa on the path of prayer. Others among the *alumbrados* built their spirituality on abandonment and insisted more and more on passivity and interior inspiration.

As happens with religious movements, exaggerated forms were soon to develop in which it was asserted that through mental prayer one frees oneself of all other ascetical duties and from the need for effort in the practice of virtue. The seeker was to renounce interior acts and exterior works and avoid thinking about Jesus Christ. All these kinds of activity, including obedience to superiors, it was said, were like roadblocks along the path to union.

Another aberration to appear was an unrestrained infatuation with ecstasy and other extraordinary phenomena. These were regarded as something to be sought. The *beata* of Piedrahita, María de Santo Domingo, had turned her monastery into a kind of center for spirituality and advanced prayer. But because of some pseudo-mystical deviations the master general of the Dominicans had to isolate her and forbid anyone in the Order to converse with her or administer the sacraments, except her confessor; neither was anyone allowed to write to her or tell others about her prophecies, ecstasies, and raptures.

In another instance, a Poor Clare, Magdalena de la Cruz, a stigmatic with a reputation for holiness, turned out to be a secret devil worshiper, after having fooled even bishops. This confirmed the popular belief that the devil uses women to deceive men, and once a preacher in condemning Teresa compared her to this 'fraud.'[10]

From the political point of view, a great effort was being

waged in Teresa's time to bring the disparate Castilians, Aragonese, and Catalans together. One of the convenient tools used in this effort was the promotion of a common faith among the people, thereby putting an end to any kind of tolerance between Christian, Moslem, and Jew. Making use as well of the common people's hatred of foreigners and their ideas and ways, the leaders sought to keep Protestants out of Spain. The inquisition, as a result, turned its attention to the illuminists and arrested the Franciscan tertiary, Isabel de la Cruz, for heresy. The following year, 1525, it condemned forty-eight illuminist propositions and issued a decree against what it considered the heresies of Luther.[11] From then on, any promotion of the interior life was open to the charge of either illuminism or Lutheranism.

With this historical situation in mind, we can understand the fears of Teresa. Through the help of a layman, Don Francisco de Salcedo, who had entered enthusiastically into the spiritual reform movement and had been practising mental prayer for about forty years, the fearful Teresa arranged to consult a priest, Gaspar Daza, known in Avila for his great holiness. As things turned out this priest proved too severe with Teresa and frightened her even more. She concluded it would be best for her not to take him as guide. Continuing, however, to discuss her spiritual life and her fears with the layman, Don Francisco, who was less frightening to her, she was encouraged. He helped her to overcome some of her defects, which she thought were incompatible with the kind of prayer she was experiencing. But soon Don Francisco himself began to have doubts.

Adding to the problem was Teresa's inability to explain her prayer. In the end, she resorted to another work, written from within the illuminist movement, by a partisan of the practice of recollection. The book entitled *The Ascent of Mount Sion* was by the Franciscan Bernardino de Laredo. Along with underlined passages from this work Teresa gave Don Francisco her first attempt at a written statement about her spiritual life, what she calls 'an account of my life and sins'.[12] Supplied with this information, Francisco went to consult the holy Maestro Daza, while Teresa awaited their verdict with anxiety, spending the days in prayer and recommending herself to the prayers of many friends. The considered opinion of these two devout souls was a hard blow. They concluded that her experiences came from the devil. Stunned, not knowing where to turn, Teresa went to the oratory and wept.

One door, however, was left open for her when the two consultors suggested she confer with a member of a new society of men religious, the Jesuits, who were frequently considered to be a part of the illuminist movement and were spiritual men knowing more about prayer than the average priest or friar.

The first Jesuit whom Teresa consulted was Diego de Cetina, an understanding priest who consoled and assured her that her prayer was from God. Feeling much better under his direction, she attributes this to the fact that 'he guided my soul by stressing the love of God and allowed freedom and used no pressure if I didn't set about doing things out of love'.[13] There was one area, however, in which he did not allow freedom; that was in prayer. Advising her to resist the passive experiences of recollection and consolation, he directed her to turn her attention to the passion of Christ. Here Teresa learned a lesson. Her passive experiences in prayer came independent of any kind of technique. At one time she had thought that for passive prayer a great deal of seclusion was necessary, as well as bodily quiet. But now she found that the more she tried to resist this prayer and distract herself, 'the more the Lord enveloped me in that sweetness and glory which seemed to surround me so completely that there was no place to escape'.[14] As a consequence she became somewhat amused by people who thought they must not stir a finger in prayer lest the quiet be disturbed.

She began to understand too the value of consulting a confessor, or spiritual director, and being open to his advice, trying even to obey him as she thought she must. The outstanding records we have of her inner life and of her mystical experience find their origin in this Catholic practice of manifesting one's state of soul to a spiritual director or confessor with the faith that God will enlighten and keep from deception the one who practises such docility to another member of the Church. She began to understand as well that it was wise to consult learned men who would be able to confirm whether or not her experiences were in accord with the teachings of Scripture.[15] From this experience, too, came the decisively clear understanding that Jesus is no obstacle to the highest contemplation, contrary to a notion she had gathered from some of the illuminist books she had read.[16]

A little later when Francis Borgia, who as Duke of Gandia had renounced all his earthly possessions to enter the Jesuits, came to Avila, Diego de Cetina and Francisco de Salcedo, still diligently keeping informed about Teresa's case, arranged a meeting between the two future saints of the Church. Francis encouraged Teresa, told her to begin her prayer with an event from the passion of Jesus, but not to resist when drawn into the passive prayer she was experiencing, in which it was impossible for her to think. Francisco de Salcedo was glad now too, Teresa adds, that in the judgement of Father Francis her experiences were from God.

The illuminations coming from this infused prayer revealed to Teresa the need for some further changes in her habits. At the same time, she felt incapable of giving up some friendships she thought she must. Discussing this matter with another Jesuit confessor, Father Prádanos, since Father Cetina had been transferred, she was told to pray over the matter and to recite the *Veni Creator*, a vocal prayer to the Holy Spirit, for light. One day (in 1555), while reciting this prayer, she experienced her first rapture and heard the words: 'No longer do I want you to converse with men but with angels'. The effects of this prayer were obvious to Teresa, and she wrote: 'May God be blessed forever because in an instant he gave me the freedom that I with all the efforts of many years could not attain by myself, often trying so to force myself that my health had to pay dearly.'[17]

The extraordinary experience of what in mystical writings is
known as the locution became a common occurrence for Teresa, and, as was to be expected, she once again submitted this
phenomenon to her confessor. He consulted others; as a result
five or six men met to discuss her spiritual state. Their unanimous decision as relayed to her by her confessor was that her
experiences were caused by the devil, that she should not receive Communion as often as she had been doing, that she
should distract herself, and avoid being alone. She became extremely fearful, dared not enter a room alone; yet deep inside
she could not feel agreement with their judgement. This latter
feeling only added to her fear because she thought it showed
lack of humility on her part. So she went on trying to force
herself to believe what they said.

Once, in a state of fear and confusion over what was then
happening to her, she heard the words: 'Do not fear, daughter,
for I am, and I will not abandon you; do not fear'. With these
words, in an instant, her fears were taken away and a wave of
courage, fortitude, and inner quiet came upon her. In addition
the fears of the devil implanted in her by the mentality of her
times left her, and she was later able to state: 'I don't understand
these fears, "The devil! The devil!", when we can say "God!
God!", and make the devil tremble.' The only thing we should
fear or be intimidated by, she concluded, is offending God.[18]

Teresa continued manifesting everything to her confessor and
trying to follow his advice, even though one priest told her not
to bother telling her experiences to her confessor if she thought
they were from God. Certainly, this would have been easier for
Teresa and freed her of much embarassment, but it did not seem
right. 'As often as the Lord commanded something of me in
prayer', she wrote, 'and my confessor told me to do otherwise,
the Lord returned and told me to obey my confessor; afterward
His Majesty would change the confessor's mind, and he would
agree with the Lord's command.'[19]

In 1559, during this period, the supreme inquisitor, Ferdinand
Valdés, out of both fear of growing illuminism and a desire to

protect the country from Lutheranism, published an index of forbidden books. Included on this index were most books on prayer written in the vernacular. Among them were books by St Francis Borgia, St John of Avila, Luis de Granada, Francisco de Osuna, Tauler, Harphius, and Denis the Carthusian. Some of them were among Teresa's favorites. Dejected over this turn of events, Teresa heard the Lord say to her: 'Don't be sad, for I shall give you a living book.'[20]

Soon after this she began to understand in a new way through what she called the intellectual vision or what we can also term mystical understanding.

> Afterward, within only a few days, I understood very clearly, because I received so much to think about and such recollection in the presence of what I saw, and the Lord showed so much love for me by teaching me in many ways, that I have very little or almost no need for books. His Majesty had become the true book in which I saw the truths. Blessed be such a book that leaves what must be read and done so impressed that you cannot forget![21]

At this time, while her confessors were urging her to pray and get others to pray that God would lead her by another path than the one she was on, Teresa had an intellectual vision of Christ. It was called an intellectual vision because something of God was understood without any image or idea. She understood that Christ was present. Distinguishing this experience from the experience she was having of God's presence in the contemplative prayer of quiet and union, she wrote:

> That vision is not like the presence of God that is often felt, especially by those who experience the prayer of union or quiet . . . in this prayer of union or quiet one understands that God is present by the effects that, as I say, He grants to the soul. . . . In this vision it is seen clearly that Jesus Christ, son of the Virgin, is present.[22]

God can teach without words, without concepts. When reading some of Teresa's descriptions of the effects of pure contemplation (prayer of union) on an individual's psyche, we must not forget all that she says in other places about the rich, noetic content of her contemplative experience. Of this new way of understanding she says:

> It is a language that belongs so to heaven that here on earth it is poorly understood, no matter how much we may desire to tell about it, if the Lord does not teach us through experience. The Lord puts what He wants the soul to know very deeply within it, and there He makes this known without image or explicit words, but in the manner of this vision we mentioned. And this manner in which God gives the soul understanding of His desires and great truths and mysteries is worthy of close attention.[23]

She compares this knowing to knowing how to read without ever having learned or studied how to read. '... the mystery of the Blessed Trinity and other sublime things are so explained that there is no theologian with whom it would not dispute in favor of these grandeurs...'[24] But this represents precisely the manner of talk that would sound an alarm for those in the Church who were trying to keep Spain Catholic. Yet Teresa insisted also that this understanding, if authentic, has transforming effects; it is accompanied by a love powerful enough to convert a person completely to good. She also confessed that it is better not to speak of many of the things understood because they would only be held suspect on account of the intimacy and friendship which God can show human beings. Unless a person has a very living faith, she surmised, he will not believe much of this knowledge that was given to her, and so she decided to speak only of certain visions that might do some good for others. A further motive for speaking of this understanding was to explain the path along which she was being led.[25]

The initial intellectual revelations were soon followed by another kind of vision, called the imaginative, in which Teresa now saw bodily forms in her imagination or fantasy. As the visions increased, Teresa's confessors doubted all the more and persisted in thinking that she was being deceived by the devil; her confessors were warned to beware of her. About this situation she wrote:

I say this so that it might be known what a great trial it is
not to have someone who has experience of this spiritual
path. .... For the opposition of good men to a little woman,
wretched, weak, and fearful like myself, seems to be nothing when described in so few words; yet among the very
severe trials I suffered in my life, this was one of the most
severe.[26]

Those she consulted warned her to resist the new favors, and
the more she resisted the more she was favored.

When I began to try to obey the command to reject and
resist these favors, there was a much greater increase in
them. In seeking to distract myself, I never got free from
prayer. It even seemed to me that I was in prayer while
sleeping.[27]

In the midst of all this misunderstanding, there was a friend
of Teresa's who did understand and believe that these experiences were from the Spirit of God. This friend was a lay-
woman, Doña Guiomar de Ulloa. Teresa received permission
to consult her and got more light from her than she did from all
the learned men. This friend arranged for Teresa to have an
interview with a friar famous for his holiness, Peter of Alcán-
tara.[28] Peter also, on account of his own mystical life, understood Teresa and explained many things to her about the various
experiences she was having. Going to Teresa's confessor and to
Francisco de Salcedo, he explained to them reasons for feeling
assured about the Carmelite nun and for not disturbing her any
more.

Teresa's advice flowing out of this experience with her directors is engagingly stated in her *Life:*

This is a mistake we make: we think that with years we
shall come to understand what in no way can be compre-
hended without experience. And so, many are wrong, as
I said, in wanting to discern spirits without having experience. I don't say that anyone who has not had spiritual
experience, provided he is a learned man, should not guide
someone who has. But he ought to limit himself to seeing
to it that in both exterior and interior matters the soul

walks in conformity to the natural way through the use of reason; and in supernatural experiences he should see that it walks in conformity with Sacred Scripture. As for the rest he shouldn't kill himself or think he understands what he doesn't, or suppress the spirit. . . . Let him not be surprised or think these things are impossible · · · but strive to strengthen his own faith and humble himself in that the Lord makes a little old woman wiser, perhaps, in this science than he is, even though he is a very learned man.[29]

An important point about all of Teresa's experiences is that they never carried with them any desire to deviate from the faith of the Church.

And with this love of the faith, which God then infuses and which is a strong living faith, it always strives to proceed in conformity with what the Church holds, asking of this one and that, as one who had already made a firm assent to these truths. All the revelations it could imagine . . . wouldn't move it one bit from what the Church holds.[30]

The first account that Teresa wrote of her spiritual life and experiences for the Dominican García de Toledo was written after she had received what she considered a special gift from God to understand her experiences and be able to explain them. It was through God's grace, she insisted, that this little old woman was made wiser in this science than learned men. 'For it is one grace to receive the Lord's favor; another, to understand which favor and grace it is; and a third, to know how to describe it.'[31]

With these graces she did much more than simply write an account of her spiritual life. While writing for her directors, she also in many ways, subtle and not so subtle, and with impressive tact, engaged in teaching them. Taking extraordinary pains to analyse and describe in careful detail the many possible experiences of the mystical life, she provided aboundant material for reflection to both the theologian and the psychologist.

Insisting on the utter impossibility of spiritual growth without inwardness, without illumination from God, without passivity, she protected many of the important theologians of her time from spoiling the spiritual renewal in Spain by reacting, out of fear of illuminism and Lutheranism, with extreme measures against the cultivation of the interior life. Furthermore, her entire life and teaching demonstrate clearly that devotion to Jesus Christ and the remembrance of his human experiences and earthly mysteries are no obstacle to the highest mystical life and prayer. The obstacle, rather, would lie in excluding him from one's life. She also gives witness that the Church, the sacraments, authority, sacramentals, vocal prayer, the many elements we associate with Catholicism do not in themselves obstruct the inward journey but foster it. That these could be misused, she had no doubt; and it was a director, whom she called 'the father of her soul', St John of the Cross, who later in much detail explained this misuse, particularly in his *Ascent of Mount Carmel*.[32] Submission to the often poor advice of her directors never resulted in spiritual loss for Teresa, though she did suffer much because of their fears and incompetence. Grace on these occasions increased. With the increase of grace comes an increase in the desire to serve; the soul becomes 'obsessed with serving the Lord'.[33]

With the extraordinary teaching, wisdom, and practical sense of this woman, the Catholic church could feel at ease in the presence of the mystical element in religion. People, even women, could practice the prayer of recollection without being deceived. Mental prayer, contemplation were important factors in any program for spiritual renewal within the church. Authentic mystical experience could be esteemed and respected as God's gift, not feared.

In our times the christian church comes into more frequent contact with the East and is beginning its dialogue with the deeply mystical religious traditions there. Appropriately, then, at this time, Teresa has become the first woman in the Catholic Church to be named a Doctor of the Church.[34] Moreover, her writings are still widely read and commented on throughout the world.

This latter fact points to the achievement of another of Teresa's goals in writing besides those of submitting to her confessors and instructing where she could: it was to attract others to prayer. For this goal, too, she received special grace, a charismatic grace known as the *gratia sermonis:*

> . . . God enlightened my intellect: sometimes with words, at other times showing me how to explain this favor, as he did with the previous prayer. His Majesty, it seems, wanted to say what I neither was able nor knew how to say.[35]

One of the requisites for being declared a Doctor of the Church is outstanding learning. A Doctor like St Jerome would come closer than Teresa to what most of us would associate with outstanding learning: a great number of languages and vast erudition on oriental and biblical matters. But gradually, in the process of naming Doctors, the Church has stressed a unity between holiness and learning. Thus we are dealing with a lived knowledge of divine things. Teresa is a Doctor because of her own living, loving experience of God and of the consequent elevated doctrine she expounds in her works.

KIERAN KAVANAUGH, OCD

The Institute of Carmelite Studies

PIERRE DE BÉRULLE:
THE SEARCH FOR UNITY

Pierre de Bérulle (1575-1629), French theologian, Cardinal, and founder of the French School of Spirituality, was instrumental in bringing Carmelite nuns into France in 1604 and became superior for life in 1614. He established the Oratory in 1611 and remained as superior until his death. The author of many works on spirituality, he is most noted for the Grandeurs of Jesus *written in 1622.*

THE CIRCUMSTANCES OF OUR LIVES profoundly shape our spirituality. This seems obvious. Often throughout history, however, we Christians have divorced religious ideas and symbol systems from their own historical setting. Then we propose them as an ahistorical model. We assume that the language and symbols that we use will speak as eloquently to another age as they do to our own. Ultimately this attempt proves fruitless. In our religious language, as in all else, we must speak out of our own experience. Thus the political, social, and economic conditions in which we live inform the articulation of our sense of relationship with the transcendent.

This is particularly clear in the case of Pierre de Bérulle, a cardinal of the Roman church and councillor to the Bourbon monarchy. Division was the most fundamental experience in his life. Born and raised in the midst of the civil and religious wars of sixteenth-century France, he felt from the very beginning of his life the religious conflict between Catholic and Calvinist. Politically, he and his family represented the two sides of the civil war; his uncles allied with the *Politique* faction and Henry of Navarre, and he with the League and the Acarie circle. In his personal life he had loyalties to both the state and the church. This became clearer as his involvements with the government increased. In his religious life he knew the tension between the active and the contemplative vocation and the call to secular priesthood or religious life. In his prayer and his spiritual writings he struggled with the integration of christian humanism into the north German mystical tradition.

Since this experience of tension and division is the most predominant theme in his life, it is not surprising to find in his writings a consistent return to the goal of unity. In the face of a world of division, disorder, and even warfare he proposed another reality of order and union. Bérulle assures his readers that everything must be seen in relationship to God. Thus, the human experience of disorder and isolation is transended. We are all drawn out of nothingness by God. We were without life and became creatures. We were without grace and became children of God. And now through Christ we are returning to God. Since everything is understood in relationship to God then ultimately what appears to be divisive and disordered can be brought within a common system and explained by its place in the whole religious scheme. Thus Bérulle could view his whole life in its relationship to God. His political and religious loyalties which might appear to be in tension are brought together into one system.

Bérulle was not satisfied with the synthesis of religious or cultural ideas which he inherited. He wished to use new language to respond to a new age. What he emphasized was first the centrality of God, that God whom we know as trinity, as persons in relationships. Then he spoke of the human person as creature and as sinner. We are thus in need of acknowledging our own dependence upon God. Yet we are powerless to do this one essential thing. We cannot unite ourselves with God, or reach across the chasm to him. We are impotent in the one thing that matters, life in union with God. Hence the crucial importance of Christ and the Incarnation is clear. The grace of God is given to Christ as mediator and to us when we are incorporated into Christ. There is a gradual progression of Bérulle's emphasis upon Christ but always upon Christ in relationship to his Father.

To understand Bérulle's emphasis upon unity it is important to consider what divisions preoccupied him. Initially his concern was with the religious conflict within France, Catholic at enmity with Calvinist. Refusing to accept this break, he considered that the heretics had torn themselves away from the womb of their mother, the church. Bérulle, immersed in this conflict, resorted to any means available, whether religious, political, or military, to control and eventually to eliminate Calvinism in France.

Although the Huguenot question is on the surface a religious one, politically the Calvinists represented the possibility of federalism within the French state. Their structure contained the seed of a republic, a thought which appalled Bérulle. He contended that all authority derived from God, not from the people. Bérulle saw the Calvinists as a constant source of rebellion, always ready to ally themselves with the disaffected within the realm, particularly with the nobility during the Recency. Later he emphasized their willingness to make alliances with the English and the Dutch, and thus to be sources of treason within France. He wrote in 1622 that 'the heresy which seduces you makes you bad Christians and bad Frenchmen at the same time.'[1]

The division between Catholic and Calvinist he described as the struggle between Christ and Satan. Bérulle identifies Christ with the Roman Catholic church.[2] Christ founded it and is always present to his church as Risen and as Eucharistic Lord. The Eucharist is precisely the sign of Christ's presence which the heretic does not possess. In his Introduction to the meditation on Mary Magdalen written for Henriette-Marie, Queen of England, Bérulle writes:

> Jesus, going to the cross, wished to create a mystery expressly in order to be in the world until the end of the world, honoring the earth with his holy presence in the Eucharist. But heresy has banished him from the earth, disparaged his mysteries, denied his word, destroyed his sacrament, and as an enemy of both Jesus and his church, has divorced itself from him, and has removed Jesus from his spouse as far as heaven is removed from the earth.

Cursed and unhappy race, enemy of heaven and of earth,
and of Jesus the God of earth and of heaven.

Jesus, therefore, who by his presence consecrates and
blesses the churches which you have seen in France, and
who receives there personally the vows and homage of his
people, is not present at all in the churches which you see in
England.[3]

Jesus is absent, he thought, from the churches separated from
communion with Rome. At a deeper level the churches in
schism and heresy are even more profoundly separated from
Christ, who is described as peaceful, humble, and obedient, offering praise and adoration to his Father. This is the role of the
Roman Catholic church, to Bérulle. Satan, on the other hand,
is seen as the source of rebellion, disorder, and disobedience.
Clearly this is Bérulle's portrait of the heretic. In the *Grandeurs
of Jesus*, Bérulle writes that heresy 'is not worthy to understand
the secret and the mystery of unity, being guided and animated
by a spirit of division.'[4] Having thus shown that only the Roman
Catholics are united to Christ, Bérulle has no difficulty in elimi-
nating the Calvinist from his world. As a part of the work of
Satan they have no right to exist.

Bérulle's lifelong preoccupation with the confessional divisions between Catholic and Protestant affected his religious
writings. His pursuit of religious unity employed several methods and they in turn influenced his spirituality, most specifically
his delineation of Christ. In the first period of his life, until he
was about 35 years old, he concentrated upon the use of logic
and reason in arguments and disputations with the Huguenots.
He published treatises illustrating the truth of the Roman Catholic position and the errors of the heretics. During some of this
time Bérulle presents Jesus as a moral guide, a sage at ease with
the representatives of pagan wisdom. Quotations from Seneca
and Virgil come as easily from his pen as the sayings of Jesus.
But gradually Bérulle recognized the inadequacy of logic and
human reason to effect conversion and restore religious unity.
He turned then to the interior and spiritual renewal of Catho-

lics, especially of priests and religious. His intent was to foster holiness and to hasten the reform of the church from within. In this period he presents Christ as priest and as the model religious, the perfect adorer of the Father, the quintessential symbol of contemplative prayer. Bérulle lays great stress upon the interior attitudes of Jesus. Fundamental to his entire perception of Jesus during the years from the first decade of the seventeenth century until 1620 is the self-emptying, the *anéantissement*, of Christ in the Incarnation.

In the last decade of his life, 1620-1629, Bérulle recognized the necessity of cooperation with the monarch in order to extirpate the Huguenots. Neither conferences nor interior renewal were effective measures against heresy in his judgment. He turned to the military and political power of Louis XIII. Bérulle's dedication to the king of the *Grandeurs of Jesus* sets up an adversary relationship between the heretics and the catholic king who defends the temples and altars of the heavenly kingdom 'for which you have clothed just and holy armies by whom you are gloriously adorned.'[5] After thus emphasizing the military role of the monarch in destroying heresy, Bérulle concludes his dedication with an exhortation to Louis to take up arms against the heretics who for sixty years have been destroying the fabric of the kingdom. 'It is time to look into an evil so great and raging which extends its poison . . . over all the . . . parts of this state which is menaced by ruin because heresy is a body which disturbs, agitates and infects the whole body of France.'[6]

The confessional division within France and the separation of many European Christians from allegiance to Rome was but one concern for Berulle. The significance and importance of heretics could be easily downplayed by identifying them with Satan. What was not as easily dealt with was the tension within his own life.

Bérulle experienced the separation of the creature and the sinner from God. In his own religious development he was concerned with coming to some union with God, breaking down the division between the human person and God. His earliest writing deals directly with this issue and throughout his life it was of paramount importance to him because union with God was the source of holiness and the means of escaping from the temporal order and from a confining and death-dealing world in which he found himself.

Raised in a family which valued the Renaissance humanist culture and then educated by the Jesuits, Bérulle displayed an initial sympathy with humanism and its focus upon man, his freedom, and his will. Dagens notes that the great question posed to the age was a lively issue within Bérulle's own family, that is 'the reconciliation of classical humanism and a Christian conception of life and human destiny.'[7]

While this was clearly a concern in his life, a reading of his later works indicates that he gradually became disaffected with too great an emphasis upon human freedom and reason. He considered this to be a revival of the Pelagian or semi-Pelagian position and he turned with increasing frequency to the writings of Augustine.

Bérulle was certainly exposed through his Jesuit education to classical humanism and the literature and debates on the relationshsip between free will and grace. It was this tension between human freedom and reliance upon God which marked his earliest writing. While still a student, aged about seventeen or eighteen, Bérulle wrote a 'Brief Exercise for Attaining Virtue' as a rule of life. It was cast in the traditional form of combat or struggle. Bérulle's rule concentrates upon the denial of self in order to find God. He examines the goal of life, which is conformity of action to the will of God. He identifies the obstacle to such conformity as the evil of self-love and self-indulgence, one of the causes of which is the multiplicity of distractions and temptations surrounding the individual. Thus Bérulle wishes to detach himself as fully as possible from these many temptations and to choose a single and immutable focus for his life, the union of his will with the will of God. He sets for himself the goal of doing what God wants in every instance, in the manner in which he wishes it done, striving always for a higher degree of perfection and denial of self. Bérulle writes:

> The source of all my actions, supernatural, spiritual, and bodily will be nothing other than the will of God; and I understand by this not only doing what God wishes, but also doing only what God wishes and in the manner in which he wishes.[8]

Bérulle desires that all his actions proceed from the will of God, the fixed and stable element in his life. Thus he will continually 'seek in all things the will of God and gain in each thing a particular victory over myself.'[9] He understands that our intellect and will have been damaged by man's fall and thus that it is very dangerous to consult our own feelings and emotions. He juxtaposes what is real and of value in God's sight to what appears to the individual as real and valuable. In this context he writes:

> Because one of the great obstacles to virtue or perfection is to think that one has it, I believe that I am always at an infinite distance from what God wants for me; and I will never be content with any of my actions, no matter how perfect they may be, what will give me a perpetual will to do things better, and to take away from myself all vain pleasure in my works is that I will propose to myself a contrary opinion and I will appropriate to myself this line from the Apocalypse: 'You say I am rich and lack nothing and you do not know that you are unhappy, miserable, poor, blind and naked.'[10]

While the emphasis is on the negation of self and union with the will of God, the tenor of his work presupposes the power of the individual to shape his or her life. Paradoxically the treatise is actually a glorification of the human will, and is founded upon it while simultaneously demeaning it.

In his search for unity in the world around him and more significantly in his own life, Bérulle experienced a 'Copernican revolution' in the first years of the seventeenth century. He alludes to this in the *Grandeurs of Jesus* of 1622.

> An excellent mind of this age has maintained that the sun is

the center of the world rather than the earth. It is immobile
and the earth . . . moves in relationship to the sun. . . . This
new opinion, which is scarcely followed in the science of
the stars is useful and ought to be followed in the science of
salvation. For Jesus is the sun immobile in his grandeur
and moving all things . . . Jesus is the true center of the
world and the world ought to be in continual movement
toward him. Jesus is the sun of our souls from whom they
receive all their graces . . . And the earth of our hearts
ought to be in continual movement toward him . . . .[11]

This understanding of Jesus as the person who fulfills the same
rôle as the sun in our planetary system, this Jesus whom Bérulle
calls the 'great star,'[12] enables Bérulle to find a unity in his life
and in his world. This centrality of Jesus begins to appear in
his writings in the seventeenth century. It emerges initially in
his retreat notes of 1602 and continues until a few months before his death in his *Life of Jesus*.

By making Christ the focal point of his life Bérulle was able
to resolve the tensions with which he lived. He was a secular
priest trying to discern whether he had a vocation to religious
life. Although he was deeply interested in the renewal of religious life and was influential in bringing the reformed Carmelite
nuns into France in 1604, he came to realize that his calling was
to the diocesan clergy. He was part of the movement after
Trent to raise the stature of the secular clergy. To this end he
established the Oratory and proposed to them the model of
Christ as priest. Christ is the perfect figure of the priest, for he
is the eternal priest from whom all priesthood derives. Bérulle
writes of 'the institution of priesthood which is the first and the
holiest state in the church of God and derives from Jesus Christ
who is eternal priest.'[13] Christ as priest offered his whole life and
death as the sacrifice of worship and homage owed to his Father.
It was the work of Christ as priest to restore the unity of man
with God destroyed by sin.

Bérulle understood his own vocation as a unique calling to
enter the only order established by Christ, not religious congregations founded by ordinary men and women. By this ordina-

tion he was called to a special intimacy with Christ and he hoped to enter the choir of Jesus in the hierarchical universe described by the pseudo-Dionysius. He tells the priests of the Oratory:

> One should believe that there is a special choir of Jesus which by participation receives the communication of the interior life which Jesus Christ lived on earth with God the Father . . . (because Jesus Christ has special souls to whom he communicates a participation in his life in a more special manner than he does to other men). And we say that these souls belong to the choir of Jesus Christ, because in order to take part in this, beyond the grace common to all, another actual and special grace is required.... . It is possible by his mercy and by his grace that we may be received also among the number of his slaves. Our life will therefore be hidden in Christ with God. What happiness it will be to participate in this life. If because of our insignificance it is excessive to aspire this high, he may deign at least to make it so that the thought of this life attracts us, he may inspire us at the same time to honor and reverence this life, and even make us desire it. . . . Let us live in our humble place until he might say to us: 'Friend, come up higher'. But God wished from all eternity that in this century our entire congregation should be received into the choir of Jesus and that I the least of all, should always occupy in it the last place by the grace of our Lord Jesus Christ and of his most sweet mother, the Virgin Mary.[14]

In a letter of 1617 to one of his priests Bérulle is very specific about the duty that the priest has in relationship to Christ.

> You ought to be an *instrument joined* to the Son of God on earth, your condition of priest and of pastor obliges you to be in that state. In order to enter it, it is necessary for you to treat with him often about it by prayer; we should be *conformed* to him by interior and exterior virtues and do this in such a way that we are a *living image* of *Jesus* on earth, as he is a *living image* of his father in heaven. It is the essence of the eternal son to be the image of his father and you know by the maxims of holy theology that you have professed that it is one of the things he has appropriated to

himself. This also ought to be one of the conditions belonging to priests that they be an *image* of the son of God on earth! For this purpose, I exhort you to think frequently about him and about his interior and exterior life on earth. Adore, love him, and pray that he will transform you into himself.[15.]

Not only is Christ the eternal priest, he is also the perfect religious. His life is given over to the Father for praise and adoration. Christ's life was one of abasement and utter obedience to God. The poverty which followed Christ from birth to death was but an expression of this obedience. Christ is sufficiency and completion in his divine nature but he chooses to 'abase himself to all the worthlessness and subjection of our nature, and even to reduce himself to begging loudly for a drop of water to quench his thirst . . .'[16] Bérulle uses Christ as a symbol for the leaving of one's life out of love for God and man. 'And who, in view of this destitution, would hold as burdensome and difficult the leaving of one's state of liberty in a former life for the love of one who has made such an abandonment and changing of state and condition for love of us?'[17]

Although Bérulle worked for the Catholic reform in France through such institutions as the Carmel and the Oratory, it was not as active groups that he especially prized them. Rather, he was primarily concerned with attitudinal change. His spirituality stresses the inner dispositions from which actions arise. What Bérulle sees as essential for union with God is taking on the interior attitudes of Christ and adhering to him, being utterly responsive to God's action and completely conformed to God's will. Convinced as he was that salvation was of God and not of man, he concentrated upon fostering an inner disposition which allowed the divinity freedom to act within the person. One must be totally handed over to God since only those who are truly empty can be filled with God. The concrete realization of this for him is the person of Christ who, although he contained within himself the fullness of divine and human life was emptied out and surrendered to his Father. For us as creatures and as sinners the acknowledgment of our emptiness is but a recognition of what is in fact the reality.

Bérulle not only described Christ's attitude toward his Father but spoke of how we can be united to Christ. In the early period of his life Bérulle considered that this could be done by imitation of Christ, but by 1602 he is already speaking of entering into Christ and adherence to him. In his retreat notes of 1602 we find him speaking of binding himself to Christ. This entering into him is made explicit in the reception of the Eucharist. There it is Christ 'who leads us and brings us close and not ourselves; it is he who has command of us and uses us, who works in us and it is not ourselves . . . and the soul does not try to direct or to dispose of itself nor to act in or of itself.'[18] The person thus united with the eucharistic Christ is given over to him and he, in turn, is given over to the Father. Christ's crucial rôle is emphasized by the individual's impotence in regard to his own salvation and union with God. Only God, acting in history through Christ the mediator, can bring about the unity of the individual with God, of creature with creator. To Bérulle, everything that is specifically human, that is, separated from God, is doomed to death and destruction and inextricably linked with sin and evil. One should be distanced as far as possible from anything that is not God and does not lead to God. One of the methods which Bérulle proposes for this is his vow of servitude by which the person can be utterly and permanently surrendered to God.

These vows, which were to cause controversy later in Bérulle's life, are a strong religious statement of the contemporary political problem of authority and order over against individual freedom and expression. From the early years of the seventeenth century Bérulle had made a political decision against individual self-expression in favor of legitimate authority and human subservience to it.

Since his interest is upon a person's interior attitudes, clearly this is what he emphasizes about Christ. In an age when groups like the Capuchins were speaking of the material poverty of

Christ, Bérulle's understanding of his poverty was much more that of an attitude of self-abasement. He spoke of Christ's humiliation in the Incarnation and the attitudes of obedience and adoration which chacterized his life and his death. Only in the last decade of his life are there any published writings on the Resurrection and the Risen Christ.

Christ's submission to his Father is intended to restore unity and order to creation. In Bérulle's view it was the heretics of his own time who had broken down this unity and created chaos, division, and disorder. Christ's obedience is the most perfect form of the reparation due God for the rebellion of the angels and the disobedience of humanity. He describes the fall of the angels as the 'greatest ruin . . . in the state of nature'[19] and obedience repairs this evil. 'And the greatest reparation that we can make to God of that which was taken away from him by the angels and by rebellious men is the entire submission and subjection that we can render to another out of love for him.'[20] And all Christians can imitate this attitude of Christ through submission to those with legitimate authority, just as Christ was obedient to everyone who had authority over him, even to a woman.

Not only did Bérulle concern himself with religious division and his own religious vocation and responsibilities, he also had major political roles in France, serving at court and in diplomatic missions abroad. Thus he must somehow deal with these multiple political dimensions of his life. He needed to see how the monarch and the political order fit into his religious system and related to his goal of unity. He began by seeing the king as a figure of Christ. He wrote of Christ in the last decade of his life as 'king and born king.'[21] Christ is the only true king and all other kingship is derived from him 'and the kings that we see are only a ray of his power . . . an image of his royalty to which everyone ought to be submitted.'[22]

It would logically follow that the king should also share in the royal work of Christ, which is the establishment and the development of his kingdom, the Roman Catholic church. Bérulle exhorts the king: 'You seek his glory, and he will establish yours. You strengthen his state, which is his church, and he will strengthen your state and your crown.'[23] The king thus participates in the regal office of Christ and works for the extension and the protection of Christ's kingdom.

Because Bérulle considered the monarch an agent of God in protecting and uniting the church he could write to Louis: 'Blessed be God who honors Saint Louis on earth in the person of Your Majesty, and wishes that his race ruin heresy in France and perhaps even beyond France.'[24] And, because the king shares in the royal authority of Christ, obedience to him and service in his court are also obedience and service rendered to Christ. There was no need to see political and religious obligations as antithetical or competitive. In Christ they were all brought together.

What conclusions can be drawn from this analysis of Bérulle's quest for unity? It is clear immediately that many of Berulle's religious ideas were derived from his own historical experience and yet they contain some important insights which transcend their particular historical situation. Jean Dagens, who devoted years of his life to the study of Bérulle, has written that 'without Bérulle something essential would be lacking to the spiritual life of France and to Christian thought.'[25] If that is true then the task of the historian is to separate out what is of contemporary value to the christian community.

In his search for unity in both his life and his world he came to the realization that 'the single goal is the knowledge of God.'[26] He asserted the centrality of God and our relationship to him. Our lives should be focused on God and not on ourselves. Now, clearly, theocentrism is not unique in the history of spirituality; Bérulle's contribution is one of emphasis. He strove to impress upon his hearers the importance of adoration and of homage to God. This insight deepened as he matured and as he concentrated less upon human effort and the conquering of one's faults to stress allowing God to work unimpeded in the soul. There was in this surrender and abandonment to God much less danger of self-preoccupation.

What he chose to emphasize about God was life and relationship. He used such words as 'seed', 'blood', 'bosom', and 'womb'.
Bérulle knew from theology and from his own prayer experience something about the mystery of God as life within the
Trinity and within creation. Yet he speaks generally only of
the Father and the Son, very rarely of the Holy Spirit. Bérulle
saw that all of life should reflect and participate in this divine
life which is characterized by unity. He dreamed of the restoration of unity to a world broken and disordered. He labored
all his life for it and it was to this end, at least from one perspective, that he formulated many of his religious ideas. Since he
found the concepts of the Renaissance to be inadequate to express fully his own experience, he needed to articulate a body
of thought which would include not only the ideas of the Renaissance, but also those of the Reformation, especially since he
had extensive dealings with the Calvinists in France.

He wanted to use insights of the Renaissance, but to nuance
them and in a sense also to transcend them. He took the vision
of the ideal man and under his pen transformed that man into
Christ. The dream that the Renaissance proposed of human
possibility and grandeur had already been realized in Christ.
Bérulle far outstripped the humanists' vision by stating that in
virtue of the Incarnation man can be transformed by grace and
can be united with God as a new creation and enter into a
wholly new mode of being by grace.

He also called for the interiorization of religion. This was of
much more concern to him than external actions. He was in
the same line as Erasmus and the reformers, placing little emphasis upon externals and much on cultivating and imitating the
attitude of Christ. This was as accessible to the unlettered and
the simple, to 'young girls', in his phrase, as it was to the scholar
and theologian. This is clearly allied with the *philosophia
Christi* of Erasmus.

Although he provided a sacramental dimension to his spirituality by stressing the sacraments as a part of one's taking on

of Christ, his specific references are to baptism and Eucharist, which does not distinguish him significantly from the reformers of the sixteenth century. He, like them, also recognized the utter need for and reliance upon grace, although Bérulle emphasized that the victory had already been won by Christ and that grace was accessible to all who wished it.

It is possible to view Bérulle's emphasis upon attitudinal change and individual transformation into Christ as his response to the failure of the Catholic party to convince the Estates General of 1614 to register the decrees of the Council of Trent as law in France. Frustration at not achieving religious unity within the realm by legislation turned his attention to influencing people's attitudes.

He strove to bring together not only the ideas of the Renaissance and Reformation, but also of the mystical literature to which he was exposed through the Acarie circle, the Biblical and patristic sources from which he drew,[27] his experiences with the Carmelite nuns, and his own prayer life. Because these ideas were very disparate, he needed to draw them together somehow and he strove by means of paradox to knit them into one fabric which was patterned after Christ. In the last few months of his life he began to write a life of Jesus. Admittedly it never progressed beyond the Incarnation but it is a superb summary of Bérulle's years of meditation upon the mystery of the God-man. In this text he describes Christ as:

> an infant Word, an infant God and a mortal and immortal God together; a God suffering and a God incapable of suffering, an eternal God and a God measured by days and moments (what Nestorius could not understand); an immense God enclosed in the womb of his mother.[28.]

Since his ideas were held together by means of paradox, Bérulle could assert two seemingly contradictory things simultaneously. This is reflected in his ideas on freedom and bondage. In our servitude to Christ we become truly free. We transfer our bondage from Satan to Christ and enter into a stability and

a permanence which will ultimately free us from further un-
faithfulness to God, from all future division and evil. Bérulle
juxtaposed life and death by stating that life languishing on the
cross was in reality the beginning of life. Life as we experience
it leads only to death. True life, eternal life, springs out of death
just as Christ was born to everlasting life in the sepulchre.

Because no individual can reach God by his or her own efforts, God comes to us, healing our divisions and raising us up
to the divinity. Christ, the eternal priest, is both the means and
the model for returning to God. By being both God and man
he restores unity and is an efficacious pledge of that unity within
one's own heart and with God which the Incarnation as a recreation brought into the world. Thus the search for unity is also
intended to achieve again the unity in ourselves who are called
to be children of God, images of him, and united forever with
him. Bérulle's image of the priest, his idealization of conformity
to Christ and the spirituality evolved from that have been the
dominant image in Roman Catholic clerical thought until Vati-
can Council II. It is significant that Bérulle's Christ and his
priest are seen only in relationship to God the Father, and are
never discussed in terms of other human beings or ministry in
the world.

Bérulle's apparent negativity toward the human and the
worldly has alienated many readers. They fail to discern the
core of his thought. Human beings are by their very nature
creatures dependent upon God. We are, as creatures, redeemed
by Christ, always in relationship to God. Not for him the agony
of the person isolated in the universe.

We are pure capacity for God, in his words. Rather than
concentrating upon the fallible and the human, Bérulle calls us
to focus our dependence upon God and our capacity for being
transformed by grace. This is his corrective to a Renaissance
over-emphasis upon human reason and freedom. His concentration upon Christ and the Incarnation supplemented the abstract Dionysian spirituality to which he had been exposed in
the Acarie circle. It also served as a counter-balance to any

Illuminist and Quietist ideas.

It is true, however, that Bérulle concentrated so fully upon God that the creature and the human were given short shrift. In his desire to be emptied of self in order to allow God to fill him with grace, creatures were often bypassed and one could accuse him of not taking human effort and this world seriously enough. His spirituality is certainly individualistic and vertical in relationship to God. Community he rarely emphasized and one's relationship to others he never discussed outside of obedience to superiors and spiritual direction.

Much as Bérulle stressed unity in his own life there is no doubt that he was a man of contrast and conflicting loyalties, with an allegiance to both the church and the state. He was either unable or unwilling to say that the response to the human condition is an unequivocal 'yes' or 'no'. To him, and to his Christ, it is both. One does not need to choose between two loyalties; one can hold them both in balance. For him there is but one God who gives authority and power to church and to state, equally and independently. There is one God who has sent to humanity one Son. And in him, and in him alone, there is life. In confronting the questions of his own time Bérulle's response was a theocentric and a Christocentric one. It was expressed in religious language, mystical metaphors, and paradox, and was focused upon the transcendent God. To Bérulle, a person's answer to ambiguity and tension came through incorporation into Christ, through union with God. But this theocentrism became less credible to the intellectual class as the century wore on. By the end of the seventeenth century the whole idea of belief in a personal, loving God and a divine redeemer was open to question. It was not that Bérulle did not recognize and experience many of the same human problems and conflicts as were seen by people at the end of the century. It was instead that he phrased his thoughts in language and with symbols that sounded hollow to later generations.

In a striking way Bérulle stood at the threshold of the new age. He is a Janus-like figure who evokes the memory of the past and the dream of the future. His preoccupation with the restoration of unity to Christendom and union with the Roman pontiff bespeak the medieval synthesis. Yet his allegiance to the new French state is equally obvious. He was a supporter of the new absolute monarchy being forged by Henry IV, Louis XIII, and Richelieu, and his occasional choice of French national interest over collaboration with Counter-Reformation countries and even papal wishes makes this clear.

He was aware of and excited by the new learning of his time, the awakening of scientific knowledge and he even incorporated references to it, especially to the theory of Copernicus, into his writings. His Christ is the ultimate science. Bérulle was part of the intellectual world around him and an associate of Descartes. He is clearly a man of two epochs, who saw the past and at times wished to re-create its unity. but who was also deeply immersed in the new age.

Politically, his spirituality for the individual Christian with all its stress upon obedience and silence and the identification of the king with the work of Christ buttressed the authority of the state. Since in his theory the monarch's power is received from God, he is free to make decisions for the good of the state and he is to be trusted and obeyed by his subjects. Just as Bérulle's Christ is noted for his obedience to authority, so also the Christian should be characterized by subservience to the rulers of the state.

Bérulle's Christ can keep all the facets of his life in balance by directing everything to the adoration of God. This is also Bérulle's self-image. But ultimately it seems that one cannot have it both ways. By the end of his life Bérulle realized that the representatives of the political and religious spheres no longer trusted one another or pursued the same goals. Richelieu chose the more overtly political path as the alliances he made during the Thirty Years' War show. And he was angered by Bérulle whose attempts to balance religious and political goals led to what Richelieu considered to be indecisiveness and political naïveté.

On the other hand there were contemporaries of Bérulle who followed his religious ideas to extremes and moved into Jansenism. Taking Bérulle's thoughts on withdrawal from the world literally, they did not keep the concomitant balance of his own political concerns and involvement in the state.

Ironically this very division between the political and the religious spheres is precisely what Bérulle was speaking of. His Christ, and he himself, were able to hold these two in balance. Recognizing the difficulty of keeping all of the various elements of our life in one unified whole he proposed his Christ as the only model and solution for this division. Subsequent history has proven Bérulle right. He was correct in his judgement that this unity is impossible to men and women without God's help. It is no wonder that Bérulle wrote about escaping this time and this place because it was luring us into division and into death, into choosing one way or the other rather than both.

Personally he lost a final struggle with Richelieu and withdrew from the court and from political life a few weeks before his death. But the eloquent and important witness of his vision remains. He proposed the possibility of unity to a world already divided and to an intellectual class that would come to choose between reason and faith. At the end of one age and the beginning of another Bérulle dared to promise that in Christ all things can be gathered into one.

ANNE M. MINTON

Weston School of Theology

FRANÇOIS DE SALES:
GENTLENESS AND CIVILITY

François de Sales (1567–1622), native of Savoy, grew up in the in-tensely religious atmosphere of Counter-Reformation Catholicism. Schooled at Paris and Padua in theology as well as civil and canon law, he took Holy Orders despite his father's plans for a career in govern-ment, and was rapidly raised to the bishopric of Geneva. Because the city itself was a Calvinist stronghold, he resided at nearby Annecy, where he was a much sought-after preacher and 'director of souls'. During his lifetime and thereafter he was noted for his gentle and gra-cious embodiment of the principles of christian charity and humanism and for his insight into both the doctrinal and spiritual theologies of his tradition. With Jeanne-Françoise de Chantal, he founded the Order of the Visitation for women and left to posterity, along with a voluminous correspondence and a wealth of diverse writings, two classic works of spirituality, Treatise on the Love of God *and* Introduction to the De-vout Life.

A NUMBER OF YEARS AGO, over a supper of brown rice and vegetables in a Trappist Abbey, I had occasion to mention the name of St François de Sales. The grizzled monk next to me shook his head irritably and spluttered into his spoon: 'Too sweet, too flowery . . . light stuff . . . if you want to know about the spiritual life . . .'; he trailed off. A youngish nun across the table who seemed to feel that my sensibilities were being of-fended, came to the saint's defense. 'I've read him, and I found him very helpful. When I was a beginner, I mean.'

These tepid evaluations of the spiritual teachings of the saint are not atypical. The literary delicacy that charmed his seven-teenth-century readers is not to today's taste. Nor is he often thought of as a guide who wrote for those advanced beyond the elementary levels of the religious life. This picture is not much challenged by the casual academic depiction of him as an unoriginal thinker who nonetheless managed to infuse a quite attractive spirit into a traditional body of teachings.

I would like to question the prevailing assumption and propose another portrayal. To be sure, François de Sales was an eclectic thinker, drawing inspiration from the vast range of christian contemplative literature in circulation in France during his lifetime. He drew from the deep springs of Spanish, Rheno-Flemish, Italian, and French spirituality as well as from scriptural and patristic sources. Since he was a bishop and his concerns were primarily pastoral, he did not see himself as a speculative theologian nor did he engage in the systematic pursuit of doctrinal clarity. And because he was an upholder of the orthodox faith against the Protestant assault, he was less interested in innovation in the spiritual life than in affirming the viability of a tradition already handed down. In these senses, he could be considered an unoriginal thinker. But while his spirituality does reflect an undeniable continuity with the past, the *spirit* that he injected into it illuminates that past with a new interior quality which so transforms its familiar face that it requires a new name.

What does this mean? Any person's spirituality is to a large extent inherited. This is especially so if he or she is to be regarded as a representative thinker in his or her tradition, as are the writers presented in this series. And any individual necessarily is a child of his or her own age, bringing the pressures of cultural change and historical circumstance to bear upon that tradition. Furthermore, each man or woman bestows upon that tradition the gift of a unique personality. If the spirituality is a living one, the person assimilates the traditional inheritance into his or her personal *gestalt*, and this, of course, modifies somewhat that which has been handed down. It also requires that the elements of tradition be reshuffled or that one or another of them perhaps be given particular stress. This, in turn, alters the entire pattern. Or perhaps the individual may add a fundamentally new insight or idea to the mixture, thus giving to a familiar palette a new range and tonality of expression. Again, the individual may not recombine the inheritance in any new way but may impart to it a particular emotional or temperamental quality, like gaiety or solemnity. Or he or she may select a new method of presenting or transmitting what is handed down.

This describes the process of transmission of any intellectual or cultural system. But, presumably, the assimilation of religious tradition is different, for here it is claimed that what is taught is to a large degree transhistorical and atemporal. The Spirit transcends time and space. But, to paraphrase St Augustine, the Spirit is ancient and yet new. In François de Sales we can see this complex interaction of past truth and present circumstance. Through his unique spirit, born of his era and temperament, we can see the ancient Spirit emerge. And at the same time that Spirit living in him becomes new.

To come to terms with this I would like first to present a general outline of his spirituality, to portray what he considered the paradigmatic approach of the human to the divine. Then, with this basic and recognizably traditional structure in mind, I want to isolate five areas in which the highly particular *spirit* of St François manifests itself, five areas in which his unique touch is perceptible. The five are: his theological perspective; his guiding insight; his character; his mode of expression; and his egalitarianism. This, I trust, will reveal the extent to which he was consistent with the past, yet at the same time a highly original figure in the history of christian spirituality.

The Spiritual Life According to St François de Sales

St François once wrote, "I am just man and nothing more'; yet when he made that apparently simple statement he left in the breathing spaces between and behind his words a wealth of wisdom unsaid. For to be man, to be fully human, is to be capable of loving God. He carefully charted in his *Treatise on the Love of God* a map by which the traveler might find a way through the landscape of human life to the journey's hoped-for end.

> Just as the divine Author and Master of Nature cooperates with and lends his firm hand to fire to rise up, to water to flow to the sea, to earth to sink beneath them and remain there—so, having planted in mankind's heart a special natural inclination not only to love the general good but to love in particular and above all else his divine goodness which is better and more lovable than all things, the graciousness of his sovereign providence required that he should contribute to these blessed ones we speak of, as much help as might be necessary for them to put into practice and make effective that inclination.[1]

The love of God is the purpose and fulfillment to which humankind was created. To incline to this love is not something foreign to human nature, but intrinsic to it; it flows naturally from the human heart. And this inclination is met on the other side by the graciously inclining Love of God himself, who desires mankind to rise to the fruition of their mutual love.[2] The lover and the beloved are alike in that the one is created in the image and the likeness of the Other and in that they receive from each other their reciprocal perfection — the one a perfection fulfilled in bestowing abundance. Their relationship François describes by this domestic metaphor:

> Mothers' breasts are sometimes so full and overflowing that they cannot endure it unless they offer them to some child. And although the child sucks the breast with great eagerness, the nurse gives it with even more ardor; the child drinks, pressed on by its need, the mother feeds, urged by her abundance.[3]

But although the inclination to love simmers just below the surface of all human experience, humankind does not have the power to catalyze that inclination into activity. Original sin has so wounded nature that both the understanding and the will — two essential elements of the soul — are paralyzed.[4] The understanding must be educated as to humankind's essential nature and destination, and the will reformed to respond to divine promptings rather than to its own misdirected urgings.

The reconstruction of the soul into its intended integrity is the task of the spiritual life. Like his predecessors in the contemplative tradition, François de Sales thought that the christian life was a gradual but radical process of personal transformation through and into the image of God known in Christ. He advised as the means to that end the essential principle of christian spirituality that is encoded in the life and death of Jesus of Nazareth — death to self and resurrection to life in God. He framed the entire picture, as will already be clear, in the language of love.

François de Sales saw the spiritual life as a continuum of love. One moves 'up' or 'down' the continuum, either nearer to or farther away from the loving perfection that is God, to the extent that one loves God above all other loves and thus perceives other loves in and through God. An ascent is required of mankind. But so far as the person is concerned, this upward movement is paradoxically also a downward movement; resurrection and crucifixion are inseparable. One dies to self-love as one surrenders to the love of God.

St François fashions the ascent in both general and specific terms. In a general sense, the movement is a dialectical process of what he calls two 'exercises' of love: complacency and benevolence.[5] Humankind's love is first a receiving and then an outflowing.

> The love which we bring to God has its beginnings in the first complacency our heart feels on suddenly perceiving the divine goodness when it begins to tend toward it.[6]

The heart is fed on this complacency and then extends beyond itself in the movement of benevolence. Praise, perseverance, and adoration on the human side are all part of this exercise of benevolence. This receiving and outpouring of love is the dynamic of the ascent. It mirrors the Love that God himself exhibits toward humankind in that the two oscillations are the same, only God's Love begins with benevolence while human-kind's begins with complacency.[7]

This general framework is augmented by a more specific detailing of the psychological dimensions of the ascent into love. Thus the saint shows us prayer or mystical theology, itself a continuum of the experience of love.[8]

> ... prayer and mystical theology is nothing else than a conversation by which the soul is amorously engaged with God in his most amiable goodness in order to unite and join herself to him.[9]

From its beginnings in meditation — or 'mystical rumination',[10] as he calls it — to the varieties of romance encountered in contemplation — which he deems 'a loving, simple and permanent attention to the spirit of divine things'[11] — the Salesian portrait of the soul is that of a lover more and more surrendered in the passion of the divine embrace.

Just as one is resurrected into God through the exercise of love so one dies to self through the same medium. The imagery of erotic surrender comes into play here. Through love of submission, St François writes, our will is united to God's good pleasure.[12] The time-honored practices of resignation and indifference are part of this submission. Likewise, our will is united to the will of God through the love of conformity.[13] The identity of the lover and the beloved are realized through obedience to the Commandments, counsels, and inspirations of God.

This is the skeleton upon which the flesh of François de Sales's spirituality rests. It is recognizable as a traditional christian anatomy of the spiritual life. Certain features are in sharp focus: the employment of the amorous language of the Song of Songs tradition, the emphasis on the reformation of the will as a primary goal of the spiritual life, the stress on the continuity between human loves and divine love, the importance given to the human inclination to love God. Nevertheless, the final product shows Salesian spirituality as an eclectic synthesis of features from a familiar repertoire.

Yet we return to the unique spirit of the saint. I would like to turn now to those five areas in which I feel that the Salesian spirit is most alive and which will give dimension and perspective to what we have so far seen.

His Theological Perspective

François de Sales cannot be properly understood unless he is viewed against the backdrop of the Catholic Reformation, that historiographic backwater much ignored in the English-speaking scholarly world.[14] He was born in an era in which the body of the Church not only recoiled and entrenched herself against Protestant attack, but an era in which she felt within herself the growing seed of reform and creative innovation. She brought to birth institutional rehabilitation as well as doctrinal definition and, most importantly for our subject, an extraordinary new spiritual energy. France, particularly in the late sixteenth and early seventeenth centuries, was energized by the new religious mood. It seems as though everyone was infatuated with the life of prayer and devotion. There were new translations of religious classics circulating, there were salons and fraternities and lay and religious interest-groups of all types forming to impart and imbibe the traditional but revitalized teachings. There were serious reform efforts in monastic orders and new congregations and orders were springing up. There was deep christian devotion at court, in education, at home.

The sources of the Church's new spiritual vitality must have been many but among the springs drawn from, one certainly must credit the Renaissance and especially Renaissance humanism. The form it took in France during this period has come to be known as 'devout humanism'.[15] In short, devout humanism is an approach to the human condition which incorporates the classical heritage of Greece and Rome and some of the historiographic tools of Renaissance scholarship as well as a certain philosophic emphasis on the importance and capability of humankind into a christian context. Its voice declares that there is in humankind a certain 'relative self-sufficiency' in its relationship to God. For our purposes here we should look at one instance of the interpenetration of this brand of humanism into the Church that is of direct importance to St François de Sales' theological perspective. This is Molinism.

Luis de Molina[16] was a Jesuit thinker whose particular formulation of the problem of grace and free will, a volatile issue of the time, caught the attention of all Europe. In the face of the Protestant doctrine of justification which denied the freedom of the human will in matters of salvation, as well as the predestinarian leanings of some of the Doctors of the Church, the question was how both to affirm the reality of the will's freedom and still safeguard traditional teachings on the efficacy of divine grace and divine prescience. Molina's solution to the problem, taken up by others and amplified, is known as Molinism. In essence, it teaches that the freedom of the will is an essential factor in the divine plan of salvation. God does not predestine men either to heaven or to hell. Nevertheless, he does have foreknowledge of all human events. Molina posits three categories of knowledge attributable to God: the purely possible, the actually existing, and the free futurible. Between the first two types of knowledge there is a middle knowledge — *scientia media* — by means of which God infallibly knows those possible events whose future occurrence is conditioned by the self-determination of man's free will. Thus whatever occurs in the future is determined by man's free choice. God is not the cause of his choice nor does God predetermine any particular choices. Nonetheless, He does see the future as it will occur.

Other Jesuit thinkers advanced the argument. God 'predestines' the elect to glory, they argued, in the sense that he foresees their merits and holiness and supplies the grace necessary for them to attain salvation. The efficacy of God's grace then does not lie in the substance of the gift of grace itself but in the divinely foreknown fact of free human cooperation with this gift. The striking humanism of this system is evident.

Molinism came finally to be the accepted Jesuit position in the free will/grace debate raging in Europe. François de Sales learned of it at Paris when he was a young student of theology. It was there, during the tumult of a spiritual crisis, that he came to adopt Molinism as his intellectual orientation.[17] This crisis I see as seminal in his career. He found himself (*à la* Luther or Pascal) in the grip of an icy fear that he might be predestined to be part of the *massa damnata*, the doomed legions of souls whose fate was to be eternal isolation from the saving face of God. Reading the great fathers Augustine and Thomas only served to make matters worse. These revered authorities taught that it was the grace of God alone, independent of individual merit, that predestined the blessed to salvation. The future saint trembled and recoiled against this doctrine. In a moving scene, he begged forgiveness of the two Doctors of the Church whose views he was rejecting and embraced the optimistic opinion of his Jesuit masters.

From then on the theological assumptions underlying his spiritual teachings were marked by this Molinist sense of the real value and freedom of the human will. It imparted to his spirituality an optimism and expansiveness that is notable. It provided him the doctrinal tools with which he rendered God infinitely encouraging and desirous of seeing the salvation of all humankind, if only they would respond to and cooperate with his proffered grace. Because of this he could later write:

> The visible sun touches everything with its life-giving warmth and, as the universal lover of all inferior things, it gives them the vigor required of them to produce; in the same way the divine Goodness loves all souls and encourages all hearts to its love without any person being hidden from its warmth.[18]

His Guiding Insight

What I consider to be the guiding insight that illuminated the nature of reality for St François is intimately connected with his theological perspective. Both were born of that early inner crisis that racked him for a period in late adolescence. Indeed, it is difficult to separate the two although they are not identical nor do they play quite the same role in his spirituality. They are joined in his person in an integral way. The insight emerged as follows. Young François was caught in the predestinarian dilemma described. To his sensitive soul it was not so much the spectre of perpetual punishment that caused him anguish as the realization that the damned would be eternally isolated from God. He felt so keenly his own love of God and so treasured his knowledge and sense of God in this lifetime that his world was wrenched apart. How, unworthy creature that he was, could he presume to be one of the elect? And how, if he was to suffer forever the separation he dreaded, could he live with that actuality? The tension was extreme. His theological resolution of the issue we have seen. On a more existential level the resolution was not so readily at hand. Unlike the young Luther, whose own spiritual struggle this recalls, the discord did not give way to the dominant chord of certainty. Rather, it resolved itself in an act of ultimate surrender to and trust in the uncertainty. 'So be it', he acknowledged, 'if I am condemned not to love you in eternity, I can at least love you with all my power during this life.'[19] It is the quality and succinctness of this insight that I believe is fundamental to any understanding of François de Sales. It is the lens through which reality became focused for him, the vision that transformed the raw clay of a life into the vigor and fullness that was his life. It was a simple insight which, like Luther's insight, straddled the abyss between the perfection that was God and the imperfection that was mankind. Before an ultimately unknowable divinity, humanity was humbled. But, thanks to the divine compassion, a pathway was forged between the two. In contrast to Luther, François de Sales saw a bridge not of faith but of love. Moreover, the bridge was not supported by God's grace alone but by humankind's innate capacity to love. Finally, one who traversed the bridge did so not with the attitude of friendship, as one who believes the promises of the friend and so travels in the certitude that those promises will be fulfilled, but with the attitude of a lover who, inebriated with desire, seeks the beloved because he or she is loved and cannot but respond, caring nothing for the end to which the love might lead.

The formulation — if I cannot love him forever, I can nonetheless love him now to my fullest capacity — reveals both the radical indifference and the dynamic engagement of the saint's insight. This is the 'pure love' that he would have known from the teachings of writers like Catherine of Genoa or Bernard of Clairvaux, a love directed solely to the beloved for the sake of the beloved alone. The remarkable thing about François de Sales is that he seems to have so profoundly assimilated the insight that it permeated his every act and word. Despite the fact that his Molinist understanding inclined him to a sunny optimism, he chose never to proceed in the spiritual life with any thought of reward or end. He turned to the present and embraced it passionately, giving himself to it with the delight and rapture of the lover who looks to nothing beyond the embrace.

He wrote of his passion to his friend and spiritual daughter, Jeanne de Chantal:

> Ah, we must once and for all give our hearts to our Immortal King and live only for him. . . . May God live in my heart! Don't you see, my heart is made for this. What ardent longings I feel for this divine love; it is true that celestial desire so fills my heart, despite my wretchedness, that it is totally given over to his Divine Majesty and nothing else. . . . If there were a single fiber of my heart not his or not cleaving to him, I would at once rip it out. . . .[20]

His Character

Pure love lends itself to a certain high-pitched performance, which, when executed by many personalities, takes on not only an ecstatic soaring quality but brings one almost to the edge of emotional and physical capacity. Indeed, François de Sales literally exhausted himself in his unreserved love of God and neighbor. He died suddenly at fifty-five, depleted by his chronic ailments and his refusal to spare himself as he served others. But despite this fact, the high key of his passion was profoundly modulated by his character. This character was of a type that gave to his insight a marvelous ease and graciousness of execution. He was above all a man of gentleness and civility and the reports of the effect he had on people reflect this.

> The manner and speech of the Blessed was majestic and serious but at the same time completely humble, as calm and candid as possibly imaginable; he was unaffected and without stiffness. No one ever heard him say anything offensive to others nor anything unsuitable or flippant. He spoke quietly, thoughtfully, deliberately, gently and wisely, always conveying his meaning but without recourse to fine phrases or any affectation; he loved directness and simplicity.[21]

It should be noted that the attractive personality he displayed was not entirely natural to him. He claimed that throughout his life he struggled against character traits that were in opposition to the gentle civility he admired. His struggle was, no doubt, very real but it went on in a very private arena for the overwhelming impression he made on his contemporaries was the one he strove to achieve.

He wished to conduct all his affairs with *douceur*. His bearing, his speech, his habits all reflect this quality, causing comments about his 'usual kind and unassuming way'[22] or his face which 'was all gentleness and peace when he looked at you.'[23] Certainly he was reflecting the current popularity of *l'honnête homme*, that cultivated figure of the fully realized gentleman who embodied in his person all the values of medieval chivalry, Renaissance learning and christian perfection. But the roots of his character go deeper than this.

This gentleness of his — 'everything through love, nothing through force' was his motto — seems to have grown out of his innate sense of proportion and balance. He was not a man given to high emotional drama nor visible ascetic exploits. He preferred instead to keep to the middle road of common sense and normal responsibility. Thus he counselled interior asceticism rather than its more flamboyant exterior counterpart.

As for myself, I could never approve the method of those

who begin with the exterior in trying to reform man, by bearing, dress or hair. On the contrary, it seems to me that one must begin with the interior. . . . Since the heart is the source of actions, so as it is so are they.[24]

And he urged the acquisition of the 'common' virtues — humility, simplicity, poverty, and the like rather than the heroic virtues so often sought after in the spiritual life.

The Blessed said that we should be very faithful to practice the little virtues and never to neglect them; that it was better to be great in God's sight by exercising this littleness than small in his eyes by cultivating the virtues that seem grand in the eyes of the world.[25]

His method of spiritual direction too reveals this sense of proportion and moderation. He never superimposed a method or an attitude upon the aspirants who came flocking to him. Instead, he gently encouraged them to follow the unique movement of divinity within themselves, taught them the strength of their own wings and then set them free to fly. Jeanne de Chantal recounts:

I noticed that he left the Spirit of God to act quite freely in the souls [that he directed], himself following the attraction of this divine spirit, directing them according to God's inspiration rather than by his own personal instructions.[26]

The result of this temperamental equilibrium was an invigorating sense of liberty in all he did. One never has a sense of labor or of violence either in his own occupations or in his direction of others. He had so little of the zealot in him, yet so much of the lover, that he managed to thread the narrow path between a self-engrossed spiritual extremism and a complacent spiritual banality.

His Mode of Expression

The specific form any spirituality takes should not be overlooked in evaluating that spirituality. The intent of the author, the audience addressed, and the particular literary form utilized will markedly determine or shape the content that emerges as a spirituality. The intent may be didactic or confessional, the author may be addressing individuals initiated into the contemplative life or not, he may be engaged in systematic theology or preaching a sermon. All this makes a difference in the final issue. François de Sales was first and foremost a pastor and a preacher. He speaks in all of his works — letters, treatises, and sermons — as a man intimately concerned with the direction of souls. As the bishop of Geneva in the era of the Catholic Reformation when concerns over the pastoral function of the episcopal office were acute, he could not be otherwise. Thus he was not concerned with systematic theology *per se*, not with chronicling his own inner experience of God, but with informing people — lay and religious alike — of the truths of the christian faith as taught by the Church and with initiating them into the life of the Spirit as known through the contemplative tradition. This he did to the end that they might assimilate those truths and that Spirit into their daily lives and make of them the matrix out of which their every act and thought proceeds.

This is not all. He expressed himself in a style unique to his spirit.[27] His æsthetic is not some mere ornament upon his thought but the vessel which gives form to content and upon which the particular nature of his thought depends for transmission. He cultivated this æsthetic at Paris and Padua where he was schooled but it can also be recognized as emerging quite naturally from the quality of his character. At its core is the perception of beauty. In France he learned that rhetoric and poetry are an internal part of logic, that argument is carried forward and made persuasive through images and metaphor. In Italy he imbibed the Renaissance atmosphere of Neo-Platonism which linked love with beauty and took as canons of truth the æsthetic categories of harmony and proportion. Furthermore, he came to see that beauty has a mission to mark out the way toward love, that creatures first ascend to God through æsthetic appreciation of the created world, although later the æsthetic experience must yield to the experience of the source of beauty alone.

Out of this theoretical posture come his writings. At first one notices that they are remarkable for their candor and directness. He speaks without artifice in the sense that he speaks directly from his own heart to the hearts of others. He understood the force of rhetoric employed with the sincerity of religious conviction. He also understood that rhetoric is a persuasive art which can move the reader or listener through texture or color. His writings are notable for their gracious use of metaphor. No spiritual issue or event of the inner life goes uncast in a new context. His prose is riddled with the unexpected turn of phrase and image.

> . . . Just as hares become white among our mountains in winter because they eat nothing but snow, so by loving and feeding on beauty, goodness and purity itself in the divine sacrament, you will become wholly beautiful, good and pure.[28]

Or again,

> Like travelers coming home from Peru, who, besides bringing back gold and silver also return with parrots and apes because they don't cost much or burden the ships, so also those who aspire to virtue do not need to reject rank and honor due them provided that it does not cost them too much care or attention or involve them in trouble, anxiety, disputes or contentions.[29]

Other writers before him had used metaphor to depict the life of the soul but none before so copiously or quite so adventurously employed fresh images. And none, I think, is so consciously leading the reader along the path to God through the evocation of beauty.

His entire tactic is intimately related to the audience he was primarily addressing.[30] François de Sales was speaking to women — women at court, in convents, in or outside of marriage. His charism was to preach to women. In fact, he considered it his God-given mission. In this he distinguished himself from many of his contemporaries in the religious life who felt that the bishop's solicitude for the 'inferior' sex was so much wasted effort or even a dangerous dalliance of sorts. This feminine preoccupation marks him once more as a man of the Renaissance, for it was in this pivotal historical era that a centuries-long literary debate about the nature of the female sex came to be weighted on the side of the champions of women. François de Sales was definitely of this persuasion.[31] His was a bold stand, for the new sense of 'feminist' life was not welcomed by ecclesiastical conservatism.

Nonetheless, he poured out his gifts upon his feminine flock, not troubling himself about the comments he might provoke. His two great works — *The Introduction to the Devout Life* and *The Treatise on the Love of God* — were written for and in correspondence with women. The former began as a series of instructions to a young wife at the French court, Madame de Charmoisy, who wished to know how to negotiate a life of devotion in an atmosphere hardly conducive to detachment and the pursuit of sanctity. The latter work was gestated in the garden of the monastery of the Visitation during conversations with the sisters there. It has been said that much of the treatise's insights into the depth of contemplative prayer were drawn from the inner experiences of those Visitation nuns.[32] It is perhaps important to point out that this women's order was co-founded by the saint along with Jeanne de Chantal, for the express purpose of creating a spiritual home for women who, while strongly drawn to a serious religious life, would not be either constitutionally or temperamentally suited for the extreme asceticism practiced in most reformed monastic orders of the day. His Visitation nuns were both the inspiration for and the embodiment of his spiritual ideals. Beyond this, François de Sales also carried on a voluminous correspondence with women in all walks of life.

It was this feminine aspect of his vocation that in part accounts for the manner in which he expressed himself. Much of his language was frankly chosen to appeal to the delicate sensibilities of his readers. In the *Introduction*, he recommends at the end of each meditation the gathering of 'a little devotional bouquet to refresh you during the rest of the day. He also made much use of the language of love extremely popular in the amorous literature of the period. He did this, of course, through the authority of the contemplative tradition which had, from early centuries, spun the allegory of the love of the human soul and its God with the threads of the *Song of Songs*. But he was aware of the literary infatuations of his directees and he used these to initiate them gradually into the deep commitment of the 'pure love' he taught.

Metaphors chosen from feminine experience pattern his writing. Pregnancy, childbirth, breast-feeding, weaning, the relationship between the young child and its mother — all are called upon to describe the spiritual life.

> See the little child to whom the mother presents her breast, it throws itself into her arms gathering and folding its tiny body in this bosom and on this loving breast, and see also the mother, how receiving it she holds it to her and as it were glues it to her bosom and kissing it joins its mouth to hers. . . . Thus our Saviour shows his most lovable bosom of divine love to the devout soul.[33]

There is also a sense in which what the era perceived as the 'feminine character' and the traits many women exhibited were put to use in his writings. He actually seemed to have preferred women as his literary subjects because they more than men seemed to embody the spiritual qualities he most valued. He especially cherished them for the hiddenness of their lives. For him, who above all stressed the interior nature of the christian life and who taught the 'common way', a woman's life could be a sterling example of sanctity.

Thus we see that his æsthetic was not merely decorative but foundational to his work. For him the perception and cultivation of beauty was the beginning of the love of God, and those whom he was called to draw to this love were those perhaps most open to the beauty of his prose. His æsthetic was a feminine æsthetic, shaped by the experiences, tastes and sensibilities of the women he so loved.

His Egalitarianism

Women were not the only usually unaddressed population to whom he spoke. Casting aside the prejudice that the life of christian perfection was cultivated primarily, if not solely, within the context of religious vows, François de Sales opened the life of devotion to an unheralded multitude of potential saints.

> It is an error, or rather a heresy, to wish to ban the devout life from the company of soldiers, the artisan's shop, the court of princes or the home of married persons.[34]

This gesture was, of course, in keeping with the reforming impulse of the Counter Reformation and was not original with him. But St François was the primary literary exponent of this egalitarian principle in the Church, the one who made the principle popular and the tradition accessible to the general public. His *Introduction to the Devout Life* was written to instruct those in lay life in prayer and the love of God in a form that could be applicable to vocations that did not require specifically religious vows.

He did one more thing that distinctively marks him off from both his predecessors and his contemporaries. He upheld marriage as a state in which sanctity could be enthusiastically pursued.[35] Not that marriage had not always been regarded as a legitimate vocation for the Christian. But marriage was sometimes seen as a lesser walk of life, not to be valued equally with the celibate life as a road for the achievement of perfection. St François challenged this notion.

The ground was broken for this idea by the upheavals of the preceding era. Wanting to rehabilitate the reputation of the married state, Erasmus, that giant figure of the Renaissance/ Reformation world, questioned the sacramental nature of the marriage bond and put forward the idea that the wedded relationship was a legal contract consisting of a 'conjugal sentiment' and thus valid outside the confines of the monastic and celibate worlds. What Erasmus wished to do was to elevate marriage above celibacy, which indeed was what happened in the Protestant milieu. But the undermining of the sacramental nature of wedded life took hold beyond the lands most caught up in the Reformation. The process was not helped by the Church's traditional predisposition to value virginity and celibacy very highly. Married persons in the Catholic Church were caught keenly between the new impulse toward a devotion they associated with those in sacramental vows and the contemporary opinion of their life state as intrinsically outside that purview.

Into the arena stepped the bishop of Geneva. He did not claim that the married state was above the celibate, but he did feel that the two alike were states in which authentic religiosity and sanctity could be cultivated. In doing this he countered one common interpretation of the function of marriage. Many of his contemporaries taught that the prime justification for wedlock was the procreation and education of children. Beyond this, it was a necessary container for the overflow of human sexuality that threatened the stability of the christian community. François de Sales spoke of marriage not only in these terms but in the terms of human friendship. The uppermost aim of the union he saw as the reciprocal perfection of each party realized day by day over the course of a lifetime. This was possible because in the saint's eyes any love could bring the human heart to God, provided it was not a love contrary to the will of God. Humankind did not have two loves — of God and of self — but one love alone which, when experienced in the context of the christian spiritual life, would be honed and shaped into the likeness of the source of all Love.

With this we bring to a close our discussion of the five areas in which François de Sales' unique spirit can be isolated: his theological perspective; his guiding insight; his character; his mode of expression; and his spiritual egalitarianism. In his person these five merge in a distinctive *gestalt* which makes of his seemingly traditional formulation of christian spirituality something wonderfully surprising and new.

The truly christian person — one who pursues life with an

eye to the attainment of human perfection — is a lover of God. He or she ascends to God through the exercise of a love that is innate but needs cultivation. Through the receptive and out-pouring dynamic of love and the practice of prayer and good works, the lover is initiated into the divine intimacy. Through the love of conformity and submission to the divine will, the lover dies to self and self-love.

Such is the plot of the drama. But a particular hero or hero-ine fulfills the story's promise! The lover is an optimistic char-acter who believes in his or her innate capacity to love God and who trusts in a God who is infinitely solicitous that that love be fulfilled. The lover also sees his or her part in the drama with a radical clarity. The meaning of the script is not in its final outcome but in its performance. Now is the time to love deeply and fully without thought of the response once the final curtain has closed. The lover is moreover a person of great breadth of spirit whose modesty, gentleness and sense of proportion hint at great interior liberty. The lover is an appre-ciator of beauty, a cultivator of a 'feminine' æsthetic and a champion of the cause of all humankind in its quest to achieve the crown of christian perfection.

François de Sales can be deemed a great master of the chris-tian spiritual path to the extent that he internalized and reflected the essential integrity and classic pattern of the wisdom on which he was nourished. The entire scope of the tradition, in both its breadth and depth, was his. He embodied in his own life and work the values and fundamental orientation upon which the tradition rests. This makes of him a profoundly tra-ditional christian thinker. But the saint was also a Christian of the Catholic Reformation, a man whose theology, whose deportment, whose literary style and æsthetic theory, whose socio-cultural opinions were to a great extent shaped by the historical reality in which he found himself. That he stood so essentially and completely for his age as well as for the gen-eral principles of christian life distinguishes him. Finally, the uniquely personal quality of his spirituality is striking. His temperament, the resonance and vibrancy of his guiding insight, his special voice and mode of communication are immediately discernible in all that he wrote or did.

To have synthesized these three levels of experience — the traditional, the historical, and the personal — in one highly complex yet exquisitely integrated spirituality is the gift of a rare lifetime. It makes St François an ideal: one who has profoundly tested the possibilities of the traditional christian life open to any individual, one in whom the ancient Spirit becomes ever new.

WENDY M. WRIGHT

The University of California — Santa Barbara

THE ABBÉ DE RANCÉ AND
MONASTIC REVIVAL

Armand-Jean le Bouthillier, abbé de Rancé (1626-1700), moved in the best social and ecclesiastical circles of seventeenth-century France, profiting to the full from his half-dozen commendatory abbacies under a system which, with royal assent, allowed clerics and even lay persons to appropriate the revenues of religious houses. Converted towards 1658 from his worldly life as an ecclesiastical dandy, Rancé divested himself of his commendatory benefices, entered the Cistercian Order in 1663, and as regular abbot of la Trappe set about renewing ancient vigor in that decadent Norman abbey. Present-day Cistercians of the Strict Observance (Trappists) trace their historical roots back to the reform initiated by Rancé at la Trappe.

THE PROPRIETY of a conference on seventeenth-century la Trappe in a seminar on the 'Roots of Modern Christian Spirituality' is none too evident to the author of these lines. Modern christian spirituality wants nothing whatsoever to do with that lugubrious norman abbey and its celebrated, *too* celebrated 'Thundering Abbot.' True, the Oxford don, A. J. Krailsheimer, shook us all back in 1974. From the pages of his meticulously documented study, *Armand-Jean de Rancé, Abbot of la Trappe: His Influence in the Cloister and the World*,[1] there emerges the figure of a reformer shocking for its specious normality: Rancé is human; indeed, almost *humane*. This is no Grendel — or so Krailsheimer would have us believe.

Fortunately, we had at that time one of the foremost authorities on post-tridentine monastic reform in France to reassure us. In his response to the disturbing Krailsheimer effort, Yves Chausy OSB concluded after several paragraphs devoted to biographical detail and monastic geography, that, 'put back in the context of his period, Rancé takes on his true dimension, which is that of a personage of secondary importance . . ."[2] For a moment we feel uneasy when Fr Chaussy qualifies this remark by immediately adding that it is by no means a negligible thing to be even of secondary importance; but calm returns with the reminder that Rancé 'is practically an unknown (for the public in general), and that no one reads his works anymore.'[3] Even more reassuring are the judgments pronounced by the dean of cistercian historians, Louis Lekai, o.cist., whose every reference to Rancé and to the peculiar spirituality of la Trappe is a tribute to the authority of his mentor in these matters, the dispassionately objective Bremond.[4] *L'Abbé Tempête*, we are convinced, will still be read when Krailsheimer's contribution has long since moldered away into the dust of our dustier library shelves.

Nor should we harbor the slightest suspicion of *parti pris* on the part of a Chaussy or a Lekai, who owe no personal allegiance to the Cistercians of the Strict Observance. The Fathers of the General Chapter of this Observance, in their assemblies international as well as regional, lead the way in disavowing any suspicion that seventeenth-century la Trappe has any relevance for contemporary monastic revival. The Abbot of Roscrea, Ireland, spoke for many when, at the 1980 General Chapter of the Order, he said with reference to the official name of the Order:

> The word 'Trappist' in our name was so unthinkable in our Region [=Ireland, Scotland, Wales, England, Australia, New Zealand] that we did not even discuss it at our Regional Meeting. However, at the end of the meeting we took a vote and opposed it almost unanimously. It is very difficult to know why the word has such connotations in our part of the world. Partly it is because we are the only Cistercians in our region, and partly it is because an image of narrow-mindedness and harshness has grown up in connection with the word. Our monasteries are not at all prepared to use that title.[5]

Still, we should avoid anything smacking of complacency,

for the situation is, in fact, a bit more complex For the past several years there has been a trickle, even a *steady* trickle of Rancéan studies by authors who, though working independently of each other and of Krailsheimer, nonetheless manifest the same revisionist tendencies as Krailsheimer. Unlike Chaussy, unlike Lekai, these writers — with one or two exceptions — enjoy no international reputation; and their organs of publication have a correspondingly limited circulation. What here disturbs, however, is the cumulative effect of this kind of writing. These authors do not *directly* attack the common doctrine, the established position. More subtly, they address themselves directly to particular questions and to sources either ignored as irrelevant by our standard authorities or else differently interpreted. The apparently non-controversial nature of much of this writing makes the emergents therefrom all the more annoying; and the mere multiplication of studies of this ilk suggests — and here I use no word stronger than *suggests* — suggests, I say, that, contrary to the assurance given us by Yves Chaussy, there is still *someone who is reading Rancé!* We have articles on Rancé and community;[6] Rancé and frequency of Communion;[7] Rancé on spiritual reading;[8] Rancé and spiritual fatherhood;[9] Rancé on discretion,[10] on the discernment of vocations;[11] Rancé and the poor;[12] Rancé and the monastic fathers of the East;[13] Rancé and the desert fathers;[14] and there is even a pretentiously long study on — strange contradiction in terms — 'The *Cistercian* Dimension of la Trappe' (italics mine)![15] The seriousness of the situation can be gauged by the fact that even a scholar of such unimpeachable authority as Fr Jean Leclercq OSB, who has otherwise served the cause of monastic studies and renewal so well, permits himself to sign his name to an article on . . . 'Rancé and Joy.'[16]

We would be overly complacent indeed to hope that the efforts of a Bremond, a Lekai, or even the General Chapter of the Cistercians of the Strict Observance, have sufficed to exorcise us of the unwanted presence; and it is here, surely, that the perceptive lines of Hughes Mearns find their full applicability:

As I was going up the stair
I met a man who wasn't there.
He wasn't there again to-day.
I wish, I wish he'd stay away.[17]

But let us adopt now a more serious tone —

RANCÉ AS A 'FIXED TYPE'

One of our problems with a phenomenon like Rancé and his monastic *praxis* at la Trappe is that, like most ordinary people, we tend to see things not necessarily exactly as they are but, to use T. E. Hulme's expression, as 'fixed types.' We have been told, and told often, that Rancé was an extremist; that he was wholly conditioned by the moral rigorism of his milieu; that he was essentially a polemicist and a bigoted one at that. 'Eccentric piety and discipline', 'novelties in the history of the Order', 'reformatory ideas', 'conspicuous deviations from the traditional interpretation of monastic vocation'—these are phrases which come naturally to Fr Louis Lekai as he writes about la Trappe and its reformer; and those of us who know and appreciate his scholarly but also eminently readable surveys of cistercian history, know that each time he has occasion to treat of the reform enacted at la Trappe under the aegis of its 'Thundering Abbot', he will vary only slightly the formula already familiar to us from his first great work, *The White Monks*, which dates from 1953:

According to de Rancé's views, monasticism was basically a form of penitential life; monasteries were like prisons; their inmates were to be considered as criminals, doomed to spend the rest of their lives in severe penances. The chief duty of the abbot was to create for his monks all types of humiliations and to encourage them to practice every self-chosen austerity even at the cost of ruining their health. The monks were never to be permitted to feel any satisfaction in their works or exercises; their proper activity was to lament their sins. The discipline of the house, menu and daily schedule were to be arranged accordingly. De Rancé and his followers multiplied the time spent in prayer, returned to hard manual labor, restored perpetual silence, and banned not only meat from their table, but also fish, eggs and butter. To a certain extent, the heroic spirit of the first Cistercians had resurged at La Trappe, but instead of the inspiration of the first crusaders, the main force behind their admirable efforts was the guilt-complex of a highly sophisticated society. The frame of their daily routine bore some resemblance to the first glorious days of Cîteaux; but for the wonderful clarity of St Bernard's contemplative spirit they substituted the gloomy and pessimistic air of contemplative rigorism.[18]

But to return to Hulme and his 'fixed types': Hulme refers to an artist who tells his pupils that they are unable to draw any particular arm because they are thinking of it as an arm; 'and because they think of it as an arm they think they know what it ought to be.'[19] So too with la Trappe. We already know what la Trappe ought to be. And what it *ought* to be is precisely what we see when we try to trace its lineaments.

A particularly memorable instance of this I recall from what happened in my own monastery a number of years ago, immediately after a conference I had given on the eastern monastic fathers and the reform of Rancé. I had kept close to my topic, and if I had spoken with admiration for the man, it was solely with respect to matters such as his childhood precociousness and his extraordinary command of Greek. Within the hour there appeared on the community bulletin-board a photocopy of an article from the *New Catholic Encyclopedia* — Fr Lekai's article on Rancé. Appended next to the heavily underlined passage about prisons, the monk as criminal, macerations of the flesh and ruined health was the laconic note: 'This is the other side of the coin.' Had I spoken of the excellence of Rancé's horsemanship — he loved to ride, and rode splendidly — the response would surely have been the same: for how could I have spoken of so disagreeable a person without depicting him for what we all know he really is? More recently a similar conference on Rancé as translator of the Holy Rule, given at a gathering of monastics and scholars, elicited not a hostile but a somewhat surprised response from one knowledgeable benedictine abbot. I had presented Rancé, he told me, in a completely new light. My own intent had been considerably more modest. I had meant only to discuss Rancé as translator of the Rule. Indeed, that is all I did discuss. But then, Rancé is a fixed type. We already know exactly what he looks like.

LA TRAPPE AS SEEN FROM VERSAILLES, CORNWALL, PARIS

I have no intention of treating even briefly of the details of Rancé's program of renewal at la Trappe. This is not because I have had occasion to touch on some of this material in other articles, but because I believe such particulars to be of minor importance in any evaluation of his monastic reform. At the level of particular observances, la Trappe remained chiefly an isolated phenomenon; and here I agree with Fr Lekai when he writes that 'Rancé's influence over the ranks of the Strict Observance during his lifetime was limited to four communities, but even at those his regulations were only partially observed.'[20] I would further like to stress that, even at la Trappe, Rance's reform survived the Revolution only in a sadly transmogrified form. The two dozen monks of la Trappe who managed to escape into Switzerland only shortly before the suppression of their abbey are beyond all praise for their heroism, their spirit of faith, their charity, and their extraordinary missionary endeavors to spread monasticism and to keep it alive in a world in the throes of revolution. But the exigencies of the apocalyptic age in which they lived, as also the exigencies imposed by their heroic but idiosyncratic leader, Dom Augustin de Lestrange,[21] contributed much to distance the latter-day Trappists from their predecessors of pre-Revolution days. The 'Trappist life' carried to points as distant as Siberia and Manhattan, and perpetuated till recent times in monasteries of the Strict Observance, owed as much to Dom Augustin as to Frère Armand-Jean of la Trappe: and this was not all to the good.

My point here is that I hold Rancé's impact to have been, not in the order of precise usages or of a particular monastic doctrine, but in the order of example or sign of a much more general sort.

Indeed, the impact of la Trappe was out of all proportion to its size. When benedictine superiors, alarmed by too many instances of trappist fever in their communities, obtained from Rome a brief against 'defections' to la Trappe, Rancé wrote ruefully that it's easy enough to see that a small monastery unable to support more than thirty-five or forty religious is incapable of causing the commotion they're complaining about . . . .'[22] Only rarely did Rancé agree to accept monks to be formed and then returned to their original community; and just as rarely did he loan monks of la Trappe to assist in the renewal of other communities. Even in these exceptional cases, there was no question of the precise regime followed at la Trappe being transposed elsewhere without modification. True, reform-minded religious and superiors frequently asked for counsel, and almost as frequently Rancé replied positively. But his advice was inevitably directed to renewal within the structures of the particular religious institutes to which his correspondents belonged.[23] Even in the case of les Clairets, the cistercian monastery for nuns which, despite his opposition, was restored to its place as a house subject to la Trappe, Rancé initially resisted the proposal that the Strict Observance be introduced in that house. Even at a later date, when the community unanimously insisted on adopting the regime of the Strict Observance, the program followed was that of the Strict Observance at large rather than of la Trappe in particular.[24] Again, when Fr Lekai tells us of Rancé's conviction that 'the reform [=Strict Observance] ought to embrace his monastic ideology' and that after he 'had realized that he was unable to impose his will upon a critical and reluctant majority of his fellow reformers, he retreated to la Trappe, where he was free to shape that community to his own image and likeness,'[25] this is a fine instance of rhetoric in function of the fixed idea. Like every other member of the Strict Observance, the recently blessed Abbot of la Trappe earnestly desired the Strict Observance program to be imposed on the Order at large — or at least on the Order in France. But as spokesman for the Reform at Rome (1664-1666), the program he defended was not of his own making, and had long since been formulated

in its general shape and in its particulars. Even the more particular and local renewal inaugurated at la Trappe from 1666
onwards was shaped only progressively, admitted of variations,
and was the result of the mutual collaboration between abbot
and community. Rancé served as center of unity, inspirer, and
catalyst; but these were functions made possible only through
the grassroots participation of the community. Moreover,
Rancé's virtually absolute authority accrued to him less from
the validity of his election as abbot than from the inner quality
of his own person. If the community verged almost on idolatry
in his regard, this was not in response to the demands of an auto-
cratic dictator, but in recognition of the christian and monastic
ideal so perfectly recapitulated and concretized in his person.
As the king's historiographer, Dom Félibien des Avaux, expressed it in a description of la Trappe written soon after a visit
there in the autumn of 1670:

> These are no timid, spineless slaves led by a valiant captain.
> These are free men, men who are generous, and who march
> after their head whom they obey with the utmost love....[26]

The temptation I must here avoid is that of going on to speak
of the dynamics of community at la Trappe, when the point
under consideration is the calculated insularity of the la Trappe
reform. Rance's responsibility was concentrated on only a very
small plot in the vineyard of the Lord; and small though this
plot was, he always put it first in his order of priorities.

That the influence of la Trappe was, one might say, in inverse
proportion to its size, is a paradox illustrative of the larger paradox that artists, writers, musicians, and even monks sometimes
throw light on universal verities for having entered at depth
into the heart of what is most particular and local. What could
be more 'local' than the geography of Yoknapatawpha County?
But in William Faulkner's stories we recognize it for what it is,
an inscape of the world of everyman. Flannery O'Connor
speaks about people and events in the accents of a young
woman from Milledgeville, Georgia; but the regional music of
her diction resonates of universal truths more richly than

would the same things said in Basic English. And what of Mauriac and that provincial regionalism of his which rarely takes him far from Bordeaux and its environs? A Maria Cross, a Thérèse Desqueyroux, a Jean Péloueyre belong to a place and time remote to us; but they nonetheless light up our own existence.

In a manner somewhat analogous, the geography of la Trappe and Rancé country, remote and particular though it seemed to be, held something of the attraction of one's home country for seventeenth-century persons in a totally different milieu. Where Rancé had gone, few dared follow. But there were many, surprisingly many, whose hearts harbored aspirations perhaps less intense than, but not unike, his own. The business bureaux of the bourgeoisie and the salons of smart society held captive countless individuals who, if things had only been different, might perhaps have . . .

I like especially one fine passage from the *Memoirs of the Duc de Saint-Simon*, a passage which becomes even more significant when kept in the context of what precedes and follows it in the narrative for 1693. Our sophisticated Duc has been telling us of his thwarted plans for marriage with a daughter of the Duc de Beauvilliers. Unblushingly he explains that it was not the girl he wished to marry — he had never so much as seen her; it was the aristocratic *family* he wished to marry into. Alas, the Duc and Madame de Beauvilliers, though sympathetic, regretfully said No.

> There was nothing left for me but to look out for another marriage. One soon presented itself, but as soon fell to the ground; and I went to La Trappe to console myself for the impossibility of making an alliance with the Duc de Beauvilliers.
>
> Although I was very young then, M. de la Trappe charmed me, and the sanctity of the place enchanted me. Every year I stayed some days there, sometimes a week at a time, and was never tired of admiring this great and distinguished man. He loved me as a son, and I respected him as though he were my father. This intimacy, singular at

> my age, I kept secret from everybody, and only went to
> the convent clandestinely.[27]

There follows an account of an unbelievably dull, unbelievably complicated lawsuit, crowned by a furious passage about the legitimization of the king's bastard sons — with a rank, mind you, just below that of princes of the blood! Schemes for an advantageous marriage, lawsuits, rage at an insult to the peerage-system — and in between a few days at la Trappe, 'the one place', he writes on another page, 'where I can breathe.'[28] The admission astonishes. Saint-Simon the snob, Saint-Simon the dilettante, Saint-Simon the ruthless observer and merciless critic of his fellow-actors in the human comedy, gravitated to la Trappe as to an oasis of sanity and peace in a world gone mad. As though fully aware of the incongruity between his public figure and his carefully concealed spiritual sensibilities, he wrote: 'This intimacy . . . I kept secret from everybody, and only went to the convent *clandestinely*.' It would be embarrassing to have others know about this temptation to sanctity. The blasé Duc of vicious wit and no less vicious pen dared not follow the older man into this region so remote to the world of the Versailles he loathed yet loved; still, it was a source of comfort and strength to know that this remote region existed; that, remote though it was, it was accessible from time to time even for the likes of a Saint-Simon; and that the abbot, for all his distancing of self from the world of Paris and Versailles, was close enough to be, as it were, his father.

This page from the *Memoirs of the Duc de Saint-Simon* is by no means alien to the insights of contemporary novelists. The plot-line of Daphne du Maurier's *The Scapegoat* is as feeble as the plot-line of *A Comedy of Errors* — only here it is a bilingual Englishman who is mistaken for a French aristocrat gone to seed. For a week the role of scapegoat for the sins of this quite 'charming, idle, and destructive French aristocrat and his family is thrust upon a lonely English traveller.'[29] The story ends as the protagonist, John, reassumes his true identity and leaves the world of St Gilles:

She came with me down the stairs, and standing there, at the dark entrance to the shop, she paused a moment before letting me out into the night, and in a troubled voice she said, 'You're not going to harm yourself in any way? You haven't said to yourself, "This is the end?"?'

'No', I said, 'it isn't the end. It may be the beginning'.

... 'And you know where you're going?'

'I know where I'm going'.

'Will you be there long?'

'I've no idea'.

'This place, is it far away?'

'Oddly enough, no. Only about fifty kilometres'.

'If they could have shown you there what to do with failure, can they also show you what to do with love?'

'I believe so ...'

I kissed her, and then I went out into the street. I heard her shut the door and bolt it behind me. I went under the Porte de Ville, and climbed into the car, and reached for my maps. They were where I had left them, in the pocket beside the driver's seat. I found the route I had marked with a blue cross a week ago. The last ten kilometres might be difficult in the darkness, but if I kept the Forêt du Perche on my right, the road would take me to the Forêt de la Trappe and to the Abbey after leaving Mortagne ....

I drove to the network of roads at the top of the town, turned left, and took the road to Bellême and Mortagne.[30]

One might be tempted to suspect — with gross injustice — that Daphne du Maurier's understanding of la Trappe is somewhat related to Chateaubriand's 'romantic conception of religious houses as hospitals for those bruised by an impossible love'.[31] But then, what are we to say to Pierre de Calan's already classic *Cosmas*? When the author decided to discourse on the ultimate verities of human existence, he chose as his setting la Trappe of the 1930s. Romanticism? The imputation is a bit unlikely in this case of a writer who has degrees in philosophy and mathematics, who has worked as a tax-inspector, who has served as Vice President of the Syndicat Général de l'Industrie Cotonnière Française and as President of Babcock and Wilcox in

France, and who is currently President of Barclay's Bank, France. As a youngster from the region around la Trappe, Pierre de Calan grew familiar with the geography of the place. As an elderly author (married with six children, and, at last count, eighteen grandchildren), it is the spiritual geography of the place which holds him spellbound.

The late Thornton Wilder never had occasion, so far as I know, to consider the phenomenon of la Trappe past or present. But his last novel, *Theophilus North*, provides categories of structure helpful for our understanding of the general significance of la Trappe and its reform. The year is 1926; Theophilus North (an acronym for 'Thornton') is on the verge of turning thirty *(Nel mezzo di cammin di nostra vita . . .)* when he goes to spend the summer working at odd jobs in the island town of Newport, an island not unlike the island of *The Tempest*, inscape of the cosmos. As young North sees it, Newport is like Troy. There are really nine cities in the single city of historic Newport, 'some superimposed, some having very little relation with the others—variously beautiful, impressive, absurd, commonplace, and one very nearly squalid.'[32] As observer and narrator of the twelve stories which take us into many of these various nine cities, T. North is citizen of none of them. The advantage, we feel, is his; his very distance enables him as observer (and here we read 'contemplative') not only to see objectively, but to participate in, and even to help direct the course of events which affect the destinies of those of whom he writes with so much love, wisdom, and quiet humor. Some denizens of a particular city within Newport live without the awareness that other cities of Newport so much as exist; others are aware of other Newports, and, indeed, would like to leave their own — but cannot. Thus Diana Bell, a tragic figure resembles, in some respects, the Duc de Saint-Simon. There is the moving scene where Theophilus brings her home by night to the back door of her family mansion: this is not the first of Diana's attempted elopements doomed from the start to end in failure.

She said, 'Hold me a minute.'

I put my arms around her. It was not an embrace; our faces did not touch. She wanted to cling for a moment to something less frozen than the lofty structure under which we stood; she was trembling after the freezing realization of the repetitions in her life.

There were servants moving about in the kitchen. She had only to ring the bell and she rang it.

'Good night', she said.

'Good night, Miss Bell.'[33]

With Theophilus, we can understand and grieve for a Diana Bell, prisoner of her own geography. But perhaps we too share North's self-avowed incapacity to understand when we see the young, radiant Eloise Fenwick making ready to pass into another country where, we know full well, we cannot follow her. Eloise has just told Theophilus of her deepest desire: 'I want to be a religious, a nun.'

I held my breath.

She answered my unspoken question. 'I'm so grateful to God for my father and mother . . . and brother, for the sun and the sea, and for Newport, that I want to give my life to Him. He will show me what I must do.'

I returned her solemn gaze.

'Eloise, I'm just an old Protestant on both sides of my family. Forgive me if I ask you this: couldn't you express your gratitude to God while living a life outside the religious orders?'

'I love my parents so much . . . and I love Charles so much, that I feel those loves would come between me and God. I want to love Him above all and I want to love everybody on earth as much as I love my family. I love them *too much*.'

And the tears rolled down her cheeks.

I did not stir.

'Father Walsh knows. He tells me to wait; in fact I must wait for three years. Mr. North, this is the last time we'll meet here. I am learning how to pray and wherever I am in the world I shall be praying for Papa and Mama and Charles and for you and' — she pointed to the guests in the tea room — 'for as many of the children of Heaven as I can hold in my mind and heart.'

During the rest of the summer our paths crossed frequently. She was disattaching herself from love of her family — and naturally from friendship — in order to encompass us all in a great offering that I could not understand.[34]

For French society of the Splendid Century, Rancé and his confrères were men who, unlike Diana Bell, had managed to break out of the deadening repetitions of an existence felt to be vacuous and without ultimate meaning. Like young Eloise, they had disattached themselves from love of family and all else, but only to encompass them all in 'a great offering' which neither society at large nor we (still less, Bremond and friends) can wholly fathom. There is a mystery here, mystery in the real sense of the word, mystery as distinct from problem. Fr Lekai's confrère, Fr Aurelius Mensáros o.cist., has referred to 'a certain mystery' which hovers over and envelops 'the personality and work of the great solitary'; but the title of the chapter in which he employs this perceptive terminology is 'The Present-day Rancéan Problem.'[35] In the categories of Gabriel Marcel, a problem or " 'puzzle' does not involve me or my feelings, it lies objectively there, and resolving it is not a matter of life and death; but a 'mystery' engages my attention and my feelings in such a way that I have to respond to it."[36] For the observer of seventeenth-century la Trappe, this abbey and its community was less puzzle than mystery.

This is not to say that even in the seventeenth century there were no *negative* critics of la Trappe. Critics there were, who loathed the place and its abbot. These extreme cases were, however, relatively few, and helped compensate, perhaps, for extreme cases of uncritical enthusiasm gone wild in the opposite direction: Rancé has had more to suffer from his friends, I fear, than from his enemies. More usually, however, criticism directed toward Rancé and his community bore on particular points, on individual morbid elements in what was otherwise perceived as a sound and admirable realization of the monastic ideal.

When Guillaume Le Roy, abbot of Hautefontaine, took his friend to task for allegedly inflicting fictitious humiliations on the brethren of la Trappe — a charge Rancé had little difficulty in refuting[37] — the accusation was in no way meant to suggest a condemnation of the whole monastic enterprise as lived at la Trappe. So also Mabillon's dignified exchange with Rancé, over the question of studies as distinct from the traditional *lectio divina*, in no way bore upon more than a single point, albeit an important point, in the program of the reformer of la Trappe. And leave it to the ever courteous Mabillon to assure his reader that, if all abbots were as enlightened as the abbot of la Trappe, and if all communities were as exemplary as the community of that 'holy abbey', then, even in the matter of this disputed question, Rancé would be right.[38]

THE FIXED TYPE AND ABSENCE OF THE POSITIVE

No reader of Rancé need fear the risk of getting lost in a tangle of rhetoric or convoluted thought. Clarity of expression and simplicity of subject matter are two characteristics of Rancé's literary style. His vocabulary in no way smacks of the esoteric, and the general impression is one of unaffected straightforwardness. But be careful! For all Rancé's simplicity of means, he is generally using technical monastic language which rings so much of the *déjà entendu* that we are apt to miss important nuances. In fact, we are apt, at times, to miss the whole point.

Let me give a single example, though in some detail. I excerpt it from a somewhat tedious book dating from the last years of the Reformer's life. His rapidly deteriorating health had forced his retirement to the infirmary in 1695, a full five years before his death. As abbot *emeritus*, he used his time and failing energies, as always, in the service of others. His first literary production from the infirmary was a two-volume work, *Maximes chrétiennes et morales*, first printed in 1698.[39] The number of maxims rises to a grand total of 1,143 texts culled, for the most part, from copies of his correspondence and earlier writ-

ings, and few of them particularly memorable. The collection
seems to strike a negative note by its very existence, for no
reader could scan the title-page without thinking straightaway
of La Rochefoucauld's celebrated *Maximes* (1665) and the
witty but cynical *bons mots* which circulated in the literary
salons in smart society. An aura of negativity hangs over us as
we thumb past the title-page and read the first of Rancé's maxims—a text doubtless positioned here as setting the tone and
summing up the chief message of all that follows. This is what
we read (and here I wish to provide the original form of the
French text, with the inconsistent accentuation and spelling of
the period):

> Heureux celuy qui vit dans un dégagement parfait des
> choses de la terre, & dans un sentiment veritable de celles du
> Ciel: L'esprit de penitence ne se trouvant, qu'où les pre-
> mieres sont entiérement détruites, & les autres vives & toutes
> presentes.

Which being translated reads:

> Happy is he who lives in perfect detachment from the
> things of earth, and in a true [or authentic] experience of
> the things of heaven; for the spirit of penitence is found
> only where the first are utterly destroyed, and the others
> are wholly living and wholly present.

Just so! We are perfectly right to bemoan the gloomy rigorism of a mind capable of penning thoughts as negative as this.
'Perfect detachment from the things of earth', which things have
to be 'utterly destroyed' if we are to have the real 'spirit of penitence'. Pessimism, contempt for the world which God created
good and which he loves. Unfortunately, thanks to our fixed
image of Rancéan doctrine, we have taken note of only one
half of the text which begins, in fact, with the diction of the
biblical beatitudes: *Heureux celui* — the *Beatus vir* of Psalm
One, and the 'Blessed are those' sayings from the Sermon on
the Mount. Rancé's *Maximes* begin with a Beatitude! This is
only speciously so, comes the objection, since the person proclaimed blessed is the man who contemns the world. Can't you

even read? I counter. Why are you lopping off the second and perhaps more significant part of the sentence? I mean the words: 'Happy is he who lives . . . in a true experience of the things of heaven.' Nowadays the Frenchman would doubtless speak of an *expérience vécue*, a 'lived experience.' *Sentiment véritable* in seventeenth-century French is not just 'sentiment' or 'idea' or 'feeling', as is clear from the concluding words of the maxim which refers to the realities of heaven as being *toutes vives et toutes présentes*, 'wholly living [or alive] and wholly present.' This is the language of experience. It is also the language of the Fathers. It is also perfectly in line with monastic texts of the *gustate et videte* kind, 'taste in an experiential act of contemplation and see.' Rancé is, in brief, proclaiming the blessedness of the man or woman for whom the kingdom to come is already a present reality.

And here we touch upon something which does indeed separate the authentic mystical and monastic tradition from the somewhat counterfeit nineteenth- and early twentieth-century counterparts. The theme of the *ferverinos* given in the chapter rooms of these later centuries tended to be along the lines of: 'Act manfully, bear with pain and suffering for love of Jesus, and persevere: heaven is coming!' Rancé, however remains firmly within the tradition in which heaven is not simply the kingdom to come, but the kingdom already inchoatively but really present. At early Clairvaux as at later la Trappe, the kingdom was perceived as still to come—and this meant a spirituality of desire and gradual growth; but the kingdom was also already present to the monk formed in the wisdom of discipline and prayer—and this meant a spirituality of joy.

There is, then, in the above quoted maxim and in countless similar pages of Rancé positive elements all too easily overlooked by the reader who, alerted by Bremond, can approach the Reformer only as a 'fixed type.'

But there is a further consideration. Does the reader really know what Rancé means by 'the things of earth'? Does the reader really know what Rancé means by 'spirit of penitence'?

Here I can only refer the reader to a few pages elsewhere, in which I treat briefly of the formula, *Monastica vita poenitentia est*.[40] For Rancé and his fellow Abstinent monks, 'penitence' or 'penance' generally stood for 'asceticism' or 'ascetic discipline' rather than the 'heroic mortifications' which feature so large in Fr Lekai's descriptions of trappist excesses. Further, Rancéan *pénitence* is rooted in the New Testament proclamation *Poenitere!* for the kingdom of God is at hand (Mt 3:2). Still further, and even more characteristically, Rancé's penitence or penance is a participation in the penitence of Jesus Christ. He writes:

> To know what the penitence of solitaries ought to be, we must consider what the penitence of Jesus Christ was.[41]

Or again:

> As the penitence of a monk owes its birth, strength, and merit to the penitence of Jesus Christ, so ought it to be a continual retracing, a faithful imitation of *his* penitence.[42]

And since Jesus' penitence is Jesus' life of self-sacrificing love culminating in the supreme manifestation of God's love and mercy on Good Friday, the monk's penance means essentially his sharing in the redemptive mystery at the very center, where the action really is. To reduce all this to flamboyant extravagance in the order of physical austerities is . . . well, not very perceptive.

In a sense the very ordinariness of Rancé's vocabulary makes it easy to overlook or distort or trivialize the authentic richness of his doctrine. In the case of Bérulle, the out-of-the-ordinary terminology and technical expressions encourage us to discover the exact meaning this great spiritual master invests in each term. Whereas with Rancé, the doctrine is tributary to the Gospel and St Paul, to John Climacus and Cassian, to St Bernard and Jean de Bernières-Louvigny; but his diction eschews anything smacking of a special technical vocabulary.

I have begun to wander a bit far afield, since, in this particular section, I am supposed to be dealing more precisely with our difficulty in discerning the more positive aspects of Rancéan thought. So let me conclude this section by citing briefly a letter written by one of the most attractive figures of the whole Splendid Century. It shows us a woman reacting in the most positive manner to a text which, for most of us, makes for grim reading indeed.

Of all the long line of mistresses to Louis XIV, Louise de La Vallière alone invites our unqualified sympathy and admiration. Here I cannot even touch on the long and painful history of her struggle to leave court and enter the Carmel at Paris. As a novice, she received from Rancé both a letter of encouragement and a personal visit on the occasion of one of Rance's last trips to Paris on affairs of the Strict Observance. Not long after her profession in 1675, one of the devout laymen who gravitated around la Trappe, Henri-Joseph de Peyre, comte de Tréville (or Troisville) read to the Carmelite nuns an account of the recent death of Fr Charles Denys, monk of la Trappe. The narrative has in it much which would qualify as 'heroic mortifications', and it would be easy enough to manipulate some of the material *á la Bremond*. But here is a passionate and noble woman of the period telling what the life and death of the austere Fr Charles Denys have to say to her. These lines are translated from Letter 15 to her great confidant, Bernardin Gigault, maréchal de Bellefonds, the unworldliest of men at the worldliest of courts:

> As a general rule, lives that are austere and filled with suf-
> fering, marvelous though they may appear, leave poor
> human nature all atremble; but it seems to me that in every-
> thing I heard yesterday there's a certain unction so filled
> with comfort and tenderness. . . . Far from taking fright
> at the rigors of penitence, one feels instead all the greater
> zeal and ardor to embrace it. Still, we're less struck with
> astonishment at so many virtues in a single individual than
> filled with wonder at the plenitude of graces God showered
> upon him. For what is it we see in this holy man? Rigorous
> austerity, yes; but an austerity coupled with extreme re-
> finement; profound humility, but also perfect innocence;
> an ardent, tender, gentle love; a peace that remains unalter-

able, no matter how many the sufferings endured for so
long a time . . . [43]

'Extreme refinement', 'ardent, tender, gentle love', 'unalterable
peace', — all so many expressions which fit less comfortably with
our fixed-type image of somber la Trappe.

But even the seventeenth-century had its own 'fixed-type'
perspectives, and these too make for possible distortions when
we try to look objectively at la Trappe in the heydey of Rancé.
I myself can never read the *Relations de la Trappe*—a long series
of short biographical sketches of the lives and deaths (mostly
the deaths) of monks of la Trappe—without seeing in my mind's
eye the splendid engraving by the hermit Frère Pacôme, who
visited la Trappe in the early eighteenth century, and turned
out a wonderful series of engravings of life at la Trappe, a picture of Rancé on his deathbed among them.[44] The monks are
assembled, grouped dramatically according to the best norms of
artistic composition. One monk covers his face in excess of
grief. Others clasp their hands or fling their arms about in suitable attitudes of affliction. Eyes roll heavenwards in ardent sup-
plication. To the left looms a huge four-poster bed large enough
to accommodate a regiment. Its billowing drapes are balanced,
to the right, by an enormous fringed curtain suspended from
the invisible empyrean — a mammoth affair such as never existed
at la Trappe. For such a curtain we have to go to the Opéra
Comique in Paris. And this, indeed, suggests what we are wit-
nessing: the death of Rancé as it might have been staged by a
Corneille or, even better, a Racine. The central figure in this
drama is, of course, the dying Reformer, artistically and grace-
fully recumbent on his bed of sackcloth and ashes. This is high
drama indeed.

I doubt that Frère Pacôme ever witnessed the death of a
Trappist. But had he done so, he doubtless would have seen it
exactly as he has depicted it in his engravings. He too had his
own artistic vision, and saw the dying Trappist as a fixed type.
Still, we would miss a great deal if we overlook the substance of
the portrayal because of our impatience with, or amusement at

the seventeenth or eighteenth-century mannerisms. The pathos and the drama are from the Splendid Century; the theological substance, the real meaning, belong to the supra-temporal order. The death of the monk on sackcloth and ashes is no lugubrious novelty from the seventeenth century. This is the way twelfth-century monks of Clairvaux died; it is the way St Martin, monk and bishop, died. The dying monk is garbed in his cowl. From his exposure to John Climacus and Cassian, he knows that the cowl has symbolized his union with Jesus crucified during the years of his monastic pilgrimage; but now it becomes his wedding garment, the sure token of his admission to the nuptials of the Lamb. His imminent final breath will merely set the seal on a death in Christ which has radically already taken place in his day to day living out of his monastic vocation. Sackcloth and ashes stand for penitence. But we might fail to note that the ashes have carefully been sprinkled in the form of a cross. The death of the monk marks the moment of his full identification with Jesus on the cross. In brief, the ritual of the death of a Trappist is an expression of the monk's plenary participation in the Paschal Mystery, the mystery of the dying and the rising of the Lord. The monk is passing through suffering and death with the Lord and in the Lord. No wonder that so many of the monks of whom we read in the *Relations* looked with eagerness to the moment when their brethren would lift them from their straw mattress and lay them on their bed of straw, sackcloth, and ashes. And let us not miss the straw. Sackcloth and ashes for the symbolism; but the straw makes for a bed more comfortable than the hard straw mattresses of the infirmary beds. A human touch, this.

Life imitates art, however; and we may take it for granted that, as Rancé lay a-dying, there was doubtless much rolling of eyes, heaving of bosoms, clasping of hands, and flailing about of arms. But this is not all there is to see for the discerning eye. The whole scene is bathed in a quiet radiance whose source is the light of the Paschal Candle. If all we see is the melancholy scene of a dying monk, this may be less than just to the objective reality we are contemplating. The aura of negativity hovering over the picture may be due more to our spiritual myopia and lack of christian culture than to any real absence of the positive in the death of the Trappist.

I suggest, then, that in addressing ourselves to la Trappe and its 'Thundering Abbot' we might find considerably more of a positive nature if (a) we learn how to read with discernment, and if (b) we take cognizance of our tendency to see only what we think we are supposed to see. All I ask for is a modicum of objectivity. Why can we not bring to our reading of the *Relations de la Trappe* the same objectivity with which we would scrutinize a newly discovered cache of thirteenth-century archival material from a hitherto unidentified cistercian convent in Calabria?

LA TRAPPE AND THE NINE (?) CITIES OF PARIS

Though Theophilus North counted as many as nine different Newports, he was never quite sure that there might not be still other Newports hidden from his discerning eye. In the case of Paris, I do not know whether young Mr North would have distinguished nine or ninety cities; but there is no doubt that the young Abbé de Rancé had it in him to move freely from one Paris to another, before finally finding his true home in a quite different country. For Theophilus North, freedom of movement from one Newport to another flowed from his contemplative objectivity; for Rancé, casual flitting about from one Paris to another was rooted in his restlessness.

He came from a family whose members had taken up residence, so to speak, in several different cities of Paris. As a member of the *famille* Bouthillier de Rancé, the young Abbé had access to many of these separate cities which made up the whole complex city of Paris of the Splendid Century. The city in which his paternal grandparents lived — and they were the best of the lot — was sparsely populated. Denis had sided with the then Huguenot Henri IV against the Catholic League, had put his pen as well as his forensic skill at the service of his king, and as *avocat* in the *Parlement* of Paris had been involved in some of the weightier matters of state. Incredibly, he refused to follow through on his advantages, lived with his large family unostentatiously below his means, and served the poor and impecunious by offering free legal services and advice. His wife, Claude Françoise de Macheot, was even more remarkable. She came from Dijon stock, and was distantly related to Jeanne Frémiot de Chantal. Orphaned at an early age, she was presented with the choice between religious life and marriage. She chose marriage, and a fine mother and wife she proved to be. She shared her husband's disconcerting lack of concern for getting ahead, turned her home into a medical dispensary for the poor, did her own shopping, supervised the devotions of her large household staff, and raised her family in what may have been an overly spartan regime to judge by the tendencies evident in the young Bouthilliers once they had achieved their majority and personal independence. All this was at a time when the lawyer class was fast becoming supremely powerful, and when almost everyone ambitioned a higher station. Denis and his wife renounced this lust for power, served God and the king and the poor faithfully, and were content. Years later, after the death of her husband, Claude-Françoise became a lay sister in the first of the Paris Visitandine convents — a mature novice aged seventy-two.[45]

Two of the Bouthillier boys became bishops. Sébastien died young as the result of sickness contracted in the exercise of his pastoral ministry. He certainly deserves at least a monograph. It was he who first taught the Abbé de Saint-Cyran the ways of mental prayer, provided a home for the up-and-coming young theologian, and was busy at work with him on a long-range program for the renewal of the episcopate and lower orders and the faithful at large when death came in 1625. This was, of course, quite some time before Saint-Cyran assumed leadership of the Jansenist movement. Perhaps it is as well that Sébastien died when he did, for his correspondence shortly preceding his death points to the stern Abbé's growing ascendency over the apostolic bishop. Had Sébastien lived, he would doubtless have been one of the first and greatest of the Jansenist or Jansenizing bishops. But Sébastien was also close, very close, to Richelieu. It was he who acted as his agent at court and in Paris when the future Prime Minister was no more than a provincial bishop; and it was also Sébastien who obtained for him the red hat from Rome.[46] So there were several cities of Paris in which this remarkable young bishop moved freely: the Paris of the devout, the Paris of court and politics, the Paris of the powerful ecclesiastics.

Sébastien's youngest brother, the Benjamin of the family, began his own ecclesiastical career humbly enough in the newly-founded Oratorians. Bérulle was a bit guarded about him — young Fr Victor's love for learning seemed a bit excessive. When Victor was offered a bishopric, he took it, even though this meant leaving the Oratory. He began his gradual ascent through successive bishoprics until, as archbishop of Tours, he had reached the upper echelons; and as archbishop of Tours he proved himself a conscientious prelate and a splendid administrator. He also loved power, and if he sincerely worked to promote the *gloire* of God, he worked even harder to promote the *gloire* of the family Bouthillier. At his death in 1670, his panegyrist found much for which to praise him truthfully; it was only on the score of Victor's personal piety that a bit of imagination had to be employed.[47] So the Paris in which Archbishop Victor moved most at ease was the Paris of worldly but capable prelates.

The two other boys, Claude and Denis, both had brilliant careers in government and at court, and both moved freely through the labyrinthine corridors of power. Inevitably, however, their careers waxed and waned according to the inconstancy of the wheel of fortune; and towards the end of their lives, mostly they waned. It was Claude who, having managed to climb the highest, also fell the lowest. The Paris of Claude and Denis, then, was the Paris of the political careerists and court diplomats.

As for the daughters, there were five of them. The eldest made a good match — less than brilliant, but more than merely respectable; and the remaining daughters opted for the convent.[48]

The daughters of Denis *fils* were similarly but more equitably apportioned cloister and hearth. Two of them married and moved in circles of smart society, while the other three entered religion. Of the three boys, Denis III was destined for an ecclesiastical career, and was already raking in sizable revenues when he died, still in pre-adolescence, in 1637. Armand-Jean, his junior by a few years (he was born in 1626) had already been tonsured as early as 1635, in prudent anticipation of his frail older brother's imminent demise. On the morrow of Denis' burial, Armand-Jean was installed as a canon of Notre-Dame de Paris, and the transfer of benefices from defunct Denis to cadet Armand-Jean was effected without a hitch. The third son, Henri, became a Knight of Malta in the place of his older brother Armand-Jean, who now became heir apparent to the family fortune. A great deal now depended on Armand-Jean; for Denis II, who had served faithfully as secretary to the Queen Mother, Marie de Medicis, tumbled mightily as of 11 November, 1630, *La Journée des Dupes*, when Richelieu at last won total ascendancy over Louis XIII, and succeeded in permanently banishing the scheming old harridan from court. The irony of it was that Denis, like all the other powerful Bouthilliers, had risen to influential position chiefly on the train of Richelieu's *cappa magna*. Years earlier Denis *grandpère* had been a second father to the young Armand-Jean du Plessis at a time when the family fortunes of the latter had reached their nadir. Once in power, Richelieu was well enough disposed to return a favor — so long as this cost no real effort and worked to his own further personal advantage. Indeed, the Cardinal had even stood sponsor at the baptism of his infant namesake; and it was to the Cardinal that the twelve-year old boy dedicated his first book, a scholarly edition of Anakreon with his own Greek *scholia*.[49]

At the age of twelve or thirteen, then, our young ecclesiastic had before him several options. Would he follow through with his flair for learning and join the ranks of the learned humanists and classicists who wore the cloth? Would he follow in the foootsteps of his godfather Richelieu and become yet another one of the ecclesiastic statesmen-politicians like his fellow boy-canons of Notre-Dame, Jean-François-Paul de Gondi (the future Cardinal de Retz) and François de Harlay de Champvallon (the future archbishop of Paris)? Would he settle rather for becoming, like his Uncle Victor, a conscientious though rather worldly prelate? Or would he settle for still less, and flit from salon to salon as yet another of those pathetic *abbés du cour* of which there were far too many? That he should aspire to true holiness in some form of pastoral ministry seems not to have been among his choices. Still, we do catch sight of him indulging in behavior somewhat at odds with his family milieu — as when, instead of turning the celebration of his first Mass into a social event, he slips off to the Carthusian monastery near the Paris Rancé *hôtel*, and celebrates the sacred mysteries in a setting of austere silence and separation from the world.[50]

My own impression is that the young Rancé was caught in something of a no-man's Paris. His studies first in philosophy and later in theology had won him his doctor's bonnet from the Sorbonne in 1654; but neither the classics nor theology held so strong an attraction for him that he was much tempted to settle down as a clerical scholar of independent means. Certainly there is little to suggest that he aspired to power at court, for he had a chronic habit of publicly championing the wrong people. To speak up as he did at the Assembly of the Clergy (1655-1657) on behalf of his friends Cardinal de Retz and Bishop François de Harlay de Champvallon, and against the omnipotent Jules Cardinal Mazarin, was the directest possible form of political suicide.[51] A truly astute politician would have been more accommodating to the exigencies of reality. Nor does Rancé seem to have been particularly noteworthy as a social butterfly. The numerous memoirs and diaries of the period in no way single him out for special attention, either as a wit or as a literary dilettante; and the most earnest effort to find evidence of real debauchery proves rather disappointing. Even the splendid story of the dissolute *abbé* discovering the corpse of his paramour, the duchesse de Montbazon, headless and pathetic to behold and waiting to be consigned to its too short coffin, has been relegated to the realm of myth;[52] so that all that remains is the likelihood of a tender attachment of the amorous *abbé* to the *duchesse,* and his shock at her sudden death from scarlet fever. That he really did know the poor woman well is certain, for the magnificent country estates of the two families lay close to each other outside Tours, and the children of the two households had been at home in either place. That Armand-Jean eventually came to know Madame de Montbazon in an even more intimate relationship is, alas, by no means unthinkable. Hers was said to be the friendliest bed in France, and even a rake as indulgent about such things as Cardinal de Retz wrote of her that he 'had never seen anyone who preserved in vice so little respect for virtue.'[53] I especially like Madame de Motteville's description of the occasion when the celebrated beauty appeared at court 'covered with pearls and one large scarlet feather.'[54] Here I steadfastly refuse to check Madame de Motteville's original text, for I fear to find that the secondary source whom I am here following may be guilty of a pious exaggeration, and that Madame de Motteville meant only to call attention to Madame de Montbazon's most striking, rather than to her only, adornment. In the circumstances, I much prefer this image of the Duchess to the engraving of her I have before my eyes as I write. Despite the attestation to her *adorables beautez* signed at the bottom of the portrait by her admirer, Jehan le Blond, Madame la Princesse Marie de Rohan, Duchesse de Montbazon, is clearly the wrong side of forty; her unevenly plucked eyebrows and her frizzled hair (her own?) need attention; and there is no denying that the good woman is running to fat. Nor is there any denying that her three children by the Duc Hercule de Rohan (forty-four years her senior) turned out remarkably well — François de Rohan-Montbazon, who formed the branch of the *princes de Soubise;* Anne, wife to the duc de Luynes; and Marie-Eléonore, abbess successively of la Trinité at Caen and then of Malnoue, and counted by historians among the *grandes abbesses* of the seventeenth century. But even when we have drawn the worst possible conclusion from what little we know about the Rancé -Montbazon relationship, the *abbé* seems to have been more of an ecclesiastical dandy than a clerical Don Juan.

I see the young Rancé, then, as an extremely talented fellow who moved freely through a good number of the many cities of Paris, but who was too torn in too many directions to be able to settle down and become a full citizen of any one particular Paris — not even the Paris of the foppish *abbés du cour.* Truth to tell, he was meant to be citizen of none of these cities. His citizenship lay in quite another country.

Rancé's spiritual itinerary in no way led straight from the Nine Cities of Paris to la Trappe, nor was there anything sudden or ostentatiously dramatic about the spiritual quest which led him so far afield from his accustomed haunts. His disgrace with God-Almighty-Mazarin and his subsequent withdrawal from the Assembly of the Clergy still in session at Paris in 1657 was certainly a traumatic experience for one who had aspired to succeed Uncle Victor as archbishop of Tours; but this was only one of a long series of deeply-felt personal losses and reversals which began when his father died in 1650 and left him head of the litigious and power-hungry *famille* Bouthillier de Rancé. Then came the deaths of his once powerful Uncle Claude and Cousin Léon in 1652 — both of them in disgrace; next, the collapse of the Fronde in 1653, with Mazarin more firmly in the ascendancy than ever; then the sudden death of Madame de Montbazon in 1657; and in early 1660 the dramatic death of the royal rake and ne'er do-well, Gaston d'Orléans, to whom Rancé had been appointed first chaplain in 1656. Meanwhile, Rancé's interior evolution was gathering momentum. If we can tax our *abbé du cour* with any real fault during this period of incipient conversion, it would be the fault of excessive dependence on others for spiritual counsel and practical advice. Simply to list and identify the persons of whom he asked counsel at this period would run to a lengthy paragraph. During 1658 and 1659, his time was spent chiefly at Véretz, his chateau near Tours, which he turned into a place of intensive spiritual retreat for himself and occasional visitors of a more serious sort. For the first time he began visiting his many benefices with a view to making amends for longstanding dereliction of his duties as commendatory superior, but also with a view to arranging for the reduction of the number of benefices held by himself personally. In the late summer of 1660, Rancé headed for the Pyrenees, where his program of conversion crystallized still further. The three bishops whom he consulted — of Comminges, Pamiers, and Alet — were episcopal counterparts of St. Vincent de Paul. All three were rightly suspected of Jansenist leanings; but, as was inevitably the case with prelates of Jansenizing tendencies, all three were remarkable for their personal piety, their poverty, their pastoral zeal, their fidelity to the reform program formulated by the Council of Trent. The advice of these bishops converged on Rancé's obligation to renounce his plurality of benefices and to make restitution for the enormous sums realized over the years from these many benefices, but lavished on the aggrandizement of family power and *gloire* rather than on the sustenance of the poor of Christ. But what was Rancé's subsequent role to be? The bishops of Pamiers and Alet saw Rancé as a future reforming bishop of their own heroic mold. The bishop of Comminges saw him rather as a reforming regular abbot of one of his many houses until then held *in commendam*. Rancé saw himself considerably more modestly than did any of the three bishops. The years 1661 and 1662 were spent chiefly in coping with the considerable problems involved in the disposal of his benefices and the dismemberment of his estate; and at last the formerly easy-going, dilettantish *abbé du cour* was free to withdraw still farther. He aspired to nothing higher than the life of a conscientious commendatory abbot living on the fringe of the poorest of his benefices, the Abbaye de la Trappe, and spending his time in prayer and penitence and spiritual reading.

Materially and morally, la Trappe had been the most abandoned of Rancé's benefices. The buildings were in ruins, and the handful of monks in residence had substituted gaming and hunting, and considerably less respectable pursuits, for the traditional practices of cistercian monastic life. Even before his retirement to la Trappe as commendatory abbot, Rancé had begun the work of restoration of the monastery plant; and he had obtained from the Abbey of Perseigne, a monastery of the Cistercians of the Strict Observance, a minuscule colony of monks to serve as the nucleus of a new community. No need to dwell at length here on this most mysterious of all the phases of the Abbé's conversion. Since the abbey whose reform he had undertaken was now populated chiefly by Strict Observance Cistercians, he undertook a careful study of the history of the origins and evolution of the White Monks, and acquainted himself thoroughly with the conflicting ideologies which at this time were pitting the 'Ancients' against the 'Abstinents' in what amounted to an internecine civil war within the Cistercian Order in France. He acted as confessor for the brethren of the newly-formed community; and in order to encourage them, he shared their fasts and began assisting at their community Mass and Office. Why not go all the way and become their regular abbot? Thet idea was not his own. At one stage he wished only to join the ranks of the nascent community as a simple monk; and it was pressure from the community itself and from his own spiritual counsellors which at last determined him to begin his year-long novitiate at Perseigne with a view to assuming the burden of regular abbot of the renewed community. He pronounced his vows at Perseigne on 26 June 1664. On 13 July he received his abbatial blessing in the cathedral at Séez, from the hands of the exiled bishop of Ardagh, Patrick Plunket; and on the next day he was home in his own monastery.

Within weeks, protesting, but protesting to no avail, he was off to Rome as one of the two delegates charged by the Strict Observance superiors with the Observance's interests in the roman settlement of the differences between the two Observances.[55] He was away for two years; and when the negotiations ended to the advantage of the 'Common' Observance, Rancé returned to la Trappe uncertain as to its future, but determined to pursue his ideal of cistercian monastic renewal based on the holy Rule of St. Benedict as interpreted by the early Cistercians. The basic thrust of this program of renewal never varied, even though it admitted of modifications and adaptations with respect to particular points. Elsewhere I have discussed some of the aspects of this reform with special reference to its cistercian dimension;[56] and I have also had occasion to treat of Rancé's theory and *praxis* as spiritual father of his community[57] (even though Rancé himself virtually eschewed the title 'Father', much preferring to refer to himself as 'Brother' of the brethren of la Trappe). What I want here to stress, however, is what I have already insisted upon, namely, that what was important about the phenomenon of the la Trappe reform is not the precise program or any of its more significant details, but quite simply the overall phenomenon itself. One might argue against the Trappist observance taken as a whole or in its parts; what one could not argue against was the *expérience vécue*, the lived experience of the brethren, which more than any verbalization by Rancé or anyone else, bore eloquent witness to the essential rightness of what was happening in that almost wholly isolated section of la Perche — a virtual islet surrounded by pools and lakes, and situated in a forested region difficult of access. Let me quote, for instance, from a lengthy narrative by the benedictine scholar Dom Claude Lancelot, addressed to Mère Angélique de Saint-Jean, abbess of Port-Royal. The letter, which describes the author's visit to the bishop of Alet, refers to Rancé as one of Nicolas Pavillon's most illustrious *dirigés*, and proceeds to speak of the reformer abbot and his community at considerable length. I do not have available Lancelot's original text, and can quote it only in the

translation by that ardent nineteenth-century evangelical
apologist for Port-Royal, Mary Anne Schimmelpenninck. No
friend to romish superstitions, Mrs. Schimmelpenninck never
scrupled to translate not so much what was actually said or
written as what *should* have been said or written had the original author been as richly graced as herself in what pertains to
the true gospel spirit. Had la Trappe appeared to her (and Dom
Lancelot) as remarkable chiefly for its monkish macerations
and austerities, her diction would have been adjusted accordingly. Monkish macerations and austerities do indeed feature
large in her account; but there is something which looms larger:

> Perhaps the most astonishing part of M. de Rancé's reform
> is, not the mere introduction of a new rule, but the total
> change, which is so soon visible in the manners, the incli-
> nations, and the very countenances of his disciples. This,
> no doubt, proves that God was of a truth with him; for
> this is a change his Spirit alone could have wrought. Few
> enter La Trappe, who do not in a short time acquire a total-
> ly new countenance and demeanour.
>
> It is impossible to describe the gravity, benignity, peace
> and love, visible in most of their aspects; or the humility,
> and yet self-possessed politeness and attention, in their
> manners. I remember when I was there, being most pecu-
> liarly struck with one of them. I think I never saw such a
> venerable, holy gravity, and yet celestial joy and love ir-
> radiate any human countenance. I could not take my eyes
> off of a countenance the most angelic I ever beheld, or
> conceived. I concluded he had been twenty or thirty
> years an inmate of this seclusion. It so happened that he
> was next day appointed our conductor. I asked his age;
> what was my astonishment at the reply, 'Six and twenty'! I
> inquired how long he had been an inhabitant of La Trappe.
> 'As a monk two years.' I then asked what he was before.
> 'Do you then forget me?' said he, smiling. I cannot express
> the surprise I felt at finding that this venerable saint, appar-
> ently fifty, was no other than a gay young captain in the
> French guards, whom I well remembered, five or six years

before, to have been one of the most elegant and dissipated young men in Paris.[58]

How much of this is Mrs. Schimmelpenninck? How much is Dom Claude Lancelot? I am unprepared to say, though I suspect most of it is Mrs. Schimmelpenninck. Further, I am quite prepared to accept the texts quoted as belonging to the literary genre of the myth. But myths, after all, take their rise as attempts to interpret and explain historical reality. What drew people to la Trappe was not the sight of penitents busy at their bloody macerations or cowled zombies shuffling around their cloister, but rather the peace and palpable joy which feature so large in almost all the eyewitness reports of the period.

By the very structure of his splendid book, *Armand-Jean de Rancé . . . His Influence in the Cloister and the World*, A. J. Krailsheimer has suggested something of the broad spectrum of society influenced by our reformer. In his treatment of 'Rancé's Influence in the Cloister', he begins by speaking of la Trappe in itself and of vocations to la Trappe; he then goes on to speak of religious of the Cistercian Order of both observances, religious of other orders, and women in religion. 'Rancé's influence in the World' deals in succession with prelates, secular clergy and Oratorians, men among 'the Great', women among 'the Great', and finally, his own family. But had Rancé followed through with his original plan of living as a conscientious commendatory abbot on the fringe of an isolated reformed cistercian abbey, I doubt that Professor Krailsheimer would have found much to say about Rancé's influence on anyone anywhere. As a theologian, Rancé was most unoriginal; indeed, he was one of the most unoriginal of thinkers; and if he ever had so much as a single important original idea, I would be grateful to have it pointed out to me. His written style is wonderful for its directness and transparency and quiet musicality; but his letters are never going to rival those of Madame de Sévigné. As spiritual director, Rancé had a genius for adapting himself to each individual; but he certainly had no distinctive 'doctrine' or 'spirituality'; and even at the level of simple discernment, he was not uniformly successful in understanding individuals or events. As a conversationalist, he could more than hold his own — so long as the conversation was a pious one; but France of the Splendid Century teemed with brilliant conversationalists, and who nowadays can quote even a single memorable *bon mot* uttered by the great man? And yet the man was truly a man of influence.

The nature of Rancé's influence was, however, of a diffused sort. It never focussed in such a way as to affect the course of events either within his own Order or in the Church or world outside. Indeed, it was rooted in what he *was* and what he stood for more than in any particular doctrine or program of monastic reform. Certainly, I here speak under correction; and what I want to say is impatient of really clear formulation. Still, it seems to me that almost everyone who dwelt in the various Nine Cities of Paris through which the restless young *abbé* had once moved could identify with him under one or more titles as one of their own. Further, significant numbers of the citizenry of those Nine Cities could recognize in themselves something of the higher aspirations which had led the *abbé du cour* from his familiar milieu to a quite new distant country. To reach that distant country was beyond the expectations of most; but it was still an encouragement and a sign of hope that so unlikely a citizen of Paris as Armand-Jean Bouthillier de Rancé could respond so wholly to an absolute ideal as to realize even now something of the peace and truth of the kingdom still to come. The preface for religious in the Roman Missal says it eloquently:

> Today we honor your saints
> who consecrated their lives to Christ
> for the sake of the kingdom of heaven.
> What love you show us
> as you recall mankind to its innocence,
> and invite us to taste on earth
> the gifts of the world to come!

This is what la Trappe was about — a return to the innocence of Eden and an anticipation of the world to come. That this also meant suffering and a sharing in the passion of Christ was an essential aspect of the present economy of salvation. But the outsider could look at la Trappe and understand that the innocence of Paradise and the peace and joy of the Kingdom are not abstract realities or mental constructs or impossible dreams. True, there must have been many such as Madame de Sévigné who could honestly say that she belonged neither to God nor to the devil — though not many were as honest as she was in admitting that this 'neither/nor' state was comfortable. Still, in time even Madame de Sévigné wanted nothing more than to surrender to the exigencies of true holiness: . . . *si mon coeur était aussi touché que mon espirit est convaincu, je serais une sainte;* . . . if my heart were touched as much as my mind is convinced, I'd be a saint."[59]

Something of this impinges on the consciousness of even a Mary Anne Schimmelpenninck, who was, we know, no friend to 'the Roman system.' In her account of Dom Lancelot's visit to la Trappe, she puts on the abbot's lips a lengthy speech about as historical as the eve-of-battle speeches recorded by Livy in his accounts of roman generals and their campaigns. 'The grand peculiarities of the Gospel are essential to all collectively,' quoth the austere reformer, 'yet no doubt, an attention to our own peculiar call, is equally essential to each individually.' Then after a long development on the varieties of religious life and vocations within the Church, he formulates what the vocation of the brethren at la Trappe really is: 'I have believed it our calling in particular, to shew the christian world, that as every worldly gift without God is empty, so God, without any worldly good, is, as of old all-sufficient.'[60]

The formula is more Mrs. Schimmelpenninck's than Rancé's; but it is, I think, essentially correct. Nor is it really very different from the splendid lines of Georges Bernanos, who wrote in 1942, at a time when people counselled prudence and discretion and compromise:

By an extraordinary abuse of language which would have
stupefied the ancient Greeks, the sense of proportion is
today confused with the prudence of imbeciles — as if
there were any other sense of proportion for a man than to
give himself without limit to values which infinitely transcend the scope of his own life.[61]

It was towards this giving himself without limit to that Love
which infinitely transcends the scope of human life that Rancé
had been moving since his childhood. No matter what the
diversions, no matter what the infidelities, his restless heart was
taking him into his own true country where he, together with
his brethren, could give himself without limit to this terrible
exigency of love. As he saw it, it was simply a question of fidelity. Circumstances had made him a commendatory abbot from
childhood, and had even led him to the priesthood. Conversion
meant, for him, becoming in truth what he already was supposed to be. Monastic life, then, and cistercian monastic life,
was the form in which this call to holiness was to be realized;
and if he interpreted cistercian life without due regard to that
sense of proportion which we so prize, this may well have been
because he felt more urgently than we the call infinitely to
transcend the scope of his own life.

Our own aspirations are doubtless less pretentious and more
realistic. Even so, this is no reason to treat la Trappe as worthy
of derision and ridicule. To come to la Trappe by way of Bremond is a bit like coming to Thornton Wilder by way of a
recent adventurous Manhattan Wooster Group play, 'Route
1 & 9 (The Last Act)'. Wilder's classic 'Our Town' is the focal
point of this production — 'Our Town', with all its truisms and
earnest praise of small-town American life. 'Route 1 & 9' begins
with an educational film about 'Our Town': platitude upon
platitude upon platitude. Next, a stage is prepared for a performance of 'Our Town' — by blindfolded stagehands who go
about their work in the spirit of high comedy while unre-
hearsed phone calls are made on stage to ensure some element
of real life. The final act is performed as a soap opera on TV

monitors. The audience views the last act as the cast throws itself into an increasingly wild party.[62] We are doubtless right to react negatively to anything in Wilder's play which suggests a racial stereotype; perhaps 'Our Town' seems a bit unreal to us who live in the age of the neutron bomb. Still, perhaps there is more to 'Our Town' than 'Route 1 & 9' suggests. And perhaps there is more to Rancé and la Trappe than what many of us can see only against the background and in the setting of our own noise and rootlessness and prudence of imbeciles.

Well, as I have already said, the propriety of a conference on seventeenth-century la Trappe in a seminar on the 'Roots of Modern Christian Spirituality' is none too evident to the author of these lines. Modern christian spirituality wants nothing whatsoever to do with that lugubrious Norman abbey and its celebrated, *too* celebrated 'Thundering Abbot' . . .

CHRYSOGONUS WADDELL, OCSO

Gethsemani Abbey

A WITNESS TO BENEDICTINE SPIRITUALITY IN THE SEVENTEENTH CENTURY

I. Formation: *1. Various influences and benedictine synthesis. 2. The decisive influence of the Maurists.* II. Doctrine: *1. The victory of the Cross. 2. The 'depths'. 3. The way of littleness. 4. Free obedience.* III. Permanent values of this teaching: *1. Christocentrism. 2. Fidelity to monastic tradition.* Conclusion: *A 'fine spirituality'.*

A publication now underway invites us to study the foundress of one of the Institutions of benedictine life which have lasted up to our own day without interruption. The publication in question is the dossier of documents concerning Catherine de Bar[1] who in the seventeenth century founded the Benedictines of Perpetual Adoration. The volumes which have already come out help us to discover one of the most remarkable spiritual works of this great period.[2] It deserves to be presented here.

I. FORMATION

1. Various Influences and Benedictine Synthesis

We need not retrace here the biography of Catherine de Bar, but can concentrate more on discerning the different traditions in which her work is rooted. Consequently we will merely recall the major dates of her life.[3] Catherine was born in Lorraine in 1614. In 1631 she entered the monastery of the Annonciades at Bruyères and was professed in 1633. A war devastated the monastery and dispersed the community. In 1639 Catherine transferred to the benedictine nuns at Rambervillers, who were under the influence of the benedictine monks of Saint-Vanne at Verdun, and was professed the following year. Obliged once more to emigrate, she went from Lorraine to France, stayed at the monastery of the Benedictines of Montmartre, founded a little monastery near the monastery of the benedictine monks at Saint-Maurdes-Fossés, came into contact with Saint-Germain-des-Près and then, in 1652, founded her Institute whose houses were soon to spread all over France, particularly in Normandy, as well as in Lorraine and Poland. After her death in 1698, the congregation spread to other european countries and numbers today forty monasteries.

In the different regions where she lived and at the various stages of her life, Catherine was marked by a good many influences. The contribution at Lorraine has been stressed by an historian specializing in the history of this province, M.P. Marot.[4] A master in the spirituality of the XVII century, L. Cognet, has given useful additional information.[5] With the Annonciades where Catherine first entered, the spirituality was mainly inspired by the Northern mystics and by Benedict of Canfield: much importance was given to interiority and the mystical life.[6] But the monastery of Rambervillers where she settled was under direct influence of the Congregation of Saint-Vanne, a severe reform, rich in doctrinal writings of a highly traditional nature.[7] The founder of this congregation, Dom Didier de la Cour, had as his disciple Dom Antoine de Lescale, who had encouraged Catherine's entry into the Benedictines.[8] In Lorraine, too, she had been helped by Canon Epiphane Louys, the premonstratensian abbot of Ettival. He kept up a correspondence with her, sent her spiritual letters, and wrote for her and her Institute two works of benedictine spirituality, one of them intended for novices. At that time there was no strict division between the different religious traditions and the greatest minds respected and encouraged traditions to which they themselves did not belong. Thus it was, for example, that a benedictine nun, Mother de Blémur, wrote a life of St. Peter Fourier, the reformer of the Congregation of the Canons Regular of St Augustine. And when the nuns from Lorraine settled in Paris they were protected by St Vincent de Paul.[9]

At Paris, Catherine de Bar lived first of all in circles which, though they depended mainly on a benedictine tradition inherited from the Middle Ages, did not exclude the wealth of spirituality transmitted by others. Effectively, the abbess of Montmartre, Marie de Beauvilliers, was on 'very good terms with the Capuchins, with the Oratorians, and among the Capuchins, in the first place, naturally, Benedict of Canfield.' For him 'the whole life of piety is summed up in the union of the will with God. God is essentially the "Divine Will" . . . .'

This tendency was completed — we are almost tempted to say corrected — by another influence which affected Catherine during her stay in Normandy: that of Jean de Bernières, founder of a retreat house called the Hermitage near the Ursuline convent where Jean had a sister. Now Bernières, together with two other priests, Father de Condren and Father de Saint-Jure, who also influenced Catherine, had a christocentric spirituality. At Saint-Maur-des-Fossés, her spiritual director was a Capuchin, Father Chrysostome de Saint-Lô, the director of Berniéres. Thus in the period preceding the foundation of her congregation, as has been pointed out by a detached expert, L. Cognet, Catherine underwent different influences which she 'assimilated in order to make a personal synthesis.'[10]

She was also the contemporary of an eminent man highly versed in things spiritual: Armand de Rancé. But he had to accomplish the reform and not simply harvest the ripe fruits. Rancé's lasting influence witnesses to the great value fact of his message in spite of certain personal character traits with which it was stamped. Happily, however, Catherine, unlike Rancé, was not a 'convert.' She has neither the complexes nor the psychological releases of a convert. She did not have to pass from a very worldly to a more austere life. Her reflexes are simply those characteristic of a nun who has grown up peacefully in her christian life and her religious vocation. And so she can help others — nuns or not — to grow in peace too, without violence, but also without weakness.

2. THE DECISIVE INFLUENCE OF THE MAURISTS

It was especially during what we might call the 'maurist

period' that Catherine de Bar, now become Mechtilde of the Blessed Sacrament, fashioned her own spirituality and gave it its permanent orientation. The idea of founding an institute which would observe perpetual adoration of the Blessed Sacrament came from Lorraine, where, as in every other place overrun by Calvinism, there sprang up a desire to make amends for the denial of the Real Presence attributed to the Calvinists. This reaction, founded on devotion or on theology, has a precedent in the history of monasticism. In the twelfth century, Alger, before entering Cluny, refuted the errors which originally came from Berengarius of Tours and were widespread in Liège at the beginning of the twelfth century.[11] In the spiritual circles she frequented, it was suggested to Mère Mechtilde that she 'found a congregation which would keep the benedictine setting, inserting into it the Adoration of the Blessed Sacrament to which it lent itself so admirably, given the liturgical bent of its piety'.[12] In this work she was greatly helped by the monks of the Congregation of Saint-Maur and particularly by those of Saint-Germain-des-Près. Since these details have been already set out elsewhere and illustrated by documents, it will be enough here merely to recall them.

The Prior of Saint-Germain-des-Près at that time was Dom Placide Roussel. It was he who, in 1656, drew up the report of the formalities concerning the Paris foundation. The nuns promised to consider him as 'their ordinary superior in all that concerned their spiritual and temporal conduct'. His successor, Dom Bernard Audebert, in 1659, confirmed that the monastery in rue Cassette came within the 'competence of his spiritual jurisdiction'. From then on Mère Mechtilde never left rue Cassette. Up to her death she kept up acquaintance with the monks of Saint-Germain, and particularly with the superior, Dom Ignace Philibert. He took care of the interests of the new monastery of benedictine nuns all the time he was in Paris, that is, until his death in 1667. 'He set up a commission of twelve members, among them Dom Audebert, superior general of the reformed Congregation of Cîteaux; they were all of the opinion that it was absolutely necessary to have a congregation given to perpetual adoration of the divine Sacrament and they charged Mère Mechtilde with the drafting of the statutes.' But, so the *Document biographique* tells us, 'unable to work at them on account of her frequent journeys she was obliged to undertake in setting up the Institute and also on account of the industry which she was obliged to put into the government of her own community whenever she was there, she found it necessary to beg him to draw up the constitutions himself. Especially moreover as he was much more acquainted with such matters than she because he had the experience of the Congregation of Saint-Maur, in which he had governed several of their first houses for a long time.'

It was to the Prior of Saint-Germain that Mère Mechtilde in 1654 proposed the blessing of a big carving in relief of the Mother of God, who was to be considered as the Superior of the Institute. A little later, on 24 August, Mère Mechtilde submitted to the Prior the act she had drawn up in order to 'dedicate' her monastery to Our Lady. In doing this, the benedictine nuns of Rue Cassette renewed an ancient devotion practised as early as the eleventh century at Marcilly, under the influence of Cluny. It is not impossible that the learning of the Maurists had something to do with the restoration of this medieval custom. Dom Bernard Audebert, a monk at Saint-Germain 'allowed the above-mentioned offering and it was renewed every year on the feast of the Assumption of the Blessed Virgin . . .'[14] The monks of Saint-Germain not only helped the nuns in the government of their community, they had a direct and lasting influence on the spiritual orientation of the whole Congregation of the Benedictines of the Blessed Sacrament. They also lent them pen and talent whenever necessary: in 1696, Dom Mabillon drew up, in the name of the Prioress, a long and beautiful circular on the death of Madame de Blémur. In 1702, an address, signed by all the nuns, made to the Prior of Saint-Germain thanked him for a talk he had given them and asked him to continue helping them. On 22 August

1668, Mère Mechtilde begged the Prior of Saint-Germain 'to approve and confirm the Bull of the erection of their Congregation obtained through Msgr de Vendôme, when he was legate', and after the approval of the Congregation and its Constitutions by Alexander VII, the benedictine nuns submitted to the Prior of Saint-Germain the formula of their profession.

In 1686, Mère Mechtilde had printed for her daughters 'The Spiritual Exercises or Practice of the Rule of St Benedict for the Use of the Benedictine Nuns of the Perpetual Adoration of the Blessed Sacrament'. This is, in fact, nothing but a work by Dom Claude Martin, 'The Practice of the Rule of St. Benedict'. This book, declared Mère Mechtilde in a letter at the beginning of the volume, 'may quite rightly be called a benedictine ethic . . . . It would suffice in itself to lead us to the perfection of our state'. Consequently, she proposed no other plan than that of Dom Claude. Nearly always she just put his own expressions into the feminine. She rarely modified the composition of the text or proposed another practice. In the chapter on stability, she adapted what had been said of stability in the Maurist congregation to enclosure proper to nuns. New chapters added in function of the specific spirit of the benedictine Nuns of Perpetual Adoration and the practices which flow naturally from this spirit — such as those entitled 'In what spirit reparation should be made' or 'Duties towards the Blessed Virgin as first and perpetual Abbess' — in no way alter the homeogeneity of the work as a whole and they fit in with the spirituality and the teachings it contains. Mère Mechtilde did not hesitate to say that 'even though every other book should be lacking, we would always find something consoling in this one', and she went on to say that it contains 'everything necessary for raising the soul to that holiness of life to which we should aspire and which is required of us by our profession'. That the rule of St Benedict was interpreted in the same way by the Maurists and the Benedictines of the Blessed Sacrament is witnessed to by the foundress herself. Dom Brachet, in giving permission to print, and Dom Claude Bretagne, then Prior of Saint-Germain, in giving his approval, confirm this agreement.

The monks of Saint-Germain greatly influenced the Benedictines of the Blessed Sacrament who spread from the rue Cassette in Paris, to different regions of France and several countries in Europe. The Paris community transferred as well. Until the Revolution, the monks of Saint-Germain helped this community even though they were generally neither chaplains nor confessors. The other houses of the Blessed Sacrament, in Rouen, Caen, Châtillon, Dreux, Bayeux, also benefitted by the help of these monks. The houses in Lorraine at Rambervillers, Toul, and Nancy were placed under the spiritual jurisdiction of the Congregation of Saint-Vanne. Two monks of Saint-Germain, Dom Guillaume Laparre and Dom Claude de Vic, busied themselves in Rome in 1705 getting the Constitutions of the Benedictines of the Blessed Sacrament definitively approved. Today the Benedictines of the Blessed Sacrament at Mas-Grenier, in the Tarn-et-Garonne department, live in the monastery once occupied by the Maurists. These nuns are keeping alive today in many places the spiritual tradition immediately inspired by that of the Congregation of Saint-Maur.

II. DOCTRINE

It is not easy to set Mechtilde's teaching in order for nowhere has she given a plan. In reading through her writings, however, we soon notice certain recurring ideas. She comes back constantly to certain points and there can be no doubt that for her they were primordial. It is precisely these points which we must try to stress here. On them the rest depends, either as natural consequences or as practical applications.

1. The Victory of the Cross

Mère Mechtilde grasped clearly that *perfection* is a key-word for St Benedict. This perfection is not a result attained once and for all, but a goal for which we must constantly strive. Such an effort implies that we root out every form of selfishness, particularly by being content with 'little things' and 'little graces', by doing 'little actions'. It is difficult here not to evoke Pascal, who says 'Do little things as though they were great on account of the majesty of Jesus Christ who does them in us and who lives our life; and the great things as though they were little and easy because of his all-powerfulness'. Here everything is 'pure simplicity', 'simple abandon', the work of the Holy Spirit who 'touches souls'. In the Gospel and the liturgy we learn that the Holy Spirit is the 'finger of God'.

Realistically, Mechtilde sets out from the experience that we all have in our fleshly heart, in the 'sinful depths which are in us' of which we become aware through temptation. Consequently, temptation is useful, as ancient and medieval monasticism always taught with astonishing insistence. All that Mechtilde teaches is full of monastic vigour even though from the seventeenth century. 'Be pressed and reduced to liquid so that the love of God flow from us'. 'Come out of self': this is the meaning of the vocation of Abraham which was for Cassian the symbol of never-ending monastic conversion. 'To tend constantly to God' is a means of staying trustful and continuing in perseverance. Mechtilde was as optimistic as she was realistic. In language which is already that of our day while yet remaining classical, she teaches that we should 'sacrifice this self' — this *ego*, we would say today — 'which alone is opposed to God in us'. This is the role of crosses in our lives. Mechtilde rarely uses the plural, as she does here, when speaking of the cross, the Lord's Cross: the mystery of suffering and victory with which we are associated as 'living members of Jesus Christ, incorporated into his deified humanity, living by his life and by his Spirit' by the grace of our baptism: 'It is no longer I who live; Christ lives in me'. All that is necessary is that we 'be faithful to the attraction of grace which draws us out of our nothingness . . . Let yourself go into nothing . . .'. Then we shall know the consolation of being 'in this blessed nothingness which frightens our nature': everything and nothing coincide — *todo y nada* —, the all of God filling our emptiness.

Here Mechtilde rises to the level of the highest mystics. And the prologue sets the tone for the rest of the work. The contents are serious and demanding, accompanied with a few archaic expressions and some poetry which make us smile a little. Yet everything is constantly centered on Jesus and his Spirit who leads us to the Father. Whatever St Benedict has to say about God is here defined and, if we may so say, personalised. The Virgin Mary is always turned towards her Son; she directs us to him and prays to him for us. The very traditional idea of the paternity of St Benedict — a theme which has also been applied to other founders of religious orders — is associated not only with the Lord but also with the Eucharist. We read in St Gregory that the Legislator breathed his last at the foot of the altar, 'ravished away from himself' by Jesus in order to be taken up to heaven. Adoration of the Blessed Sacrament is here explicitly mentioned and associated with the idea of 'reparation', recognised by renowned present-day theologians as having a profound signification.[16] But in all this work there is no unduly exaggerated devotion. We have here what we may rightly style 'classical christianism'.

2. THE DEPTHS

We must now deal in more detail and more insistently with certain points of application of the doctrine which we have briefly reviewed. It does not seem untimely to draw attention, on the one hand, to the consistency of all that follows the prologue, and, on the other, to certain problems relative to the application of this doctrine. We have here indeed a real spirituality, with a practical side relevant even today.

One of Mechtilde's strongest convictions led her to speak frequently of what she called the 'depths', 'our depths'; she uses too the words 'deep', 'deeply'. This recalls what the Rhineland mystics — whose influence on the Ecole Française is well-known — named the *Grund*: man's centre where his selfishness lies and which, once emptied and purified, becomes the place of the divine indwelling. The 'depths' are really what should be, and we must constantly revert to them; Mechtilde speaks of returning to the depths. This is nothing but self-knowledge, which is as important in her teaching as it is in that of St Bernard. 'Let us return to our heart', he wrote more than once, quoting a psalm: *redire ad cor;* or, referring to what the Gospel says about the prodigal son: *ad se reversus*, he came back to himself. 'Enter into yourself, into your interior, remaining at the feet of the majesty of God; that is where you will find him'. There is nothing theoretical about all this. Like Bernard, Mechtilde sets out from 'experience'; she is fond of using this word and also the verb 'to experience'. She is well acquainted with our amusements, the things Pascal called distractions. She knows too that the opposite to the 'depths' is self-elevation, 'the sentiment of our own worth. Pride makes us climb up. We must come down'. How? By having the pole of attraction which is self-love in the depths of our heart replaced by love of Jesus Christ, 'this divine centre where we must enter'. We have to substitute his 'reign', his 'empire' — as the vocabulary of the century of Louis XIV puts it[17] — for our self-interest. 'The Spirit of Jesus Christ', 'our Lord and his divine Spirit', must come and dwell within us and govern us in all things. We must 'desire this reign', then judge all things 'in relation to Him'. The 'Sacred Heart' is mentioned only once. The style, though different from that of Margaret Mary Alacoque, is no less fervent. Certain pages, greatly inspired by St Paul, betray a loving obsession with Jesus Christ: a summary would betray the fervour of all this and give too pale an image of it.

Our return to the Father in Christ and by his Spirit will only come about as an effect of grace, the grace of faith whose seed is planted in us at baptism and which guides us throughout life. Hence the stress laid on attention in everything to the movings, more precisely, to the inspiration, of grace: 'God gives movement to the soul . . . pray in such manner as to be given movement'. Do everything 'in faith': this leads first of all to prayer, continual prayer. Before finding expression in certain interior activities — though these also favor it —, prayer is an attitude of being present to God, 'adhesion to God'. Mechtilde liked to use the play of words *adorer et adhérer* (to adore and to adhere). One of the densest pages in her writings can be summed up in two words: 'await God'. From such a life of prayer, prayer activities flow quite naturally and simply, that is to say, without any complications. When Mechtilde mentions this life, she adopts the themes and sometimes even the very words of monastic tradition from the Fathers to the Middle Ages, and perhaps particularly of the twelfth century: For example, she describes the texts which serve for *Lectio divina* as 'silent preachers',[18] or she says that divine office is total prayer, committing the whole being, including the senses, or again she shows that perpetual adoration is a way of continuing the *laus perennis*. And she comments on the very little St Benedict says about prayer. In order to practise the prayer of simplicity, she recommends that we 'leave the different methods to one side . . . Avoid prayer which gives you a headache'. Prayer is like a mystical desert where 'we meet the Bridegroom'. The nuns are to be faithful to that 'souvenir of God' to which Fr. I. Hausherr has devoted so many pages. They are to keep up 'the gentle habit of doing things not out of tender love, but by faith'. And all this is constantly linked to the feasts and the mysteries celebrated in the liturgy. Even those short but frequent ejaculatory prayers by which the soul rises up to God and which St Benedict recommends are given a charming equivalent: 'Make a little loving return . . .', 'the mind gives God a little wink . . .'. The pages Mechtilde wrote on prayer are probably the most beautiful of her whole work. She talks as a specialist in the matter. Her expertise is guaranteed first by her own personal experience, but also by the fact that it is completely in keeping with the most ancient and the most constant spiritual tradition of Christendom.

3. THE WAY OF LITTLENESS

When speaking of humility, Mechtilde used the language of the Gospel. Her favorite terms were those expressing littleness and all the variations to which it lends itself. Like St Gregory and the Fathers, she knew of 'compunction'. But rather than use these latinate words, she preferred words of her own times which are much more expressive for the seventeenth century and our own: 'Let us be consumed, remain exposed to the Blessed Sacrament, be plunged in God' — and, notice, being 'plunged' evokes the image of the 'depths'. Be 'entirely and continually disengaged'. Only once does she use the words 'holy indifference', but she speaks of our 'simple gaze' on God, one which is free of any 'seeking of ourselves'. With St Paul, she says: 'Die to self and live to God'. 'Divest oneself' without any secret complacency. Live as if in exile, in a foreign land, in poverty; awaiting all things from God, desire him, even when he remains silent. 'If your depths are crucified . . .'. 'Be annihilated to self in order to be united to God', 'be a capacity for God', 'who loves little, humble, lowly, annihilated souls' and 'deep littleness'. Be the owner of nothing, 'possess nothing by attachment'. And still more: 'be nothing' [St Bernard said: *annullari*], 'lose everything' in view of union with God, for 'the possession of God'. Live 'in a childlike simplicity because we know our own self-truth'. Here again we cannot help linking this teaching with what St Bernard says in his treatise *On the Steps of Humility*. Dwell in 'deep littleness', and there, deep down, taste God and his mercy. . . Be 'clothed with God even unto inexpressible penetration'. Mary's *Magnificat* was the song of her lowliness and her exaltation. This robust mosaic of phrases could be further enlarged. But each of those citations is fully meaningful when replaced in the context: a mystique of annihilation, stamped with patience and tranquillity.

Jesus is the model and the source of this patience. This is one of the forms of this spirit of childhood which seventeenth-century French devotion to the 'Child King' favoured and expressed.[19] Not only does Mechtilde use the formula 'spirit of childhood', but she sometimes links the idea to Jesus in a way which to us seems unusual, even though it has antecedents in the patristic tradition and in the Rule of St Benedict: 'Go to our Lord like a little child. He is your father who truly loves you

. . . ? It has always been correct christology to attribute to the
Son of God the sentiments of a father waiting for his sons to
come back.[20] And immediately Mechtilde goes on to show
that she has a right view of the paschal mystery when she speaks
of 'being entirely clothed with the Spirit of Jesus Christ, because entirely annihilated in him'.

Considered in the light of such depths, daily sufferings are, so
to speak, surface incidents. It is not that we do not feel them
keenly, but they are never to be sought for themselves or provoked in any way. In a commentary of the Rule composed
during the baroque period in form of 'emblems' each one of
which was topped by a short inscription, one of the most frequent symbols was the wounded heart: it is represented as being
crushed between the anvil and the hammer, pierced with an
arrow, crowned with thorns, painful in every way possible.[21]
We see nothing of this in Mechtilde's writings: she took no rest
in suffering, but in acceptation, silence, obedience, thanksgiving, the happiness of a soul who 'flies towards God'.

Presence to God is more than voluntarism, and yet with all
that there is no trace of quietism, simply a serene acceptance of
all that God wills. Penance is nothing but sharing in 'the abandonment of Jesus' during his passion. When a soul is 'stabilised
in God', in 'a prodigious deprivation', it can in all circumstances
keep the peace of the risen Christ. St Bernard said 'God is
tranquil and tranquilises all things'. Mechtilde writes of the
'soul possessing this tranquility': 'God contemplates himself in
the depths of this soul. He imprints there his divine perfections'.

4. Free obedience

Two basic observances of the monastic life are mentioned insistently if not frequently: silence and obedience. On silence
Mechtilde retains especially, as in all the rest, the 'deep' meaning: it is a sharing in the silence of Jesus, his silence before his
birth when he was still lying in Mary, then his silence during
his passion. And, like Bossuet, she quotes this short Gospel sentence 'But Jesus remained silent *Ipse autem tacebat*'. Her con-

cept of obedience may well today raise a problem which in former times did not exist. The words 'blind obedience' need to be understood correctly, and several texts help us to this correct comprehension. According to the teaching of St Benedict followed by Mechtilde, obedience is a gift from God: 'It is God who gives you the strength to submit.' To submit is an activity, not a passivity, a submission to oppression. When Mechtilde says, 'I no longer have any will', the entire context proves that she does indeed have a will, but what she means is that she no longer acts except in 'relation to Jesus Christ.' Observances, she says, are 'carriers of grace', not in themselves, but if they are practised 'in view of Jesus Christ.' Consequently the formulas praising 'total liberty' are just as forceful as those commending obedience.

Of particular observances, Mechtilde did not consider so much superficial exactitude as the depth of the intention. She urges that we never neglect 'a little interior reproach' for it opens us up to grace. 'Rectify your intentions.' In this area the demands of God and of the spiritual advisor are limitless. All that follows is perfectly moderate. Mechtilde could be quite outspoken when she noticed a lack of self-denial, but she also had the art of recalling, not only the kindness and the mercy of God, but also his justice and his truth. She preaches joy, security and peace and thus frees her nuns and her friends from any excessive tendency to austerity. She has a sense of physical weakness: 'Do not deprive yourself of fruit, you need a little refreshment. Take a little wine too with your water. Eat and be joyful because to serve God you need a holy liberty which comes from a free heart.' And she wrote to the superior of another religious: 'Consult the doctors about her Lent, I do not think she is able to observe it.'

With moderation we find mercy, indulgence, compassion: 'Be tender for the suffering of your neighbour', and again 'You will gain nothing, except by always giving way.' This keen sense of the limits of every woman and every man inspired Mechtilde to a charming translation of St Benedict's words *multorum servire moribus*: 'adapt yourself to the temper' of each and everyone. Finally, the sense of the 'need of souls' which we find expressed so intensely in the volumes of her correspondence is conveyed also by what she says in commenting on the Rule about prayer, conversations in the parlour, and letters to be written. Her practical sense, her desire to serve appear in the efforts she makes to do away with the dowry which was then a condition for being admitted to the monastic life.

III.

THE PERMANENT VALUES OF THIS TEACHING

1. CHRISTOCENTRISM

Two characteristics sum up the major traits of this spirituality. First of all there is an authentic *christocentrism*, that is to say, one which conforms to the purest theological and spiritual tradition of the Church. It is to be explained by the influence of Bérulle, Condran, and Olier — the great representatives of the *école française* of the times — but above all the influence of Scripture and particularly of St Paul. All this was integrated into a general inner attitude fashioned by the liturgy. Of course devotion to Christ is centered around the Eucharist — the mystery about which so many monks had written from the ninth to the twelfth century[22] — but the Jesus who is there celebrated and adored is considered, as in the liturgy, under his pascal aspect. Mère Mechtilde taught her nuns, 'You are dead and your life is hidden in Jesus-Christ.'[23] A traditional theme, if ever there was one.[24] And she taught as well its indispensable complement: the passage from death 'to the new life of Jesus Christ, which is the very grace of christianity.' Baptism incorporates us into Christ and makes us participants in his priesthood, his 'quality of priest and victim.' In the eucharistic sacrifice, Christ offers himself and we offer ourselves with him and in him. That is the royal priesthood of the faithful.

This seems to be the heart of her doctrine — and it is the teaching of the Church — expressed after the fashion of her times and with a remarkable constancy. She went to great pains to point out that this status of 'victim' which she gave her daughters was nothing new, but a title received from and stamped upon the soul by Jesus Christ at baptism. It is as we have seen, none other than the priesthood of the faithful.

Perpetual adoration was, for Mechtilde, not only homage to the eucharistic presence, but also 'a universal renewal of our whole life and of all our actions', 'actual adoration.' It is the practice, the means, and the sign of the paschal life, the fruit of the Eucharist for spreading the grace of the sacrifice in us and in the world. In this way Mechtilde linked adoration and reparation. For, let it be noticed, 'reparation' made to Christ in the Eucharist is always presented by her as a participation in the mystery of the Redemption in our modest place as re- deemed creatures, as members of a Church which continues this redemptive work 'until he shall come again.' Mechtilde insisted especially on this point: 'It is only a Jesus Christ who can make reparation for his glory and that of his Father.' There lies the secret: 'become, each of us, Jesus Christ.'[25] This is quite the opposite of a sentimental and selfish piety. The greatest representatives of the monastic tradition would feel at home with such teaching.

2. FIDELITY TO MONASTIC TRADITION

Another outstanding characteristic of Mère Mechtilde's teaching is her attachment to monastic tradition. She some- times alludes to the texts of the Fathers read in community or during Office. It should be remembered that her writings are backed-up by the learning of the Maurists. She rarely quoted names of authors such as Augustine and Condran. But she knew of others, either by first-hand information or because they were read in the monastic circles of her times. Amongst biblical models she went directly to those whom monastic tradition recognized as having a special meaning for monks and nuns: Abraham, St John, St Paul, Mary Magdalen.

As to the Rule of St Benedict, Mère Mechtilde retained all

its basic observances. Contemporaries remarked that her nuns 'follow the Rule of St Benedict in its most precise strictness',[25] they 'bring to life the ancient Rule of St Benedict and the pristine stictness of its observance — and it pleases God to raise up from time nuns who, aspiring to a holy reformation of their Order, serve as instruments to provide it.'[26] In this way they deserve to be called the 'reformed religious' of this Order.[27]

Lastly, Mère Mechtilde came back instinctively, because she knew the tradition to which she belonged, to many a practice which had been handed down without interruption from the Middle Ages: this has already been pointed out in connection with our Lady Abbess.[28] The same is true of the devotion to St John associated with Mary at the foot of the Cross,[29] of the clothing *ad succurrendum* which allowed people living in the world to 'die in the Habit of the Order',[30] of the symbolism of this habit, sign of 'a life hidden from the world and separated from the world' and a reminder of the Cross of Christ.[31]

CONCLUSION

A *'fine spirituality'*

In the spiritual direction which she, like so many other women in the Church did, Mechtilde excelled in giving very practical advice, full of psychological insight and common sense. But in her writings we find much more than that: there is a real spiritual teaching. Her distinctive mark could be summed up in a few words: a mystique of the constant presence to God by means of poverty of heart. Not that this is unique to Mechtilde; she shares this characteristic with all the greatest witnesses of spiritual theology. When she speaks of it, however, she has the accents of intense faith which make her message useful to her contemporaries and valid for us, too. This faith went so far as to 'congratulate' a deceased person for having at last 'arrived', as St Benedict says in the last word of his Rule. This is the goal of the 'conversion of manners' to which so many interpreters of the Rule have striven to give an acceptable meaning. Mechtilde merely says that St Benedict, especially in Chapter IV, *On the Instruments of Good Works*, 'teaches us to repress our manners by the virtues'. And at the end, she brings together in a splendid synthesis, all those major realities which ought to penetrate our lives: the Incarnation, the Gospel, the Spirit, the Church, the Eucharist.

'Everyone wants to be spiritual and with the finest spirituality'. Mechtilde gave this old christian word its real meaning, making it something which is not opposed to matter or corporality (we saw that she had a concern for health) — but the contrary to a life according to the flesh, that is to say, to nature inclined to sin. In the seventeenth century words such as 'spirituality', 'mystic', and 'love' were sometimes used with abuse, to such an extent that certain authors found it necessary to qualify them and to speak of 'pure love' or 'true mystic'. Mechtilde smiled quietly at this sort of fashion, and it is probably because she was aware of its dangers that she scarcely ever used such vocabulary. For her, in keeping with the language used by St Paul, 'fine spirituality' means living according to the Spirit of Christ, and she requires it in her writings from beginning to end, with a simplicity which leaves no doubt to the quality of the experience underlying the message. There is no useless rhetoric: 'Humility does not consist in having humble thoughts, but in bearing the weight of our truth which is the abyss of our extreme wretchedness when it please God to make it known to us . . .'. And herein lies the true charism of Mère Mechtilde: 'God has given me a tenderness and something I cannot define for suffering and afflicted souls, so that I have them always before my mind. . . . It seems to me that God made me for such souls. . . '. Is that not why we feel her so close to us?

JEAN LECLERCQ

Clervaux

JOSEPH HALL, *THE ARTE OF DIVINE MEDITATION*, AND ANGLICAN SPIRITUALITY

Joseph Hall (1574-1656) was Bishop of Norwich in the Church of England, which had separated from Rome during the sixteenth-century Reformation but retained Catholic forms of government and worship. Standing mid-way between the Catholic-minded and the Puritans, who argued for wider-sweeping reforms in polity and doctrine, Hall represents the Anglican appeal to intellect and affection, moderation, and the 'beauty of holiness'.

ANGLICAN SPIRITUALITY during its formative years in the reigns of Elizabeth I and James I was imbued with meditative piety. This piety involved far more than treatises on and works of meditation identified as such. Sermons, eucharistic devotions, poetry, and occasional, reflective essays all served as vehicles for the practice of meditation. In addition, those who preached and wrote were steeped in the Scriptures and worshiped daily with the *Book of Common Prayer*, through which much of their biblical knowledge came. Indeed, it is not too much to say that during the reigns of Elizabeth and James the *Book of Common Prayer* came to dominate Anglican spirituality. The meditative practices of individuals were thus influenced by and, I would say, rooted in that corporate worship prescribed by law. The Word of God, proclaimed, preached, and dramatized in Prayer Book offices and sacraments, inspired that meditation which is the subject of this paper.

In order better to understand the nature of the meditation which lay at the heart of nascent Anglicanism, we turn to Joseph Hall, his *Arte of Divine Meditation*, and the examples he provides, principally his meditation on the christian life. Without altogether denying the influence of Ignatian, Salesian, and other forms of post-Tridentine meditation practised in

England, I am convinced that the influence of a native tradition of meditation was more pervasive and more influential. At the turn of the century, this tradition found overt and self-conscious expression in the revision of Roman Catholic treatises on meditation, making them conform to the native tradition, and in original manuals for meditation, such as the *Seven Treatises* of Richard Rogers (1603) and Hall's *Arte* (1606).[1] If we focus here upon Hall's manual it is because a methodical treatment of the subject by an influential Anglican divine, and bishop, is helpful to us in discerning the meditative element in Anglican spirituality in diverse works ranging from sermons to poetry. We shall also be concerned with an author who acknowledges historical continuity, basing his understanding in the *Devotio Moderna* of the late middle ages. Lastly, he is a bishop who stands at the boundary between Puritan and Anglo-Catholic segments of nascent Anglicanism. There were many people more Puritan than he and many more Anglo-Catholic. The definition of Protestant meditation provided by Barbara Lewalski, as focusing on the Bible and on application to the self, aptly describes the more Puritan works of meditation. The more Anglo-Catholic works focused on Word *and Sacraments*, as does the *Book of Common Prayer* which the most extreme Puritans much despised, and tends to emphasize corporate as well as individual application.[2] Anglicanism is broader and more complex than many critics are willing to acknowledge. Joseph Hall is Anglican — partaking of the full, although variegated, tradition of Anglican spirituality. We turn first to a brief consideration of his life.

Biographical Considerations

Joseph Hall (1574-1656), the bishop of Norwich, was born and grew up at Ashby-de-la-Zouch, in the shadow of Henry Hastings, the Puritan Earl of Huntingdon,[3] and went to Emmanuel College, Cambridge, a Puritan stronghold. Yet, as a priest of the Church of England, this devoted son of the church enjoyed such preferment that he ascended to the episcopacy,

an office much reviled by presbyterian Puritans and by Sepa-
ratists, for whom the notorious Martin Marprelate spoke and
wrote. At the Synod of Dort in 1618, Hall mediated the quarrel between Calvinists and Arminians and preached a sermon
in Latin advocating moderation and mutual charity. As Bishop
of Exeter he aroused the suspicions of Archbishop William
Laud by showing favor to Puritans, but in 1640 he defended
the Church of England before an hostile parliament and was
convicted of high treason and committed to the Tower of
London. He was subsequently released, went to his see of
Norwich, labored there until expelled, and lived the remainder of his long life in retirement at a house rented in the village
of Higham, within his diocese. He died at eight-two in 1656.
The *Arte of Divine Meditation* was but one amongst his many
works. A prolific writer, Hall wrote while at Cambridge and
published satires in English verse patterned on the works of
Latin satirists.[4] His verses were widely heralded in his day and
have commanded considerable attention in our time, but they
are not to be compared to his *Arte*, his many meditations, including three centuries written before 1606, and his sermons.

An Introduction to the Arte

The *Arte of Divine Meditation* was quite possibly Hall's
most influential work. It was first published in 1606, reprinted
in 1607 and 1609, and was thenceforth to be found in Hall's
Opera, including thirteen editions before 1650. Furthermore,
the *Arte* was adopted and elaborated upon by Isaac Ambrose
in his *Prima, Media, and Ultima* (1659) and by Edmund Cala-
my in his *The Art of Divine Meditation* (1680). Finally, the
Arte influenced the greatest of all English treatises on meditation, that found in the fourth part of Richard Baxter's *The
Saints Everlasting Rest.*[5]

Whence did the inspiration for Hall's *Arte* come? He had,
before 1606, written three centuries of *Meditations and Vowes*,
'homely Aphorismes,' moralistic rather than devotional. It
would seem that Hall had a strong urge toward meditation, but

was searching for the right style. He found that for which he searched on the continent, discovering there a 'Rule of Meditation' which he adopted and adapted. That rule came not from Ignatius of Loyola, Francis de Sales, or any other post-Tridentine source — Hall was, if anything, anti-Roman and anti-Jesuit; while in the Low Countries, he argued with a Jesuit named Costerus, scoffed at images of the Virgin, and generally scorned all Roman Catholics.[6] What he discovered during his journey was the *Rosetum exercitiorum spiritualium et sacrarum meditationum* of John Mombaer (Mauburnus) first published in 1494 and subsequently in 1504, 1510, 1603, 1610 (in an altered edition), and 1620. The 'Scale of Meditation of an Author, ancient, but nameless' which Hall describes, with the first half of the scale, in chapter sixteen of the *Arte*, is that found in the *Rosetum* and derived by Mombaer from Wessel Gansfort, who first set it forth in his *Scala Meditatoria*, written somewhere between 1486 and his death in 1489. It is most likely Mombaer to whom Hall refers when in his dedication to Sir Richard Lea he says: 'In this Art of mine, I confess to have received more light from one obscure nameless Monk, which wrote some hundred and twelve years ago, than from the directions of all other writers.'[7] The *Rosetum* was published anonymously one hundred and twelve years prior to Hall's *Arte*.

F.L. Huntley has argued that 'the obscure nameless Monk' was not Mombaer but someone else, possibly the Pseudo-Bonaventura whose *Meditations* on the life of Christ were published in 1494, but most likely Thomas à Kempis whose *De imitatione Christi* was published in 1492. The chief reason for looking beyond Mombaer has to do with Hall's saying in chapter sixteen, when referring to the *Scala Meditatoria*, that this complex method is 'allowed by some authors, [but] rejected by us.'[8] In fact, Hall relies upon the *Scala*, modifying that part of it concerning preparation and understanding, but adhering closely to the latter part concerning the affections and conclusions. What, then, does Hall mean when he says that he rejects the *Scala* of Wessel Gansfort in Mombaer's *Rosetum?* It could be that he is seeking to put his reader at ease by saying that his method is not as complex and demanding as it might be. But it is more reasonable to assume that Hall has some understanding of the spirit of meditation among the Brethren of the Common Life, to whom Gansfort and Mombaer belonged, knowing how foreign a rigid *Scala* is to those who prefer Augustine to the Scholastics. He could have derived his understanding from reading more of the *Rosetum* than the part containing the *Scala*.[9] He could have been guided by his reading in Gerson to which he refers, and in others of the Windesheimers, and he could have discovered the *Rosetum* with the assistance of a follower of the *Devotio Moderna*, someone who warned him against an overly-rigid approach to meditation and against using and recommendng the *Scala* as though one could meditate only according to its specifications. That is to say, it would seem that Hall found the *Scala* useful in providing a rule; he especially applauded its emphasis on the affections. But he still believed in the efficacy of external meditations and was convinced, as he says more than once, that any set of rules must be considered flexible and be adapted to individual needs. Hall himself did not follow the *Scala* in detail, except in the exempla he provided on life and death. He was concerned in the *Arte* to derive what he could from the *Scala*, but he did not wish to see his readers adopt it whole.

R.R. Post points out that both Wessel Gansfort and John Mombaer were providing an aid to meditation in the *Scala*, that 'users of this method need not keep too strictly to the models; they have a choice',[10] and that to meditate could mean for the Windesheimers either meditation for a specific time, reflection upon 'Christ's passion or on one of the last things' leading 'to the complicated method of Wessel Gansfort, adopted by Mombaer', or simply rumination. This last 'is not a methodical, well deliberated activity, but a perpetual and constantly active state of being mindful of God or of Christ, a constant search of the heart intended to assure that the Devotionalists carried out their prayers, hours, study, work, eating and any recreation in the proper spirit.'[11] Such rumination has been emphasized among the Devotionalists from the beginning. The development of a method concerned with a stricter interpretation of meditation developed later and was largely the work of Wessel Gansfort. Post considers the method to be 'complicated and artificial . . . anyone who could not succeed in applying this method lost heart and abandoned both method and interpretation.'[12]

It is evident that Hall did not adhere to the method in his meditations following the publication of the *Arte*.[13] In writing to Mr Robert Haye, Hall recommended a simpler form of meditation. The devout Christian at the end of each day is admonished 'cheerfully and constantly, both to look up to God, and into our hearts; as we have to do with both: to God in Thanksgiving, first; then in Request.' By this he meant that we should meditate upon God's favor to us, first considering 'these external, inferior, earthly graces', and then, remembering God's spiritual favors, we are to consider those favors, raising our affections with our thoughts.' Finally, we are to mount higher, into heaven, acknowledging 'those celestial graces' of our soul's 'election to glory, redemption from shame and death', the intercession of our Saviour, preparation of our soul's place, staying there awhile upon the meditation of our 'future joys.' 'This done, the way is made for your Request. Sue now to your God, as for grace to answer these mercies, so to see wherein you have not answered them.'[14] He ends with a detailed self-examination, with resolution to a better life. If this be considered a form of meditation, as Hall seems to have considered it, then much that we know of as personal devotions in the works of Lancelot Andrewes, John Donne, George Herbert, and others, must be acknowledged as meditative.

In fact, as Huntley has pointed out, Hall wrote of at least three kinds of meditation, each conforming to a portion of the *Arte*: 'occasional meditations', extemporal in character and caused by some external occurence or reality; deliberate meditation, carefully planned, chiefly concerned with the intellect;

and deliberate meditation, chiefly concerned with the affections. The first might be 'On the sight of a lark flying up' or 'On hearing of music by night',[15] the second might be some careful exegesis of a biblical text, such as that on Ephesians 3:14, 19, called 'Meditation on the Love of Christ',[16] the third might be 'The Breathings of the Devout Soul', addresses made to God but with constant concern for the state of the soul and thus of the affections ('Ah, my Lord God, what heats and colds do I feel in my soul!').[17] The three modes of meditation concern three books, as is suggested by chapter twelve of the *Arte*: 'The Book of Creatures', 'The Book of Scriptures', and 'The Book of the Soul', the first coming from God the Father, the second from God the Son, and the third from God the Holy Spirit.[18] The three kinds obviously belong together, as the *Arte* indicates, but are separable in practice. Less obviously, they represent three emphases in Anglicanism: a concern for the created order as the sphere of God's continuing operation; a concern for Scripture interpreted by reason; and a concern for the personal and practical application of God's truth, revealed in nature and through Scripture, to and by the individual soul. That Hall emphasized the last is natural, for Anglicanism emphasized moral behavior and Richard Hooker emphasized the end or purpose for which God's laws are provided.[19]

It is with this background in mind — and principally with the knowledge that Hall did not adhere rigidly to the *Scala* — that we turn to a detailed examination of the *Arte*, on the basis of which we shall be able to explore more fully the sources of his understanding of meditation and thus the relationship of such an understanding to Anglican Spirituality.

AN EXAMINATION OF HALL's Arte of Divine Meditation (1606)

Divine meditation, Hall said in the *Arte*, 'is nothing else but a bending of the mind upon some spiritual object, through divers forms of discourse, until our thoughts come to an issue.[20] Involving the whole of life, active as well as contemplative, meditation is appropriate, even necessary, to everyone and not just to those who are cloistered. By means of meditation we search out and conquer the enemy within and fortify ourselves against any re-entry, we learn to utilize those means that fit us 'to all good duties', we gain self-knowledge and power to control our lives, gaining 'more light unto our knowledge, more heat to our affections, more life to our devotion', and we turn from love of earthly things toward heavenly comforts. By means of meditation 'we see our Saviour, with Stephen; we talk with God, as Moses' and 'are ravished, with blessed Paul, unto Paradise; and see that heaven, which we are loth to leave, which we cannot utter'.[21]

Hall realized that meditation involves both knowledge and the affections, but he was convinced that 'God's School is more of Affection, than Understanding', and that in his time the problem was not that people had much zeal but little knowledge so much as it was that many had 'much knowledge, without zeal'.[22] Here Hall identified a fundamental issue in his time and it is certain that not all Anglicans would agree with his analysis of the problem.[23] Hall then wrote of two kinds of meditation: extemporal and deliberate. He was most concerned for the latter, but he recognized the existence and value of the former. Hall had known extemporal meditation, such meditation as is 'occasioned by outward occurences offered to the mind', is without definite rules, and is imbued with a sense of awe. We may, for instance, observe a watercourse running by amongst the pebbles, as did St Augustine, note that at times it seems to run silently and at other times 'in a shriller note', and be brought to meditate with awe on 'the excellent order, which God hath settled in all these inferior things'.[24] He warned against superstition in such meditation but he was equally concerned for those whose dulled sight prevents them from reading 'God's Great Book':

> the heaven rolling above thy head, in a constant and unmovable motion; the stars so overlooking one another, that the greatest shew little, the least greatest, all glorious; the air full of bottles of rain, or fleeces of snow, or divers

forms of fiery exhalations; the sea, under one uniform face, full of strange and monstrous shapes beneath; the earth so adorned with variety of plants, that thou canst not but tread on many at once with every foot; besides the store of creatures, that fly about it, walk upon it, live in it.[25]

Here there is at least one root of that natural theology which was influenced by Anglican spirituality and in turn influenced its further development.[26]

In this treatise Hall's attention was fixed on deliberate and not extemporal meditation. Writing of deliberate meditation Hall had in mind that which is 'wrought out of our own heart' (and thus not occasioned by externals) that which is Platonic and Augustinian and not Aristotelian and Scholastic. But while centered upon intuitive groping into the soul, far beyond sense perception, and thus profoundly subjective, such meditation is in need of rules based in part on the experience of others and in part on our own personal experience in the past. These rules (and he thus outlines the rest of his treatise) involve 'first the Qualities of the Person fit for meditation; then the Circumstances, Manner, and Proceedings of the Work'[27]

When considering necessary qualities, Hall emphasized repentance, relying here chiefly upon Jean Gerson.[28] It is contrition that chiefly matters in this work of repentance and it is over-scrupulosity that emerges as the chief obstacle to the final working out of repentance.[29] Next, the person must be free from the distractions of worldly cares, the better to focus his thoughts, leaving his cares at the door, not renouncing them. Thirdly, constancy is required, constancy in practice and in matter, that is, in dwelling upon the same thought 'without flitting, without weariness, until it have attained to some issue of spiritual profit', although he urged that this not be done without abatement. Hall advised a mingling of labor with meditation, employing a wide variety of activities, and yet he emphasized that we must persevere in meditation to a fruitful issue.[30]

As to circumstances, Hall discussed place, time, and bodily

gestures with the same pastoral concern. As to the first, Hall acknowledged that God may be encountered anywhere and that different places suit different persons. As a rule, however, a place where one may be solitary is best. Following the advice of some 'great Master in this Art',[31] Hall was again chiefly concerned with concentration versus distraction.[32]. Where time is concerned, Hall preferred the evening, but the important consideration was that it be an apt time. Sunday is suggested as a propitious time for meditation: 'for the plentiful instruction of that day stirreth thee up to this action, and fills with matter; and the zeal of thy public service warmeth thy heart to this other business of devotion.'[33] Here Hall acknowledged the critical importance of public worship to the practice of meditation, a fact to be kept in mind as we proceed.[34] As to bodily gesture, Hall laid down the simple rule that it be reverent. Different postures appeal to different persons: Gerson preferred to sit with his face turned up toward heaven, Hall preferred to walk while meditating.[35]

After considering the qualities required and the circumstances, Hall turned to the matter, or subject, of meditation. He objected to three types, which people naturally meditate upon: that which is carnal and involves self-gain to the detriment of others; that which is focused upon natural phenomena without any spiritual issue; and that which is given over to 'forms of government and rules of state.' Hall thus indirectly attacked people who are lost in sin, those preoccupied with the new science to the exclusion of spiritual matters, and all machievellians and erastians. It is not that such matters cannot enter into our meditations — the first for repentance, the second as revelatory of God's Great Book of Nature, and the third as matter of serious concern for justice — but the safest way is 'to keep the track of divinity', meditating on the divine essence and persons, attributes and works, with humility. The best matters concern those most capable of affecting the heart and stirring up devotion, namely:

Christ Jesus our Mediator, his incarnation, miracles, life,

passion, burial, resurrection, ascension, intercession, and
the benefit of our redemption, the certainty of our election,
the graces and proceeding of our sanctification, our glorious estate lost in our first parents, our present vileness, our
inclination to sin, our severall actuall offences, the temptations and sleights of evil angels, the use of the sacraments,
nature and practice of faith and repentance, the miseries of
our life with the frailty of it, the certainty and uncertainty
of our death, the glory of God's Saints above, the awful-
ness of Judgment, the terrors of hell, and the rest of this
quality.[36]

Meditation, that is, is 'wrought out of our own heart' as we
consider ourselves in relation to God's deeds on our behalf and
God's will for his chosen. Meditation is a necessary work of
sanctification, involving remembrance of God's grace in Christ
for us, repentance of our refusal of that grace, and the intention
to live by grace alone. Meditation is thus not contemplation so
much as it is the fitting of the Christian for life and death.

Having said this by way of preliminary consideration, Hall
then turned to the three parts of meditation proper: (1) the entrance, (2) the proceeding, and (3) the conclusion. The entrance consists of prayer and the choice of a subject for meditation. Prayer is the opening of the heart to God that God may
speak to us in our meditation.[37] Such prayer should not be long
but it should be fervent and it should be that our 'meditation
may be guided aright and blessed', that we may avoid distractions, ending with the hope that 'our souls and lives' may be
bettered by this exercise'. Hall's description could easily be
used to construct a short prayer. The choice of subject involves
the mind 'recollecting itself', making choice of subject and rejecting all obstacles. At this point Hall began a meditation, his
first example, this one concerned with the christian life. Exemplum II, at the end of the treatise, concerns christian death.
These are the chief subjects and most illustrative. The meditation begins with the meditator addressing himself: 'What wilt
thou muse upon, O my soul?' and concluding, 'wherein

shouldest thou rather meditate, than of the life and glory of God's Saints?' His concern is for the state of his own soul, but in order to consider that aright he must focus upon the souls of God's saints in general and make application to himself at each step along the way.

The proceeding is next, but as a preliminary Hall reveals that he has been influenced by the *Scala Meditationis* of Gansfort as found in Mombaer's *Rosetum*, although he does not reveal the authorship, if he knew it. Hall presents the first part of the *Scala*, consisting of (1) the preparation and (2) the proceeding in or engagement of the human understanding. In the spirit of the *Devotio Moderna* Hall expressed suspicion concerning the complexity and seeming rigidity of the method, he even speaks of rejecting it, and yet he proceeds to follow its outline, modifying the proceeding in the understanding, but following the proceedings in the affections step by step. Of the proceeding in the understanding he wrote: 'I would rather to require only a deep and firm Consideration of the thing propounded: which shall be done, if we follow it in our discourse, through all or the principal parts of those places, which natural reason doth afford us.'[38] His attitude is further revealed in the presentation of three premonitions: (1) that not everyone should be bound 'to the same uniform proceeding', (2) that those who meditate are not bound to follow every step as laid down in that which follows, and (3) that when we bog down at any particular place in the proceeding we not stick there and be prevented from going on.

In the first part, concerning understanding, we begin with a description of the subject chosen ('Who are the Saints, but those, which, having been weakly holy upon earth, are perfectly holy above? . . . What is their life, but that blessed estate above, wherein their glorified soul hath a fruition of God?'), followed by a division of the subject. The division is to be 'easy and voluntary', not complex and rigidly structured, 'whereby our thoughts shall have more room made for them, and our proceeding shall be more distinct'.[39] Thus life in general may be divided for the purpose of meditation into the natural life, the life of grace, and the life of glory. When applied to our own particular lives this process represents one of development, or spiritual formation, and the possibility exists that persons on the way toward the life of glory may be at different stages of development.[40]

The division having been made, we are advised to examine the matter before us in terms of those 'principal places and heads of reason, which nature hath taught', beginning with causes. The principal cause of eternal life, Hall says, is God. the same who gives us our natural or temporal life. But we gain eternal life not without some action on our part. Hall put the paradox this way: 'as he will not save thee without thy faith, so thou canst never have faith without his gift'.[41] Here Hall is in agreement with Anglican teaching, such as that of Hooker.[42] From causes we proceed to effects, and principally to the joy that belongs to those upon whom God bestows eternal life. He next turns to consider the subject or purpose of that meditated upon ('the Paradise of God') and the appendances and qualities of the same. In his example the latter concerns being with parents, family, friends, angels, and Christ — perpetually. He proceeds through understanding to compare his subject with that which is contrary to it. In his meditation on the life of the saints, he thinks of misery on earth, sin, and hell. As previously he had thought of that which caused him to praise and thank God, now, with God's love enabling him, he thought of the dangers that beset him, and principally of his own sin, and there arose within him a holy fear such as Hooker wrote of and repentance and the comforting thought that he is not among the reprobate.[43] Next he considered likenesses or similitudes and meditated upon eternal life as

> both a kingdom and a feast. A kingdom: *He, that over-comes shall rule the nations; and shall sit with me in my throne:* O blessed promotion! O large dominion and royal seat ... A feast: *Blessed are they, that are called to the marriage-supper of the Lamb:* feasts have more than necessity

of provision, more than ordinary diet; but marriage-feasts
yet more than common abundance; but the marriage-feast
of the Son of God to his blessed Spouse, the Church, must
so far exceed in all heavenly munificence and variety, as the
persons are of the great state and majesty: there is new
wine, pure manna, and all manner of spiritual dainties ... [44]

We are then invited to consider the titles and names of that
meditated upon, and finally, the testimonies of Scripture, a fitting conclusion, for 'in matters of God, none but divine authority can command assent.'[45] With that the first part of the meditation ends.

Hall then turns to that which he professes to be paramount:
the Affections, '*Wherein is required, A Taste and Relish of
what we have thought upon*.'[46] This is the 'very soul of meditation; whereto all that is past serveth but as an instrument. A
man is a man, by his understanding part; but he is a Christian,
by his will and affections.'[47] In the first part of meditation we
see (understanding involves sight); in the second part we taste,
feel, and are affected by the sweetness or bitterness of our subject and are brought to exclaim, as in the example: 'O blessed
estate of the Saints! O glory not to be expressed, even by those
which are glorified! O incomprehensible salvation ... .'[48] This
passionate response is followed by contrition or 'Humiliation';
'But, alas, where is my love? where is my longing? where art
thou, O my soul?' and a hearty wish for that which we see and
begin to taste but because of sin have not attained. This is that
contrition which Hooker defined as 'a corrosive desire to have
done other than we have done,'[49] and is followed by confession.
Hall notes that which I have elsewhere called the essential
rhythm of the *Book of Common Prayer*:[50]

it is to be duly observed, how the mind is, by turns de-
pressed and lifted up, being lifted up with out estate of
Joy, it is cast down with Complaint [contrition]; lifted
up with Wishes, it is cast down with Confession: which
order doth best hold it in ure and just temper; and maketh
it more feeling of the comfort.[51]

After Confession comes Petition whereby we request at God's hands that 'which we acknowledge ourselves unable, and none but God able to perform.'[52] It is of interest to note that in the example, Hall returned to the figure of light, associated with understanding, as he has pointed out: 'O thou, that layedst clay upon the blind man's eyes, take away this clay from mine eyes; wherewith, alas, they are so daubed up, that they cannot see heaven.' Petition is followed by *'vehement Enforcement of our Petition'*:

> Oh, let me see heaven, another while; and love it much more than the earth, by how much the things there are more worthy to be loved. O God, look down on thy wretched pilgrim, and teach me to look up to thee; and to see thy goodness in the land of the living.[53]

At the conclusion there comes, first, Confidence (cheerfully expressed) in gaining that for which we have prayed, and then Thanksgiving and Recommendation 'of ourselves to God: wherein the soul doth cheerfully give up itself, and repose wholly upon her Maker and Redeemer; committing herself to him, in all her ways . . . desiring, in all things, to glorify him, and to walk worthy of her high and glorious calling.'[54] With the thanksgiving the gradual descent from the mountain top into the valley of ordinary experience begins. Hall was evidently concerned, as other spiritual masters have been, in making the transition from a powerful spiritual experience to routine existence without losing that which was gained in the experience, and he advised, 'like as physicians do in their sweats and exercise, that we cease not over-suddenly; but leave off, by little and little. The mind may not be suffered to fall headlong from the height; but must descend, by degrees.'

The epilogue is an exhortation to the use of meditation. Hall had in mind, among others, those preoccupied with worldly business, with no time for meditation:

> Unto this only neglect, let me ascribe the commonness of that Laodicean temper of men; or, if that be worse, of the dead coldness which hath stricken the hearts of many,

having left them nothing but the bodies of men, and vizors of Christians; to this only THEY HAVE NOT MEDI-TATED. It is not more impossible to live without a heart, than to be devout with meditation.[55]

There follows, then, the second example, this one on death.[56]

MEDITATION AND ANGLICAN SPIRITUALITY

The most obvious form of meditation in nascent Anglican-ism had to do not with formal exercises in meditation such as those of Hall's on life and death but with sermons preached in the public services of worship of the church. Preaching, whether Puritan or Anglo-Catholic, was generally composed of preparation — the presentation of a biblical text and prayer — the explication and exposition of the text, together with proofs, and the application of both text and exposition to the lives of parishioners, with intent to arouse the affections. It is evident here that the sermon and Hallsian meditation are fundamentally similar. The arousal of the affections is the end and purpose of both sermon and formal meditation. In part this is so because both are influenced by rhetorical conventions and in particular rhetorical style. Thomas Wilson, with reference to rhetoric in a treatise published in 1553, wrote: 'Affections ... (called Pas-sions) are none other thyng, but a stirring, or forcing of the mynde, either to desier, or elles to detest, and lothe any thyng more vehemently than by nature we are commonly wonte to doe.'[57] But this pervasive concern for the arousal of the affec-tions had theological roots also. Richard Hooker, writing of the sermon, said:

> So worthie a part of divine service we should greatlie wronge, if we did not esteeme preachinge as the blessed ordinance of God, sermons as keyes to the kingdom of heaven, as wings to the soule, as spurres to the good affec-tions of men, with the sounde and healthie as foode, as psysicke unto diseased mindes.[58]

In the few sermons that have come down to our time from Hooker we can readily note how the learned divine sought to engage the affections of his auditory. For instance, in a sermon on Jude, vv. 17-21, having set forth his text and having brought forward related texts, he said:

> Which of you will gladly remain or abide in a mishapen, a ruinous, or a broken house? And shall we suffer sin and vanity to drop in at our eyes, and at our ears, at every corner of our bodies, and of our souls, knowing that we are the temples of the Holy Ghost? Which of you receiveth a guest whom he honoureth, or whom he loveth, and doth not sweep his chamber against his coming? And shall we suffer the chamber of our hearts and consciences to lie full of vomiting, full of filth, full of garbage, knowing that Christ hath said, 'I and my Father will come and dwell with you?'[59]

In such a vein he continued until, in a manner typically Anglican, he concluded:

> Blessed and praised for ever and ever be his name, who perceiving of how senseless and heavy metal we are made, hath instituted in his Church a spiritual supper, and an holy communion to be celebrated often, that we might thereby be occasioned often to examine these buildings of ours, in what case they stand. For sith God doth not dwell in temples which are unclean, sith a shrine cannot be a sanctuary unto him; and this supper is received as a seal unto us, that we are his house and his sanctuary; that his Christ is as truly united to me, and I to him, as my arm is united and knit unto my shoulder . . . therefore ere we put forth our hands to take his blessed sacrament, we are charged to examine and to try our hearts whether God be in us of a truth or no . . . .[60]

In this as in other sermons, Hooker provided intellectual food for the mind, true to his reputation as learned and judicious, but his attention was fixed upon arousing the affections so that when the congregation departed the church building its members had both substance and cause for further meditation.

John Jewel, the famed bishop of Salisbury and author of the *Apologia Ecclesiæ Anglicanæ,* strove to arouse the affections in a sermon on Romans 13:12; when meditating on the Christian as feeding on Christ, he exclaimed: 'O brethren! O that we had senses to feel this food, that we could savour of the bread of life, and taste and see how sweet the Lord is! He that thus tasteth of this bread shall live for ever.' He then butressed this exhortation with carefully chosen passages of a similar nature from John Chrysostom, Arnold of Bonneval (whom he cited as Cyprian), and Bernard of Clairvaux, sources themselves indicative of the Augustinian mode of meditation.[61]

The sermons of those whom I am calling for convenience sake Anglo-Catholics are replete with proofs or supporting quotations from Scripture and the Fathers, ancient and medieval, indicating the seriousness with which Anglican divines took the appeal to history and the primitive church as well as to Scriptures. We are also made aware of the fact that far from having been delivered extemporaneously, these sermons were carefully crafted, according to deliberate plans, their phrases fined and refined. Such care was taken because these preachers understood the power and influence of the Word preached to the lives of individuals and the community.[62]

The supreme example of the sermon as art form is provided by Lancelot Andrewes, the Caroline bishop of Winchester. Among his most famous sermons there is one frequently cited, carefully analysed by Blench.[63] It was given on Good Friday in 1597 at the Court of Queen Elizabeth I. Its text is Zechariah 12:10: '*And they shall look upon Me, Whom they have pierced*'. The sermon, written in the 'modern style' but with medieval fulness, consists of exordium, division, confirmation, and conclusion. In the exordium the text is explained as referring to Christ and his passion, and we are enjoined to look upon him and his piercing. The division is then made between sight itself (*Quem transfixerunt*) and the act of seeing (*Respicient in Eum*). That part of the sermon called the confirmation provides the major portion of the whole, combining both an appeal to the intellect and an appeal to the affections. Andrewes does this by presenting the piercing of Christ and analyzing its meaning, which is his appeal to the intellect. Simultaneously he enjoins us to look upon that piercing with application of its meaning to our lives; thus he appeals to the affections. His listeners are asked to look upon Christ, *Respice et transfigere*, 'look and be pierced' with lamentation and mourning, *Respice et transfige*, 'look upon Him and pierce . . . that in thee that was the cause of Christ's piercing, sin and the lusts thereof', *Respice et dilige*, 'look and be pierced with love of Him that so loved thee, that He gave Himself in this sort to be pierced for thee', *Respice et crede*, look and believe, trust in Him, *Respice et spera*, look and hope, *Respice et recipe*, look and receive the water and blood flowing from His pierced side (the water in baptism, the blood in the sacrament of Christ's Body and Blood, for the blood of the New Testament 'will run in the high and holy mysteries of the Body and Blood of Christ . . . There may we be partakers of the "cup of salvation" ') and finally, *Respice et retribue:*

> And shall we alway receive grace, even streams of grace issuing from Him that is pierced, and shall there not from us issue something back again, that He may look for and receive from us that from Him have and do daily receive so many good things?[64]

With that, then, Andrewes moved to his conclusion. We place Christ before our mind's eye and He looks upon us with love and mercy. We ask,

> How we shall know when Christ doth thus respect us? Then truly, when fixing both the eyes of our meditation 'upon Him that was pierced', — as it were one eye upon the grief, the other upon the love wherwith he was pierced, we find by both, or one of these, some motion of grace arise in our hearts; the consideration of His grief piercing our hearts with sorrow, the consideration of His love piercing our hearts with mutual love again.[65]

This remarkable sermon is itself a meditation and it was a means of inspiring, arousing, that quite private and personal meditation to which Hall referred in his *Arte*. It begins in contempla-

tion and ends in an exhortation to action. Those who attended
upon sermons such as this one, whether at the royal chapel or
in a country parish church, had cause to be deeply interested in
meditation, interested in Hall's *Arte* and other works of the
genre. They can also be expected to have read sermons if they
were literate, the sermons of the great Puritan preacher, Henry
Smith the 'silver-tongued', or sermons such as those of John
Donne, Lancelot Andrewes or Joseph Hall. Sermons were immensely popular, heard and read, becoming the basis for the
cultivation of the personal spiritual life and an influence for
good upon the cultivation of the godly kingdom.[66]

Reading Andrewes' sermon on Zechariah 12:10, one might
suspect Ignatian influence in the way Andrewes dwelt upon
seeing the passion, placing us there before the cross, but the
influence could have been that of the Windesheimers, of medieval piety, and of medieval liturgical drama, such as the traditional observances of Maundy Thursday and Good Friday.
But we need not even look that far. In the Sacrament for Good
Friday, according to the Elizabethan *Book of Common Prayer*,
in the context of which Andrewes preached, the Epistle was
from Hebrews 10 ('by means of the blood of Jesu, we have
liberty to enter into the holy place') and the Gospel was the
entire passion narrative from John, culminating with the sol-
diers thrusting the spear into the dead body of Christ, 'and
forthwith there came out blood and water.'[67] Thus it is not the
sermon alone that we should have in mind. It is the public
worship of the church as found in the *Book of Common Prayer*,
its daily offices and its sacraments. Thus if we start with Hall's
Arte and his occasional and deliberate meditations, we are inclined back of them to the preaching of the church, and ultimately arrive at that public worship in which sermons are
delivered. Anglican spirituality is rooted in, inspired by, and
governed by its corporate worship. The primary manual for
private devotions in the Church of England is the *Book of
Common Prayer* and all that flows from it.

When we differentiate this Anglo-Catholic spirituality from

that of the Puritans, we note that non-puritan meditation focused on the sacraments as well as on the Word, which is understandable when we take into account the Prayer Book emphasis on sacraments.[68] Many of the most clearly meditative writings of such divines as we have considered thus far concern the Eucharist. In 'A Treatise of Sacraments', constructed out of a series of sermons preached at Salisbury Cathedral, John Jewel said: 'Let us set before our eyes that dreadful tragedy [Christ's passion], and the causes and effects of his death, that so our hearts may be the rather moved to yield that allegiance, obedience, and reverence which is due'.[69] He proceeded to paint the picture: 'Let us remember', he said, 'Christ was forsaken, scorned, buffeted, crucified, and left upon the cross: he was "a worm and no man, a reproach among men." '[70] Having presented the sight to the mind, he then asked, 'Where is the power of Christ's death now? Where is the force and power of his word?' He had Christ give the answer:

> Behold, O man, thus have I sought thee: these things I suffer for thy sake, that thou shouldest eat my flesh and drink my blood, and be made one with me, that thou mightest come into me and I into thee. I have made thee a member of my body, bone of my bones, flesh of my flesh. Thou that wallowest in thy sins . . . what might I do for thy sake, to save thee that I have not done? What might I suffer and have not endured it? O be a partner of my death, that thou mayest have part in my resurrection.[71]

Jewel then cried out in response, on behalf of all present and all reading his treatise:

> Let us die with Christ, let us be crucified unto the world. Let us be holy eagles and soar above. Let us go up into the great parlour and receive of our Lord the cup of the new testament . . . Let us offer up our bodies a living, pure, holy, and acceptable sacrifice to God. So shall we be partakers of the death of Christ.[72]

In his sermon and in the treatise that preserved it, we have a meditation not only on the passion but on the Eucharist, for the Gospel is set forth, the Word proclaimed, as the passion is depicted (equivalent to the *pro-anaphora*). Christ comes to us, assuring us that the word is lively, the Gospel true, and that if we would fully partake of that which is promised we must yield to Christ, become a partner to his death, and thus rise with him in his resurrection (this is equivalent to the *anaphora*). And finally, Jewel provides the only appropriate response, the people's oblation, echoing the very words of Prayer Book Eucharist. To meditate upon Christ, thus, is to be one with him and live as becomes those who are bones of his bones and flesh of his flesh.

A further example is provided by Richard Hooker when, at the end of a very intellectual argument concerning Christ's presence in the Eucharist in Book V of his *Lawes*, he reaches for the most eloquent and affective way of putting his convictions and convincing his readers. Thinking that he is quoting Cyprian, he quotes Arnold of Bonneval: [73]

> the verie letter of the worde of Christ giveth plaine securitie that these mysteries doe as nailes fasten us to his verie crosse, that by them wee draw out, as touchinge efficacie force and vertue, even the blood of his gored side, in the woundes of our redemer wee there dip our tongues, wee are died redd both within and without, our hunger is satisfied and our thirst for ever quenched, they are thinges wonderful which hee feeleth, great which hee seeth and unhard of which he uttereth whose soule is possest of this pascall lamb and made joyfull in the strength of this new wine, this bread hath in it more then the substance which our eyes behold, this cup hallowed with sollemne benediction availeth to the endles life and wellfare both of soule and bodie, in that it serveth as well for a medicine to heale our infirmities and purge our sinnes as for a sacrifice of thanksgiving, with touching it sanctifieth, it enlightneth with beliefe, it trulie conformeth us unto the image of Jesus Christ.... [74]

In this way, the entire chapter concerning 'the sacrament of the body and blood of Christ', is a meditation, beginning with the intellect, ending in the affections. It is because this is so that Hooker cannot be relegated to the congregation of learned and dry theologians who have so often and so fruitlessly disturbed the church. Theological thinking was to him meditative thinking, affective thinking, thinking whose end and purpose was to advance Christians to greater maturity in Christ.

The meditative element in the writings of Jewel and Hooker concerning the sacraments is clearly similar to that of Andrewes in his sermons where he focuses upon Christ,[75] and in his *Preces Privatæ* as he prays:

> Remembering therefore, o sovran Lord, even we,
>   (in the presence of thy holy mysteries)
>   the saving sufferings of thy Christ,
>   his quicknening cross . . .
> we beseech Thee, o Lord,
>   that with the witness of our conscience clean,
>   receiving our share of thy hallowed things,
>   we may be united to the holy body and blood of thy Christ,
>   and receiving them not unworthily
>   may have Christ indwelling in our hearts,
>   and be made a temple of thy Holy Ghost.[76]

That such a prayer and meditation draws on the Liturgy of St Basil and the *Horologion* is not surprising when we remember how Anglicans intellectually and affectively grounded themselves in the early church. What is to me most noteworthy is the way in which Andrewes adheres to a meditative style in both sermons and private devotions.

Without any difficulty we may pass to the poetry of Donne and Herbert, a prominent example of private devotions rooted in the *Book of Common Prayer*. Barbara Lewalski has pointed out that Donne knew Hall when the latter was rector at Hawstead, Sir Robert Drury's country estate. Hall, himself a poet, wrote the poetic preface to Donne's *Second Anniversarie*, 'and almost certainly that for the *First Anniversarie* as well.'[77] Donne's *Devotions upon Emergent Occasions* combine both occasional and deliberate meditation in a Hallsian manner. Both the *Anniversarie* poems and the *Devotions* are occasional, the first occasioned by the death of Elizabeth Drury, the second by the poet's illness. Both are deliberate meditations, the first on 'the frailty and decay of this whole world' and 'the incommodities of the soule in this life and her exaltation in the next', and the second on the 'complex relationship of sin and sickness'.[78] Donne's Holy Sonnets are clearly meditative. If we take the 1633 sonnets alone, it would seem that we have a meditative sequence related to the Sacrament of Christ's Body and Blood.

A. The stage is set: preparatory prayer. Sonnet 1.

B. The agony: contrition with pleading for sacramental grace. Sonnets 2-5.

C. Transition: defiant faith. Sonnet 6.

D. The Cross of Christ: the means of grace. Sonnets 7-9.

E. Conclusion: Participation in Christ. Sonnets 10-12.

Here A. clearly concerns preparation as in Hall's scheme. B. involves repentance, the major precondition both to meditation and to participation in the sacrament. C. is transitional — a strong assertion of faith in the face of assailing doubts. D. is the subject of the meditation proper and the heart of eucharistic devotion. E. is the end and purpose of all, both meditation and sacraments, Sonnet 11 quietly affirming:

> Wilt thou love God as he thee! then digest,
> My Soule, this wholesome meditation,
> How God the Spirit, by Angels waited on
> In heaven, doth make his Temple in thy brest . . . .[79]

It is, perhaps, too much to suggest that Donne was deliberately writing here a meditative series of poems for use in relation to the Eucharist, but when we turn to Herbert there need be no hesitation in saying that the gentle priest and poet was composing something useful when he wrote *The Temple*. Stanley Fish has argued persuasively that *The Temple* is a kind

of catechism.[80] In *The Priest to the Temple* Herbert revealed
that the best catechesis involves not learning by rote but rather
by the socratic method whereby the catechizer 'will draw
out of ignorant and silly souls, even the dark and deep points
of Religion'.[81] As Fish puts it: 'the goal is the involvement of
the reader in his own edification . . . and the shape is the bringing of the reader "by questions well ordered" to "that which
he knows not"'.[82] Of interest here is that *The Temple* as a kind
of catechism involves in important ways the Hallsian process
of meditation. For instance, the catechist is prepared in the
Church Porch and then proceeds to confront the heart of
christian faith when, entering the church, he sees the Altar and
contrition is aroused:

> A broken A L T A R, Lord, thy servant reares,
> Made of a heart, and cemented with teares:
>> Whose parts are as thy hand did frame;
>> No workmans tool hath touch'd the same.
>>> A H E A R T alone
>>> Is such a stone,
>>> As nothing but
>>> Thy pow'r doth cut.
>>> Wherefore each part
>>> Of my hard heart
>>> Meets in this frame,
>>> To praise thy name.
>> That if I chance to hold my peace,
>> These stones to praise thee may not cease.
> O let thy blessed S A C R I F I C E be mine,
> And sanctifie this A L T A R to be thine.[83]

This is immediately followed by the long poem, 'The Sacrifice',
which is derived from the medieval *Improperia* or *Reproaches*
of Good Friday and the responsories for Matins on Maundy
Thursday, Good Friday, and Holy Saturday. Here the poet
presents the subject of meditation, which is the passion of
Christ, Christ directly confronting the reader, making us present at the event and calling forth responses of contrition and

thanksgiving. Thus, for instance, Christ addresses us:

> Oh all ye, who passe by, whose eyes and minde
> To worldly things are sharp, but to me blinde;
> To me, who took eyes that I might you finde:
>   Was ever grief like mine? [84]

At the end of this drama, the contrite Christian responds with praise when considering the death of Christ, the source of salvation, from whose pierced side the sacraments do flow, Christ's woe, 'man's weale.' The poems that follow, making up the bulk of the collection known as *The Temple* involve the believer grappling with the meaning of the divine drama, while the affections are more and more deeply engaged, and the necessary submission to divine love and all its implications begun are carried toward completion. *The Temple* is as a whole a lengthy meditation. Along the way there is such material for meditation as the ordinary Christian may be expected to be able to engage in without being overtaxed, but also without being able to escape the inevitable realization that God's love requires our submission in the participation whereby we and the earth are renewed.

Elsewhere I have argued that Herbert's *The Temple* was formatively influenced by the *Book of Common Prayer*.[85] But indeed the Elizabethan Prayer Book was critically influential in all that pertains to meditation and spirituality among those non-puritans whom we have been referring to as Anglo-Catholics. The English lived day by day in the midst of that holy routine prescribed by the Prayer Book. The tone of the book is established in its preface, where emphasis is placed on the orderly and regular reading of Scripture, that the clergy 'by often reading and meditation of God's Word [should] be stirred to godliness themselves, and be more able to exhort others by wholesome doctrine, and to confute them that were adversaries to the truth.'[86] Morning Prayer begins with preparation, prayer and contrition, confession, and absolution. It then proceeds to instruction of the mind, in lessons and canticles, providing the devout with subject matter for meditation, and it ends with

the Creed, the Our Father, versicles and prayers, and the response of the faithful, engaging their affections and directing
them toward newness of life.[87] The Holy Communion service
is more complex. It begins with preparation, the collect for
purity and self-examination through the recitation of the Ten
Commandments. There follow propers, subject matter for
meditation, including collects, epistle, and gospel. The Creed
is both a summary of the Gospel and, with the 'I believe', an
affective response. Then comes the sermon in which subject
and response are rehearsed, explained, exposited as we have
observed, intellect and affections both being engaged, but always with some degree of newness of life as the purposed outcome. In the light of this sequence offerings are made, money
and prayers, for the 'whole state of Christ's Church militant
here in earth.'[88]

Then the process begins again, with preparation involving
exhortation, confession, and absolution. The subject matter
for meditation follows, being both the central action of the
liturgy and the passion of Christ in which the liturgy is rooted.
Actions and words dramatize to the faithful the infinite, healing, life-giving love of God on the cross. The faithful are
drawn into, engaged, in the drama as they receive the body
and blood of Christ, the heavenly mysteries that preserve their
bodies and souls unto everlasting life. Their affections now engaged by the sacrificial love of God in Christ, the faithful respond, offering 'ourselves, our souls and bodies, to be a reasonable, holy, and living sacrifice unto thee, humbly beseeching
thee, that all we which be partakers of the Holy Communion,
may be filled with thy grace, and heavenly benediction.'[89] It
remains to sing out 'Glory be to God on high' and to be dis-
missed with the blessing.

The sermons, treatises, and poems we have considered all
manifest their dependence, in varying degrees, upon this holy
routine. It is instructive to realize that all is centered upon the
moving of the affections; Hooker says as much more than once
in his defense of the *Book of Common Prayer* against Puritan

objections, arguing persuasively that the intent of the Eucharist is to change lives not bread and wine.[90]

Conclusion

Hall's *Arte* illuminates Anglican spirituality and can be regarded as a helpful aid to meditation, one grounded in the traditions of Augustine and the *Devotio*, rather than in the *Exercises* of Ignatius of Loyola. But the foundation of Anglican spirituality is the *Book of Common Prayer*, the corporate worship of the Church of England, the preaching of the Word and the administration of the Sacraments; and principally that preaching occurred in the context of the sacrament of the Body and Blood of Christ.

As extensions of this public exercise aimed at the intellect in such a way as to arouse the affections aright, there were devotional works for use by individuals. Such a work was Henry Bull's *Christian praiers and holy meditations* (1570; first published in 1566) and in time there appeared the immensely popular *Preces Privatæ* of Lancelot Andrewes. Hall himself, as we have observed, composed numerous collections of meditations for individual use. In recent years we have been discovering that poetry, such as Donne's Holy Sonnets, Herbert's *The Temple*, Crashaw's Sacred Poems, and Vaughan's *Silex Scintillans* were regarded as resources for private meditation. Hall's *Arte* was an aid, agreeable to Anglicans because, although it was not to be used legalistically, it addressed both intellect and affection, placing emphasis on the latter, as did the *Book of Common Prayer*.

It can indeed be argued that Anglican spirituality is fundamentally concerned with intellect and the affections, and their relationship. Anglicans from Hooker, to Jeremy Taylor, to Bishop Butler, to Frederick Denison Maurice, and on down to persons of our own time have emphasized reason and have insisted that in spiritual matters the mind must not be neglected, that we must be reasonable in all things, that we must search the Scriptures utilizing every good tool available to us, that we must test the spirits and not naively assume that every spirit is holy, and that we must learn to distinguish carefully between that which is essential to salvation and that which is indifferent (*adiaphora*). But the reason to which Anglicans appeal is not arid intellect; it is the right reason of christian humanism, the moral law of reason of Richard Hooker, and the eye of the spirit of Samuel Taylor Coleridge. Such reason has been intended to move the affections, to inform and direct the will towards the Good, the True and the Beautiful, and thus God. The end in view has been restored, renewed, redeemed persons and communities — nothing less than the forming or reforming of societies as the *societas christiana*.

Meditation in Anglican spirituality is not passive contemplation, then, but the deliberate opening of mind and heart to the grace of God, the affections being moved, the will activated. Hall's *Arte* helps us to understand this, but it must never be regarded as the complete expression of Anglican meditation. For that wholeness we begin by looking to the *Book of Common Prayer* and from thence to all that is dependent upon it. As an aid, the *Arte* was highly regarded in the seventeenth century and has its value now.

JOHN BOOTY

Episcopal Divinity School
Cambridge, Massachusetts.
[now: *School of Theology*
 The University of The South]

PURITAN SPIRITUALITY: THE TENSION OF BIBLE AND EXPERIENCE

'Puritans' were those English protestants, usually of Calvinist leanings, whose concern for popular religion — as against institutional religion — led them to seek to purify the Church of England of its vestigial 'popery' by emphasizing the individual's confrontation of the word of God in Scripture, by simplyfying worship and stressing preaching, and by abolishing episcopal government within the established church. Their failure to achieve the last resulted in their separation from the English church.

FOR MORE THAN FIFTEEN years I have been actively researching the phenomenon known as Protestant Scholasticism, mainly in its Continental expression. In the course of that study I have found it necessary to do a good deal of work on Puritan Scholasticism, as regards both its development and its characteristic expression. In the course of that study I have been increasingly impressed by the relatively greater emphasis placed by the English Puritans upon piety, upon inward religion, than by the French and Swiss Calvinists with whom I am most familiar. I have become convinced that this relatively greater stress upon inward religion has the greatest influence upon the type of religious literature produced by the Puritans, a type of literature which has no close parallel in either Swiss or French Protestantism. I have consequently undertaken a study of Puritan spirituality with the greatest interest and enthusiasm. While my primary task has been to read as much as possible in the primary sources, starting with the sixteenth century Puritans, I have sampled the secondary literature and would like to mention those contemporary authors whom I have found the most helpful. To begin with, I have found the work of Professor Geoffrey Nuttall indispensable. In my judgment Nuttall must be recognized as the 'Dean' of Puritan Interpreters. There is only one problem: he works in the wrong century for my immediate purposes, most of his work having to do with the seventeenth century.[1] I have also found J. Sears McGee's *The Godly Man in Stuart England*[2] to be one of the better books available on the topic; unfortunately he, too, works in the wrong century. John Ray Knott, Jr.'s *The Sword of the Spirit*[3] is a superior presentation of the Puritan view and use of the Bible. Both Leonard Trinterud's *Elizabethan Puritanism*[4] and H.C. Porter's *Puritanism in Tudor England*[5] are valuable anthologies with useful introductions. Porter's *Reformation and Reaction in Tudor Cambridge*[6] is a perceptive, if somewhat opaque, presentation. Of the more purely historical accounts I have found the work of Patrick Collison,[7] Wallace MacCaffrey,[8] and, recently, Winthrop Hudson[9] most useful. Finally, I should mention my debt to articles by Jerald Brauer,[10] J. I. Packer,[11] Nuttall,[12] Trinterud,[13] and Ronald Vander Molen.[14]

The purpose of this paper will be, first, to place the movement solidly in its historical context; and second, to present Puritan spirituality as much as possible in its own terms. In no way should this effort be viewed as proposing a definitive interpretation, but it is intended to be provocative and suggestive of certain tendencies which need careful attention in any consideration of English Puritan views. I shall make particular effort to identify and to separate out certain attitudes and characteristics which appear to me to be crucial and central to the Puritan spirit.

As everyone who is in the least way knowledgeable of studies having to do with Puritanism knows, great debate rages and much ink continues to be spilled over the problem of definition of the term so as to distinguish Puritan from Anglican.[15] In fact, a survey of the secondary literature could lead one to conclude that there were no Puritans! In the late 1960s Charles and Katherine George argued the impossibility of distinguishing Puritan and Anglican on the basis of doctrine.[16] Everett Emerson doubts whether it is possible to make any general statements about Puritan economic theory, social theory, or even a Puritan style.[17] I can only say that if there were no Puritans and no distinctions which make Puritanism an identifiable historical movement, then we have been the victims of an unbelievably effective academic hoax, one which makes the so-called Pilt-down Man hoax a very minor perturbation.

What this academic double-talk illustrates is that in order to get to the heart of the movement it is necessary to cut through many layers of sectarian religious and secular myth as well as through a good deal of questionable historical interpretation. In terms of the scholarly world, one of the factors which has most distorted our picture of Puritanism has been the enormous interest which Puritanism has for some reason generated among scholars in many disciplines, so that the field of Puritan studies has become practically a profession unto itself. The quite na-tural consequence has been a plethora of studies on every topic under the sun, a great many of which have focused on, and stressed, those aspects of Puritanism which were at best periph-eral and occasional. I am firmly of the opinion that *the failure to mark well and distinguish carefully the essential features of the movement from the occasional actions of some members of the movement has been perhaps the major cause for confusion among scholars about the nature of Puritanism.* Because some of these occasional actions were of major importance in the course of English history, they have captured the attention and become the focus of a great amount of scholarly investigation, and have led to the unwarranted conclusion that such was what the Puritans were all about. The outstanding case in point, of course, is the so-called 'Puritan Revolution' of the 1640s. As a result of this remarkable and epochal event, scholars have launched an energetic campaign to discover and analyze the political, economic, and social ideas of the Puritans, a quest which has led the preponderance of Puritan scholars to spend all of their time and efforts on what is essentially a sideroad at best. Not that this quest has not produced valuable and valid historical analyses — indeed some of these studies are brilliant and help immediately in our understanding of the seventeenth century world —, but at the same time they have bedeviled the field of Puritan studies by suggesting that political and social measures give us the real shape of the Puritan. It is appropriate, I believe, to remind ourselves that the present day political actions of the so-called 'Moral Majority' do not define and illustrate the essence of evangelical Christianity today any more than the actions of the 'political Puritans' defined and illustrated the essence of Puritanism. Now I want to make clear that I have no problem with those who find a revolutionary ideology in Puritanism; my misgivings arise only when the religious impulses which lie behind Puritan ideology are given short shrift and when we are left with the impression that political or social or economic considerations were the driving force of the movement. I am in complete agreement with Gordon Rupp who argues that,

> Too little attention has been paid to their spirituality, to what they have to say of Christian experience, of their devotion to Christ, and about the joy of the Christian religion. But the evidence is abundant, at almost every level of religious and theological writing. It is time to look at Puritanism from the other side of the [Christopher] Hill . . . .[18]

A second major factor which has bedeviled our understanding of Puritanism is the generally unsympathetic and unsavory, even hostile, caricature of the Puritans which has prevailed from the sixteenth century to our own day, perhaps especially in the popular mind, but also among the intellectuals. H.C. Porter notes that 'By the end of Elizabeth's reign the idea was commonplace among intellectuals of the Puritan as curious, silly, and hypocritical.'[19] This view seems quickly to have become the traditional one. Because this 'traditional view of Puritanism has been fostered by a romantic novelist like Scott and by a rhetorical historian like Macauley for whom it was natural to paint only the decadent Puritanism,'[20] it becomes particularly pernicious for the very reason that even the scientific researcher is conditioned to read the Puritan writers looking for the unsavory side. It is past time that we repudiate the oft-repeated definition of H. L. Mencken that 'Puritanism is the haunting fear that someone, somewhere, may be happy.'[21]

A third factor hindering our understanding has been a failure to utilize an adequate historical method in the study of Puritanism, a failing which, I must say, often characterized theological studies of the movement. Of course there is need to tread lightly at this point since we all fail here, but most of us ought to do better. There are at least two areas here which need more attention:

(1) The eternal problem of reading back into Puritan ideas and history certain presuppositions which *our experience* tells us are important. We have often attributed to the Puritans religious beliefs and practices which stem from later groups such as the Methodists, the holiness movements, and even from the *mentalité* of the Victorian period. An example of this type of misperception is, of course, the celebrated issue of Puritanism and alcoholic beverages. Perry Miller and others have shattered once and for all, we hope, the myth that the Puritans were teetotalers, but the important question is, How did the myth arise? Or perhaps better, the really important question at the moment is, How many other such myths have been and continue to be perpetrated as a result of our reading back into Puritanism those belief systems and practices which are, *we think*, characteristic of persons holding the kind of religious faith we find in the Puritans?

(2) The need to take into account the essentially medieval reference of Puritan language and thought. 'The world in which the Puritan grew up', observes Geoffrey Nuttall, 'was still nominally a *mundus Christianus*, with the State and the Church ideally one.'[22] Thus we should not find it strange if the Puritan naturally reflects the medieval belief that every part of his life can be and should be ordered around an intensely religious ideal. Again, if we find the Puritan all too inclined to argue and debate, we must remember that this is nothing but the theological equivalent of the chivalric duel of the medievalist,

that he is simply sharing the *mentalité* of his age which held that one's honor can never allow a challenge to be ignored. Or again, if we find the Puritan unusually zealous to defend the honor of God and of His Word, we must remember that in the age of chivalry for one to lose his honor was to lose simply everything.

II

With this kind of introduction, I have obviously made it incumbent upon myself to make at least some general reference to the historical context in which Puritanism should be understood. It is axiomatic that to establish even the general historical context is not necessarily easy. But if we accept the common position that Puritanism as a distinct historical movement began in the mid 1560s — and I see no reason to argue with this position — then there are at least five broad issues which must be 'factored into the equation'. These will be mentioned only in the briefest fashion even though each deserves extended comment and illustration.

First, and perhaps foremost, as I intimated above, the essentially medieval character, mind set, and value system of the movement must be kept in mind. Thirty years ago Leonard Trinterud observed that 'what seems to be emerging [in Puritan Studies] is an account of Puritanism in which the heritage from medieval English thought and life is the controlling factor'.[23] I am convinced that we have yet to appreciate the implications and the extent of the medieval reference of the Puritan.

Second, and closely associated with the need to appreciate fully the medieval reference of Puritanism's ideology, is the need to appreciate and investigate fully the role of the influence of Wyclif's ideas, as passed through the Lollards, on those of the Puritans. Though this influence is often given lip service in the literature, rarely is there solid content or comparative data presented to support the assertion. Yet, a recent article by Charles Brockwell, Jr. does initiate a pattern to be emulated and, one hopes the results of such studies will be then digested

into the analyses and interpretations of Puritanism.[24] Brockwell's illuminating study compares the responses of Bishop
Reginald Pecock (d. ca. 1460) to the Lollards with that of
Richard Hooker to the Puritans, demonstrating an affinity
which can hardly be accidental. Brockwell argues that 'At the
heart of both Lollard and Puritan nonconformity was their
stout insistence upon the right to interpret the Bible in their
own way, no matter what scholars might demonstrate or prelates might demand',[25] and shows further the almost exact position of Lollard and Puritan upon a host of issues.

Third, much more generally accepted and applied is the
recognition that the principles and theological emphases of the
Continental Reformation play a significant role. The Puritans
certainly regarded themselves as an integral part of the Reformation in England — perhaps as *the* integral part. Moreover,
of course, we must constantly remind ourselves of the 'political'
manner in which the break with the Roman Catholic Church
occurred in England and the effect which this had on the formation of the Puritan party.

Fourth, and again an item quite generally recognized, the
impact and influence of the Renaissance on the movement was
very considerable. One can safely argue, I believe, that without the educational interest which it excited, the Bible in the
vernacular which it helped promote, the general mood and
atmosphere of dissent which it fostered, the individualism
which it helped sponsor, the new social and economic climate
which it helped bring about, the new sense of values which it
promoted, and the discontent with corrupt practices in politics
and religion which it helped produce, the tender plant of Puritanism would have wilted and died in the first heat of Summer.

Fifth, there was the great impact of the Marian exiles on the
nature of the difference between Anglican and Puritan, a factor
which has also been duly recognized as of late.[26] The Prayer
Book debate and the intimate contact with the leaders of the
Reformed (Calvinistic) Church were powerful shaping factors
which significantly altered some of the original impulses of

Puritanism, and, if I am not mistaken, in the event changed the course of Puritan spirituality.

III

Before moving now to a consideration of Puritan spirituality *per se*, I would like to suggest, without development, a series of characteristics which I believe are more or less unique to Puritanism — at least unique if compared to the major Protestant groups of the sixteenth and seventeenth centuries. At least these qualities struck me as new and unusual after a long period of time of being accustomed to Calvinist and Lutheran attitudes. If I mistake not, they make up some of the unwritten assumptions which lie behind the Puritan program and are therefore of utmost importance in the development of the distinctives of Puritan spirituality.

1. *Naïveté:*

It is striking how convinced is the Puritan that his ideas on reform and the christian life are the true New Testament pattern. It is equally striking how sure the Puritan is that just getting the Bible into the hands of the people will bring about the reform and even unity which is consistent with the Word of God. Any honest reading of the Bible will unquestionably dispel the darkness of the age and of the spirit. Light cannot fail to overcome the darkness. There is apparently no thought given to the possibility that the Bible would be differently interpreted by its readers.

2. *Simplicity:*

Closely related to the *naïveté* of the Puritan is the trait which is perhaps best described as simplicity. There is, according to the Puritan, nothing at all complicated about either the message or the organization of the christian church. Indeed, many of the problems which the church faces stem from the complications and complexities introduced by the rational schemes of the theologians or the machinations of self-seeking prelates.

Thus the Puritan concern for simplicity led to a pervasive distrust of intellectuals and clerics.

3. *Separatism:*

A third recurrent theme in Puritan literature which becomes thereby an identifying trait is the constant call to 'come out from among them and be separate.'[27] This trait is found pervasively even among those groups who do not become part of the Brownist or Separatist sect. The celebrated Cartwright-Whitgift debates nicely illustrate this tendency within Puritanism to separatism. When Whitgift charges that

> These men separate themselves also from the congregation, and will communicate with us neither in prayers, hearing the word, nor sacraments. They contemn and despise all those that be not of their sect as polluted, and not worthy to be saluted or kept company with. . . .[28]

he is pointing to a fundamental aspect of Puritan spirituality — if you will, to its monastic impulse. I find very instructive the comparison of Puritanism and Cistercian reform developed in Geoffrey Nuttall's article on the Puritan spirit through the ages. It is perhaps not merely coincidence that an oft-repeated theme among the early Cistercians was that of *puritas*.[29]

4. *Seriousness, or Severity:*

A fourth characteristic is the gravity with which the Puritan approached all aspects of life. William Tyndale speaks for the movement, I believe, when in his Prologue to the book of Exodus, after admonishing his readers to 'Cleave unto the text and plain story' he says: 'And note every thing earnestly, as things pertaining unto thine own heart and soul.'[30] Or elsewhere he will say: 'As thou readest, therefore, think that every syllable pertaineth to thine own self, . . .'[31] When this was combined with the aforementioned belief that everything in life is a religious happening the result was a world of thought where seriousness is characteristic of the spiritual pilgrimage.[32]

5. *Spiritism or Mysticism:*

The final trait I would note is the emphasis upon the mystical communion of the individual soul with God. Nuttall's 'The Holy Spirit in Puritan Piety' and his 'Puritan and Quaker Mysticism' are excellent statements of this aspect of Puritanism. It is fairly well known, of course, that Luther had drawn heavily upon mystical writers, but I was surprised to find this element so strongly stated in these allegedly 'Calvinist' Puritans. The aforementioned strongly anti-intellectual predilection of the Puritans surely contributes to this striking sensitivity and affective bent of Puritan spirituality. This helps account for the predominance of the uneducated lay person, and especially of women, in the movement. Among others, Porter notes the appeal to women, observing that '. . . Grindal and Hooker would have recognized as an instance of their conviction that puritanism was of special appeal to females'.[33]

Puritanism, while a distinct historical entity, was basically a spirit and not in any sense an organized movement, though in the later stages of this spirit an organization was necessary. Brown is correct in saying that Puritanism 'was not so much an organized system as a religious temper and a moral force, and being such it could enter into combinations and alliances of varied kind'.[34] Because it was fundamentally a spirit, an attitude of mind, *a spiritual outlook,* a mode of life, Puritanism was of far greater consequence as a religious expression than as an institution.

It is necessary to emphasize that Puritanism began as a movement of reaction, with many of the excesses which accompany reactionary movements. It partook of that spirit which protested the abuses in the Roman Catholic Church, but it took its shape and form as an historical movement from its reaction vs. 'Romish remainders' in the Elizabethan English Church. Specifically, the issue of clerical dress in 1564 was the catalyst which brought the Puritans together and made of them a distinct religious group. They agreed that the matter of dress was an indifferent matter in and of itself, but they were terribly concerned that the division between the 'religious' and the lay, to which they were violently opposed, would be maintained.

Since Puritanism began as a reaction, as seems to be natural in reactionary movements it attracted a remarkable variety of personalities and thus was characterized by an unbelievable complexity and dissimilarity. It is amazing that men as different as William Dell and Richard Baxter could ever be considered part of the same movement, yet it is true that they were because of their common beliefs and common goal. There were present in the movement great extremes in viewpoint — from the most radical mystic or spiritualist to the hyper-rationalist. It is this exceeding complexity of viewpoints which causes extreme difficulty in either defining the movement or in adequately analyzing its character.

Obviously, then, Puritanism is not marked by simple relationships to the various areas of life and therefore one makes definitive statements about 'Puritan spirituality' only with a great deal of audacity. Puritan attitudes on politics, on social problems, on economic changes and even on questions of theology are not any one consistent testimony. Yet the attitudes which we see exhibited with regard to these problems do seem to present a certain, even a remarkable, continuity. These attitudes have, by and large, been all fashioned by the same causes and impulses which gave them a common denominator, or common denominators, at the beginning. The specific way in which the Puritan expressed himself or herself in relation to that common denominator will vary over time, however. The points of emphasis and concern of a Puritan in 1570 are really quite different from those a Puritan would express in 1650. And this change is not by any means solely a result of the Civil War of the 1640's. No, the changing nature of Puritanism, *and* of the Anglicanism against which Puritanism struggled, had been a factor from the very first. Polemic often brings change, especially to the character of a movement, and the Puritan was always involved in polemic. But perhaps even without the polemic atmosphere the eventual division of Puritanism into the three rather distinct strands of rationalism, moralism, and mysticism would have occurred, for these tendencies were present in rather delicate balance from the very first.[35]

My reading suggests that the writings and influence of William Perkins (d. 1602) were decisive in changing the character of Puritanism; that means that we may rather conveniently and neatly divide Puritanism into Tudor Puritanism and Stuart Puritanism. It is beyond the scope of this paper to defend this hypothesis, but I would note that Perkins provided a learned, scholastic-type theology which effectively eliminated the lay, common person expression which was so strong in the early years.

What follows, then, has its primary reference to the essence of *Tudor Puritanism*. If you need terminus points, they are from William Tyndale who provided the translation for the first printed English Bible, and Arthur Dent, a little known 'Preacher of the Word of God in Essex' as he calls himself.[36]

When we address the question, What *was* the common denominator which gave Puritanism a recognizable continuity?, we come to the matter proper of Puritan spirituality. Though the Puritans are known and have been studied for many things — their biblicism, their piety, their ascetic tendencies (which in spite of Max Weber's arguments I find very like medieval asceticism), their individualism (which is presumably an outworking of the Reformation principle of the priesthood of all believers), their godly discipline, their extreme moralism, their mystical tendencies, their inordinate zeal, their church polity, and their overwhelming emphasis on preaching, though all of these are used to define Puritanism, it is my belief that when all is boiled down to basics, there are two poles at the heart of Puritan spirituality — the Bible as the living word of God, and a lively sense or experience of the Spirit of God. These two poles are, however, not really separable.[37]

There is a delicate balance to be maintained between these two poles. And the history of the movement points up the need for this healthy tension. When the Puritan overstressed experience — as certain did — this led to grave doubts about assurance and therefore to an excessive interest in the *syllogismus prac-*

ticus and cases of conscience. When he overstressed Scripture as God's law book — as certain did — this led to legalism and sterile theological/philosophical systems.

Religious experience, or a lively encounter with God, is the crucial element in Puritan spirituality. Indeed Puritanism is animated by 'a devotion of the heart, of Christian experience.'[38] The activity which characterized Puritan spirituality was remarkable and encompassed every aspect of life. The oft-believed notion, so forcefully promulgated by Weber and Troeltsch, which attributes this zeal to the Puritan doctrine of predestination is false. They were not trying to prove their election but were, rather, only outliving an inworked experience of God's grace. In the words of J.C. Brauer, 'The Puritan did not engage in his rigorous action to prove his own election. On the contrary, this activism and reforming zeal *arose also from the personal conversion experience*. Once he experienced the redemptive love of God in the new birth, the Puritan was possessed of a spirit that would not let him rest.'[39]

That their zeal and activity came from an experience of grace is evident in their own writings. John Bunyan says in his *Grace Abounding* that he preached 'what I felt, what I smartingly did feel . . . what I saw and felt.'[40] Again, he says that the seven abominations in his heart he does continually feel.[41] His personal experience of the Gospel truths was all-important to him. Richard Sibbes states that 'the sense of the love of Christ in pardoning of sins will constrain one to a *holy violence* in the performing of all duties.'[42]

The activity produced by this existential encounter of God's redemptive love also produced their most obvious characteristic — the dissatisfaction with that which they considered half-way reform. Their conversion led them to desire a New Testament type church and so to push the reformation to its furthest extreme. Because of this Tawney is undoubtedly correct when he says, 'Puritanism, not the Tudor secession from Rome, was the true English Reformation, and it is from its struggle against the old order that an England which is unmistakably modern emerges."[43] They did push through thoroughgoing reformation principles. Though they lost the battle (in that the English Church was never permanently reformed according to their ideals) it may well be said that they won the war, for they attained a permanent place for their principles on the English scene (not to mention the American) in the church groups which are a product of the movement and which continue to this day.

Before leaving this experiential aspect of the Puritan movement we would do well to note that this very phenomenon produced an emphasis on the Holy Spirit which is probably not found in any other christian tradition of the period. It culminated in John Owen's great work on the Holy Spirit, pretty much an opening of virgin territory. He even tells us that he knew of no other such work and this was not because he was unfamiliar with the literature of the historic church. He nevertheless gives us a very thorough treatment of the subject at hand and shows the centrality of this doctrine in all areas of the christian life. The importance of the Holy Spirit in Puritan thought has been brilliantly set forth by Geoffrey Nuttall in his most important work on Puritanism.

The influence of this characteristic personal experience with God was tremendous in giving cohesion to the movement and in giving it a distinctiveness. Obviously there were those in the Anglican Church who experienced just as dynamically the grace of God, but it was not at all as universal as it was in Puritanism. This experience made *every Puritan a pilgrim* in this life and produced his other-worldly emphasis which has often been recognized. This is brilliantly portrayed in Bunyan's *Pilgrim's Progress* but was by no means limited to Bunyan.

Thus the 'encounter' was of the highest moment in Puritan spirituality. Maclear notes that this experiential note which 'sounded again and again in Puritan sermons, diaries, biographies, and guides to the spiritual life attained its climax in the conversion experience, which was not an ornament but a norm of the religious life.'[44] One way in which this norm worked itself out is the way it influenced the Puritan use and view of the Bible. Not only did he see the Bible in all its parts as a spiritually dynamic and immediately applicable Word of God to the individual soul, but he also felt that without this conversion experience the Bible remained a closed book, that the individual who had not had this spiritual encounter with God in Christ could never understand the Bible no matter how much scholarly effort he expended or how many scholarly experts he read or consulted.

We come, then, to the second distinctive characteristic of Puritanism — the unusually strong emphasis on the Bible as the living, convicting, healing, word of God. This is the basis of which one author calls their 'notorious scripturism'.[45] This has been quite universally recognized, and the traditional presentation runs something like this:

Obedience to God was all-important in the Puritan way of thinking. But to obey God, he had to know his will. This will he found revealed in the Bible. This is made plain by the second question of the Westminster Shorter Catechism. The Bible was their only authority. Brown says, 'The fundamental idea of Puritanism in all its manifestations was the supreme authority of scripture brought to bear upon the conscience as opposed to an unenlightened reliance on the priesthood and the outward ordinances of the Church'.[46] Tatham, expressing the same idea, says, 'The keynote of the Puritan position was the acceptance of the Bible as the one infallible authority before which all institutions in the Church must stand or fall . . . the Puritans . . . demanded the abolition of all for which the Bible offered no positive warrant'.[47] This latter idea was, it is argued, a step beyond that which the Reformers had taken.

Thus, the argument goes, the doctrine of the infallibility of the Scriptures was not questioned.[48] It was simply an accepted fact. Richard Baxter presumably speaks for the movement when he says, 'The Holy Spirit, by immediate inspiration, revealed unto the apostles the doctrine of Christ, and caused them infallibly to indite the Scriptures'.[49] Any reform movement must establish an authority for itself, and the authority of the Puritans was the Infallible Book.

I have very grave difficulty with this portrayal of the Puritan view of the Bible. It lacks, it seems to me, any real appreciation for the essence of Puritan spirituality, at least in the Tudor period.[50] It is true, of course, that the authority of the Reformation groups, in all its phases and in all geographical locations, was the Bible. Certainly all the reformers accepted the Bible as the Word of God to man. But, perhaps as a result of his place within a Protestant context already, the Puritan did not stress the Bible as authority as the primary issue, but rather as the place where man encounters God — or perhaps better, as the place where God encounters man. Said otherwise, the Bible is not a static source of doctrine and theory, but a living Word where man finds spiritual sustenance and healing. What is being said, then, is not that the Bible was not used as an authority for faith and practice, but that this use was very much subordinate to the 'spiritual use'. The distinction may seem to be drawn too sharply, but it would be to distort the nature of Puritan spirituality not to insist upon the point. It is the power of the Word of God to convert the soul and the immediate relevance of the Word of God to every modern problem which strikes the dominant note sounded in Tudor Puritan writings.

The contemporaneity and immediate relevance of every part of the Bible relates integrally with the feeling that the Bible is a book for a common person, not just for the learned. Learning does not provide any particular advantage, for use of the Bible was a spiritual, not an intellectual, matter. The Puritan, in Bronkema's words, 'regarded the Bible as the people's Book. The uneducated could read it and imbibe its spirit. All parts of the Bible were of equal validity, commands for Israel hold also for us.'[51] So the great use to which the Puritans put the Bible was the reformation and ordering of life. Their severe morality was also basically the outcome of the application of the Scriptures, especially of the Old Testament. Because they were primarily interested in the reformation of life, there was very little emphasis as such on doctrine. The important matter for the Puritan was how the Bible affected his life and this was how he used it.

With this in mind, it follows, of course, that the vernacular Bible was central to the Puritan program. Without the Bible available to the common people a fundamental element of the Puritan spirit could not have developed. At this point, the work of William Tyndale becomes especially important. By providing the vernacular translation he provided this essential source to all literate Englishmen and thus removed the source of spirituality from the exclusive domain of the educated and the clerical groups. When Tyndale in his prologues – in a curious, seemingly uncomprehended contradiction of the principle that the Bible needs no human interpreter – gives guidance for the reader of the biblical book in question, he always stresses its spiritual use. In the 'Prologue to the Pentateuch' he states: 'It is not enough . . . to read and talk of it only, but we must also desire God, day and night instantly, to open our eyes, and to make us *understand and feel* wherefore the scripture was given, that we may apply the medicine of the scripture, every man to his own sores; . . . .'[52]

The Bible, he believes, has 'but one simple, literal sense' and throughout he stresses that its blessings 'shalt thou evermore find in the plain text and literal sense.'[53] The reader of the Bible is to 'Cleave unto the text and plain story' and likewise 'beware of subtle allegories.'[55] The plain, literal text is to be interpreted spiritually; this will bring a feeling of God's direction:

> . . . first seek out the law that God will have thee to do, interpreting it spiritually, without gloss or covering the brightness of Moses' face; *so that thou feel in thine heart* how that it is damnable sin before God not to love thy neighbour that is thine enemy as purely as Christ loved thee; and that not to love thy neighbour in thine heart is to have committed already all sin against him.[55]

So the plain, literal sense is in fact the spiritual sense, and the effect of its reading is the production of a feeling faith. Such faith 'is a lively thing, mighty in working, valiant, and strong, ever doing, ever fruitful; so that it is impossible that he who is endued therewith should not work always good works without ceasing.'[56] Its effect 'maketh a man glad, lusty, cheerful, and true-hearted unto God and unto all creatures; whereof, willingly and without compulsion, he is glad and ready to do good to every man, to do service to every man. . . .'[57] This faith, this experience of God in the soul, in turn permits the Scripture to be read with edification and perception:

> . . . he which is sound in the faith shall at once perceive that the judgment of the heretics is corrupt in their expositions, as a whole man doth feel at once, even with smelling to the meat, that the taste of the sick is infected.[58]

So the dynamic nature of the Bible, interpreted simply and spiritually, is fundamental to Puritan spirituality. It is true that early in Elizabeth's reign a very different tradition emerges with John Jewel, whose 'A treatise of the Holy Scriptures' is nothing but a panegyric on the authority, utility, necessity, delectability, etc. of the Bible — if you will, an academic, theological discourse on the doctrine of Scripture —,[59] but Jewel is representing the Continental Reformed influence as a result of his exile. The more dynamic portrayal, with its emphasis on feeling, is still clearly seen in the very early seventeenth century in the writings of Arthur Dent. Dent is true to the tradition coming from Tyndale when he writes that 'it is one thing to know the Historie and letter of the Scriptures, and another thing to *beleeve* and *feele* the power thereof in the heart, which is onely from the sanctifying spirit which none of the wise of this world can have.'[60] By the time of Dent, of course, the pervasive concern with assurance was in vogue, but Dent's response remains true to the position of the dynamic quality of the word of God and its affective impact on the soul.

> But you must learn to know out of the Scriptures, that all outward honesty and reighteousnesse, without the true knowledge and inwarde feeling of God, auayleth not to eternall life.[61]

Thus we find two poles, mystical experience and a view of the Bible as a dynamic, living, relevant message from God, at the heart of Puritan spirituality. What did this mean for the history of the movement? There is no room here to address this question in detail, but I will venture a general comment.

The fervor with which he took the position, as well as the position itself which the Puritan took on these two poles of his spirituality, led to a great many of the radical aspects of Puritanism. To propagate the idea that even the uneducated could read the Bible with spiritual benefit and without need of interpretation or instruction proved very disruptive in the sixteenth century. The relations of the movement with Anglicanism, the many splinter groups spawned by Puritanism, and the complete inability of the Puritans to unite forces even during the Commonwealth period prove its endemically disruptive character. One of their more adamant positions was that a full system of church government could be discovered in the New Testament. The Anglican could not accept the Bible as a guide for each detail of life. He interpreted the Scripture as setting forth the general principles of the faith but thought that questions such as the specific form of church government were not definitively spelled out there. Man, being a rational creature, was given the freedom of using such order of worship and polity as would best fit the situation;[62] to use the Bible to substantiate every detail of life whether personal or with relation to the community of believers, was a misuse of God's Word. The Puritan, who found a spiritual message in every part of Scripture, could not understand or appreciate the idea of a book which provides only the general principles of the faith. If the Bible speaks to us immediately, if it is a living, contemporary word from God, then it must be applied immediately and minutely. To hold that God did not provide a definitive word for the polity of the church was inconceivable.[63] The result of such a position could only be a device which would permit men to make crucial alterations in the Word of God. Such consequences would deny the living, dynamic quality of the Bible. The Puritan could not live with such an alternative, especially since his mystical experience of the presence of God was so real.

BRIAN ARMSTRONG

Georgia State University

PIETIST SPIRITUALITY: SOME ASPECTS OF PRESENT RESEARCH

Pietism was a reaction within German protestantism to the then dominant speculative scholasticism and intellectualized faith. Its call for personal conversion, holiness of life, scripture reading, meditation, quiet prayer, and pastoral counselling brought it into conflict with the religious establishment, whether Lutheran or Calvinist, and influenced many persons beyond Germany and the Westphalian churches. Many pietist groups sought refuge in North America in the eighteenth century.

So SIGNIFICANT was the Pietist awakening of late seventeenth and early eighteenth-century Protestantism that a modern student of the movement is able to state, 'To write the history of Pietism is to write the history of modern Protestantism.'[1] From its beginning under Philipp Jakob Spener at Frankfurt-am-Main in 1675 to the end of the first major period of its growth in 1727 with the death of August Hermann Francke, Spener's colleague and successor in Halle-am-Saale, Pietism had spread throughout all Protestant denominations in the German-speaking world,[2] had begun to influence anglophones, and had forced a restructuring of Protestant social, intellectual, and ecclesiatical institutions, private and public attitudes to personal redemption, worship, devotion, missionary work, the concept of the responsibility of the church to society, church and state relations, and the significance of denominational positions. Moreover, as it developed, it helped to establish the foundations of modern biblical studies, and even before its renewal in the nineteenth century *Erweckungsbewegung*, it had influenced aspects of German music, literature, and philosophy.[3] It is difficult, for example, to consider Kant's concern with the categorical imperative, the moral proof for God's existence, and the trans-

cendental structures of thought aside from his Pietist background. Likewise Schleiermacher's emphasis on religious 'feeling' is related to his Pietist education. Nor can Pietism easily be
separated from the rise of Methodism; and for students of nineteenth-century American revivalism and twentieth-century
Evangelicalism, the history of Pietism provides analogues useful
for a fuller understanding of these later movements.[4]

PIETISM: AN HISTORICAL OUTLINE

Despite the problems in defining so wide-reaching a movement there is agreement on its general historical shape. Certainly there were many 'Proto-Pietist' individuals and groups within Protestantism, but the Pietist awakening itself can be dated
precisely. On September 8, 1675 Philipp Jakob Spener (1635-
1705), the Lutheran chief minister in Frankfurt-am-Main, published an introduction to the sermons of an earlier Lutheran
preacher and author, Johann Arndt (1555-1621), and entitled
his piece *Pia desideria, or Heartfelt Desire for a God-pleasing
Reform of the True Evangelical Church, Together with Several Simple Christian Proposals Looking Toward this End.*[5]

The introduction, despite its brevity, was immediately popular, and quickly appeared in numerous editions, including a Latin version. It began with an outline of the corrupt conditions
in the church, blaming civil authorities, clergy, and laity for the
situation. The treatise then sketched Spener's hopes for better
times and outlined proposals to correct the abuses it noted.
Spener required first that thought be given to a more extensive
use of the word of God. The Holy Scriptures, particularly the
New Testament, should be read more diligently by both clergy
and laity. Small groups should be established and should meet
regularly. These conventicles (*eccesiolae in ecclesia*), Spener
hoped, would provide an atmosphere for the mutual edification
of devout believers. Secondly, Spener proposed the renewal
of the concept of the spiritual priesthood of all believers so as
to overcome a 'presumptuous monopoly of the clergy' and, as
a result, a 'slothful clergy.'[6] Thirdly, Spener insisted that 'it is

by no means enough to have knowledge of the Christian faith, for Christianity consists rather in practice."[7] This requirement of *praxis pietatis* was central to the Pietist program. It consisted, Spener taught, in love of God and neighbour. 'Love', he stated, 'is the whole life of a man who has faith and who through his faith is saved, and his fulfillment of the laws of God consists in love.'[8] Fourthly, Spener called for a less polemical attitude towards persons who held other religious positions. Pure doctrine is important, he argued, but it is maintained, not by dispute and logical precision, but by repentance and holiness of life. As a result he proposed a restructuring of religious training in the universities, advising that the Aristotelian scholasticism of Protestant Orthodoxy be set to the side and more attention be given to holiness of life, prayer, meditative reading (among which he lists late medieval mystical compositions), catechetics, homiletics, and pastoral counselling.

Basic to Spener's proposals was a theology which required experiential verity at every point in the believer's life. The true believer, Spener and his Pietist colleagues held, will be convicted of his sinful state, repent, experience a new birth, and live in progressive devotion to God and love for neighbour. Under Spencer's disciple and colleague August Hermann Francke (1663-1727) the experience of sin and repentance (*Busse*) and of the new birth (*Wiedergeburt*) was emphasised. Francke played a leading role in diseminating Pietist ideas and at the University of Halle he created institutions in keeping with the Pietist vision: an orphanage, educational programs for young and old, hospital care, a printing press, a mission program, and social service work.

Pietist conventicles were soon found everywhere. In some locations, they received the help and approval of local pastors; in others they opposed the religious establishment of which they were initially a part and separated from the religious groups legitimated by the Treaty of Westphalia in 1648 (viz., Lutheranism, Calvinism, and Roman Catholicism). These Radical Pietists, as opposed to the Church Pietists who remained

loyal to the structures of their Lutheran or Calvinist parent
bodies, were as a result often persecuted as a 'fourth species of
religion'. Radical Pietists, chief among whom was Gottfried
Arnold (1666-1714), were much attracted to mystical, Quietist, and Boehmist ideas and often emphasised visionary and
other parapsychological experiences. Almost all radicals made
a clear division between the religious establishments (the members of which they associated with pharisees and hypocrites)
and the spiritual church of truly reborn believers who, directly
illuminated by the Holy Spirit, had no need to depend on the
dead letter of ritual, theological science, and canon law. Many
Radical Pietists fled to America where they flourished in the
religious tolerance of Pennsylvania in particular.

Antagonism to Pietism developed as rapidly as the movement
itself. Opponents saw it, particularly its tendency to separatism, subjectivism, and individualism, as destructive of Germany's socio-religious balance, a balance won only after the
horrors of the Thirty Years War and at the beginning of the
Pietist turmoil, maintained precariously for only twenty-five
years. Moreover, Pietism looked to its opponents like indiffer-
entism. Spener, for example, was much influenced by English
Puritan and continental Calvinist writers, did not speak out
clearly enough against the mystical spiritualism of Jacob Boehme (1575-1624) and his followers, had been in contact with
the separatist Jean de Labadie, and in his emphasis on the need
for christian holiness seemed to reject the central Lutheran
doctrine of forensic justification. The Pietist emphasis on repentance, assurance of new birth, and personal growth in holiness struck many theologians as supporting a concept of justification based on merit and as a rejection of Luther's *simul iustus
et peccator* paradox.

In spite of fierce opposition, however, the movement pros-
pered. An especially interesting development occurred when
Ludwig Nikolaus, Count von Zinzendorf (1700-1760), invited
the persecuted remnants of the former Hussite movement, the
Bohemian Brethren or Moravians, to his Saxon estates in the

1720s. There the Moravians were renewed on a Pietist model and spread to other areas of Germany, England, and the English colonies of Georgia and Pennsylvania. First in Georgia and later in London, John Wesley (1703-1791) came into contact with these Pietists and there and on a later trip to Germany was influenced by their theology.

In Württemburg, Pietism developed conventicles which have lasted to the twentieth century. These Pietists early manifested a particular interest in biblical study as witnessed by their most important representative, Johann Albrecht Bengel (1687-1752) and to a lesser extent by Friedrich Christoph Oetinger (1702-1782). By Oetinger's day, however, Pietism had begun to change. The early Pietists had stood in opposition to Protestant Scholasticism or Orthodoxy. By the late eighteenth-century, the Orthodox and the Pietists stood united against the Enlightenment at the same time as they incorporated those universalistic elements in Enlightenment thought which eventually led to Romanticism. It was Neo-Pietists, men such as Johann Caspar Lavatar (1741-1801) and Heinrich Jung-Stilling (1740-1817), who attracted authors as significant as Johann Wolfgang von Goethe and who laid the foundations for the nineteenth-century Pietist renewal in Germany.

The Problem of Definition

An historical outline of Pietism such as the one here presented makes the problems in its definition immediately evident. Where is one to date the beginning of the awakening? The publication of the *Pia desideria* can be precisely dated, but it was in its initial form an introduction to Arndt's sermons, and there is little in Pietism not already in Arndt's works and in the works of many other writers influenced by him. Moreover, Spener had already established the distinctive Pietist conventicles five years before the publication of the *Pia desideria*. Likewise it is difficult to ascertain when Pietism ends. The contemporary New Testament scholar, Ernest Käseman still finds it necessary to carry on dialogue with Pietism,[9] Pietist conventicles are still active in Germany, and the movement continues to shape Protestant development.

Nor can Pietism be geographically, linguistically, or denominationally defined. Spener was a Lutheran, but his program was actively pursued in Reformed and Radical Reformation circles. Pietism began in Germany, but had many followers in Scandinavia, Switzerland, the Netherlands, England, and America. Sociological definitions of the movement, even within its first half century are equally difficult. It is not always simple to distinguish separatist Pietists from those who remained loyal to a denomination, and the term 'Radical Pietism' is many times almost impossible to apply with accuracy. It is often difficult as well to distinguish between Pietists and other groups such as Boehmists, Philadelphians, Inspirationalists, and in some instances even Mennonites and Schwenkfelders. If such confusion arises over sociological definitions, it is not surprising that agreement is seldom reached on a proper theological definition of Pietism or on whether it is to be theologically defined at all.

Such problems are not modern. The earliest Pietists too were perplexed, as were their opponents. But what has made a definition, indeed a description, of Pietism most problematic for all students of the awakening is that, until very recently, it has almost always been discussed in a polemical setting. The bitter controversies of the eighteenth-century, particularly the attacks on Pietism by Lutheran Orthodox writers such as Valentine Ernest Loescher, have continued in some form to our own century. In the mid-nineteenth century, the question of Pietism was taken up by Albrecht Ritschl, the most important Lutheran theologian of his day. Unfortunately, Ritschl's three volume history of the movement (*Geschichte des Pietismus*) was a theological exercise under the guise of scientific history, but an exercise so impressive and powerful that most of its conclusions were accepted for almost a century.[10] In his 'Prolegomena' Ritschl associated Pietism with late medieval piety, particularly Franciscan piety, and with Anabaptism (then still interpreted by most historians under the adjective *schwär-merisch*, emphasised Pietism's mystical elements, its associations with Roman Catholic piety, and its attachment to Calvinism, and he attacked it from his Lutheran perspective accordingly. In many ways Ritschl was at the mercy of his sources. His knowledge of Anabaptism was based on the Swiss Reformer Heinrich Bullinger's attacks on it, and his association of Anabaptism with Pietism may have been influenced by his reading of Max Goebel's study of christian life in the Rhine-Westphalia area. Goebel's work was sympathetic to the Radical Reformation, Proto-Pietism, and Pietism, and tended to highlight mystical elements in these movements and to tie them to the spirituality of the late middle ages.[11]

The modern study of Pietism begins only after the second world war and most studies have appeared since the mid 1960s. The most important journal dedicated to the movement, *Pietismus und Neuzeit*, published its first volume in 1974. The journal has appeared under the direction of the 'Historical Commission for the study of Pietism'[12] which oversees as well a series of studies on the movement,[13] a bibliographic series, and a text series.[14] A central figure in the modern study of Pietism was Martin Schmidt, who insisted on a theological definition of Pietism and focussed attention on its Lutheran rather than its radical aspects.[15] The result has been that few studies of Radical Pietism have been undertaken. A second scholar deserving special attention is the American F. Ernst Stoeffler, who in two fine volumes, *The Rise of Evangelical Pietism* and *German Pietism in the Eighteenth-Century*, traced the sources of Pietism in the Calvinist, Puritan, and Lutheran traditions and outlined the development of the movement to the end of the eighteenth century.[16] Stoeffler's works have all the shortcomings of surveys and are to some degree encyclopedic in nature, but their value must not be underestimated and his work, which draws attention to and popularises the distinctiveness of Pietism in America, deserves special recognition.[17]

PIETISM, PROTESTANT SCHOLASTICISM, AND THE *Ordo Salutis*

A recent study of Pietism in Augsburg begins with the commonplace that the history of Pietism cannot be written for some years yet because of the amount of work still remaining to be done.[18] Any generalized comments regarding it are therefore ill-advised; as a result I have chosen to devote the remainder of this paper to one aspect of Pietist thought, namely Pietism's use of Protestant scholasticism as reflected in its use of the scholastic doctrine of the *ordo salutis* (order of salvation), and to conclude with some brief comments on other major areas of research into Pietism requiring closer attention.

The Pietist division between true reborn believers and dead, hypocritical mouthers of confessions tended after the Enlightenment attack on Orthodoxy and the Romantic affirmation of individual feeling to shape the way in which Pietists and others read Pietist history. Thus Pietists have been described by themselves and others as opposed to Protestant Orthodoxy or Scholasticism. The Pietists are thus seen as pastoral, the Orthodox as scholarly; the Pietists as practical and affective, the Orthodox as speculative; in most extreme descriptions, the Pietists as *Gottesgelehrten*, the Orthodox as *Schriftsgelehrten*. Radical Pietism in particular accentuated this division, which was then read back into Lutheran history. As a result, histories of Protestant Scholasticism and histories of Proto-Pietism were written.[19] But such a division is far too simplistic. Because of it Arndt is generally seen as the 'father of Pietism' and John Gerhard (1582-1637) as a scholastic, yet Gerhard supported Arndt when the latter was attacked. Moreover, there are strong theological ties from Arndt to Protestant Orthodoxy and from Orthodoxy to Pietism. It is therefore not surprising that Orthodoxy should have joined with Pietism at the end of the eighteenth century to oppose the Enlightenment, or that scholastic theologians such as David Hollaz (1648-1713) were already influenced by Pietism at the beginning of the century. The division between the two movements was not as precise as earlier writing suggests. A review of the Lutheran doctrine of the *unio mystica* (mystical union) within the framework of Lutheranism's theology of the application of redemptive grace to the believer (*ordo salutis*) makes this point even clearer.

Nineteenth and early twentieth-century Lutheranism rejected the mystical elements within the tradition, especially as those elements were manifested in Pietism, regarding them as the result of foreign influences from late medieval spirituality (brought in by Arndt) and of Spanish-Jesuit piety (introduced in prayer literature).[20] Against this tendency Werner Elert insisted that mystical terminology was not introduced into Lutheranism in the seventeenth-century, but was already present in Luther.[21] Later scholarship substantiated this claim, pointing to the way in which the three-fold mystical path had been 'democritised' prior to the sixteenth-century and how Luther made use of this democritisation.[22]

For Luther the three-fold path did not proceed from the purgative through the illuminative to the unitive life but, turned on its head, began with the unitive life. All descriptions of the union of the believer with God in earlier writings were, as a result, used by Luther to describe the gracious union of every believer with Christ through faith alone. *Exstasis* for him is the rapture of the mind into the clear *cognition of faith*[23] and *excessus* is the experience of being lifted up *in faith alone* into unity with God in Christ.[24] Once he established that the mystical union was a union in Christ by faith alone, Luther could go on to describe that union in terminology borrowed from the mystics. Every believer is united with Christ in such a way that the two are one as the bride and bridegroom are one. Luther speaks always within a forensic framework; the union is the result of God's declaration of justification accepted by faith. Any love which returns to God is psychological. It does not make the believer better or more deserving of merit; the believer remains always a sinner and yet justified.

Johann Arndt followed Luther's pattern but extended it by making more ample use of earlier mystical literature. Large

sections of his *True Christianity* are translations and paraphrases of Tauler, the *Theologia deutsch*, Angela of Foligno
and other mystics.[25] In the section of *True Christianity* entitled
'On the Union of the Believers with Christ their Head', Arndt
outlined in fourteen chapters an order by which the redemptive effects of the saving death and resurrection of Jesus are
applied in the life of the believer.[26] The first two describe the
believer's election, the third vocation, the fourth illumination,
the fifth conversion, the sixth regeneration and justification
(Arndt here treats repentance and faith), the seventh the mystical union of the believer with Christ, the eighth and nineth
renovation, the tenth preservation, and the fourteenth glorification.

This order, technically known as the *ordo salutis*, did not
remain solely within the so-called Proto-Pietist domain, but
was amplified by the Protestant Scholastics. Of the Lutheran
scholastic works treating the topic, the *Theologia Didactico-
Polemica* (1685) by Johann Andreas Quenstedt[27] is the most
exhaustive and best represents the culmination of orthodox
teaching on the subject of mystical union. Quenstedt initiates
his discussion of the *ordo* with a treatment of redemption, and
then outlines questions relating to the call, regeneration, and
conversion, before developing an article on justification. It is
only after this article that he treats penance and confession, the
unio mystica (the mystical union of the believer with Christ),
and renovation — changing, to a degree, Arndt's order. By
making regeneration precede conversion, and penitence grow
out of justification, Quenstedt is able to insist more strongly
that the process of salvation is totally God's work and man's
power has no part in it. Regeneration by the Spirit's guidance
leads to a quickening, a conversion. Penitence is possible only
for those who are justified in Christ and thereby know their
shortcomings; it is, therefore, closely related to renovation.[28]

In addition, Quenstedt points out that the whole process occurs in a moment (*in instantu*), in a mathematical point of time,
from God's point of view.[29] All parts of the *ordo* are bound to-

gether in the act of faith, the agent by which Christ's merits are ascribed to man. From man's point of view, however, the *unio* can be seen as growing out of justification. This union can be understood in two ways. It can refer to that general union of man in creation, but in the *ordo* it is understood as a special union generously given to be fully enjoyed in glory. It is a spiritual union, as distinguished from a carnal union, and one of substances, but not a substantial union. It is initiated by the entire Trinity, its instrumental cause is the word and sacraments, its medium the faith of the believer.

Just as, from man's point of view, the *unio mystica* grows out of justification, so renovation rises from the union.[30] Elsewhere in his work, Quenstedt outlines the exact relationship between renovation and this union,[31] but in no way does he allow for the possibility of growth toward a union in love of God on the part of the *viator*. For Quenstedt, renovation is dependent on the co-operation of man, *justus* indeed — and thereby able to play a role in such renewal — but always *peccator*.

The movement from Arndt as a 'Proto-Pietist' to Quenstedt as a 'scholastic' continues in the work of, among others, the radical Pietist Gottfried Arnold[32] who had studied under Quenstedt. Early in his career, Arnold wrote a large study of the early Church entitled *Die Erste Liebe*.[33] According to the title, the volume was intended as a true portrayal of the practical faith and life of the first Christians according to the authentic documents of the period, and was written to call Christians back to their forsaken first love (Revelation 2:4), the love manifested prior to the Constantinian decline. The work was written as an aid to those reborn Christians who wished to understand God's will for the Church. The clearest indications of the concerns of that will are found in those persecuted and suffering witnesses to the truth (*Zeugen der Wahrheit*) in the early Church and thereafter. They are to serve as models for all christian endeavours. The reader of history, Arnold contends, must be open to the leading of the Spirit in his interpretation of the texts, for it is the divine which is working in history and it is the divine, as a result, which is the best guide to history's meaning.[34]

A cursory reading of Arnold's study suggests that it is opposed to scholastic Orthodoxy in every way. It upholds history against philosophic theology, opposes systematisation of christian experiential faith, and requires practical love and holiness along side of and, to some degree, above true faith. A closer look, however, indicates that Arnold is still working within the theological structures established by his teacher Quenstedt. Book One of *Die Erste Liebe*, although intended as a presentation of early christian theology, is based on the Lutheran *ordo salutis*, and the thought of the book is invigorated by direct contact with the works of Johann Arndt. The argument of this first book is carefully outlined. It progresses through two major movements, the first of which is recapitulated and more deeply developed in the second. The first is primarily concerned with establishing the general progression of the *ordo* according to its external manifestations; the second treats of inner spiritual change and growth. Two final sections comprise a third movement; each reviews the *ordo* once more, adding depth and breadth according to their differing emphases, the renewal of God's image in man, and the union of man and God in love.

Arnold begins the first section of his argument in proper Lutheran fashion with a statement on God's call to sinful man. Faith comes through preaching which announces the word of grace in Christ and directs man to turn from self and the world to God (*vocatio*). Illumination by the Holy Spirit follows; this gives knowledge of sin, and the punishment necessitated by God's law. The result is that past wrongs are admitted and rejected (conversio), and a new regenerated life is undertaken by that faith in Christ which justifies man and leads him to knowledge and certainty of the mercy of God. All this is solely a gift of God for which man merits nothing. Renovation of life follows upon this changed attitude; sin is hated and truth is sought without hypocrisy. Renovation is experienced by the Christian within the christian community to which he is led by the Holy Spirit. It grows out of a mystical union of the believer with Christ, understood in the first instance, as in Luther and Arndt, as a union into his body, the church, through baptism. Like his predecessors, Arnold insists that the union is directed toward God in love.[35]

Having thus presented the general pattern of redemption portrayed, as he believed, in the primitive church, Arnold returns to an earlier stage of the redemptive process according to the Luther *ordo*, the stage of illumination, and begins to work through the *ordo salutis* again, this time in greater detail, placing the emphasis more directly on the inner man, rather than on the external manifestations in inner change that he chronicled in the first section of his work. Under the topic illumination, he calls his reader's attention to this change of emphasis, noting the role of the inner spiritual voice which will continue in the believer to his death. This inner voice he opposes to the outer dead letter, but in proper fashion he also indicates the necessary use of the outer word of Scripture.[36]

A discussion of the new birth (*Wiedergeburt, conversio*) follows, as expected, the treatment of illumination. The new birth is the *sine qua non* of christian life, a supernatural act worked solely by the divine to the increase of a holy life and the renewal of the image of God in man (*regeneratio*). Borrowing heavily from Arndt, Arnold developed the latter's teaching within a three-fold anthropology. A Christian is body, soul, and spirit. The spirit is God's gift, His image and likeness received in faith (*justificatio*). It is through this spirit that the image of God is renewed at conversion, and it is toward the fulfilment of that image that the soul is directed for final perfect renewal in heaven.[37]

Through the spirit as well, man is made like the angels and united with God (*unio mystica*). Man thus becomes a participant in the very nature of God, but pantheism is avoided:

> This communion with God [the early Christians] considered high and powerful, but they had no thoughts of de-

fining the new birth as a divinisation in the purest sense
from 2 Peter 1:4. They did not believe that man became
God in his nature when he was renewed to the image of
God . . . . 'He who clings to God is one spirit with Him;
this occurs when man is swallowed up in faith . . .' This
and similar passages the ancients made use of to explain
their understanding not of a change into the divine being
but a divine illumination or enlightenment, the goal of the
divine mystery through which man comes near to God and
is divinised.[38]

In such participation man receives the gifts of the Spirit, chief
among which is faith. Arndt's emphasis on the fruits of faith
as love for God and neighbour and patient endurance, preserved in hope for a blessed eternity then follows.[39]

In this second development of his theme, Arnold has made
use of the scholastic teaching on the union of the major stages
in the *ordo* 'in one moment of time.' The believer by faith is
reborn and regenerated; he is renewed toward the image of
God and united with the divine. He is complete in this new
birth 'in a moment of time' in that he knows and loves his
Maker, but such love naturally seeks its object; in a renewed
life, a pious walk according to the teachings and example of
Jesus, obedience to God's will and law, and the shunning of sin,
it progresses to ultimate perfection lived out in full love, trust,
hope, humility, and praise toward God, both here, and finally
and completely in glory.[40]

Faith is for Arnold an act which progresses experientially in
love from the time of the new birth through to its completion,
full renovation, and perfect union.

> [The early Christians] knew that human nature, even in
> its sinfulness always desires something upon which it can
> cast its love; that the heart moves according to certain
> stirrings and affections; that one desire always overcomes
> another and one grows out of another. After they had
> known the true and only life-giving source in their en-
> lightenment and had begun to enjoy it, the love and incli-
> nation of their spirit had to rest in that source and become

> a true piece and witness of true Christianity. Love for God was, for them, a living being in the soul which joined together two things in the closest way . . . namely the loving heart of the child and the loving Father in heaven.[41]

Such love gains its end only in heaven, but it can achieve ecstatic insights while on earth, although its ultimate goal here is peace and joy in the Holy Spirit.

> He who has reached a high grade of love, discovers that the Lord's promises were true for those who loved Him, those whom He yet at this time fills according to His wisdom. He will be overcome and almost drunken, indeed, swallowed up and imprisoned in another world as if it were not able any longer to know his own nature.[42]

With this emphasis, Arnold was able to uphold a strongly mystical approach. His approach, however, was always stated in terms of incomplete or complete love for God in Christ. In his system, as in Arndt's and Luther's before him, mystical union was for those in whom Christ dwelt and who dwelt in him by faith; it defined, in fact, only that indwelling. It was marked by the fruits of faith and was completed in heaven whither Christians were drawn as chaste brides of Christ.[43]

The doctrine of the *ordo salutis* and the *unio mystica* is only one among many topics which Pietists like Arnold learned from their scholastic forebearers and which the scholastics shared with their 'Proto-Pietist' contemporaries. A full study of the Orthodox concern with *praxis*, both in devotion and social action remains to be done, but preliminary investigations in this area indicate that the Orthodox were not purely intellectual and solely speculative as the later Pietist offensive claimed.[44] Moreover, there remains much work to be completed on the Pietist influence on later scholastics. An interesting comparison can be drawn, for example, between Arndt's early description of the *ordo salutis* and the scholastic outline of it maintained by David Hollaz. Nor is it surprising that Hollaz's *Evangelische Gnaden-Ordnung* was popular among Pietists.[45] Its sub-title makes clear the reason why, entitled as it is 'How a soul is brought down from its own righteousness and piety to an understanding of its sinful misery, is led to the miraculous sweetness of Jesus and comes by faith to forgiveness of sins and a pious life? When one realises that seventeenth-century Lutheranism was not as stratified and divided as has sometimes been suggested, later Lutheran attraction to Jacob Boehme and Spener's and other Pietist's defenses of the Görlitz shoemaker become clearer. Elsewhere I have attempted to show how Boehme's thought can, in part, be interpreted within traditional Lutheran theology and need not be reduced solely to Paracelsean, kabbalistic, and mystical spiritualist categories.[46]

SOME FURTHER AREAS FOR STUDY

Basic for the study of any religious group or movement are bibliographic guides, dependable editions, and textual and philological-literary studies of primary sources. For students of Pietism they are still badly needed. *Die Historische Kommission zur Erforschung des Pietismus* in 1972 published a register to the works of the Württemberg Pietists in the sixteenth and seventeenth-centuries as the first volume of its *Bibliographie zur Geschichte des Pietismus*, but no further volumes have at present been announced.[47] A complete bibliographical listing of Spener's and Francke's works will apparently be available only along with the critical editions of their writings, now in progress.[48] Lesser figures are even more poorly served, and this shortcoming often hinders a proper interpretation of their thought. One example, of special interest to students of spirituality, indicates this clearly. In 1732 a Palatinate baker, weaver, and pastor, Johann Conrad Beissel, moved to the wilderness area some six miles north of present Lancaster, Pennsylvania, and in a very short time established there the most significant Pietist monastery, the Ephrata Cloister. From 1732 to its closing in 1812 the Cloister housed at times up to three hundred celibates, male and female, attracted a number of married associates, was visited by major religious and political figures, developed a distinctive art and musical theory (discussed in Thomas Mann's

Dr Faustus), pursued an active printing program (over eighty titles were published), maintained the art of manuscript illumination, and encouraged the composition of theological treatises, devotional writings, and hymns.[49] A daughter house, Snowhill, near Quincy, Pennsylvania, existed until the last celibate died there in 1896. The study of Ephrata is important for students of Pietism because the movement arose out of the separatist Pietist community of the Schwarzenau Brethren (now the Church of the Brethren) and because its attachment to Boehmism, Inspirationalism and Anabaptism as well as to the Reformed Church helps us to understand the theological, not to mention the sociological, dynamics involved in the awakening. Moreover, Ephrata offers good insights into Pietism in America, its hopes, ideals, and developing relationships to the American political and social vision. The significance of Ephrata spirituality in its own right as well as with study and understanding of Pietism has often been noted, but almost all studies of the Cloister to present have been carried out by persons interested in colonial American, particularly 'Pennsylvania Dutch', folklife. As a result, discussions of Ephrata's theology are often neglected or its theology is read in light of nineteenth-century developments in American religion. Seldom have studies of Ephrata spirituality been based on a full study of the texts available, for despite the fact that Ephrata was important enough to deserve an article in the English translation of Voltaire's *Philosophical Dictionary*[50] and that its second Prior Peter Miller was an active and respected member of the American Philosophical Association, it was not until 1944 that a bibliography of works printed at Ephrata appeared (a bibliography now long out of date), and no full list of Ephrata manuscripts has been completed. How important such a bibliography could be for the study of Ephrata is indicated by the work of Guy T. Hollyday who in the summer of 1970 completed a preliminary list of Ephrata music manuscripts alone; at that time he had located over fifty completed codices.[51] The 'nunnery' at Snowhill still contains many manuscript letters and

hymns as well as printed books; how much material in addition
to this remains in the possession of the last remaining married
members of the community is not known.[52]

Contemporary technological developments in microprint
and bibliographic information services make it possible to study
a community like Ephrata and other colonial American Pietist
groups as never before. Since the American Antiquarian Society's (Worcester, Massachusetts) publication on microcard
of all books printed in America prior to 1800, any student almost anywhere in the world can take up rare Ephrata texts
without entering the state of Pennsylvania. Any supporting
materials required a student can locate quickly enough in most
cases in the *National Union Catalogue* (Pre 1956 imprints) and
obtain in microform from the institution listed. Since so many
Pietists from so many denominations came to America in the
eighteenth-century, it is not surprising that a student is seldom
disappointed in his search for books on this continent. But at
the point modern technological advances are at their best, they
are also at their worst. So much trust do we put in such systems
that when a microcard simply prints under the title of a work
an eighteenth-century publisher's advertisement for that work
(meaning that the work has not been located), it is too often
taken for granted that the piece is irretrievably lost. For students of Pietism, such a supposition need not be accepted.
Many extremely popular Pietist works did not find their way
into public institutions (The National Union Catalogue list-
ings for Starck's *Gebetbuch* give no indication of that work's
popularity[53]) and many remain in private or small and still not
fully catalogued public collections.[54] Thus, for a century,
students of Gottfried Arnold maintained that his work on the
speech of angels (a work of importance for understanding his
later mystical theology) was lost; a letter to libraries near the
city in which he lived resulted in the discovery of a copy of
the 'lost' work.[55]

Next to the location and complete listing of Pietist books *and*
manuscripts (it is too often forgotten by students of post-six-

teenth-century theology that the manuscript culture is still with us), there remains a great need for accurate critical editions of Pietist writings. The willingness of publishers to print facsimile editions is praiseworthy (although the texts themselves are often much less expensive if simply photocopied in some form), but it is based often on the premise that Pietist writings are 'wild' texts, that is, that authors then were popularizers and not careful thinkers or scholars. To some degree this premise is true, but when it is, the need for a critical annotated edition is greater than before, particularly for those Pietists who borrowed freely from other spiritual authors. In this latter case, if one knows exactly how the Pietist author consciously or unconsciously altered his original text, one can gain fuller insights into the author's spiritual orientation. The appearance of a work in facsimile tends to discourage a critical edition of the same work and to fix the opinion that any further textual or source study is of little use. Fortunately, within the last five years a series *Texte zur Geschichte des Pietismus* has been established and now includes important works by Francke and Oetinger even though some of these have appeared or are announced to appear in facsimilie editions.[56]

Discussions regarding the sources of Pietism touch four areas in addition to the question of the relationship between Protestant Orthodoxy and Pietism already briefly considered. There remain the questions of the influence of late medieval mysticism, of seventeenth-century Quietism, of the Reformed Church, and of the Radical Reformation. A more detailed discussion of the first two I leave for the paper to follow. Our understanding of the impact of the Reformed Church (in its English Puritan, Dutch Pietistic Calvinist, and German Reformed Pietist forms) has been aided by the work of Stoeffler and the biographical study of the early Spener by Johannes Wallman.[57]

What ties are there between the disparate groups of the Radical Reformation (particularly the Anabaptists [Mennonites] and the Schwenkfelders) and the Pietists? The question is troubled by many historiographical and theological difficulties, not the least of which are a continuing controversy over a proper definition of Anabaptist and Mennonite, and the problem of describing adequately the so-called Radical Reformation or groups within it such as the Schwenkfelders who deliberately rejected definition.[58] Simply because Ritschl was opposed to Pietists and was partially pleased to attack them by association with Anabaptism does not mean that his suggestion that the two groups have morphological ties is to be rejected out of hand. Furthermore, every study which takes up the question of Anabaptism-Pietism must beware of entrapment by the impressive work of Robert Friedmann, *Mennonite Piety Through the Centuries*,[59] a series of papers which, however valuable they are for documenting the Mennonites' use of Pietism and Pietism's entrance into that tradition, must always be read with a clear view of Friedmann's implicit thesis: Pietism corrupted the purity of the Anabaptist vision and must be distinctly separated from that vision. As regards Schwenkfelder Pietist ties, the problems are of yet another order. There are many morphological similarities between Schwenkfeld's spirituality and the Pietist program and Schwenkfelders were closely tied to Lutheran Pietism from the beginning. Indeed, one could claim that the Schwenkfelder renewal in the late seventeenth-century is directly related to the impact of Pietism on its members. It is not surprising that when they came under persecution in 1719 the Schwenkfelders fled to Görlitz, particularly to the Pietist Lutheran Church of Melchior Schöffer, and to the estates of the Lutheran Pietist Count Zinzendorf.[60]

But the need for research and study on all these questions concerning Pietism's sources defines only one area of research yet to be done. Many thematic studies must be undertaken, not the least of which is a proper description of Pietist eschatology. Spener's *Pia desideria* was written in what he called 'a hope for better times'. He expected that the Protestant Church, persecuted by Catholic Babel, would reform and then face a new millenial age. His program was developed with this eschatological context and it is within this context that one can interpret the social action programs of Halle, Pietist missionary zeal, its attraction to visionary and mystical literature, and its interest in utopian projects.[61] An interesting study could as well be done on Pietist hermeneutics and biblical studies from within this context. Bengel, so often noted for his careful 'scientific' biblical studies was also deeply involved in eschatological speculation,[62] as were the radical Inspirationalists at Berleberg who completed an eight volume folio edition of the Bible which included their own translation and mystical commentary.[63] The use of this Bible not only among Pietists but also among many other German-speaking groups still remains to be studied, as does the hermeneutical theory of Oetinger (his *Inquisitio* has recently been reprinted with a stimulating introduction by Hans Georg Gadamer).[64] For persons interested in England and the English-speaking Americas such studies will almost certainly alter our view of the early work of the Society for the Promotion of the Gospel and the Society for the Promotion of Christian Knowledge.

Pietism's importance in German literature and language is likewise to be reviewed. We have available an excellent study of Pietism's effect on German language, particularly on German vocabulary,[65] but almost unstudied is its relation to and reshaping of baroque poetry, the genres of the biography, autobiography, and personal journal as well as the literary impact on historiography and historical themes (in particular the theme of the Constantinian fall of the Church). It will be some years before we can ascertain fully Pietism's importance for German philosophy and later theology. Kant, Goethe, Schelling, Hegel, Novals, Schleiermacher, and Kierkegaard were all in some way affected by the movement.[66] Tillich studied under Martin Kähler at Halle, where Pietism was still strong, and Barth's early work is in dialogue with Pietism.[67] Only after such questions are treated will we be able to ascertain properly Pietism's sociological impact in Germany and through its English-speaking descendants in America. Then perhaps we can begin to understand what its role was in generating and supporting a sense of social duty so strong that the love it required for God and fellow man could with seeming ease be transferred to national idols and chauvinistic ideals.[68]

PETER C. ERB

Wilfrid Laurier University
Waterloo, Ontario

THE MEDIEVAL SOURCES OF PIETISM:
A CASE STUDY

THERE IS A POPULAR APPROACH to Pietism, now over a century old, which links the movement closely to Roman Catholic sources. It notes the many pietist uses of medieval or seventeenth-century Catholic texts, particularly mystical and quietist texts, suggests that this use is the result of Pietism's predisposition to Catholic theology, and then either, negatively, attacks it as rejecting the protestant principle of justification by grace through faith alone or, positively, praises it for initiating ecumenical dialogue.[1]

To analyse the merits and problems of such approaches for the pietist movement as a whole is impossible in so short a paper as this and perhaps beyond the limits of the present state of pietist studies. A beginning can be made, however, by discussing the use of medieval texts in the work of one representative Pietist. Among pietist students of medieval, sixteenth, and seventeenth-century Catholic writings, the most significant was the Lutheran historian, poet, theologian, and pastor, Gottfried Arnold (1666-1714).[2] Arnold, rather than another Pietist, has been chosen for several reasons. He was by far the most learned of all the Pietists and of all of them made the most extensive use of Roman Catholic writings. This fact has seldom been appreciated, attention having been earlier devoted to Arnold's patristic and protestant studies.[3] Moreover, with the exception of Spener and Francke, Arnold was the most influential of the first generation pietist 'theologians' and was the most influential author in establishing a pietist historiography. In addition, Arnold, unlike any other writer of his day, best reflects both conservative and radical wings within the pietist awakening.

GOTTFRIED ARNOLD: A BRIEF BIOGRAPHY

An outline of Arnold's career can be briefly given. Born in Annaberg, Saxony in 1666, he attended the university of Wittenberg, and on graduating in 1689, he obtained a position as tutor in Dresden. There he was in close contact with the conventicle of Philipp Jakob Spener. A man of precise piety, Arnold soon found himself in conflict with less meticulous believers. When an opportunity arose to take a position at Quedlinburg, he moved.

The Quedlinburg to which Arnold came in 1693 was, and for some years would remain, the centre of religious radicalism. In this milieu Arnold wrote and edited his first books on church history. Of these the most important was *Die Erste Liebe* (1696), an immediately popular portrayal of the thought and life of the early Church. In 1697 Arnold was invited to teach history at Giessen, but one year later, disillusioned with the university, he resigned his position and returned to Quedlinburg. His resignation was followed by the publication of his *Unparteiische Kirchen-und Ketzer-Historie* (1699-1700) in which he developed the theory of the Constantinian fall of the church and maintained that in many cases in history the true Church was represented by those pious, reborn Christians who were attacked as heretics, and that the heretics were in fact those members of the established church who demanded precise doctrinal agreement and persecuted all who did not conform in every detail. What offended Arnold's contemporaries were not only the principles of his *Historie*, but the associated facts of his career at the time. In a defense of his resignation from the university, he had harshly attacked the institutional Church, and in the same year as the *Unparteiische Kirchen-und Ketzer-Historie* was printed, *Das Geheimnis der göttlichen Sophia* appeared, seemingly upholding a radical Boehmism which disparaged the established church and taught a perfectionism so extreme as to counsel a return to the pure celibate life of Edenic Adam. The controversy raged for two years and then, in September 1701, Arnold accepted a position as a court preacher in Alstedt and married. If his resignation from Gießen ended the first major period of his life, the second ends with his marriage. During the third period, from 1701 to his death in 1714, Arnold dedicated himself to his pastoral work, and continued publications which by his death numbered over fifty titles.

Among Arnold's works were many editions and translations of Roman Catholic authors. These included the complete works of Ruusbroec (1701), Angelus Silesius' *Cherubinischer Wandersmann* (1701, 1713), the letters of Cardinal Petrucci (1702), the *Confessio amantis* of Gertrude More (1702), the *Spiritual Guide* of Molinos (1699, 1712, 1713), selections from Madame Guyon's works (1701, 1707), and the works of Thomas à Kempis (1712). Three editions of the Macarian homilies appeared in Arnold's life (1697, 1699, 1702), and from 1700 to 1701 he published a collection of letters, *Auserlesene Sendschreiben*, and edited the *Vitae Patrum* and a collection of biographies, *Das Leben der Gläubigen*, which introduced German Protestant readers to many patristic and medieval authors and to John of the Cross, Teresa of Avila, Jeanne-Françoise de Chantal and Brother Lawrence of the Resurrection. In 1702 Arnold's *History of Mystical Theology*, heavily indebted to the work of Pierre Poret (d. 1719), appeared in both Latin and German.[4]

Arnold's Early Use of Medieval Texts

Very few references to medieval authors appear in Arnold's works prior to his *Unparteiische Kirchen-und Ketzer-Historie*, and these are to Bernard of Clairvaux;[5] the medieval section of that work is very weak.[6] In his discussion of the thirteenth and fourteenth centuries, for example, medieval spiritual authors are only briefly listed. Only the sermons of Tauler, the *Theologia deutsch*, and the *Imitatio Christi* does he seem to have known at first hand. His treatment otherwise depended on

secondary sources and was shaped by his perceived opposition
between the truly reborn mystical writers and the hypocritical
scholastics; thus, Bonaventure is treated with Aquinas as a
'wretched' (*elende*) scholastic.[7]

The next significant work printed by Arnold in which medieval authors play a role is his *Poetische Lob-und Liebes-Sprüche*
of 1700. Much of this collection of poetry is based on an earlier
work by the Strassburg Schwenckfelder Daniel Sudermann (d.
1631).[8] Sudermann made extensive use of medieval spiritual
authors in his work and provided for his poems a lengthy series
of notes which quoted fourteenth-century German mystics and
which were reprinted by Arnold.

From 1700 on Arnold's use of medieval authors increased.
His *Auserlesene Sendschreiben* contained German selections
from Ruusbroec, Suso, and Thomas à Kempis.[9] His *Vitae
Patrum* included short biographies of Bernard of Clairvaux and
Thomas Aquinas, a reprint of the German edition of the *Meis-
terbuch*, a German translation of Pomerius' life of Ruusbroec,
and the à Kempis lives of Gerard Groote, Florentius, and Arnold of Schoonhoven.[10] His *Leben der Gläubigen* included
biographies of Angela of Foligno and Nicolas von der Flüe;
printed and ascribed to Flüe was Eckhart's *Von Abgeschiedenheit*.[11]

Each of the articles in Arnold's *Historie und Beschreibung
der Mystischen Theologie*[12] provide brief biographical information on an author, a list of his works, and in some cases earlier
positive judgements. Almost no information is provided on
either spiritual or intellectual relationships between authors. Of
twelfth-century writers, Bernard of Clairvaux receives the
fullest treatment, but discussion does not extend beyond bibliographic information and the quotation of earlier judgements
regarding his work.

Some attempt was made to indicate the existence of a cistercian school by listing in order the major disciples of Bernard.
Arnold knew some of William of St Thierry's works and may
have seen the sermons of Guerric of Igny, but his knowledge

of them seems to have come through Johann Bona (1609-1674), as did his knowledge of Aelred of Rievaulx. Arnold's attempt to draw the cistercian authors of the twelfth century together into a school fails, in that he used the designation 'friend of Bernard' to describe all the cistercians and Hugh and Richard of St Victor as well. Anselm is treated more carefully, and Hildegard of Bingen noted.

Arnold's chapter on the thirteenth century is the briefest, and most of it is devoted to Bonaventure, whose significance was by this time clear to Arnold. How closely he knew Bonaventure's work is difficult to say. His lengthy list of the great Franciscan's compositions is taken from Maximillian Sandaeus' (1578-1656) *Theologia Mystica*,[13] which Arnold consulted at numerous places. Albert the Great and Thomas Aquinas receive brief treatments. Gertrude the Great and Mechthild of Hackeborn are mistakenly discussed under the fourteenth-century rubric, and Angela of Foligno is listed as a sixteenth-century writer.

Suso is the first major fourteenth-century author listed and praised. Arnold was acquainted with the Anselm Hoffmann translation of Surius' Latin translations and believed as a result that the *Book of the Nine Rocks* was by Suso. Arnold's knowledge of Eckhart was, and remained, scanty. He knew only the scattered texts in the Tauler edition which went under Eckhart's name and therefore spent little time discussing him. Tauler and Ruusbroec received his fullest attention. The work of the Strassburg Dominican was known to Arnold in numerous editions. He accepted without question the authenticity of the *Nachfolgung des armen Lebens Christi*, the *Medulla Animae*, the meditations on the life and passion of Christ, and the book on inner contemplation. In the list of judgements on Tauler, he made some attempt to step beyond his normal process of quoting general praises for the life and doctrine of a mystic, but even in this case he made no comment on the writer's theology beyond a brief statement that the Dominican taught that a believer should advance in the christian life.

With Ruusbroec the case is similar. The Dutch mystic's works are listed as they appear in the 1692 Cologne edition of Surius' translation. Reference is made to the Pomerius life as printed in the *Leben der Alt-Väter*, but, surprisingly, no indication of the 1701 translation is to be found. In describing Ruusbroec's theology, Arnold added to his earlier notes concerning Tauler only that Ruusbroec's teaching was directly inspired by God, that its depth and difficulty is not to be a cause for its rejection, that Ruusbroec spoke against the corruption of the clergy, loved meditation on the name of Jesus, as did Tauler, and that he had taught the truth as understood by the protestant tradition before the rise of Protestantism.[14] A short section is devoted to Gerhard Zutphen, and a very short note is included on Gerhard Groote. Fuller discussions are given of Catherine of Siena and of Bridget of Sweden.

The articles on fifteenth-century authors are longer than others in the volume, but this is in keeping with the extent of writing done by many of the writers of that period whom Arnold includes. Sixty works, for example, are ascribed to Gerson from the 1606 Paris edition of his works. The *Imitatio Christi* is not his, Arnold adds; the spiritually-enlightened reader, it is his contention, will be aware that the style and spirit of the *Imitatio* is very similar to that displayed in the works of Thomas à Kempis which are listed in full as they appear in the 1680 Cologne edition. The *Imitatio's* value, he believed, is testified to both by its popularity — it was translated into numerous languages — and by the love many Catholics and Protestants had for it. Controversy has also raged over the authorship and value of the *Theologia deutsch*, Arnold notes, but in this case, as well, the popularity of the work among spiritually astute readers sets all questions regarding its value at rest for him. Briefer studies are devoted to other fifteenth-century spiritual writers: Laurence Guistiani, Catherine of Bologna, Denis the Carthusian, John of Schonhoven, Harphius, and Savonarola. For information on Nicolas of Flüe, Arnold refers his reader to the *Leben der Altväter* [sic].

ARNOLD'S CONCEPT OF MYSTICAL UNION:
HIS LATER USE OF MEDIEVAL MYSTICS

By 1703, Arnold had gained a good knowledge of late medieval spirituality. The importance this knowledge was to have for his work during the highly productive last ten years of his life can be especially noted in his most significant theological study, the *Wahre Abbildung des Inwendigen Christentums*, published in 1709.[15]

Arnold's spirituality is to be studied as that of a man of faith seeking ever deeper understanding of the mystery of his faith-union with Christ. Understanding that union's nature, he believed, would lead to an ecstatic mystical experience of love for the One who had initially wrought the union, and understanding its operation would bring the believer to a knowledge of God's will for himself and for the Church.

All examples of believers who had experienced such union in the past may be studied, Arnold stated. The enlightened reader need have no fear of papal teaching, for the Spirit within the believer will testify to the truth in earlier writings. In addition, many Protestants have testified to the value of medieval and Roman Catholic authors. Although Scripture is the final judge of all religious experience, medieval and Catholic writers may serve as a mirror in which true and false Christianity may be reflected.

As the source and end of all spirituality, the Trinity leads man to consider his creation, primal state, and fall. By meditation on the heights of his glorious origin, the believer comes to understand better the depth of his fall, and the possibilities open to him in Christ. Man's dignity is based on the nature of man's soul, the breath of God in man. Toward this breath man must turn.[16] Arnold rejects all pantheistic overtones. The soul is the breath of God, not a part of his being; it is mutable, whereas He is immutable. Ruusbroec in particular was a help to Arnold in making this distinction between God and creatures.[17]

It is in this context that Arnold discusses the spark of the soul, the *füncklein*, a term he borrows directly from the medieval mystics. Man was created to develop the Trinitarian ground or spark in himself. In his original Edenic state man was, Arnold believed, like the angels: he was filled with divine wisdom, holiness, freedom, balance (of 'temperatures' — Arnold is here making use of Boehmist imagery), and was lord of all, but his memory, understanding, and will turned from the divine to consider the confusion about him. Now fallen he cannot find peace until he turns back toward life and lives once again in it. Arnold made use of medieval authors in his discussion of the results of the fall, first among which is the loss of the divine image. Loss is not the best word in this case, Arnold admits, although he is willing to use it; better words would be 'suppressed', 'narrowed', 'covered', or 'darkened', for the spark cannot be lost. It is, he writes, quoting a Taulerian sermon, so deeply impressed upon the soul that it can in no way be extinguished;[18] God's likeness, on the other hand, is the fullness of light toward which the spark is directed, and it is this which is lost in the fall.

Arnold's discussion of the Edenic state and man's fall from it raises two problems which cause major difficulty in the interpretation of Arnold's work. One of these concerns the nature of his anthropology. Does not emphasis on the spark of the divine in man, matched with his call for radical moral change, suggest a positive view of man out of keeping with the words of the Lutheran *Formula of Concord* on this point?[19] Secondly, does Arnold not at times support a synergism unacceptable within the Lutheran framework? Central to the consideration of either of these questions is a review of Arnold's concept of the nature and method of theology. Neither question — that of anthropology or that of free will — is treated by him outside the context of faith. In Arnold's view, true theology is faith in the guise of another discipline, be that discipline history, literary criticism, or philosophy. All theological discussion, in his opinion, is intended for the believer, the newborn enlightened Christian whose faith searches for greater understanding of theological mysteries so as to embody itself in the world in both a practical and a speculative way.[20]

All discussions of the original state of man are intended for the believer, the Christian who has experienced repentance for past sins and the new birth. Extensive treatment of man's perfect Edenic state is to inspire the man of faith to direct his steps toward the full perfection of that state of thankfulness and hope. Arnold never considered the possibility of such a return simplistically. Man's total corruption is emphasized in a typical Lutheran fashion, to avoid any sense of an overly easy solution and to increase man's sense of gratitude for redemption.

Arnold's use of the concept of the spark of the soul is to be understood similarly. Not defined as a material part of man, the spark is understood by him as a mark of original perfection and as a continual reminder of man's proper direction. The passages referring to this spark in Arnold are not directed to questions of man's essence but to questions of his orientation. The *Theologia deutsch* in particular is called upon to support this contention.[21] Like Luther, Arnold insisted that the will of man is bound, and accordingly he upheld the necessity of grace in Christ for human redemption. Through the Spirit's work in him, a believer can know, Arnold insisted, quoting Ruusbroec, that he is called to be a child of God.[22] Despite this emphasis on the bound will, however, Arnold did uphold, in a paradoxical manner, the free will of man. The Spirit will work, he wrote, quoting Ruusbroec and others, only in an obedient, pure heart which desires the Spirit's gift.[23] As they stand Arnold's words seem to be out of keeping with those of the *Formula of Concord* which discuss the free will.[24]

Arnold's statements are not, however, to be read outside his Lutheran context. Arnold was no Pelagian; when he comments on free will his purpose is purely pastoral, as is that of the *Formula of Concord* in its discussion of God's election.[25] Arnold did not intend to suggest that by purifying one's intentions one may attain to salvation; he meant to point out only that God is not unjust in his condemnation of the unrighteous.

It is all too easy to misinterpret Arnold's position on the doctrine of grace because of his near refusal to clarify terms. Arnold was certainly aware of the *Formula of Concord's* distinction between the nature of free will in fallen man and that in
regenerated man,[26] but he took this for granted in the *Wahre
Abbildung*, rather than explain it fully. Regenerated man is expected, according to Lutheran Pietist doctrine, to use his free
will to grow in grace, to employ the third use of the law.[27]
When discussing free will and grace in the redeemed man,
Arnold placed emphasis on the free will to a degree which, if
he had been discussing the same question in relation to fallen
man, would be heretical. In the seventh chapter of the *Wahre
Abbildung* for example, Arnold examines the role of the Holy
Spirit in the conversion of fallen man. As we have already
noted, he insists on the necessity of the Spirit for fallen man's
redemption. All discussions of man's preparation, the strength
of his free will, and the value of his activity occur after this
section, indicating that they are not to be understood in any
way as causal factors in man's salvation.[28]

God's election is made operative, writes Arnold, following
the traditional Lutheran *ordo salutis*, in his calling (*vocatio*) of
the sinner through the words of Scripture and of the preacher.
The call makes effectual the sinner's knowledge of Law and
Gospel. What the redeemed sinner discovers is the inevitable
conflict between his desire to live according to the new demands of Law and Gospel and his attraction to the carnal ways
of the flesh. The spiritual and physical trials accompanying
this dual attraction are all characterized by the term *Anfech-
tungen;* to describe these the Taulerian writings in particular
are used.[29] References to medieval authors on guidance in spiritual trial are surprisingly few; whereas Luther noted Gerson
regularly on the topic, Arnold makes no reference to him whatever.

God's election and call of the sinner to a holy life is continued
in His illumination (*illuminatio*) of the chosen soul through the
Holy Spirit. It is the Spirit which prays in such a soul and pro-

duces the fruit of that prayer. The prayer of the Spirit is an ever present supernatural aspect of the Christian's life; on this Kempis and Tauler agree.[30] It aims solely toward heaven, helping man, according to Tauler, to overcome the evils of this world,[31] remain obedient to God, and endure suffering in patience, strength, and resignation.

Regeneration (*regeneratio*) follows illumination and is characterized by a denial of self and the things of this world.[32] In regeneration one suffers and dies with Christ, becoming spiritually poor, but in it also one rises with Christ in faith, becoming united with one's Saviour in light, freedom, and purity.[33]

By faith one is justified (*justificatio*) before God. Christ becomes his life; with him, Arnold writes, citing Ruusbroec and Tauler, the believer shares a communion so close that he dies and experiences all things with his Lord.[34] Christ's reception in the heart of man is the true Gospel; it is secret, hidden from us, as Bernard and others had written.[35] It is given in the same manner to all, and according to Ruusbroec, may be directly experienced.[36] Christ is united with all creatures in a general way, writes Arnold, but to the believer he is present in a special way.

Following this discussion, Arnold proceeds to describe more fully the nature of the faith union with Christ (*unio mystica*) and to make wide use of medieval sources to do so.[37] How one can so receive Christ is unknown, but it occurs in faith, according to Ruusbroec and others.[38] Through the power of this union, the believer is redirected to the Father, learning first through the pattern established by the incarnate Jesus of Nazareth. At this point in his argument, Arnold sums up his concept of the birth of Christ in the soul in a chapter composed almost entirely of quotations from Bernard, Tauler, and Ruusbroec. Christ is born in the soul with election, born properly in faith, and born daily in every act of renovation by the believer.[39]

The first fruit of this union, according to Arnold, is the assurance[40] that one is united with God. And, following the traditional description of mystical union established by Bernard and popularized by later writers, Arnold goes on to describe the relationship between God and the believer as fire and white-hot iron, wind and water, sun and air.[41]

Another way of describing the mystical union and its fruits is in terms of love. Love comes from the Father and must of necessity return to him. This return, wrote Tauler, comes out of faith; love is eternal, but progresses by stages in the believer's life until it reaches its fulfilment.[42] Arnold did not attempt to enumerate these states consistently. To understand this love, or word, of God, the believer must so turn inwardly with his whole heart as to live the unitive life to the fullest, to experience its heat and fire when it most completely controls him. As this union in love grows, it heals the believer and makes him holy, until, sunk in God, the believer finds victory in all the trials of this life and rejoices in the ecstatic sweetness of divine love.[43]

'There is no end in describing the holy and most precious matter, namely [the nature of] divine love', wrote Arnold, introducing his chapter on the spiritual marriage between God and the soul.[44] His statement is important, for it makes clear his understanding of the term 'spiritual marriage'. This term is simply another way of describing every believer's faith-union with Christ: it is not the end of the Christian's life, reached after arduous loving; it is not the consummation of love, but rather a general description of the whole life of love.

In the last section of the *Wahre Abbildung*, however, Arnold began to move beyond his earlier discussion characterizing the mystical union in itself and in its results. As he proceeded in his argument, he took ever more interst in the relative perfection of the various aspects of the union. Thus, although all Christian believers rest in the peace of the Spirit, Arnold placed great emphasis on the deeper rest possible for mature Christians. The goal of mystical union is glorification, yet this term is not used by Arnold to mean man's glorification in the first place. United with God and directed by the Holy Spirit to understand the mystery of that union, the believer at the height of his maturity glorifies the Holy Trinity which is the source of his spiritual life. As the Father was the chief agent in calling the beginner in the christian life to the Son, and the Son was the chief agent in renewing man in conversion and union, so the Spirit directs the youth in Christ to develop maturely, to learn experientially to understand more fully the mysterious purpose of the Trinity united with him, and thus to glorify his Triune God.

Tauler and Arnold: A Comparative Survey

In the some five hundred pages of the *Wahre Abbildung*, Arnold quotes from medieval authors, in most cases with lengthy extracts, over six hundred and fifty times. Of these quotations, Tauler accounts for almost one half. Over one quarter are taken from Ruusbroec, and almost another quarter from Bernard of Clairvaux. Almost all the sermons now accepted as Tauler's were available to Arnold in the 1703 Frankfurt edition, but they were heavily edited. A parallel edition of the Frankfurt 1703 and Ferdinand Vetter editions of the sermon on the three births (*see addendum below*) makes this immediately clear. That there is some question as to whether or not this is a Tauler or an Eckhart sermon need not delay us.[45]

Almost from the first line of the 1703 edition's text of this sermon on the three births, a reader is aware of the 'pietistic' tone. Whereas Tauler was describing a religious experience which takes the believer 'out of himself' (*usser ime selber*) in love, the later edition makes no mention of this and describes the love experience rather as one of joyous triumph and thankfulness. It is the experience, according to the 1703 edition, of a 'soul rooted in true faith' (*recht-glaubigen Seele*) rather than a 'good' soul. The adjective 'true' is added to modify love, and 'heartfelt' to modify experience, adding to the pietistic dimension. Likewise, the birth which Tauler says is found (*bevinden*) in the soul is described as experienced (*fühlen* in the 1703 edition) after one has turned to it in the new birth (*kehret und wendet*). The 1703 edition insists as well on the necessity of faith for such an experience (*die glaubige Seele*) and adds a description of the activity of the soul *in Gott*. Rather than speaking about the new birth, the 1703 edition wishes to teach (*lehren*) concerning it, so that the parishioners (*Pfarrkinder*) listening to the sermon or meditating on it might be directed (*weisen*) to experiential knowledge of it (*erkennen*).

The remainder of the parallels noted in the addendum printed below are self-explanatory. All indicate that a Pietist approaching this Tauler text for the first time had ample reason to believe that the medieval mystic agreed fully with him. As a result, one may not charge Arnold with deliberately misinterpreting his text. The edition of Tauler which Arnold had went a long way in predetermining his interpretation of that author, and the nuances of the 'modernization' of the Tauler sermons suggested to Arnold that Tauler's theological system was the same as his own.

That Arnold was mistaken in this supposition is demonstrable. For example, like Tauler, Arnold too makes a sharp distinction between the exterior and the interior man; Arnold's distinction is between the old and the new man. Arnold defines the mind (*gemute*) as the spirit (*geist*) given to the new-born believer as the act of faith,[46] and, quoting Luther on Romans 7:22, he writes, 'The internal man is here called the spirit born out of grace, which here, in holy men, strives against externality',[47] referring his reader to a Tauler passage.[48] But the significant difference between Tauler and Arnold must not be overlooked. The spirit or *gemute* for Tauler is part of every man; for Arnold it is granted only to the new man, the man in Christ. Secondly, Arnold's Lutheranism is evident in his rejection of any possibility of a natural path from man to God; Arnold relates the spirit to the spark of the soul[49] and to the image of God, whereas Tauler uses both these latter images to describe the ground (*grunt*) of the soul.[50]

Tauler often describes the ground of the soul in terms of a spark (*funkelin*) which both incites and attracts the soul to itself, although he uses the image of the spark primarily when he is referring to the operative aspect of the ground (*grunt*), that is, when he is more concerned with associating ground (*grunt*) with the mind (*gemute*).[51] In the ground (*grunt*), in itself, man finds God — God dwells in it — and because reason may not enter there, Tauler may only speak of the God discovered in the ground (*grunt*) in negative terms. God cannot be understood by reason; He is beyond it.[52] The most common of these negative terms for God are groundlessness (*abgrund*) and wilderness (*wuste*). At other points Tauler uses such words as darkness (*finsternus*) and nothingness (*nichts*).[53]

For Tauler, however, reason has a positive role to play in the lower stages of one's journey toward spiritual perfection. To come to God one must learn to detach oneself from things (*abgeschiedenheit*). The proper use of reason is the first step back to one's origin.[54] Arnold can accept no such position. He is very insistent that natural reason since the fall is totally and irreparably false.[55] Only in the redeemed man can reason have any vitality, and then, Arnold suggests, one must be circumspect in his use of it.[56] It is not reason but the spirit which directs one away from the things of the world, allows one to become detached (*abgeschieden*) and resigned (*gelassen*). Both detachment and resignation are the work of grace.[57]

Arnold then did not distinguish between spirit (*geist=gemute*) and ground (*grunt*) in the way Tauler did; the Lutheran Pietist related all images of the spark of the soul to the spirit (*geist*), and his emphasis on a unity of simple love for God rather than on a search for simple unity in God, as well as his Lutheran concern with forensic justification, mitigated against the development on Arnold's part of a doctrine of the ground (*grunt*) of the soul as a part of man. For Tauler, mind (*gemute*) and ground (*grunt*) were different aspects of the same reality, but for Arnold the spirit (*geist*) was evident only in the life of every believer, not, as in Tauler, in every man. Arnold thought that this spirit came from the Holy Spirit — it is the Spirit's gift — but not that it was in any way a piece of the divine in man; it is solely a new inclination toward God, who can be known and enjoyed only in glory. The spirit lives in the believer, and the believer may turn with it in its (the

Spirit's) orientation toward a holy life. By directing his attention ever more fully toward this goal, the believer may experience and know the ecstatic joy of life in God and love for him, but such joy and love is always the believer's psychological joy and love resulting from his own experienced knowledge that he is living ever more fully according to God's will; it is not the result of his having attained experience or knowledge of the Spirit itself, that is, Christ's life in him, and certainly not of the divine unity.

As extensive as was Arnold's use of late medieval mysticism, there is no indication that he embraced directly the thought of these writers. His use of these writers is always within the context of Pietism; radical that Pietism was, but it was also Lutheran. Central to understanding Arnold and his use of medieval texts is a proper interpretation of his doctrine of the *ordo salutis*. That doctrine, rooted in Luther and Arndt and shaped under later scholasticism, Arnold developed somewhat to suit his peculiar interests. Since all stages of the *ordo* were believed to occur in a mathematical point of time, Arnold was able to uphold a doctrine of forensic justification, while at the same time pastorally directing believers to growth in Christ and toward a relative perfection. It was both an imitation of Christ and a conformity to him. As one modern writer has defined it:

> The imitative life of Christ involves both God's activity, through the Spirit, in conforming man to His image in Christ (*conformitas*), and man's focusing of his moral and spiritual attention on the exemplar, Christ (*imitatio*).[58]

At the basis of this imitative life is divine love. That love flows from God to man, and under its influence the believer is drawn back to God as a student in the school of experimental knowledge where he is taught to set aside all other loves for the world and for oneself.[59]

What is clear, at least from a study of Arnold's use of medieval texts, is that Pietism's extensive interest in Roman Catholic sources did not indicate a predisposition to Catholic theology, nor did the use of those texts detract from the Protestant principle of justification by grace through faith alone. In fact, the opposite is true; medieval and other Catholic compositions were reinterpreted by Pietists within their already established theological framework, firmly rooted within Protestantism. As a result Pietism cannot be simplistically claimed as a forerunner of modern ecumenism. Unfortunately, the opposite is the case. Pietism did use Catholic texts, but within a context of anti-Catholic prejudice. One need go no further than Spener's *Pia desideria* to demonstrate this. In that work the senior Pietist leader continually associated the Roman Catholic Church with Babel and Antichrist,[60] and attacked it for evil which, although still found among Protestant churches, 'can rightfully be laid at the doorstep of the Roman Church'.[61] In his introductions to Tauler he praised the work of medieval authors, but his commendation was almost always given with a warning that the authors wrote in times of great darkness, some of which remains in their writings.[62] Moreover there are numerous fiercely polemical attacks on Catholicism in Spener's other writings.[63] Pietism was in general, no more open to ecumenical dialogue in the modern sense of the term than was the Protestantism which preceded it. Indeed, Pietism tended to step aside from such dialogue. As Martin Schmidt describes pietist ecumenicity:

> Its appeal was made, not to doctrine, nor to the more or less skilful diplomacy of ecclesiastical politicians. Here there were no public discussions of theological problems, no synods; detailed plans for union of the Churches are regarded as of secondary importance. All the leading ideas and views of earlier ecumenical activity are, for the Pietist, unusable and worthless. He rejects the idea that doctrine is the heart of Christian faith; he rejects the idea of the state Church; he rejects the institutional incorporation of the Church in liturgy, sacrament, and Church polity — or at least without any great difficulty finds it possible to do without them all.
>
> The decisive thing for him is that consciousness of spiritual fellowship which Pietism has taken over from the mystical traditions of 'spiritualism', but which, with incomparable

energy, power of conviction, and vigour, it sets in the centre of the stage. Pietism regards itself as a manifestation of
ecumenical reality, or rather as the actual incorporation of
the ecumenical idea. For this reason its ecumenical activity
always gives the impression of spontaneous recognition of
an already existing reality, even when its plans of action
are carefully and deliberately matured.[64]

As a result of such an attitude, denominational differences were
not overcome, but deepened. Anti-Catholic feeling remained
and divisions between Christians widened: divisions between
true and false believers, between reborn believers who lived by
the Spirit in their hearts and mere formal accepters of creed
who understood only the dead letter. The true believers, it was
understood, would recognise one another under the direction
of the Spirit, in whatever institutional framework they existed,
Protestant, Radical, or Catholic. Theological precision was of
secondary importance and was supposedly set aside; but theological system is nevertheless ever present in the act of faith and
relegation of it to a secondary position inevitably placed theology itself under the control of sociological dynamics and
political machinations.

PETER C. ERB

Wilfrid Laurier University
Waterloo, Ontario

ADDENDUM: PARALLEL TEXTS
OF TAULER'S SERMON 'ON THE THREE BIRTHS'
FROM THE FRANCKFURT 1703 TAULER
AND VETTER EDITION

[Important differences are italicized; significant omissions in
either text are bracketed].

Franckfurt 1703 Edition	*Vetter Edition*
[69] Heute begehet man in der gantzen werthen Christenheit dreyerley	[7] Man beget húte drier leige geburt in der heilgen cristen-heit, in der ein ieglich

Geburten/ in welcher ein
ieglicher Christen Mensch so
grosse Freud und Wonne *haben*
solte/ dasz er für hertz-
licher Liebe/ [*für frölichem*
Jauchzen/ *für freudenreicher*]
Dancksagung/ ja für innig-
licher Freude [*seines*
Hertzens hüpffen und]
springen solte. Und warlich/
wer bey sich selbsten noch
seine Freude hieraus fühlet
und hat/ der mag sich [wohl
für Leid und Traurigkeit]
fürchten.

Die erste und oberste
Geburt ist/ da der himml-
ische Vater gebieret seinen
eingebornen Sohn/ also dasz
er mit ihm ist ein einiger
gleich-wesentlicher ewiger
GOtt/ [und doch eine sonder-
bare] und von ihm unter-
schiedene Person. Die
andere Geburt ist/ da die
jungfräuliche Mutter einen
Sohn aus ihrem Leib gebieret/
in unverletzter Keuschheit/
ohn alle Sünde und Gebrech-
lichkeit. Die dritte Geburt
ist/ da Gott zwar warhafftig/
aber doch geistlicher weise
mit Lieb und Gnaden/ alle Tag
und Stunde geboren wird in
einer *rechtgläubigen* Seele.

Die drey Geburten
begehet man mit den drey
Messen/ so an diesem hohen
Fest gelesen werden. Denn

cristen mensche so grosse
weide und wunne *solte nemen*
daz er rehte von wunnen solte
[*usser ime selber*] *springen*
in iubilo und in minnen, in
dangnemekeit und inrelicher
fröude, und weler mensche des
nit in ime bevint, der mag
sich vörhten.

Nu di erste und die überste
geburt daz ist das der himel-
sche vatter gebirt seinen
eingebornen sun in götlicher
wesenlicheit, in persönlicher
underscheit. Die ander geburt
die man húte beget, das ist
die müterliche berhaftekeit
die geschach megdelicher
kúschikeit in rehter luterkeit.
Die dirte geburt ist daz Got
alle tage und alle stunde wurt
werlichen geistlichen geborn
in einre *güten* sele mit gnoden
und mit minnen.

Dise drie geburte beget man
húte mit den drien messen.
Die erste singet man in der
vinster naht, und get an:

die erste Messe singt man
mitten in der finstern Nacht/
und fängt also an: Der HErr
hat zu Mir gesprochen: Du
bist mein Sohn heute/ [(das
ist/ von Ewigkeit)] hab ich
dich gezeuget: Und diese
Messe bedeut die verborgene
Geburt/ welch in der Finstern/
das ist/ in der verborgenen
unbekandten Gottheit
geschicht. Die andere Messe
hebt also an: Das Licht
scheinet heut über uns.
Diese Messe bezeichnet den
Glantz der vergötterten
menschlichen Natur/ [das ist/
wie S. Paulus spricht/ dasz
Gott in Fleisch offenbaret
ist.] Diese Messe wird zum
[70] theil in der Nacht/ zum
Theil am Tage gesungen: weil
die Geburt/ darvon sie
handelt/ zum Theil bekandt/
zum Theil aber unbekandt
gewesen ist. Die dritte
Messe singt man am hellen
Tage/ und fangt also an:
Puer natus est nobis: Ein
Kind ist uns geboren/ ein
Sohn ist uns gegeben. Sie
bedeut aber und zeigt an
die holdselge liebliche
Geburt/ die alle Tag und
Stunden/ ja auch alle Augen-
blick geschehen soll/ und
· geschicht in einer jeglichen
rechtgläubigen Seele/ wahn
sie in [wahrer] Liebe und

dominus dixit ad me, filius
meus es tu, ego [8] hodie
genui te; und dise messe
meinet die verborgene geburt
die geschach in der vinsterre
verborgenre unbekanter got-
heit. Die ander messe get an:
lux fulgebit hodie super nos,
und die meinet den schin der
gegötteter menschlicher
naturen, und die messe ist
ein teil in vinsternisse und
ein teil in

dem tage, sú waz ein teil
bekant und ein teil unbekant.
Die dirte messe singet man in
dem kloren tage, und die get
an: puer natus est nobis et
filius datus est nobis, und
meinet die minnencliche
geburt die alle tage und in
allen ougenblicken sol geschehen und geschiht in einre
ieglicher *güten* heilgen selen,
ob sú sich darzü kert mit
warnemende und mit minnen,
wan sol sú diser geburt in ir
bevinden und gewar werden,
daz müs geschehen durch einen

[hertzlichem] Auffmercken
sich darzu kehret [und wendet.] Denn soll [die gläubige
Seele] diese Geburt in ihr
fühlen und erkennen/ so musz
sie alle ihre Kräffle [in
GOTT] richten und kehren.
Und wenn sie das thut/ *so
schencket sich GOtt der
Seelen dermassen zu eigen in
und durch diese dritte
Geburt/ dasz sie nichts
eigeners haben kan/ als
eben ihren GOtt Heyland
CHristum:* wie denn die
göttliche Wort solches hell
und klar anzeigen/ als da es
heisset: Ein Kind ist uns
geboren/ uns ist ein Sohn
gegeben/ das ist/ disz
geborne Kind und Sohn ist
unser: es ist unser gantz
und gar eigen über alles:
Dann es wird ohn unterlasz/
zu allen Zeiten und Stunden
in uns geboren.

   Nun von dieser
dritten und letzten Geburt/
[welche aber sehr lieblich
und freudenreich ist]/ habe
ich mir diszmal am ersten zu
lehren fürgenommen/ [und auch
meine liebe Pfarrkinder zu
weisen]/ wie wir konnen und
sollen dar zu gelangen.
[Damit wir aber etlicher
massen erkennen mogen]/ wie
diese Geburt gantz adelich
und fruchtbarlich geschehe/

inker und widerker alle ir
krefte, *und in diser geburt
wurt ir Got also eigen und
git sich . ir als eigen über
alles daz eigen daz ie oder ie
eigen wart.* Daz wort daz
sprichet: ein kint ist uns
geborn und ein sun ist uns
gegeben; er ist unser und
zümole unser eigen und über
alle eigen, er wurt alle zit
geborn one underlos in uns.

Von diser minnenclichen
geburt, die dise leste messe
meinet, von der wellent wir
nu aller erste sprechen. Wie
wir herzü kummen süllent das
die edel geburt [in uns]
adellichen und fruhtberlichen
geschehe, daz sullent wir
leren an der eigenschaft der
ersten vetterlichen geburt,
do der vatter gebirt sinen
sun in der ewikeit, wan von
überflüssikeit.

so müssen wir *mit Fleisz
bedencken* die allererste und
oberste Geburt/ da GOtt der
Vater seinen eingebornen Sohn
in der Ewigkeit [zeuget und]
gebieret. Denn aus dem
unendlichen Uber[71]flusz des
überschwenglichen Reichthums
seiner Güte/ hat GOtt sich
nicht können enthalten/ er
hat sich müssen ausgiessen/
und andern mittheilen. Denn
des guten Natur und Eigen-
schafft ist/ wie S. Augustinus zeuget/ dasz es sich
ausgiesse/ und andern
mittheile. So hat nun GOtt
der Vater sich ausgegossen/
*indem er von Ewigkeit her
seinen Sohn also geboren hat/
dasz er zwar eines göttlichen
Wesens mit ihm/ und doch
gleichwol die andere Person
in der einigen und ewigen
Gottheit* ist/ hernacher hat
GOtt sich auch ausgegossen in
alle Creaturen/ darum spricht
S. Augustinus abermal: Weil
GOtt gut ist/ so sind wir
auch gut: und alles guts/ so
die Creaturen in und an sich
haben/ kommt gantz und eigent-
lich her von der wesentlichen
Gütigkeit des Schöpffers.

des überwesenlichen richtümes
in der güte Gottes so enmöhte
er sich nút inne enthalten er
müste sich uzgiessen und
gemeinsamen, wan als [Boecius
und] sant Augustinus sprechent
daz Gottes nature und sin art
ist daz er sich uzgiesse, und
alsus hat der vatter sich
uzgegossen *an dem usgange der
götlichen personen*, und vor
hat er sich entgossen an die
creaturen. Darumb sprach sant
Augustinus: 'wan Got güt ist,
darumb sint wir, und als daz
alle creaturen gütz hant, daz
ist alles von der wesenlichen
güte Gottes allein.'

Notes

APOCALYPTIC TRADITIONS
THIRTEENTH-CENTURY RELIGIOUS LIFE

BIBLIOGRAPHY

E. Randolph Daniel, *The Franciscan Concept of Mission in the High Middle Ages.* Lexington, The University of Kentucky, 1975.

M. D. Lambert, *Franciscan Poverty.* London, S.P.C.K., 1961.

Gordon Leff, *Heresy in the Later Middle Ages,* Vol. I. New York, Barnes and Noble, 1967.

Bernard McGinn, *Apocalyptic Spirituality.* New York, Paulist Press, 1979.

——————————, *Visions of the End. Apocalyptic Traditions in the Middle Ages.* New York, Columbia University, 1979.

Marjorie Reeves, *The Influence of Prophecy in the Later Middle Ages. A Study in Joachimism.* Oxford, Clarendon Press, 1969.

Bernhard Töpfer, *Das kommende Reich des Friedens.* Berlin, Akademie-Verlag, 1964.

NOTES

1. The most influential work in this camp has been that of N. Cohn, *The Pursuit of the Millennium.* In the second edition (Oxford, 1970) Cohn admits: 'Millenarian sects and movements have varied in attitude from the most violent aggressiveness to the mildest pacifism and from the most ethereal spirituality to the most earthbound materialism. And they have also varied greatly in social composition and social function' (Introduction, unpaged).

2. Thus a statement like that of Y. Talmon: 'Most millenarian movements were subterranean and amorphous popular revolt movements', would not be correct as a generalization regarding the medieval period. See 'Pursuit of the Millennium: the Relation between Religious and Social Change', *Archives européenes de sociologie* 3 (1962) 127.

3. I have tried to advance a typology of the political uses of apocalypticism in my book *Visions of the End: Apocalyptic Traditions in the Middle Ages* (New York, 1979), 28-36; and I have discussed the spiritual values in *Apocalyptic Spirituality* (New York, 1979) 7-16.

4. Cohn seems to suggest this by claiming that many of the would-be messi-

ahs he treats were 'former members of the lower clergy'; see *Pursuit of the Millennium*, 'Introduction', unpaged.

5. *Prophecy in the Later Middle Ages* (Oxford, 1969), 'New Spiritual Men', 133-292.

6. H. de Lubac in *La postérité spirituelle de Joachim de Flore. I. de Joachim à Schelling* (Paris, 1978) 48-9, n. 6, has plausibly suggested that Joachim took the term *viri spirituales* signifying the perfect interpreters of Scripture from Augustine. The term is also found in other authors, e.g., Honorius Augustodunensis, *Comm. in Cant. Cant.*; PL 172:490B.

7. B. McGinn, 'Joachim and the Sibyl', *Cîteaux* 34 (1973) 103-7.

8. *Designat puer iste castissimus ordinem monachorum, qui proprius est, ut dixi, Spiritus sancti, inchoatus a beatissimo Benedicto....* Chap. 1 (p. 10) from C. Baraut's edition of this text in 'Un Tratado inédito de Joaquin de Fiore', *Analecta Sacra Tarraconensia* 24 (1951). Subsequent references will be to the chapter and page numbers of this edition.

9. E.g., chaps. 1 (p. 10), 10 (pp. 25-6), and 18 (p. 42).

10. E.g., chaps. 7 (pp. 20-2), 11 (p. 28), 25 (p. 54), and 45 (p. 85).

11. Chap. 15 (pp. 36-7).

12. The fullest description of the two in this text is to be found in chap. 43 (pp. 82-3).

13. See 'Joachim and the Sibyl', 107.

14. See Reeves, 140-44, for a list of textual references and a discussion of the two orders in Joachim's works. I mention here only one key text, *Expositio in Apocalypsim* (Venice, 1527; photomechanical reprint 1964) ff. 175ᵛ-76ʳ, with translation available in my *Visions of the End* (New York, 1979) 136-7.

15. The best account of the order's history is F. Russo, *Gioacchino da Fiore e le Fondazione Florensi in Calabria* (Naples, 1958). See also F. Caraffa, 'Florensi', *Dizionario degli Istituti di Perfezione* (Rome, 1977) IV, cc. 79-82. Joachim appears to have modelled his order on the Cistercians, but the florensian customs have not survived.

16. *The Theology of History in St. Bonaventure* (Chicago, 1971) 39.

17. The best studies of this *figura* are H. Grundmann, *Neue Forschungen über Joachim von Fiore* (Marburg, 1950) 85-121; and M. Reeves and B. Hirsch-Reich, *The Figurae of Joachim of Fiore* (Oxford, 1972) 232-48. An illustration of the figure and translation of the text is available in B. McGinn, *Apocalyptic Spirituality* (New York, 1979) 142-8.

18. *... in ipsa erit pater spiritualis qui preerit omnibus, cuius dispositioni et arbitrio omnes obtemperabunt.* L. Tondelli, M. Reeves, and B. Hirsch-Reich, *Il Libro delle Figure* (Turin, 1950) I, Tavola XII.

19. Joachim certainly believed that the papacy would continue to exist in the coming *status* (Reeves, 396-7); and a passage in the *Liber Concordie* (Venice, 1519; photomechanical reprint 1964) f. 89ʳ, interprets the domination of Joseph over his brothers as the concord of the domination of the papacy in its spiritualized (monasticized) form in the third *status*.

20. E.g., *Expositio*, f. 22ʳ; *Liber Concordie*, ff. 57ᵛ, 66ᵛ-67ᵛ, 71ᵛ.

21. On Benedict as the *germinatio*, see e.g., *Liber Concordie*, ff. 8ᵛ, 56ᵛ-57ʳ. Reeves, *Prophecy*, 138, note 1, gives a list of texts.

22. 'The Abbot and the Doctors: Scholastic Reactions to the Radical Eschatology of Joachim of Fiore', *Church History* 40 (1971) 34-5.

23. E.g., in *Expositio*, ff. 175ᵛ-176ʳ, both orders seem monastic, but in *Expositio*, ff. 146ʳ-147ᵛ, one is monastic and one clerical. In *Liber Concordie*, f. 80ʳ, they are a clerical and a lay order.

24. *Prophecy*, 242.

25. In IV Sent. d. 43, q. 1, a. 3, quaest. 4, sol. II, ad 3.

26. Reeves, *Prophecy*, 145.

27. As E. R. Daniel reminds us in his *The Franciscan Concept of Mission in the High Middle Ages* (Lexington, 1975), Joachite ideas are not the only form of eschatology used by the Franciscans; but insofar as the Franciscans moved from general expectation of the End and their hopes for the universalization of the model provided by Francis to a pronounced apocalypticism convinced of the imminence of history's crisis, I believe their ideas took on a more Joachite cast than Professor Daniel is prepared to admit. See also Daniel's paper 'St. Bonaventure: Defender of Franciscan Eschatology', *San Bonaventura, 1274-1974* (Rome, 1974) IV, 793-806.

28. For the account that follows, besides the rich material in Reeves, see also G. Leff, *Heresy in the Later Middle Ages* (New York, 1967) Vol. 1, Part 1, 'Poverty and Prophecy', 51-255. Something of the wealth of literature devoted to this history can be gleaned from these works.

29. E.g., *In Hieremiam* (Venice, 1525) f. 23ʳ.

30. E.g., *In Hier.*, ff. 14ʳ, 43ᵛ, 59ʳ, 60ᵛ.

31. The case was first argued in 'The Abbot Joachim's Disciples and the Cistercian Order', *Sophia* 19 (1951) 355-71; and was subsequently attacked by B. Töpfer in *Das kommende Reich des Friedens* (Berlin, 1964) 108-24. Reeves returned to the defense of her position in *Prophecy*, 148-58. More recently, F. Simoni has defended the franciscan authorship in 'Il *Super Hieremiam* e il Gioachismo Francescano', *Bullettino dell'Istituto Storico Italiano per il Medio Evo*, 82 (1970) 13-46.

32. *Spiritualiter: Petrus praedicatores: Iacobus conversos eorum. Ioannes alter ordo minorum: qui ab ipsis angelis minorabitur paulo minus: quia novissimus. In Hier.*, f. 13ʳ. Reeves, *Prophecy*, 156-8, note 2, suggests that this passage is a gloss that has crept into the text.

33. 'Il *Super Hieremiam*', 30.

34. As argued by E. R. Daniel, 'A Re-Examination of the Origins of Franciscan Joachitism', *Speculum* 43 (1968) 671-6. Salimbene in his *Chronica* (MGH. SS. XXXII:236) tells the story of a florensian abbot fleeing the wrath of Frederick II, who brought the works of Joachim to the franciscan house at Pisa. Older studies, such as that of E. Benz, *Ecclesia Spiritualis* (Stuttgart, 1934) 175-7, have seen in this event the origins of Franciscan Joachitism.

35. This is evident from Salimbene's *Chronica*, e.g., 20-21, 101, 266-7, 288-9, 415, 580, 640. Emphasis on the mendicants' apocalyptic role couched in Joachite language is also found in the *Expositio in Apocalypsim* of the german Franciscan, Alexander of Bremen, written about 1248-50. See Reeves, *Prophecy*, 178.

36. On John of Parma, see G. Bondatti, *Gioachinismo e Francescanesimo nel Dugento* (S. Maria degli Angeli, 1924) 60-111.

37. See M. Lambert, *Franciscan Poverty* (London, 1961) 61-6.

38. *Et omnibus fratribus meis clericis et laicis praecipio firmiter per obedientiam ut non mittant glossas in regula neque in istis verbis dicendo: Ita volunt intelligi.* K. Esser, *Die Opuscula des hl. Franziskus von Assisi* (Grottaferrata, 1976) 444. I have made use of the translation of R. B. Brooke, *The Coming of the Friars* (New York, 1975) 119.

39. This characterization is partly adapted from J. Moorman, *A History of the Franciscan Order* (Oxford, 1968) 94.

40. It has recently been suggested that John, or someone in his immediate circle, was responsible for the final Joachite edition of the *Vaticinium Sibillae Erythraeae*. See Paul J. Alexander, 'The Diffusion of Byzantine Apocalypses in the Medieval West and the Beginnings of Joachimism', *Prophecy and Millenarianism. Essays in Honour of Marjorie Reeves* (Essex, 1980) 87-91.

41. The text of the Encyclical of 1255 (*Salvator seculi*) can be found in L. Wadding, *Annales Minorum* (Rome, 1732) III: 380-3. For a partial translation, see *Visions of the End*, 164-5.

42. There is one text, *Liber Concordie*, f. 67ʳ, where Joachim speaks of poverty as a special characteristic of the Church of the third *status*.

43. It is mentioned in texts like *In Hier.*, f. 28ᵛ.

44. On this issue, see Lambert, 102-9.

45. *Arbor vitae crucifixae Jesu* V, 3 (Venice, 1485) f. 210ᵛ. The passage actually says that John held that the sixth *status* of history began with Francis, though Ubertino goes on to say that John must have meant that Francis was the Angel of the Sixth Seal. *Hic* [John] *autem plenissime asserebat sicut et ego auribus meis indignis ab eius sancto ore audivi quod sextum signaculum in Francisco et eius statu accipiat ortum et quod in confusione vite et regule sue per transgressores filios et eius faventes malo prelatos debebat iniquitas ecclesia* [sic] *consummari.*

46. In Joachim the Angel had been identified with the Roman Pontiff of the time of the crisis of the second *status* (*Expos.*, f. 120ᵛ; *Conc.*, f. 56ʳ). For a study of this theme, see S. Bihel, 'S. Franciscus fuitne Angelus Sexti Sigilli?', *Antonianum* 2 (1927) 59-90.

47. See R. B. Brooke, *Early Franciscan Government* (Cambridge, 1959) 255-72.

48. Brooke, 260.

49. The Protocoll of the Anagni Commission was edited by F. Ehrle, 'Das Evangelium aeternum und die Commission zu Anagni', *Archiv für Literatur-und Kirchengeschichte* 1 (1885) 49-142. For a partial translation, see *Visions of the End*, 165-6.

50. Ehrle, 101, 131.

51. Ehrle, 112, contains the complaints of the investigators about the unwonted exaltation Joachim granted to the coming order of the time of transition; later (115) the Commission expresses fears of the depression of the clerical life in the *status* to come. More damning are the excerpts of suspect points from the *Introductorius* made by the Paris Masters, among which we find:

Tertium est, quod ordo parvulorum erit ille in quo implebitur praedicta pro-missio Apostoli [i.e., domination from sea to sea in the *status* to come]. See Matthew Paris, *Chronica*, 'Additamenta', Rolls Series VI: 338.

52. *Prophecy*, 188.

53. E.g., M. Lambert, 103-25; and E. R. Daniel, 'St. Bonaventure: A Faithful Disciple of St. Francis? A Re-Examination of the Question', *San Bonaventura*, II, 174-80. The later Spirituals, especially Angelo of Clareno, were largely responsible for the myth of the opposition between John and Bonaventure.

54. *Early Franciscan Government*, 272.

55. Ratzinger has amply demonstrated the Joachite character of Bonaventure's views of history. See also my paper, 'The Significance of Bonaventure's Theology of History', in David Tracy, ed., *Celebrating the Medieval Heritage. Journal of Religion. Supplement*, 58 (1978) 564-81.

56. E.g., *Legenda major*, Prologus and chap. 13 (*Opera omnia* VIII: 504, 545).

57. E.g., Coll. II, 17; XV, 11, 20, 22; XVI, 1. For some selections in translation, see *Visions of the End*, 197-202.

58. Especially in Coll. XVI.

59. Coll. XVI, 16.

60. *Iste est ordo seraphicus. De isto videtur fuisse Franciscus. . . . Et in his consummabitur Ecclesia. Quis autem ordo futurus sit, vel iam sit, non est facile scire. . . . Et dicebat, quod illa apparitio seraph beato Francisco, quae fuit expressiva et impressa, ostendebat quod iste ordo illi respondere debeat, sed tamen pervenire ad hoc per tribulationes.* Coll. XXII, 22-3 (*Opera omnia* V, 440-1).

61. See, e.g., Coll. XVI, 2.

62. I agree with Ratzinger, 35-55, on the future character of the *ordo seraphicus* in this key text despite the arguments of E. R. Daniel, 'St. Bonaventure, Defender of Franciscan Eschatology', that Bonaventure is speaking here of a state of life rather than a definite order. Daniel's argument seems to me to have two weaknesses. First, while it is useful to invoke the witness of the earlier *Itinerarium* to explain the importance of Francis' stigmata and the stages of ascent that lead up to it, there is a much greater degree of historicization of these themes in the *Collationes*. The pattern that was established on an individual and a-temporal basis in the *Itinerarium* was expanded to an interpretation of the development of the religious life in the Church's history in the later work. Second, the context of the passage speaks throughout of orders as definite institutional forms of religious life. The *ordo seraphicus* may be a state, but it is also an order as well.

63. Olivi's *Lectura in Apocalypsim* has thus far not received a modern critical edition. There are partial witnesses in two versions of the excerpts made for the Papal Commission which condemned the work in 1326. These may be found in S. Baluze, *Miscellanea* (Lucca, 1761) II: 258-76; and I. von Döllinger, *Beiträge zur Sektengeschichte der Mitteralters* (Munich, 1890) II: 527-85. In addition, I have made use of Rome, Bibl. Angel. MS 382. On the condemnation of the text, see D. Burr, *The Persecution of Peter Olivi*. Trans. Amer. Phil.

Soc. N.S., 66, 5 (1976). For some translated excerpts, see *Visions of the End*, 208-11.

64. ... *habuit etiam in manu, i.e., in pleno opere et in plena possessione et potestate, libellum evangelii Christi apertum, sicut patet ex regula, quam servavit et scripsit et ex statu evangelico, quem instituit.* ... von Döllinger, 560 (see Bibl. Angel. MS 382, f. 73ra). On Francis as the Angel of the Sixth Seal in Olivi, see R. Manselli, *La Lectura super Apocalypsim di Pietro di Giovanni Olivi* (Rome, 1955) 210-19.

65. E.g., von Döllinger, 560, 569-70, 572-3.

66. For Olivi's views on the role of the *viri spirituales*, see Leff, 129-34; and Burr, 19-20, 23, 84-5.

67. E.g., von Döllinger, 564-7.

68. ... *qui ordo evangelicus est tamquam homo rationalis ad imaginem Dei factus, et ipse subjicet bestias et omnem terram, et preerit piscibus et avibus, i.e., omnibus ordinibus quinto tempore formatis* (von Döllinger, 531). Reeves, *Prophecy*, 199-200, stresses Olivi's belief in a more perfect future.

69. E.g., *Huic ordini prefato datur potestas et discretio regendi ecclesiam illius temporis* ... (Bibl. Angel. MS 382, f. 75ra), See Burr, 23, as well as the text cited by H. Oberman in 'Fourteenth Century Religious Thought: A Premature Profile', *Speculum* 53 (1978) 90. The Commission that investigated Olivi's Commentary in 1319 certainly believed that he thought that papal authority would be ceded to the Franciscans in the age to come. See the *Littera magistrorum*, art. 47, in S. Baluze, *Miscellanea* (Lyon, 1761) II, 268.

70. Burr, 70-2, points out Olivi's rejection of the sectarian position implied in some of the Spirituals' denial of the legitimacy of Celestine's abdication.

71. *Heresy in the Later Middle Ages*, 1:152.

72. Ubertino stresses the triumph of Franciscan poverty in the coming age in V, 12 of the *Arbor vitae crucifixae Jesu* (Venice, 1485; photomechanical reprint, 1961), ff. 238v-40r.

73. V, 8 (*ed. cit.*, ff. 230r-33r). See the translation in *Visions of the End*, 212-4.

74. For this group, see A. Frugoni, *Celestiniana* (Rome, 1954). Angelo told the history of the group in his *Epistola excusatoria* which is translated in *Apocalyptic Spirituality*, 159-72.

75. This was recognized by Olivi, who condemned the separation of Angelo's group from the order. See his 'Letter to Conrad of Offida', in *Historiches Jahrbuch*, 3 (1882) 658-9; and his *Questiones super evangelicam perfectionem*, q. 16, as cited in F. Ehrle, 'Die Spirituellen, ihr Verhältnis zum Franciscanerorden', *Archiv für Literatur-und Kirchengeschichte* 3 (1887) 619, n. 3.

76. See the account given in Bernard Gui's *Practica inquisitionis* (ed. G. Mollat *Manuel de l'Inquisiteur*, [Paris, 1964] 1:144-6), and the examples cited in Reeves, *Prophecy*, 205-6, 213.

77. The well-known vision ascribed to James of Massa is a good illustration. See Angelus a Clarino, *Chronicon seu historia septem tribulationum ordinis Minorum* (ed. A. Ghinato; Rome, 1959) 119-22.

78. Leff, *Heresy* 1:191, stresses the fact that the Spirituals were still fighting for the Church: 'It cannot be overstated that it [the Spirituals' ideology] was

founded upon a desire to regenerate the church, not to destroy or replace it'.

79. In contrast to the amount of materials on franciscan apocalyptic, very little has been done on dominican involvement with apocalyptic and millenarian ideas. H. Haupt has some remarks in 'Zur Geschichte der Joachimismus', *Zeitschrift für Kirchengeschichte* 7 (1885) 401-6; the fullest account is in Reeves, *Prophecy*, 161-74.

80. The story is first recorded in 1256 by Gerard of Fracheto in his *Vitae Fratrum* edited in *Monumenta Ordinis Praedicatorum Historica* 1 (1897) 13, and was taken up by later dominican sources.

81. . . . *novissime diebus istis in fine seculorum duos nostros Ordines in ministerium salutis, prout indubitanter creditur, suscitavit, vocans ad eos viros non paucos, et ditans eos donis coelestibus, per quod non solum suam, sed aliorum efficaciter possent operari salutem, verbo pariter et exemplo.* . . . *Hi sunt illae duae stellae lucidae, quae secundum Sibyllinum vaticinium habent species quatuor animalium, in diebus novissimis nomine Agni vociferantes in directione humilitatis et voluntarie paupertatis.* Wadding, *Annales Minorum* III, 380-1. See the discussion in Reeves, *Prophecy*, 146-7.

82. Cited in Reeves, *ibid.*

83. See *Expositio magni prophete Joachim in librum beati Cyrilli* . . . (Venice, 1516) ff. 46ᵛ-47ʳ.

84. Reeves, *Prophecy*, 169.

85. On Brother Arnold, see E. Winkelmann, ed., *Fratris Arnoldi de Correctione Ecclesiae Epistola* . . . (Berlin, 1865); on Robert, J. Bignami-Odier, 'Les visions de Robert d'Uzès, O.P.', *Archivum Fratrum Praedicatorum* 25 (1955) 258-310.

86. L. Oliger published a version of this vision in his 'Ein pseudo prophetische Text aus Spanien über die heiligen Franziskus und Dominicus', *Kirchengeschichtliche Studien P. Michael Bihl, O.F.M.* (Kohner, 1941) 13-28 (unavailable to me). Dietrich of Apolda (*c.* 1225-98), a Saxon hagiographer, used the vision in his *Acta ampliora S. Dominici Confessoris* (AA SS Aug. I: 622-4). Dietrich also makes reference to Joachim's prophecy of the Dominicans (*op. cit.*, p. 570).

87. *Instauratae sunt rotae, et funiculus Francisci, et catena Dominici eis indissolubiliter insertae sunt, et earum splendor in septuplum coruscabat.* Dietrich, 623.

88. The possible relation between this vision and the famous 'Chariot vision' of *Purgatorio* XXXII, a connection hinted at by some previous investigators, has never been systematically explored.

89. Salimbene in his *Chronica*, 290-3, feels compelled to show that they were not predicted by Joachim. See Reeves, *Prophecy*, 242-3.

90. Töpfer, 318-9. For the contrary position, see C. Violante, 'Eresie urbane e eresie rurale in Italia dall'XI al XIII secolo', *L'eresia medievale* (Bologna, 1974) 179, 182-3.

91. Bernard Gui, *De secta illorum* . . ., edited by A. Segarizzi in *Rerum Italicarum Scriptores* IX, 5 (Città di Castello, 1907) 17-36. Selections are available in *Visions of the End*, 227-9.

92. D. M. Soloman, 'The Sentence Commentary of Richard Fishacre and

the Apocalypse Commentary of Hugh of St. Cher', *Archivum Fratrum Praedicatorum* 46 (1978) 373-6.

93. . . . *angelus Ephesi fuit beatus Benedictus et congregatio monachorum fuit sua ecclesia. Item, angelus Pergami fuit beatus Silvester papa et clerici fuerunt sua ecclesia. Item, angelus Sardis fuit beatus Franciscus et fratres Minores fuerunt sua ecclesia. Item, angelus Laodicie fuit beatus Dominicus et fratres Praedicatores fuerunt sua ecclesia. Item, angelus Smirne fuit frater Gregorius Parmensis que a supradictis occisus. Item, angelus Tyatire est ipse frater Dulcinus dyocesis novarensis. Item, angelus Phyladelphie erit praedictus papa sanctus, et iste tres ecclesiae ultime sunt ista congregatio apostolica in istis diebus novissimis missa.* Bernard Gui, 22. In the same letter written in 1300, Dolcino advances a theory of the history of the world involving four *status* instead of the customary Joachite three.

94. Bernard Gui, 24.

95. *Item, dicit quod omnes persecutores sui predicti prelatis cum ecclesie erant in brevi occidendi et consumendi, et qui ex eis essent residui converterentur ad sectam suam et unirentur ei, et tunc ipse et sui in omnibus prevalerent.* Bernard Gui, 20.

96. In his final years Dolcino also apparently came to identify himself with the coming Holy Pope. See Töpfer, 304; and Reeves, *Prophecy*, 246.

97. See, e.g., G. Constable and B. Smith, *Liber de diversis ordinibus qui sunt in æcclesia* (Oxford, 1972), especially the 'Introduction'.

98. M. Hill, *The Religious Order* (London, 1973) 85-103.

99. Francis's belief that the Gospel alone was the center of his observance is evident in the Rule, the Testament, and in a host of the stories circulated about him, e.g., *Scripta Leonis, Rufini et Angeli,* ed. R. B. Brooke (Oxford, 1970) 94. For the background to this evangelical emphasis, see M.-D. Chenu, *Nature, Man and Society in the Twelfth Century* (Chicago, 1968) chap. 7.

100. Anselm of Havelberg, *Dialogues I,* ed. G. Salet (Paris, 1964), especially 34-44, and 116-8.

101. Reeves, *Prophecy*, 247, cites examples of survival into the fifteenth century.

102. See *The Social Teaching of the Christian Churches* 1:328-82 (Harper Torchbook ed.) for an analysis. Troeltsch's treatment of the Franciscans (355-8) highlights the problems of this application.

103. See chap. 2, 'An Ideal Type of the Religious Order', 19-60.

104. *The Religious Order*, 4-5.

105. E.g., his remarks on the Franciscans, 29-30, 95-100.

DEVOTIO MODERNA ATQUE ANTIQUA
THE MODERN DEVOTION AND CARTHUSIAN SPIRITUALITY

NOTES

1. *The Turning Tide: Tradition and Innovation in the Fifteenth Century* was the theme of an international symposium on the fifteenth century held in Regensburg, Germany from August 11-16, 1982.

2. Jürgen Moltmann, *Umkehr zur Zukunft*, (München: Chr. Kaiser Verlag, 1970) 114-118.

3. A. Hyma, *The Christian Renaissance: A History of the 'Devotio Moderna'*, (2nd edition, New York: Archon Books, 1965). A Hyma, *The Brethren of the Common Life* (Grand Rapids, 1950). L. Spitz, *The Religious Renaissance of the German Humanists* (Cambridge, 1963). L. J. Richard, *The Spirituality of John Calvin* (Atlanta: John Knox Press, 1974).

4. A. Hyma, *The Christian Renaissance*, 309ff.

5. L. Spitz, *The Religious Renaissance of the German Humanists*, 7.

6. L.J. Richard, *The Spirituality of John Calvin*, 12, 33, 36 ff.

7. R.R. Post, *The Modern Devotion: Confrontation with Reformation and Humanism* (Leiden: E. J. Brill, 1968).

8. Ibid., 676-80.

9. A. Hyma, *The Brethren of the Common Life*, 19.

10. *Conclusa et proposita non vota*, in: Thomas à Kempis, *Opera Omnia*; ed. M. J. Pohl, 7 vols. (Freiburg, 1902-1921) 17:88.

11. Ibid., p. 91.

12. Guigo I, *Meditations of Guigo, Prior of the Charterhouse*, trans. John J. Jolin (Milwaukee: Marquette University Press, 1951) 46-47.

13. Ibid., pp. 13-14, 50.

14. *De Simonia ad beguttas;* ed. W. de Vreese (The Hague: 1950) 25.

15. *Gerardi Magni Epistolae*, n. 56; ed. W. Mulder (Antwerp, 1933) p. 243.

16. *Epistola* 9; p. 238.

17. *Conclusa et proposita non vota;* ed. Pohl, 7:97ff.

18. Ibid.

19. Guigo I, *Meditations*, p. 46.

20. K.C.L.M. de Beer, *Studie over de spiritualiteit van Geert Groote*, (Brussels: Nijmegen, 1938) 290-299.

21. In Archief voor de Geschiedenis van het Aartsbisdom Utrecht, 10 (1882) ed. J.F. Vregt, pp. 383-427. Critical edition of *Omnes, inquit artes* by Th. van Woerkum; typed copy in University Library of University of Nijmegen.

22. Post, p. 318.

23. *Ibid.*

24. *Ibid.*

25. *Ibid.*, p. 320.

26. *Ibid.*, p. 321.

27. *Ibid.*, p. 318.

28. *Ibid.*, p. 322.

29. *De reformatione virium animae;* ed. de la Bigne, *Bibliotheca veterum Patrum* 5 (Parisiis, 1624). Gerard of Zutphen, *The Spiritual Ascent*, trans. A. Landau (1907).

30. *The Spiritual Ascent*, c.l; trans. Landau, p. 2.

31. *Ibid.*, c.2;8.

32. Lucien J. Richard, *The Spirituality of John Calvin*, p. 20.

33. G. Zerbolt, *The Spiritual Ascent*, c. 27, pp. 55-60.

34. *Ibid.*, c. 27; p. 59.

35. *Ibid.*, c. 43; p. 193.

36. *Ibid.*, c. 198; p. 26.

37. Post, p. 327.

38. Guigues II Le Chartreux, *Lettre sur la Vie Contemplative* (L'échelle des moines), Douze Méditations. Ed. with introduction by Edmund Colledge and James Walsh. SCh 163. (Paris, 1970). English translation by Colledge and Walsh, *Guigo II. The Ladder of Monks and Twelve Meditations.* Cistercian Studies Series, Nbr. 48 (Kalamazoo: Cistercian Publications, 1981).

39. Ibid., Ch. II, p. 84 (CS 48:67-8).

40. Ibid., Ch. XII, pp. 106-108 (CS 48:79-80); Ch. XIV, p. 112 (CS 48:82).

41. Giles Constable, 'The Popularity of Twelfth-Century Spiritual Writers in the Late Middle Ages', *Renaissance Studies in Honor of Hans Baron*, edd. A. Molho and J. Tedeschi (DeKalb, IL: Northern Illinois University Press, 1971) 5-28.

42. Post, 328.

43. *Ibid.*, 3 f.

44. 'The Original Constitution of the Brethren of the Common Life at Deventer', in A. Hyma, *The Christian Renaissance*, 2nd. ed., Appendix C, pp. 440-476. (Hereafter referred to as 'Constitution').

45. E. Margaret Thompson, *The Carthusian Order in England* (New York: MacMillan & Co., 1930).

46. 'Constitution', Cap. I, p. 442.

47. *Ibid.*, Cap. IX, p. 448.

48. *Ibid.*, Cap. XXXVII, p. 472.

49. Thompson, *The Carthusian Order in England*, 20-21.

50. *Ibid.*, p. 35.

51. 'Constitution', Cap. II, pp. 442 f.

52. Thompson, 358 f.

53. *Ibid.*, 23 f.

54. 'Constitution', Cap. VI, p. 445.

55. Thompson, 34.

56. *Ibid.*

57. 'Constitution', Cap. XVI, p. 454.

58. Jean Leclercq, *The Love of Learning and the Desire for God* (New York: Fordham University Press, 2nd. rev. ed., 1974) pp. 33-56.

59. Giles Constable, 'The Popularity', 5-28.

60. Bernard of Clairvaux, SC 61:3 trans. Kilian Walsh & Irene M. Edmonds, *On the Song of Songs*, Cistercian Fathers Series, 31 (Kalamazoo: Cistercian Publications, 1979) 143.

61. *Supra*, notes 11-15; 32. See also: Darrell R. Reinke, 'The Monastic Style in Luther's *De Libertate Christiana*', *Studies in Medieval Culture*, X, edd. John R. Sommerfeld & Thomas H. Seiler (Kalamazoo: Medieval Institute Publications, 1977) 147-154.

62. Leclercq, *The Love of Learning*, 19 f.

63. David Curtis Steinmetz, *Misericordia Dei: The Theology of Johannes von Staupitz in Its Late Medieval Setting* (Leiden, 1968) 139.

64. This is the conclusion reached by Darrell R. Reinke in *Luther, The Cloister, and the Language of Monastic Devotion* (Diss. Washington Univer-

sity, 1972). See also, by the same author: 'Martin Luther: Language and Devotional Consciousness', in *The Spirituality of Western Christendom*, ed. E. R. Elder (Kalamazoo: Cistercian Publications, 1976) 152-168.

65. Post, 680.

THE CLOUD OF UNKNOWING
AND MYSTICA THEOLOGIA

NOTES

1. I agree with James Walsh, trans., *The Cloud of Unknowing* (New York, 1981), intro. pp. 2-9, that none of the arguments adduced against Carthusian authorship is sufficient. Walsh has shown in what way the circumstances of the text's composition point to Carthusian authorship, and has brought forward the slight external evidence available. I think the configuration of *The Cloud*'s sources suggest Carthusian authorship. This point, without special reference to the question of authorship, will be treated in this study.

2. References to pseudo-Dionysius' *De mystica theologia* will be to the Latin text assembled by the editor in *Deonise Hid Diuinite and other Treatises on Contemplative Prayer Related to The Cloud of Unknowing*, ed. Phyllis Hodgson, EETS 231 (Oxford 1955 for 1949, repr. 1958). See p. 95. In his translation of the work, the author of *The Cloud* renders these phrases, 'streite & litel . . . of short seiinges', p. 4.

3. Aldous Huxley, *Grey Eminence: A Study in Religion and Politics* (New York, 1941) pp. 62-66.

4. *Deonise Hid Diuinite* and *A Tretyse of þe Stodye of Wysdome* are edited by Hodgson in *Deonise Hid Diuinite*, pp. 2-10, 11-46, respectively.

5. These three works are edited by Hodgson in *Deonise Hid Diuinite*, pp. 47-59, 61-67, 79-93, respectively.

6. *Deonise Hid Diuinite*, p. xxxvii.

7. See Guigo II, *Scala claustralium*, ed. Edmund Colledge and James Walsh (*Lettre sur la vie contemplative*) (Paris, 1970). Colledge and Walsh restore the epistolary genre of this seminal monastic work. A Middle English translation of this work, *A Ladder of Foure Ronges by the which Men Mowe Wele Clyme to Heven*, is edited by Hodgson, *Deonise Hid Diuinite*, pp. 100-117. For remarks on this translation, see *Lettre*, ed. Colledge and Walsh, pp. 45-52.

8. *De mystica theologia*, p. 94.

9. For Cicero's distinction between *oratio* and *sermo*, see *Orator*, with trans. by H. M. Hubbell (Loeb Classical Series, 1942) 19, 63-64, pp. 352-53. For the themes in Seneca's letters to which I have referred, see *Ad Lucilium epistulae morales*, 3 vols., with trans. by R. M. Gummere (Loeb Classical Series, 1953) XXXVIII, I, pp. 256-59 (*sermo* creeps into the soul, appeals to reason rather than passion); XL, I, pp. 262-71 (letters suited to communication of like-minded friends; plain, unadorned style appropriate to speech that 'heals the mind', contrasted with speech that pleases a crowd; the spiritual *medicus*); XLI, I, pp. 272-78 (God is to be found within the soul); LV, I, pp. 365-73 (soli-

tude, tranquillity of spirit, fruitful leisure, spiritual friendship communicated by letters); LXXV, II, pp. 136-47 (the spiritual *medicus*, appropriateness of *sermo* for self-revelation, self-knowledge); XCII, II, pp. 446-70 (conformity of reason to divine reason, reason's control of the passions, tranquillity of spirit, the good lies in election of the will). XCV, III, pp. 58-104 (extended comparison between the art of medicine and philosophy of the soul; conformity with the divine will); XCVI, III, pp. 104-107 (conformity with the divine will). In XCV, 57, pp. 92-93, Seneca says 'Actio recta non erit, nisi recta fuerit voluntas, ab hac enim est actio. Rursus voluntas non erit recta, nisi habitus animi rectus fuerit, ab hoc enim est voluntas'; see note 54 below. On this aspect of the Stoics' thought in general and Seneca's in particular, see André-Jean Voelke, *L'Idée de volunté dans le stoicisme* (Paris, 1973). For the christian absorption of Seneca's thought, see José Antonio Franquiz, 'The Place of Seneca in the Curriculum of the Middle Ages', in *Arts libéraux et philosophie au moyen âge: Actes du Quartième Congrès International de Philosophie Médiévale* (Montreal, 1967) pp. 1065-72. For Seneca's theory of therapeutic speech, conducive to self-knowledge, see A. Guillemin, 'Sénèque directeur d'âmes: III. Les Théories littéraires', *Revue des études latines*, 32 (1954) 250-74.

10. *Epistola ad fratres de Monte Dei*, I, 9, 25-I, 9, 27; PL 184:323-25. See J. M: Déchanet, '*Seneca noster*, des Lettres à Lucilius à La Lettre aux Freres du Mont-Dieu', in *Mélanges de Ghellinck* (Gembloux, 1951) pp. 753-66. Since it was addressed to Carthusians, William's *Epistola* was a part of Carthusian literature. In the late Middle Ages, the work was usually attributed to Bernard of Clairvaux.

11. Augustine, *De doctrina christiana*, ed. G. M. Green, CSEL (Vienna, 1963) I, 14, pp. 15-16; William of St. Thierry, *Epistola ad fratres*, I, 9, 26; PL 184:324. For the therapeutic theme in Augustine, and its classical source, see Rudolph Arbesmann, 'The Concept of "Christus Medicus" in St. Augustine', *Traditio*, 10 (1954) 1-28.

12. *The Book of Privy Counselling*, in *The Cloud of Unknowing and The Book of Privy Counselling*, ed. Phyllis Hodgson, EETS, O.S. 218 (Oxford, 1944 for 1943, repr. 1958) pp. 139-39. All quotations from *The Cloud* and *The Book* are from this edition. Henceforward citations of these texts will be made in the body of the paper.

13. Walsh, trans., *The Cloud of Unknowing*, pp. 52-53.

14. Jean Leclercq, *The Love of Learning and the Desire for God*, trans. C. Misrahi (New York, 1961) p. 181.

15. The author's use of the term 'writing' perhaps echoes the *dictamen* of the *ars dictaminis*, the medieval art of letter writing.

16. See *The Cloud*, ed. Hodgson, p. 183 n. 14/13, where Methley's annotation is quoted. Edmund Colledge's and James Walsh's ' "The Cloud of Unknowing" and "The Mirror of Simple Souls" in the Latin Glossed Translations by Richard Methley of Mount Grace Charterhouse' is scheduled to appear in *Archivio italiano per la storia della pietà*.

17. On the eremitic tradition among the Carthusians, see Yves Gourdel, 'Chartreux', *Dictionnaire de spiritualité* 2 (Paris, 1955) especially 705-711. Gourdel quotes a fourteenth-century Carthusian author: 'La vie cartusienne,

quoiqu'elle doive étre jugée érémetique en raison de la place préponderante et de la dignité plus grande de l'élément érémentique, est composée de la vie solitaire et de vie commune' (711).

18. See M.-D. Chenu, *La Theologie au douziéme siècle* (Paris, 1957) pp. 172-78; Grover Zinn, 'Book and Word. The Victorine Background of Bonaventure's Use of Symbols', in *S. Bonaventura, 1274-1974*, II (Grottaferrata, 1973) pp. 143-69.

19. James Walsh, '*Sapientia christianorum:* The Doctrine of Thomas Gallus, Abbot of Vercelli, on Contemplation' (Ph.D. dissertation, Gregorian University, Rome, 1957). Robert Javelet, 'Thomas Gallus ou les Écritures dans une dialectique mystique', in *L'Homme devant Dieu: Mélanges offerts au pere Henri De Lubac*, 2 (Paris, 1964) pp. 99-110.

20. Hugh's *Mystica theologia* is printed in the *Opera omnia sancti Bonaventurae* (Rome, 1586-96) volume VII, pp. 699-730. See especially the *Quaestio unica*, pp. 726-30.

21. Rudolph's *De septem itineribus aeternitatis* is also printed in *Opera . . . Bonaventurae* (Rome, 1586-96) VII, pp. 145-96.

22. Walsh, trans., *The Cloud of Unknowing*, pp. 23-26. As Walsh points out, in lieu of an edition we are indebted to J. P. Grausem, 'Le "De contemplatione" de Guiges du Pont', *Revue d'ascetique et de mystique*, 10 (1929) 259-89.

23. For an extended treatment of the tradition of the three modes, see Kent Emery, Jr., 'Benet of Canfield: Counter-Reformation Spirituality and its Mediæval Origins' (Ph.D. dissertation, University of Toronto, 1976) pp. 148-249.

24. In *Deonise Hid Diuinite*, 3, the author translates the title *Symbolica theologia* 'þe Gadering of Deuine Sentence', p. 7 (Latin text, p. 97). This rendering reflects Hugh of St Victor's definition of *symbolum*. We quote, because Hugh's contrasting term, *anagoge* is also illumining for *The Cloud*, as we shall see: 'Symbolum est collatio formarum visibilum ad invisibilium demonstrationem. Anagoge autem ascensio, sive elevatio mentis est ad superna contemplanda . . . Ex his vero duobis generibus visionum, duo quoque descriptionum genera in sacro eliquio sunt formata. Unum, quo formis, et figuris, et similitudinibus rerum occultarum veritas adumbratur. Alterum, quo nude et pure sicut est absque integumento exprimitur. Cum itaque formis, et signis, et similitudinibus manifestatur, quod occultum est, vel quod manifestum est, describitur, symbolica demonstratio est. Cum vero pura ett nuda revelatione ostenditur, vel plana et aperta narratione docetur, anagogica.' Hugh of St Victor, *Expositio in Hierarchiam Coelestem s. Dionysii Areopagitae*; PL 175-941.

25. *Deonise Hid Diuinite*, 3, pp. 7-8; *De mystica theologia*, 3, p. 97 (*In symbolica autem theologia, quae sunt a sensibilibus ad divina Dei nominationes*).

26. *Deonise Hid Diuinite*, 3, pp. 7-8.

27. *Deonise Hid Diuinite*, 3, p. 8; *De mystica theologia*, 3, p. 96.

28. *Deonise Hid Diuinite*, 1, p. 3. The Latin text of Sarracenus (pp. 94-95) reads: 'circa mysticas visiones forti contritione et sensus derelinque et intellectuales operationes, et omnia sensibilia et intelligibilia, et omnia non exsistencia et exsistentia; et sicut possibile, ignote consurge ad ejus unitionem qui est super omnem substantiam et cognitionem'.

29. For the distinction *infra rationem*, *supra rationem*, and implied *in ratione*

see Richard of St Victor, *Benjamin minor*, 74; PL 196:53; for the distinction *extra se, intra se et in se,* and *supra se,* see Bonaventure, *Itinerarium mentis in Deum, Opera omnia,* cura PP. Colegiia s. Bonaventura, V (Quaracchi, 1891), I, 4, p. 297.

30. *Deonise Hid Diuinite,* prol., p. 2, 11.25-28. See the note by Hodgson, p. 121, n. 2/25.

31. *Benjamin major,* I, 7; PL 196: 72-73.

32. *A Tretyse of þe Stodye of Wysdome,* pp 54-6. Richard of St Victor, *Benjamin minor*, 73; PL 196:52: 'In tanta namque quotidiani conatus anxietate, in hujus modi doloris immensitate, et Benjamin nascitur, et Rachel moritur, quia cum mens hominis supra seipsam rapitur, omnes humanae ratiocinationis, angustias supergreditur. Ad illud enim quod supra se elevata, et in extasi rapta, de divinitatis lumine conspicit, omnis humanae ratio succumbit. Quod est enim Rachelis interitus, nisi rationis defectus?'

33. *A Tretyse of þe Stodye of Wysdome,* p. 42. See Richard of St Victor, *Benjamin minor*, 72, 78; PL 196:51-52, 55-56.

34. Bonaventure, *Itinerarium* I, 4, p. 297; I, 7, p. 298.

35. Walsh, trans., *The Cloud of Unknowing,* pp. 52-53, implies that *The Cloud* was written for a novice.

36. Augustine, *De Trinitate libri XV,* ed. W. J. Mountain auxiliante Fr. Glorie, *Corpus Christianorum* L (I-XII), La (XIII-XV) (Turnhout, 1968), XV, 27, 49, p. 531: 'Quantum uero attinet ad illam summam, ineffabilem, incorporalem immutabilemque naturam per intelligentiam utcumque cernendam, nusquam se melius regente dumtaxat fidei regla acies humanae mentis exerceat quam in eo quod ipse homo in sua natura melius ceteris animalibus, melius etiam ceteris animae suae partibus habet, quod est ipsa mens cui quidam rerum inuisibilium tributus est uisus, et cui tamquam in loco superiore atque interiore honorabiliter praesidenti iudicanda omnia nuntiat etiam corporis sensus, et qua non est superior cui regenda est nisi deus.'

William of St Thierry, *Epistola ad fratres de Monte Dei,* II, 2, 5; PL 184:341: 'Nullam vero dignius et utilius exercitium est homini eam habenti, quam in eo quod melius habet, et in quo caeteris animalibus, et caeteris partibus suis praeeminet, quae est ipsa mens vel animus. Menti vero vel animo, cui caetera pars hominis regenda subdita est, nec dignius est aliquid ad quaerendum, nec dulcius ad inveniendum, nec utilius ad habendum, quam quod solum ipsam mentem supereminet, qui est solus Deus.'

Liber de spiritu et anima, 11; PL 40:786: 'Rationale et intellectuale lumen, quo ratiocinamur, intelligimus et sapimus, mentem dicimus, quae ita facta est ad imaginem Dei, ut nulla interposita natura ab ipsa veritate formetur. Mens enim ex eo dicta est quod emineat in anima.'

37. Richard of St Victor, *Benjamin major,* I, 6; PL 196:71.

38. Hugh of Balma, *Mystica theologia,* pp. 726-30.

39. See Hugh, *Mystica theologia,* 2, 2, *De triplici anagogia,* pp. 704-710: 'Tantum autem per artem huius theoricae scientiae lumen acquiritur, & tanto sapientiae dilitatio in scripturis, ut quot verba in nova & veteri Testamento, quot creaturae in mundo, tot habeat anima intelligentias, vel sermones, totum ad Deum ad punctum amoris omnia referendo, ut postea apparebit' (p. 704).

40. *Liber de spiritu et anima*, 9; PL 40:785: 'Duplex est quidem vita animae; alia qua vivit in carne, et alia qua vivit in Deo. Duo siquidem in homine sensus sunt, unus interior reficitur in contemplatione divinitatis, sensus exterior in contemplatione humanitatis. Propterea enim Deus homo factus est, ut totum hominem in se beatificaret, et tota conversio hominis esset ad ipsum, et tota dilectio hominis esset in ipso, cum a sensu carnis videretur per carnem, et a sensu mentis videretur per divinitatis contemplationem. Hoc autem erat totum bonum hominis, ut sive ingrederetur sive agrederetur, pascua in factore suo inveniret (Jn 10:9); pascua foris in carne Salvatoris, et pascua intus in divinitate Creatoris.' See Rudolph of Biberach, *De septem itinerius aeternitatis, Prol.*, d. 1-6, pp. 145-50. Characteristically, Rudolph's progress is threefold (sensible, intelligible, affective-mystical): 'Ego sum ostium sensui, per corporale obiectum, Videte, inquit, manus meas, & pedes meos. Ego sum ostium intellectui, per fidem reseratum. Unde in Isaia dicitur: Nisi credideritis, non intelligetis. Ego sum ostium voluntati, per charitatem apertum. *Charitas non vult scire medium inter se & dilectum* immo, ut dicit Hugo, Amor sive charitas suo acumine omnia penetrat, donec ad dilectum veniat' (pp. 145-46). By such acute love, Mary penetrates the 'obscure' humanity to Christ's divinity (*The Cloud*, 17, p. 47).

41. From the twelfth century on, one discovers many terms, nearly synonymous but interpreted variously by different authors, for the highest part of the soul, for example, besides *mens*, *apex mentis*, *scintilla animae*, *synderesis*, *apex affectus* (Hugh of Balma). For William of St Thierry, *animus* and *mens* are synonymous (see note 36). The *Liber de spiritu et anima* equates *mens* and *spiritus*, distinguished from *anima* (see 10; PL 40:736). This equation was common; see M.-D. Chenu, 'Spiritus, Le vocabulaire de l'âme au XIIᵉ siècle', *Revue des sciences philosophiques et théologiques*, 41 (1957) 217-19. However, some, such as the author of the twelfth-century *De discretione animae, spiritus, et mentis*, sharply distinguished *spiritus* and *mens*. The author of this treatise founds his distinction on a scriptural passage, and identifies *spiritus* with *cor*: 'Inter spiritum enim et mentem manifeste dividit Apostolus in *Epistola* ad *Corinthos prima* ... In Evangelio mens ab anima discernitur, ubi Deus *ex toto corde* et *ex tota anima* et *ex tota mente* diligi praecipitur. Si autem et nomine cordis spiritus ibi intelligitur, sic ipsius quoque ab utraque illarum discretio innuitur.' See the text edited by Nicholas M. Haring, 'Gilbert of Poitiers, Author of the "De discretione animae, spiritus et mentis" commonly attributed to Achard of Saint Victor', *Mediaeval Studies*, 22 (1960) 26, 179. The author of the treatise, who despite Haring's argument seems to be Achard of St Victor (J. Chatillon, 'Achard de saint Victor et le *De discretione animae spiritus et mentis*', *Archives d'histoire doctrinale et littéraire du Moyen Âge*, 31 (1964) 7-35), demotes *spiritus* and associates it with *imaginatio*; see *De discretione*, ed. Haring, 42, 183. The source for this association, is Augustine, *De Genesi ad Litteram*, XII, 24, 51; PL 34:474-75. Whoever wrote *De discretione*, Bonaventure seems to have used the text, while restoring *spiritus* to a purely spiritual power. See *Itinerarium*, I, 4, p. 297: 'Secundum hunc triplicem progressum mens nostra tres habet aspectus principales. Unus est ad corporalia exteriora, secundum quem vocatur *animalitas* seu sensualitas; *alias* intra se et

in se, secundum quem dicitur *spiritus*; tertius supra se, secundum quem dicitur *mens*. —Ex quibus omnibus disponere se debet ad conscendendum in Deum, ut ipsum diligat *ex tota mente, ex toto corde*, et *ex tota anima*, in que consistit perfecta legis observatio et simul cum hoc sapientia christiana.'   •

The author of *The Cloud* seems to use the terms 'spirit' and 'mind' synonymously.

42. See Augustine, *De Trinitate*, IX, 4, 4, p. 297, IX, 4, 7, p. 299, and IX, 5, 8, pp. 300-301, where he states that *mens* embraces *amor* and *notitia* in one indistiguishable act and is the one *essentia* of the soul. In X, II, 18, pp. 330-31, Augustine says that *mens* binds *memoria, intelligentia*, and *uoluntas* in one *substantia*, one *essentia*. *Memoria* is nearly identified with *mens* in this text.

43. See the texts in note 42, and *De Trinitate*, XIV, 10, 13, pp. 440-41, and XV, 6, 10, p. 474.

44. *De Trinitate*, XII, 3, pp. 357-58. In XV, 7, 11, p. 475, Augustine explains why 'non igitur anima sed quod excellit in anima mens uocatur.'

45. *De Trinitate*, IV, 15, p. 187; XII, 14, 23, p. 376; XV, 1, 1, p. 460. In the last text, Augustine, as will William of St Thierry after him, identifies *mens* and *animus*, and distinguishes this higher part from *anima*.

46. See *De Trinitate*, XIV, 7, 10, p. 434, where Augustine observes that the unified act of *mens* seems most like memory: 'Nam si nos referamus ad interiorem intellegentiam qua se intellegit et interiorem uoluntatem qua se diligit, ubi haec tria simul sunt et simul semper fuerunt ex quo esse coeperunt siue cogitarentur siue non cogitarentur, uidebitur quidem imago illius trinitatis et ad solam memoriam pertinere.' Throughout book X of the *Confessiones*, Augustine speaks of *memoria*, the *ipsius animi mei sedem* (X, 25, 36) in terms strikingly similar to those which define *mens*.

47. See note 36. For *mens* knowing and loving itself in an indistinguishable, simultaneous act, see *Liber de spiritu et anima*, 23; PL 40:801; in this unified act *mens* is an image of the Trinity, 24; 804; *mens* embraces the soul's powers, and is especially related to memory ('Mens universorum capax, et omnium rerum similitudine insignita; Memoria etiam mens est ... Mens autem vocata est, quod emineat in anima, vel quod meminerit'), 11; 786, and 24; 803; *mens* distinguished from *anima* but identified with *spiritus*, 24; 803. Here the author quotes Augustine, *De Trinitate*, XII, 3, pp. 357-58 directly: 'Quapropter non anima, sed quod excellit in anima, mens vocatur, tanquam caput vel oculus' (803-804).

The attribution of *De spiritu et anima* to Augustine is, of course, anachronistic, but not perverse. At least medieval authors acknowledged, or recognized, their primary source of inspiration. On the question of authorship, see the discussion of Bernard McGinn, ed. *Three Treatises on Man: A Cistercian Anthropology*, CS24 (Kalamazoo, 1977) pp. 65-67.

48. *Liber de spiritu et anima*, 11; PL 40:786.

49. *Liber de spiritu et anima*, 11, 52; PL 40:786, 817.

50. *Liber de spiritu et anima*, 24; PL 40:803 ('In essentia namque est simplex, in officiis multiplex').

51. *Liber de spiritu et anima*, 52; PL 40:818.

52. *Liber de spiritu et anima*, 24; PL 40:804.

53. *Iohannis Cassiani Conlationes XXIIII*, ed. Michael Petschenig, *CSEL* XIII (Vienna, 1886) I, 5, pp. 10-11. Cassian says that a monk should pursue his end (*finem* = eternal life) by directing his *intentio* in a straight line towards the proper 'fixed target' (*scopos* = purity of heart), as athletes aim their *iacula vel sagittas*. Cassian's distinction between the monk's 'end' and the 'fixed target' at which he should aim in order to attain it is based on the beatitude, 'Blessed are the pure in heart, for they shall see God.'

54. Robert Pouchet, *La Rectitudo chez saint Anselme: Un itinéraire augustinien de l'âme a Dieu* (Paris, 1964), *passim* (Augustine, Gregory, Anselm, Grosseteste, Bonaventure, etc.).

55. Rudolph of Biberach, *De septem itineribus aeternitatis, itin.* I, d. 1-6, pp. 150-54.

56. *Confessions*, Texte établi par Pierre de Labriolle, II (Livres IX-XIII, Paris, 1969), XI, 11, 13, p: 305. Since it is unavailable to me, I am unable to cite Luc Verheijen's new *Corpus Christianorum* edition of the *Confessiones*.

57. *Confessions*, XI, 14, 17, p. 308: 'Si ergo praesens, ut tempus sit, ideo fit, quia in praeteritum transit, quomodo et hoc dicimus, cui causa, ut sit, illa est, quia non erit, ut scilicet non uere dicamus tempus esse, nisi quia tendit non esse?'

58. *Confessions*, XI, 13, 15, p. 307.

59. *Confessions*, XI, 15, 20, p. 310: 'Si quid intellegitur temporis, quod in nullas iam uel minutissimas momentorum partes diuidi possit, id solum est, quod praesens dicatur; quod tamen ita raptim a futuro in praeteritum transuolat, ut nulla morula extendatur.'

60. *Il Convivio, Le opere di Dante Alighieri*, 4th ed. (Oxford, 1924), I, 12-13, pp. 249-50.

CONTINENTAL WOMEN MYSTICS
AN ASSESSMENT

NOTES

1. Lucia of the Incarnation, 'The Western Spiritual Tradition', *The Way*, Suppl. 16 (1972) 16. Also see Conrad Pepler, 'The *Scale*', *Life of the Spirit*, 3 and 4 (1949) 509.

2. *De probatione spirituum*, i, 15, discussed in Eric Colledge, '*Epistola solitarii ad reges*: Alphonse of Pecha as Organizer of Birgittine and Urbanist Propaganda. *Medieval Studies* 17 (1956) 44-6.

3. Mary Jeremy Finnegan, *Scholars and Mystics* (Chicago: Henry Regnery Company, 1962) 101.

4. Lucy Menzies, tr. *The Revelations of Mechthild of Magdeburg (1210–1297) or The Flowing Light of the Godhead* (London, New York, Toronto: Longmans, Green and Co., 1953), IV/13, 108.

5. Menzies, I, 3.

6. Menzies, IV/2, 98.

7. Menzies, V/12, 135.

8. Linda Eckenstein, *Women Under Monasticism* (Cambridge: Cambridge University Press, 1896) 336.

9. F. P. Pickering, 'A German Mystic Miscellany of the Late Fifteenth Century in the John Rylands Library', *John Rylands Library Bulletin*, 22 (1938) 476-81.

10. Colledge, 40-4.

11. Ernest W. McDonnell, *The Beguines and Beghards in Medieval Culture. With special emphasis on the Belgian scene* (New Brunswick, N.J.: Rutgers University Press, 1954) 7.

12. McDonnell, 399.

13. Colledge, 43.

14. Ruth J. Dean, 'Manuscripts of St. Elizabeth of Schönau in England', *Modern Language Review*, 32 (1937) 62-71; 'Elizabeth, Abbess of Schönau, and Roger of Ford', *Modern Philology*, 41 (1944) 209-20.

15. Theresa Halligan, 'The Revelations of St. Matilda in English: *The Booke of Gostlye Grace*', *Notes & Queries*, 21 (1974) 443-6; (critical edition) *The Booke of Gostlye Grace of Mechthild of Hackeborn* (Toronto: Pontifical Institute of Mediæval Studies, 1979).

16. William P. Cummings, ed., *The Revelations of Saint Birgitta*, EETS O.S. 178 (London: Oxford University Press, 1929).

17. Phyllis Hodgson and Gabriel Liegey, eds., *The Orcherd of Syon*, Vol. I, EETS O.S. 285 (London: Oxford University Press, 1966), (critical edition); Phyllis Hodgson, '*The Orchard of Syon* and the English Mystical Tradition', Sir Israel Gollancz Memorial Lecture, *Proceedings of the British Academy*, 50 (1964) 229-49.

18. Marilyn Doiron. 'Margaret Porete: *The Mirror of Simple Souls*, A Middle English Translation', *Archivio italiano per la storia della pietà*, 5 (1968) 241-355. Also in this same issue see Edmund Colledge and Romana Guarnieri, 'The Glosses by "M.N." and Richard Methley to *The Mirror of Simple Souls*', 357-82.

19. Carl Horstmann, ed. 'Prosalegenden: Die Legenden des MS. Douce 114', *Anglia*, 8 (1885) 102-96.

20. I am indebted to Professor Roger Ellis, University of Cardiff, for a copy of his article, ' "Flores ad fabricandam . . . coronam": An Investigation into the Uses of the *Revelations* of St. Bridget of Sweden in Fifteenth-Century England', scheduled to appear in *Medium Aevum*.

21. Norman F. Blake, '*The Form of Living* in Prose and Poetry', *Archiv*, 211 (1974) 300-8; 'Varieties of Middle English Religious Prose', in Beryl Rowland, ed., *Chaucer and Middle English Studies in Honor of Rossell Hope Robbins*, (London: George Allen and Unwin, 1974) 348-56. For a further discussion of Middle English mystical manuscripts, see Valerie M. Lagorio, 'Problems in Middle English Mystical Prose', in A.S.G. Edwards and Derek Pearsall, eds., *Middle English Prose: Essays on Bibliographical Problems*, (New York and London: Garland Publishing, Inc., 1981) 128-48.

22. Pickering, 455-8. Also see Adolf Spammer, *Über die Zersetzung und Vererbung in den deutschen Mystikertexten*. Diss. Giessen, 1910, on fifteenth-century compendia of mystical texts.

23. Barnabas Ahern, 'Christian Perfection, Contemplation, and Purgatory', *American Ecclesiastical Review*, 118 (1948) 81.

24. Anna Groh Seeholtz, *Friends of God: Practical Mystics of the Fourteenth Century* (New York: Columbia University Press, 1934) 127.

25. Rufus Jones, *The Flowering of Mysticism: The Friends of God in the Fourteenth Century* (New York: The Macmillan Company, 1939) 161.

26. Oskar Pfister, 'Hysterie und Mystik bie M. Ebner', *Zentralblatt für Psychoanalyse*, I, 19, Heft 10/11, p. 11.

27. Jones, 164.

28. Friedrich von Hügel. *The Mystical Element of Religion as Studied in Saint Catherine of Genoa and Her Friends*. 2 Vols. (London: 1908; 2d. ed. 1923; rpt. James Clark, 1961) I, 223; II, 32-40.

29. Benedict Groeschel, 'A Discussion of Mystical Phenomena', in *Catherine of Genoa. Purgation and Purgatory. The Spiritual Dialogue*, tr. Serge Hughes (New York, Ramsey, Toronto: Paulist Press, 1979) 7-14.

30. Kenneth Wapnick, 'Mysticism and Schizophrenia', *Journal of Transpersonal Psychology*, 1, No. 2 (1969) 49-67.

31. Lucy Menzies, *Mirrors of the Holy. Ten Studies in Sanctity* (London: A. R. Mowbray & Co., Ltd.; Milwaukee: The Morehouse Publishing Co., 1928) xx.

32. Catherine of Siena, *The Dialogue*, tr. Suzanne Noffke (New York, Ramsey, Toronto: Paulist Press, 1980) Chap. 78, 144.

33. For a comprehensive study of these *vitae*, their content and significance, see Walter Blank, *Die Nonnenviten des 14. Jahrhunderts*, Diss. Freiburg, 1962. Concerning the Lowland mystics, see Brenda M. Bolton, '*Vitae Matrum*: A Further Aspect of The Frauenfrage', in *Medieval Women*, ed. Derek Baker (Oxford: Basil Blackwell, 1978) 253-73.

34. Halligan, *Booke*, 41.

35. Bruce W. Hozeski, '*Ordo Virtutum*: Hildegard of Bingen's Liturgical Morality Play', *Annuale Medievale*, 13 (1972) 45-69 (contains a modern English translation); and 'Hildegard of Bingen's *Ordo Virtutum*: The Earliest Discovered Liturgical Morality Play', *The American Benedictine Review*, 26 (1975) 251-9.

36. Jones, 35.

37. Odo Egres, 'Mechthild von Magdeburg: *The Flowing Light of God*', in E. Rozanne Elder, ed., *Cistercians in the Late Middle Ages* (Kalamazoo, Mich.: Cistercian Publications, 1981) 35.

38. Grete Lüers, *Die Sprache der deutschen Mystik des Mittelalters im Werke der Mechthild von Magdeburg* (Munich, 1926; rpt. Darmstadt: Wissenschaftliche Buchgesellschaft, 1966); Mary A. Ewer, *A Survey of Mystical Symbolism* (London: SPCK; New York: Macmillan Co., 1933); Hester McNeal Reed Gehring, 'The Language of Mysticism in South German Dominican Convent Chronicles of the Fourteenth Century', Diss. University of Michigan 1957; Wolfgang Riehle, *The Middle English Mystics*, tr. Bernard Standring (London, Boston and Henley: Routledge & Kegan Paul, 1981); George W. Tuma, *The Fourteenth Century English Mystics. A Comparative Analysis*, 2 Vols., Elizabethan and Renaissance Studies 61 and 62 (Salzburg, 1977).

39. Ray C. Petry, 'Social Responsibility and the Late Medieval Mystics', *Church History*, 21 (1952) 3-19.

40. Richard Kieckhefer, 'Mysticism and Social Consciousness in the Fourteenth Century', *University of Ottawa Quarterly*, 48 (1978) 185.

41. Petry, 41.

42. Finnegan, 169-70.

43. Menzies, *Mirrors*, xi.

44. Wapnick, 53.

45. See the extensive discussion of this matter in Richard Woods, *Mysterion. An Approach To Mystical Spirituality* (Chicago: The Thomas More Press, 1981) 159-73.

46. Catherine of Siena, *Dialogue*, Chap. 86, p. 89.

47. Finnegan, 134.

48. Katherine Dyckman and L. Patrick Carroll, *Inviting the Mystic, Supporting the Prophets* (New York/Ramsey: Paulist, 1981) 82-3.

49. Menzies, *Revelations*, VI/21, p. 189.

50. Sebastian Bullough, 'Catherine the Dominican', *Life of the Spirit*, 15 (1961) 447-52.

51. Eckenstein, 333.

52. McDonnell, 399-400.

53. Hodgson, '*The Orcherd of Syon*', 237-40.

54. Dean, 'Elizabeth, Abbess of Schönau, and Roger of Ford', 209.

55. See Valerie M. Lagorio and Ritamary Bradley, *The 14th-Century English Mystics: A Comprehensive Annotated Bibliography* (New York and London: Garland Publishing, Inc., 1981) 41-52.

56. James C. Franklin, *Mystical Transformations. The Imagery of Liquids in the Work of Mechthild von Magdeburg* (London: Associated University Presses, 1978) 24.

57. McDonnell, 291-5.

58. Peter Dronke, *Poetic Individuality in the Middle Ages. New Departures in Poetry, 1000–1150* (Oxford: Clarendon Press, 1970) 150-92, 197-8.

59. Stephen Axters, *The Spirituality of the Old Low Countries*, tr. Donald Attwater (London: Aquin Press, 1954) 11.

61. Alice Kemp-Welch, 'Mechthild of Magdeburg. A Thirteenth-Century Mystic and Beguine', in *Of Six Medieval Women* (London: Macmillan and Co., Ltd., 1913) 77.

61. Norman F. Blake, '*Revelations* of St. Matilda', *Notes & Queries*, 218 (1973) 32-5.

SAINT TERESA OF AVILA
SIXTEENTH-CENTURY SPAIN

BIBLIOGRAPHY

The Collected Works of St Teresa of Avila. Translated by Kieran Kavanaugh and Otilio Rodriguez. Vol. 1: *The Book of Her Life, Spiritual Testimonies, Soliloquies.* Washington, D.C.: Institute of Carmelite Studies Publications,

1976. Vol. 2: *The Way of Perfection, Meditations on the Song of Songs, The Interior Castle*. Washington, D.C.: ICS Publications 1980.

The Complete Works of St Teresa of Jesus. Translated and edited by E. Allison Peers. New York: Sheed and Ward, 1946.

The Letters of St Teresa of Jesus. Translated and edited by E. Allison Peers. London: Burns Oates, 1951.

Auclair, M. *Teresa of Avila*. Translated by Kathleen Pond. New York: Pantheon Books, Inc., 1953.

Clissold, Stephen. *St Teresa of Avila*. London: Sheldon Press, 1979.

Efrén de la Madre de Dios and Otger Steggink. *Tiempo y Vida De Santa Teresa*. Madrid: Biblioteca De Autores Christianos, 1977.

Walsh, William T. *Saint Teresa of Avila*. Milwaukee: Bruce, 1943.

Adolfo de la M. de Dios. 'Espagne: l'Age d'or.' In *Dictionnaire de Spiritualité*. Paris: Beauchesne.

Alvarez, Tommaso della Croce. '*Santa Teresa e i movimenti spirituali del suo tempo*.' In *Collana Fiamma* Viva, Vol. 4. Rome: Teresianum, 1963.

Andrés, Melquiades. *La Teología española en el siglo XVI*. 2 Vols. Madrid: Biblioteca De Autores Christianos, 1976 & 1977.

Elliott, J.H. *Imperial Spain 1469-1716*. New York: The New American Library, 1965.

Egido, Teofanes. '*The Historical Setting of St Teresa's Life*.' In *Carmelite Studies*, Vol. 1. Washington, D.C.: ICS Publications, 1980.

Hoornaert, Rodolpe. *Sainte Thérèse, Ecrivain: Son Milieu, Ses Facultés Son Œuvre*. Paris: Desclée de Brouwer, 1922.

Llamas Martinez, Enrique. *Santa Teresa de Jesús y la Inquisición Española*. Madrid: C.S.I.C., 1972.

Pacho, Eulogio de la Virgen del Carmen. 'Illuminisme.' In *Dictionnaire de Spiritualité*. Paris: Beauchesne.

NOTES

1. See The *Collected Works of St Teresa of Avila*, tr. K. Kavanaugh and O. Rodriguez, Vol. 1 (Washington: ICS Publications, 1976), *Life*, ch. 1, no. 4.

2. See *Life*, ch. 3, nos. 4-7.

3. See *Life*, ch. 4, no. 7.

4. See *Life*, ch. 5, no. 8.

5. See *Life*, ch. 9, nos. 7-9. A statue of the suffering Christ also evoked a strong response in Teresa at this time and contributed to the decisive change in her life.

6. *Life*, ch. 23, no. 1.

7. Ibid., no. 2.

8. The effort in the Spanish reform movement to return to the primitive sources as an indisputable means to living the Gospel may be distinguished into two periods: a voluntary effort in each religious order that lasted till 1494, and obligatory reform imposed by Cisneros and authorized by Alexander VI in 1494. Around a thousand Franciscans who refused to accept this imposed reform left Spain for Africa. See Melquiades Andrés, *La Teología Española en el Siglo XVI*, 2 Vols. (Madrid: BAC, 1976 & 1977) I:246-247.

9. One can understand how the *conversos* would experience a certain antipathy toward the excessive attention that was given by many Christians to external practices and ceremonies and were even scandalized by the pagan customs that were mixed with the celebration of christian feasts. Thus the religious of *converso* origin stressed the interior path of recollection. This emphasis on the interior life was later seconded by those promoting reform as well as by the humanists and the followers of Erasmus.

10. Certain reforms among the Dominicans and Franciscans were linked with *beatas* and visionaries. It became difficult to distinguish between heroic virtue and the fraudulent. In general, the Dominicans of the period were slow to admit any kind of extraordinary mystical phenomena; the Franciscans did so more easily.

11. The forty-eight propositions were not the articles of a creed confessed by *alumbrados*, but were rather propositions of determined individuals. Taken together they indicate a climate of thinking and acting. It was said that more authority was given to Isabel de la Cruz than to St Paul. Basically these people were looking for an easy way to union with God without the mediation of the Church or good works.

12. *Life*, ch. 23, nos. 12-14.

13. *Life*, ch. 24, no. 1; see also ch. 31, no. 17.

14. Ibid., no. 2.

15. See *Life*, ch. 34, no. 11; ch. 33, no. 5; ch. 25, no. 13.

16. See *Life*, ch. 24, no. 2.

17 Ibid., no. 8.

18. See *Life*, ch. 25, nos. 18, 21, 22; ch. 26, no. 1.

19. *Life*, ch. 26, nos. 4-5; see also ch. 31, nos. 12-13.

20. *Life*, ch. 26, no. 5.

21. Ibid.

22. *Life*, ch. 27, no. 4. The use of the word vision can be misleading; nothing is seen, but something is understood in a way that transcends ordinary conceptual understanding. In Teresa's doctrine these visions, revelations, and locutions are not essential to spiritual growth and, though esteemed as gifts from God, should not be sought. See *Life*, ch. 21 no. 11; ch. 29, no. 4.

23. *Life*, ch. 27, no. 6.

24. Ibid., no. 9.

25. See ibid.

26. *Life*, ch. 28, no. 18.

27. *Life*, ch. 29, no. 7.

28. See *Life*, ch. 30, nos. 2-3.

29. *Life*, ch. 34, nos. 11-12.

30. *Life*, ch. 25, no. 12.

31. *Life*, ch. 17, no. 5.

32. See her letter to Madre Ana de Jesús, December 1578: *The Letters of St Teresa*, tr E. A. Peers, Vol. 2 (London: Burns Oates, 1951), pp. 624-625.

33. *Life*, ch. 20, no. 23.

34. On September 27, 1970 by Paul VI.

35. *Life*, ch. 18, no. 8.

PIERRE DE BÉRULLE
THE SEARCH FOR UNITY

NOTES

1. Bérulle, 'Dédiez au Roy', *Discours de l'État et des Grandeurs de Jésus, Œuvres Complètes* Reproduction de l'édition princeps (1644) (Montsoult: Maison d'institution de l'Oratoire, 1960) Tome I, p. 134.

2. Bérulle, letter 'Aux Carmélites Résidant à Bordeaux et Restées Fidelès aux Supérieurs', January 15, 1623 in Jean Dagens, (ed.), *Correspondance du Cardinal de Bérulle* (Paris: Desclée de Brouwer, 1937) Tome II, p. 347. 'l'église, qui est le royaume du ciel et l'état du Fils de Dieu . . . '.

3. Bérulle, *Œuvres Complètes*, (note 1) Tome I, p. 549.

4. Bérulle, *Discours de l'État et des Grandeurs de Jésus, Œuvres Complètes*, Tome I, p. 203.

5. Bérulle, 'Dédiez au Roy', *Discours de l'État et des Grandeurs de Jésus, Œuvres Complètes*, Tome I, p. 130.

6. *Ibid.*, p. 138.

7. Jean Dagens, Introduction to *Correspondance du Cardinal de Bérulle*, (note 2), Tome I, p. x.

8. Bérulle, 'Bref Exercise pour parvenir a la vertu' in Michael Houssaye, *M. de Bérulle et les Carmélites de France, (1575-1611)* (Paris: Henri Plon, Editeur, 1872) p. 106.

9. *Ibid.*

10. *Ibid.*

11. Bérulle, *Discours de l'État et des Grandeurs de Jésus, Œuvres Complètes*, Tome I, pp. 171-72.

12. *Ibid.*, p. 172.

13. Bérulle, 'Projet de l'Érection de la Congrégation de l'Oratoire de Jésus' [fin de 1610] in Jean Dagens (ed.), *Correspondance du Cardinal de Bérulle*, Tome I, p. 119.

14. Bérulle, *Collationes congregationes nostrae*, Bibliothèque nationale, ms. lat. 18210, November 1, 1613, pp. 165-66. For an analysis of this subject see Michel Dupuy, *Bérulle et le Sacerdoce: Étude Historique et Doctrinale, Textes Inédits.* (Paris: Éditions P. Lethielleux, 1969) especially pp. 100-105.

15. Bérulle, letter to Monsieur le Curé de St-Saturnin, June 11 [1617] in Jean Dagens (ed.). *Correspondance du Cardinal de Bérulle*, Tome I, p. 241. Emphasis is Bérulle's.

16. Bérulle, letter 'A une Religieuse' [Vers 1615?] in Jean Dagens (ed.), *Correspondance du Cardinal Bérulle*, Tome I, p. 196.

17. *Ibid.*, p. 197.

18. Bérulle, 'Œuvres de Piété' CXCVI Retraite de M. de Bérulle, *Œuvres Complètes* (Paris: Éditions Migne, 1856) p. 1297.

19. Bérulle, letter 'A une Religieuse', Vers 1615?, *op. cit.*, Dagens (ed.), *Correspondance*, p. 197.

20. *Ibid.*, p. 198.

21. Bérulle, 'Dédiéʒ au Roy', *Vie de Jésus, Œuvres Complètes,* Tome I, p. 430.

22. *Ibid.*

23. *Ibid.,* p. 432.

24. *Ibid.,* p. 433.

25. Jean Dagens, Introduction to *Correspondance du Cardinal de Bérulle,* Tome I, pp. ix-x.

26. Michel Dupuy, *Bérulle, Une Spiritualité de L'Adoration* (Tournai: Desclée, 1964), p. 51.

27. Cf. William M. Thompson, 'The Christic Universe of Pierre de Bérulle and the French School', *The American Benedictine Review* 29:4 (December, 1978) pp. 320-47.

28. Bérulle, *Vie de Jésus, Œuvres Complètes,* Tome I, p. 502.

FRANCOIS DE SALES
GENTLENESS AND CIVILITY

BIBLIOGRAPHY

PRIMARY SOURCES CITED

Œuvres de Saint François de Sales. Édition complète d'après les autographes et les éditions originales. Par les soins des Religieuses de la Visitation du Premier Monastère d'Annecy. Annecy, 26 vols. 1892-1932. (Abbreviated as A. in notes.)

Ste. Jeanne-Françoise Frémyot de Chantal. Sa Vie et ses Œuvres. Edition authentique publiée par les soins des Religieuses du Premier Monastère de la Visitation Sainte-Marie d'Annecy. 8 vols., Paris, 1874-79. (Abbreviated as Ch. in notes.)

TRANSLATIONS OF THE WRITINGS OF FRANÇOIS DE SALES

Library of St. Francis de Sales. Translated and edited by H. B. Mackey o.s.b. London, 1883-1910.

1. Letters to Persons in the World; 2. Treatise on the Love of God; 3. The Catholic Controversy; 4. Letters to Persons in Religion; 5. Spiritual Conferences; 6. Mystical Explanation of the Canticle of Canticles; Depositions of Ste. Jane Frances de Chantal in the Cause of the Canonization of St. Francis de Sales, by his friend Pierre Camus, Bishop of Belley.

Introduction to the Devout Life. Translated by M. Day. New York: Dutton, 1961.

Introduction to the Devout Life. Translated by J. K. Ryan. New York: Doubleday, 1953. 4th edition 1972.

On the Preacher and Preaching. A Letter by Francis de Sales. Translation and introduction by John K. Ryan. U.S.A.: Henry Regnery Co., 1964.

St. Francis de Sales in His Letters. Edited and translated by the Sisters of the Visitation, Harrow-on-the-Hill. St. Louis, Mo.: B. Herder Book Co., 1933.

St. Francis de Sales. Selected Letters. Translation and introduction by Elisa-

beth Stopp. New York: Harper and Bros., 1960.
A Selection from the Spiritual Letters of St. Francis de Sales. Translated by the author of 'Life of St. Francis de Sales, etc.' London: Rivingtons, 1871.
Treatise on the Love of God. 2 vols. Translated by John K. Ryan. Rockford, Illinois: Tan Books, 1974.

OTHER WORKS OF INTEREST

Bedoyere, Michael de la. *François de Sales.* New York: Harper and Bros., 1960.
Brémond, Henri. *A Literary History of Religious Thought in France From the Wars of Religion Down to Our Times.* Vol. I Devout Humanism. Vol. II The Coming of Mysticism. New York: MacMillan Co., 1930.
Calvet, J. *La littérature religieuse de François de Sales à Fénelon.* Paris: Les editions Mondiales, 1956.
Julien-Eymard d'Angers. *L'humanisme crétien au XVIIe siècle: St. François de Sales et Yves de Paris.* La Haye: Martinus Nijhoff, 1970.
Lajeunie, E. J. *Saint François de Sales. L'homme, la pensée, l'action.* 2 vols. Paris: Editions Guy Victor, 1964.
Schueller, Th. *La Femme et le Saint. La femme et ses problèmes d'après Saint François de Sales.* Paris: Les Editions Ouvrières, 1970.
Stopp, Elisabeth, translator. *Saint Francis de Sales: A Testimony by St. Chantal.* London: Faber and Faber, 1967.
Vincent, Francis. *Saint François de Sales, Directeur d'âmes.* Paris: Beauchesne, 1923.

NOTES

1. *Traité de l'Amour de Dieu,* I, XVI; A. IV, 77.
2. *Ibid.,* I, XVI; A. IV, 84.
3. *Ibid.,* I, XV; A. IV, 75-76.
4. *Ibid.,* I, XVII; A. IV, 80-83.
5. *Ibid.,* V, I-XIII; A. IV, 255-299.
6. *Ibid.,* V, III; A. IV, 263.
7. *Ibid.,* V, VI; A. IV, 275.
8. *Ibid.,* VI, I-XV; A. IV, 301-361.
9. *Ibid.,* VI, I; A. IV, 304.
10. *Ibid.,* VI, II; A. IV, 310.
11. *Ibid.,* VI, III; A. IV, 312.
12. *Ibid.,* IX, I-XVI; A. V, 109-163.
13. *Ibid.,* VII, I-VII; A. V, 59-107.
14. Even Louis Bouyer in his three volume *History of Christian Spirituality,* (Eng. trans., New York: Desclée and Co., 1963), sideskirts the issue, speaking only briefly of sixteenth century Spain and not at all of France. There is, of course, Henri Brémond's classic study, *Histoire Littéraire du Sentiment Religieux en France depuis la Fin des Guerres de Religion jusqu'à nos Jours,* (Paris: Bloud et Gay, 1921). English trans. K. L. Montgomery, (New York: MacMillan, 1930). But the fact remains that the historiographic thrust of the English world bypasses the era. For a thoughtful essay on the topic see H. Outram Evennett, *The Spirit of the Counter-Reformation* (Cambridge: University Press, 1968).

15. This term, coined by Brémond, has come under question as a legitimate rubric for the phenomena that Brémond wants to isolate. A sane evaluation of the issue and a clearer definition is supplied by Julien-Eymard d'Angers in his *L'Humanisme Chrétien au XVIIe Siècle: St. François de Sales et Yves de Paris*, (La Haye: Martinus Nijhoff, 1970). Also, on the relationship between the saint and the Renaissance see J. Calvet, *La Littérature Religieuse de François de Sales à Fénelon* (Paris: Les Editions Mondiales, 1956).

16. On Molina and Molinism see Anton C. Pegis, 'Molina and Human Liberty' in *Jesuit Thinkers of the Renaissance*, edited by Gerard Smith (Milwaukee, Wisc.: Marquette University Press, 1939), pp. 75-131 and Joseph H. Fichter, *Man of Spain: Francis of Suarez* (New York: MacMillan Co., 1940).

17. For an analysis of St François' relationship to this theology consult Francis Vincent, *Saint François de Sales, Directeur d'âmes* (Paris: Beauchesne, 1923).

18. *Traité*, II, VIII; A. IV, 112-113.

19. This is the version of the saint's struggle recorded by Calvet, p. 23.

20. *Teneur de la déposition de la Venerable Mère Jeanne-Françoise Freymot de Chantal* in Ch. II, 26, 124-125.

21. *Ibid.*, Ch. II, 46, 221.

22. *Ibid.*, Ch. II, 16, 110.

23. *Ibid.*, Ch. II, 11, 109.

24. *Introduction à la Vie Devote*, III, 23; A. III, 216-217.

25. *Teneur*, Ch. II, 30, 154.

26. *Ibid.*, Ch. II, 40, 200.

27. Th. Schueller, *La Femme et le Saint: La femme et ses problèmes d'après Saint François de Sales* (Paris: Les Editions ouvrières, 1970), pp. 55-104 has a discussion of the Salesian æsthetic upon which what follows is based.

28. *Introduction*, II, 21; A. III, 122.

29. *Ibid.*, III, 4; A. III, 145.

30. This is the subject of Schueller's book.

31. There is evidence that François de Sales' opinions on the subject of women formed the theological justification for the feminist position taken by Marie Le Jars de Gournay (d. 1645), an early champion of the equality of the sexes. Schueller, pp. 220ff.

32. Brémond goes so far as to claim that the *Treatise* is a soul portrait of Jeanne de Chantal and that her mentor owes to her his insight into the depth of the contemplative life.

33. *Traité*, VII, I; A. V, 6.

34. *Introduction*, I, 3; A. III, 20-21.

35. Schueller, pp. 155ff.

THE ABBÉ DE RANCÉ
MONASTIC REVIVAL

NOTES

1. Clarendon Press, Oxford, 1974 [= Krailsheimer, *Rancé*].

2. In 'Un livre sur Rancé', in *Cîteaux: Commentarii Cistercienses* 26 (1975) 221.

3. *Ibid.*

4. H. Bremond, *L'Abbè Tempête* (Paris, 1929); trans. by F. Sheed, *The Thundering Abbot* (London, 1930).

5. *General Chapter OCSO Masculine Branch, 1980: Minutes of the Sessions,* p. 166 (*pro manuscripto*, s.l., s.d.).
[NOTE: Here we must make a distinction, and an important one. The Fathers of the General Chapter just referred to are indeed embarrassed by the appellation 'Trappist' as a name convertible with 'Cistercian'. Quite different, however, is the same General Chapter's concern to protect the Order's exclusive legal right to the name 'Trappist' for *trade mark* purposes 'Trappist' as applied to beer, cheese, and chocolate is a hallmark of excellence.] See *Ibid.*, pp. 44-46.

6. L. Aubry, 'Personne et Communauté: Rancé et la Trappe', in the *pro manuscripto* collection of papers, *La Communauté: Laval - Septembre 1976* (s.l., s.d.) pp. 225-251 (1-27).

7. D. Pezzoli, 'L'Abbé de Rancé et l'esprit de la pratique eucharistique', *Collectanea O.C.R.*, 22 (1961) 138-147.

8. Sr Marie-Raphael, 'La *lectio divina* selon Rancé', in *Tamié 79. La Lectio Divina. Rencontre des Pères-Maîtres et Mères-Maîtresses bénédictins et cisterciens du Nord et de l'Est de la France a l'Abbaye de Tamié (Savoie) du 22 au 27 janvier 1979* (s.l., s.d.) pp. 302-335.•

9. C. Waddell, 'The Abbot as Spiritual Father in the Writings and Pastoral Practice of Rancé', in *Abba: Guides to Wholeness and Holiness East and West,* CS 38 (1982) 158-204.

10. D. Pezzoli. 'L'Abbe de Rancé. Textes sur la discretion', in *Collectanea,* 24 (1962) 259-263.

11. D. Pezzoli, 'Le Discernment des vocations monastiques par l'abbé de Rancé', *Collectanea* 22 (1960) 37-48.

12. C. Waddell, 'Notes on Seventeenth-century la Trappe and the Poor', *Monastic Exchange,* 8 (1976) 56-62.

13. C. Waddell, 'The Eastern Monastic Fathers and the Reform of Rancé', *One Yet Two. Monastic Tradition East and West,* CS 29 (Kalamazoo, 1976) 423-439.

14. L. Aubry, 'Les Pères des déserts à la Trappe', *Cîteaux,* 32 (1981) 167-214.

15. In *Cistercians in the Late Middle Ages.* Studies in Medieval Cistercian History VI. CS 64 (Kalamazoo, 1981) pp. 102-61.

16. 'La joie dans Rancé', *Collectanea,* 25 (1963) 206-15.

17. As quoted in S. I. Hayakawa, *Language in Thought and Action* (New York - Burlingame, 1964, 2nd ed.) p. 199.

18. L. Lekai, *The White Monks. A History of the Cistercian Order* (Okauchee, Wisconsin: Our Lady of Spring Bank, 1953) 106-107.

19. Hayakawa, *Language,* p. 199.

20. L. Lekai, *The Rise of the Cistercian Strict Observance in Seventeenth Century France* (Washington, D.C., 1968) 170.

21. The death of Fr Jérôme du Halgouët in 1977 deprived the Order of its most knowledgeable expert on Dom Augustin de Lestrange and his period.

See his remarkable series of articles, 'Pierres d'attente pour une histoire de l'Ordre dans la première moitié du XIXème siècle', in *Cîteaux*', 17 (1966) 89-118; 18 (1967) 51-75, 240-262; 19 (1968) 74-93; 20 (1969) 38-68; 21 (1970) 23-61, 279-299; 22 (1971) 61-92; 23 (1972) 91-113; 26 (1975) 57-81, 185-215, 284-315; 27 (1976) 56-84; 28 (1977) 48-93.

22. As quoted in Krailsheimer, *Rancé*, p. 156.

23. The chapters in Krailsheimer's study, 'Religious of the Cistercian Order' (Ch. 7, pp. 123-151) and 'Religious of Other Orders' (Ch. 8, pp. 152-175) and 'Women in Religion' (Ch. 9, pp. 176-210), provide many instances of this.

24. The question is discussed at length in the section 3. 'Les Clairets Adopts the Reform: 1692,' in C. Waddell, 'Armand-Jean de Rancé and Françoise-Angélique d'Etampes Valençay: Reformers of les Clairets,' to be published in the collection of papers, *Medieval Religious Women: The Cistercians* (Cistercian Publication, 1984?).

25. Lekai, *The Rise*, p. 169.

26. [Félibien des Avaux], *Description de l'abbaye de la Trappe* (Paris, 1671) 81.

27. W.H. Lewis (ed.), *Memoirs of the Duc de Saint-Simon* (New York, 1964) 8-9.

28. François-Régis Bastide devotes a number of perceptive pages to the importance of la Trappe in the life of the duc de Saint-Simon in his *Saint-Simon par lui-même*, Coll. Ecrivains de toujours (Paris, 1967) 87-97.

29. From the jacket description of the Penguin Book edition (1962; reprint 1966).

30. *Ibid.*, pp. 319-320.

31. The expression is Peter Hebblethwaite's, from his Introduction to his translation of Pierre de Calan's *Cosmas or the Love of God* London, 1980).

32. T. Wilder, *Theophilus North*, paperback ed. (Avon, New York, 1974), p. 23.

33. *Ibid.*, p. 54.

34. *Ibid.*, pp. 180-1.

35. The author's study, 'L'Abbé de Rancé et la règle bénédictine,' in *Analecta S.O.C.*, 22 (1966) 161-217, is helpful chiefly for its bibliographical information.

36. See pp. 8-9 of Peter Hebblethwaite's Introduction to the book described above, footnote 31.

37. See F. Vandenbroucke, 'Humiliations volontaires? La pensée de l'Abbé de Rancé', *Collectanea*, 27 (1965) 194-201.

38. Mabillon, *Traité des Etudes monastiques* (Paris, 1691) pp. 3-4.

39. There was a second edition by the same printer (Delaune, Paris) in 1702.

40. See C. Waddell, 'The Cistercian Dimension', pp. 120-1, and 144-5.

41. From Rancé's most important work, *De la sainteté et des devoirs de la vie monastique*, first printed in 1683, and frquently thereafter. The citation is from Ch. 12, 'De la pénitence', p. 262 of the edition of 1846 (Paris).

42. *Ibid.*, p. 261.

43. Translated from the life and edition of Louise's letters by J. Lair, *Louise de la Vallière* (Paris, 1881).

44. Pacôme, *Description du plan en relief de l'Abbaye de la Trappe presente au Roy Par le Frere Pacome, Religieux Solitaire* (Paris, 1708). The engraving of the death of the holy abbot is on a double-page between pp. 61 and 62.

45. Biographical details for both Denis and his wife come from Mère de Chaugy's necrological notice of Soeur Claude Françoise, Archives Visitation d'Annecy, Série: Vies n° 5, pp. 479-503.

46. Our Sébastien is the 'Bouthillier' who appears frequently in Philippe Erlanger's, *Richelieu. The Thrust for Power*, trans. P. Wolf (New York, 1968). But the richest source of bibliographical information on him may be found by following up the references under 'Bouthillier ou Le Bouthillier' in J. Orcibal, *Jean Duvergier de Hauranne, Abbè de Saint-Cyran et son temps (1518-1638)*, Les origines de Jansénisme III (Paris, 1948) pp. 233-4.

47. Brief biographical details about Victor are in Krailsheimer, *Rancé*, p. 218. Victor was one of the truly great prelates of Tours, and deserves further study — if not as a contribution to hagiographical studies, perhaps as a contribution to sociological investigations: the role of the great prelate in French society.

48. Information from the necrological notice referred to above, footnote 45.

49. Contrary to the current drift of scholarly opinion, there is no reason to assume that this edition is more the work of the young boy's tutors than it is his own. It would be a remarkable achievement for any scholar at any age; but it is, in point of fact, chiefly a work of compilation. Definitions and clarification of terms form the substance of the commentary; and the edition simply proves that Rancé knew from an early age how to consult a lexicon. Indeed, his later polemical discussions were probably affected by his early training in word-hunting. For Rancé, debate meant largely quoting 'authorities'.

50. See the account by L. Dubois, *Histoire de l'Abbé de Rancé et de sa Réforme* (Paris, 1866) 1, pp. 56-57.

51. The Acts and Minutes of the Assembly, prolix though they are, are also remarkably discreet whenever touching upon matters concerning personalities in high places. Clues as to Rancé's activity during the first year of meetings are to be gleaned from memoirs and related sources. This phase of his pre-conversion period is of considerable interest, and calls for more detailed study.

52. For a recent judicious appraisal of the evidence, see Krailsheimer, *Rancé*, pp. 6-7, 10-11.

53. As quoted in J.H.M. Salmon, Cardinal de Retz. *The Anatomy of a Conspirator* (New York, 1970) p. 62.

54. *Ibid.*

55. Excellent document collected by T. Nguyên-Dình-Tuyên, 'Histoire des controverses à Rome entre la Commune et l'Etroite Observance de 1662 à 1666' *Analecta Cisterciensia*, 26 (1970) 3-247.

56. See footnote 15, above.

57. See footnote 9, above.

58. M.A. Schimmelpenninck, *Select Memoirs of Port Royal* (4th ed., London, 1835), 2:355-6.

59. See the remarkable series of quotations excerpted by J. Cordelier, *Mme*

de Sévigné par elle-même, Coll. Ecrivains de tourjours (Paris, 1967) 138-43.
60. Schimmelpenninck, *Select Memoirs*, p. 358.
61. As quoted by Robert Speaight, *Georges Bernanos. A Study of the Man and the Writer* (New York, 1974), p. 16.
62. Description based on the review by David Sterrit, 'Wooster Group defies convention in latest multimedia effort', in the 'Arts/Entertainment' section of the *Christian Science Monitor*, Monday, 1 March, 1982.

BENEDICTINE SPIRITUALITY
OF THE SEVENTEENTH-CENTURY

NOTES

1. I have written on the spiritual work of Mère Mechtilde in 'Une école de spiritualité bénédictine datant du XVIIe siècle: les Bénédictines de l'Adoration Perpetuelle' in *Studia monastica* 18 (1977) 433-53, with the publication of some unedited letters: 'Lumières nouvelles sur Catherine de Bar', ibid. 20 (1978) 397-408; and in *Introduction à Catherine de Bar, à l'écoute de S.Benoit* (Rouen 1980) 3-17.

2. The volumes of the writings of Mère Mechtilde which have already been published are: *Catherine de Bar, Mère Mechtilde du Saint-Sacrement. Document biographique. Ecrits spirituels*. 1610-1670 (Rouen, 1973) This basic work will be cited hereafter by the abbreviation *Catherine de Bar, Lettres inédites*, (Rouen, 1976); *Fondation de Rouen*, (Rouen, 1977); *A l'écoute de S. Benoît*, (Rouen, 1980). The publishers are the Benedictines, 14 Rue Bourg l'Abbé, F-76000, Rouen.

3. A chronology of the life of Mère Mechtilde is given in *Catherine de Bar*, p. 325, and a *bibliography, ibid.*, 329-31; to this should be added Y. Chaussy, *Les Bénédictines et la réforme catholique en France au XVIIe siècle* (Paris, 1975) 371-7; a brief but compact bibliography of Mère Mechtilde.

4. *Catherine de Bar*, Préface, p. 7-21.

5. 'Conference faite à l'Institut Catholique de Paris le samedi 8 février 1958', *ibid.*, 23-33.

6. L. Cognet, *ibid.*, p. 24-5.

7. 'Spiritualité vanniste et tradition monastique', in *Revue d'ascétique et de mystique* 36 (1960) 214-31 reprinted in *Spiritualité occidentale 2, Témoins* (Paris, 1965); translated in *Espiritualidad occidental. Testigos* (Salamanca, 1967).

8. *Catherine de Bar*, pp. 238, 98.

9. *Ibid.*, 20-21.

10. *Ibid.*, 26.

11. L. Brigue, 'Alger de Liège', in *Studia eucharistica DCC Anni a condito festo Sanctissimi Corporis Christi 1246-1946* (Antwerp, 1946) 50-60.

12. *Catherine de Bar*, 28.

13. 'Saint-Germain-des-Prés et les Bénédictines de Paris', in *Revue d'histoire*

de l'Eglise de France 43 (1957) 223-30; this special number of the review has also been edited under the title *Mémorial du XIVe centenaire de l'abbaye de Saint-Germain-des-Prés* (Paris, 1959).

14. *Catherine de Bar*, 238 and 98. Cf. 'Notre Dame abbesse', in *Priez sans cesse, Trois cents ans de prière* (Paris, 1953) 175-7, and M. Pigeon, 'Sainte Marie, abbesse', in *Cîteaux* 26 (1973) 68-9.

15. The ideas set out in paragraph two and the quotations which are made there are taken from *A l'ecoute de S. Benoît*.

16. For example. A. Chapelle, SJ, 'L'adoration eucharistique et la réparation' in *Vie consacrée* 46(1974) 338-54.

17. In 'La royauté du Christ dans la spiritualité française du XVIIe siècle', in *La Vie spirituelle*. Supplément, I (1947) 216-29 and 291-307, I have quoted texts.

18. Cf. L. Gougaud, 'Muta praedicatio', in *Revue bénédictine* 42 (1930), 170-71.

19. Cf. *La royauté du Christ*.

20. This has been shown by A. Borias, 'Le Christ dans la Règle de saint Benoît', in *Revue bénédictine* 82 (1972) 109-32.

21. B. Galiner, *Regula emblematica S. Benedicti* (Vienna, 1780).

22. Bibliography in 'Les méditations eucharistiques d'Arnaud de Bonneval', in RTAM 13 (1946) 40-56.

23. Cited in *Catherine de Bar*, p. 118.

24. See, for example, *Pierre le Vénérable* (Saint-Wandrille, 1946) 91-4: 'La vie cachée'; G. Penco, 'Il monastico sepolcro di Cristo', in *Vita monastica* 17 (1913) 99-109.

25. Cited in *Catherine de Bar*, 234.

26. *Ibid.*, 235.

27. *Ibid.*, 249.

28. See note 14 above.

29. *Catherine de Bar*, 185. Cf. 'Dévotion et théologie mariale dans le monachisme bénédictin', in *Maria. Ètudes sur la Sainte Vierge*, II, (Paris, 1952) 557-58, 577.

30. *Catherine de Bar*, 194; cf. 'La vêture "ad succurrendum" d'après le moine Raoul', in *Analecta monastica; Studia Anselmiana*, 3 (Rome, 1955) 158-68.

31. *Catherine de Bar*, 198; cf. *La vie parfaite* (Paris-Turnhout, 1948). 128-9.

JOSEPH HALL
ANGLICAN SPIRITUALITY

NOTES

1. See Barbara Kiefer Lewalski, *Donne's Anniversaries and the Poetry of Praise; The Creation of a Symbolic Mode* (Princeton, N.J.: Princeton University Press, 1973) 75-81.

2. The corporate aspect of Anglican spirituality is stressed in *The Godly*

Kingdom of Tudor England: Great Books of the English Reformation, ed. John Booty (Wilton, Conn.: Morehouse-Barlow, 1981); see especially Chapter One.

3. See Claire Cross, *The Puritan Earl: The Life of Henry Hastings Third Earl of Huntingdon*, 1536-1595 (London: Macmillans, 1966), especially 122-23. There is no denying the early and strong Puritan influence on Hall.

4. There is a good discussion of this in Frank Livingstone Huntley, *Bishop Joseph Hall 1574-1656* (Cambridge: D.S. Brewer, 1979) Chapter two.

5. Barbara Kiefer Lewalski, *Protestant Poetics and the Seventeenth Century Religious Lyric* (Princeton, N.J.: Princeton University Press, 1979) 150, and Louis Martz, *The Poetry of Meditation* (New Haven: Yale University Press, 1954) 332.

6. Huntley, *Hall*, pp. 72-73.

7. Joseph Hall, *Works*, ed. Josiah Pratt, 10 vols. (London, 1808) 7:43.

8. Huntley, *Hall*, pp. 76ff; Hall, *Works*, 7:56. For the *Scala*, see Wessel Gansfort, *Opera* (Gronigen: Excudebat Ioannis Sussius, 1614)) 287-289.

9. See, for instance, the *Rosetum* (Basle: J. Parvius et J. Scabelerus, 1510), Alph. 2.C (*Affectionis subtrahendae causae*), Alph. 4. A.B.C. (*Meditatio est oranti necessaria*), and Alph. 46, which contains the *Scala* but also much more on meditation.

10. R.R. Post, *The Modern Devotion*, Studies in Medieval and Reformation Thought, 3 (Leiden: E.J. Brill, 1968) 545.

11. Ibid, p. 547.

12. Ibid., p. 546.

13. See, for example, Hall's 'Select Thoughts or Choice Helps for a Pious Spirit', *Works*, 7:245-305.

14. Epistle 8 of Decade III, of Hall's Letters; *Works*, 7:190-192.

15. Huntley, *Hall*, p. 81; *Works*, 6:137, 145.

16. Hall, *Works*, 7:227.

17. Ibid., 7:318.

18. Huntley works out the implications in his *Hall*, pp. 82-84. See Hall, *Works*, 7:53-54.

19. See H.R. McAdoo, *The Structure of Caroline Moral Theology* (London: Longmans, Green and Co., 1949) Chapter one. Hooker's strong emphasis on purpose begins with his definitions of law in *Of The Laws of Ecclesiastical Polity*, Book I, Ch. 2, sec. 1; *Works*, Folger Shakespeare Library Edition, Vol. 1, ed. G. Edelen (Cambridge: Belknap Press of Harvard University Press, 1977) p. 58.

20. Hall, *Works*, 7:45.

21. Hall, p. 44.

22. Hall, p. 45.

23. Both Jewel in his sermon on Ps 69:9 (*Works*, ed. J. Ayre, Parker Society, Vol. 2, [Cambridge, At the University Press, 1847] 1004ff), and Hooker in his *Lawes* (Pref. 3.10) protest against persons driven by zeal without knowledge. It is imperative for Anglican spirituality that intellect and affections be held together, either in balance or in tension.

24. Hall, p. 46.

25. Hall, p. 47.

26. See Hooker, *Lawes*, II.1.4, where the theologian demonstrates his deep appreciation for God's revelation 'in the glorious works of nature', and the impressive treatise of John Ray, the seventeenth-century naturalist, *The Wisdom of God Manifested in the Works of the Creation* (London: R. Harbin for William Innys, 1717). And see Richard S. Westfall, *Science and Religion in Seventeenth Century England* (New Haven: Yale University Press, 1958), especially Chapter five.

27. Hall, p. 47.

28. Hall speaks of Gerson as 'that worthy Chancellor of Paris', and refers to the 'hill of meditation' and the 'ladder of contemplation'. He probably knew Gerson's *La Montaigne de Contemplation*. See Gerson, *Œuvres Complètes*, ed. Mgr. Glorieux (Paris: Desclee & Cie, n.d.), 7:16-55.

29. See Hooker, *Lawes*, VI.3.2-6. This is the classic Anglican statement on repentance. See also McAdoo, *Caroline Moral Theology*, Chapter Five.

30. Hall, pp. 49-50. Hall advised relaxing the mind by working with the hands, mixing parts as comedians do, 'that the pleasantness of the one may temper the austereness of the other' (p. 50).

31. Huntley, *Hall*, p. 80, suggests that the 'great Master' may be Bernard or Gerson, but prefers to think it is Thomas à Kempis.

32. Hall, p. 51.

33. Hall, p. 52.

34. See below, pp. 225-227.

35. Hall, p. 53.

36. Hall, p. 54.

37. Hall writes: 'prayer maketh way for meditation; meditation giveth matter, strength, and life to our prayers; by which, as all other things are sanctified to us, so we are sanctified to all holy things' (p. 55). See Jean Gerson, *Selections from A Deo exiuit, Contra curiositatem and De Mystical Theologia speculativa*, ed. Steven E. Ozment Leiden: Brill, 1969) 65-6.

38. Hall, p. 57.

39. Hall, p. 58.

40. In a way reminiscent of Hooker's description of the christian life (*Lawes*, V.56.10), Hall states: 'In this life here, may be degrees; there, can be no imperfection. If some be like the sky, others like the stars; yet all shine' (p. 58).

41. Hall, p. 59.

42. Hooker related justification and sanctification to the same critical moment of salvation without denying either the importance of the former or the necessity of the latter. See Hooker's 'A Learned Discourse of Justification,' Section 21 (*Works*, 7th Keble ed. [Oxford, 1888], 3:507-508).

43. See Hooker, *Lawes*, VI.3.2.

44. Hall, pp. 63-4.

45. Hall, p. 65. In his example he cites Rev 21:4, Rom 8:18, and Ps 31:19.

46. Hall, p. 65.

47. Hall, p. 66.

48. *Ibid.*

49. Hooker, *Lawes*, VI.3.4.

50. John Booty, *Three Anglican Divines on Prayer: Jewel, Andrewes, and Hooker* (Cambridge: Cowley Publication, 1977) p. 9.

51. Hall, p. 67.

52. Hall, p. 68.

53. Hall, p. 69.

54. Hall, p. 70.

55. *Ibid.*

56. Hall, *Works*, 7:73-80. In the margins Hall identifies the different divisions of the meditation as provided in the *Arte*.

57. Thomas Wilson, *The Arte of Rhetorique, for the use of all suche as are studious of Eloquence* (London, 1533), fol. 71ᵛ. See also sig. a.i.ᵛ-a.iiᵛ.

58. *Lawes*, V.22.1. Note the utility of sermons in Lewalski, *Donne's Anniversaries*, p. 87

59. Hooker, *Works* (1888), 3:686. See J. W. Blench, *Preaching in England in the Late Fifteenth and Sixteenth Centuries* (New York: Barnes and Noble, 1964) 190-192 for further examples.

60. Ibid., pp. 686-687.

61. Jewel, *Works*, Parker Society 2:1042; see also pp. 1090, 1054-56.

62. This is clearly the situation with regard to *Certaine Sermons or Homilies* (1547), the so-called First Book of Homilies. See John Wall in Chapter two of *The Godly Kingdom*, ed. Booty.

63. Blench, *Preaching*, 108-111.

64. Andrewes, *Ninety-Six Sermons*, Library of Anglo-Catholic Theology (Oxford, 1841) 2:134.

65. Ibid., p. 137.

66. See Blench, *Preaching;* Horton Davies, *Worship and Theology in England*, 1, *From Cranmer to Hooker* (Princeton, N.J.: Princeton University Press, 1970). Chapter Six (On Anglican Preaching) and Chapter Eight (On Puritan Preaching), and Irvonwy Morgan, *The Godly Preachers of the Elizabethan Church* (London: Epworth Press, 1965) pp. 107 ff. on Henry Smith.

67. *The Book of Common Prayer 1559: The Elizabethan Prayer Book,* ed. John E. Booty (Charlottesville, Va.: The University Press of Virginia for the Folger Shakespeare Library, 1976) 150.

68. See *The Godly Kingdom*, Ch. 3, and the title page of the Prayer Book, *Book of Common Prayer 1559.*

69. Jewel, *Works*, Parker Society, 2:1122.

70. *Ibid.*, p. 1123.

71. *Ibid.*, pp. 1123-1124.

72. *Ibid.*, p. 1124.

73. Hooker found *De coena Domini* in the Cyprian *Opera* (Geneva: Excudebat Ioannes le Preux, 1593) where it was annotated by Simon Goulart, the Calvinist-humanist theologian. It is in fact a part of Arnold of Bonneval's (fl. c. 1144) *De cardinalibus Christi operibus*. See Jean Leclercq, OSB, 'Les méditations eucharistiques d'Arnauld de Bonneval', *Recherches de Théologie ancienne et médiévale*, 13 (1946) 40-56.

74. Hooker, *Lawes,* V.67.12.

75. Especially the sermon on Zech 12:10 in *Ninety-Six Sermons,* Library of Anglo-Catholic Theology, 2:119-137.

76. *The Private Devotions of Lancelot Andrewes,* ed. F.E. Brightman (New York: Living Age Books; Meridian Books, Inc., 1961) 123.

77. Lewalski, *Donne's Anniversaries,* p. 83.

78. Ibid., p. 109.

79. John Donne, *The Divine Poems,* ed. Helen Gardner, 2nd ed. Oxford: Clarendon, 1978) 11. I am dependent on Dame Helen's arrangement of the sonnets of 1633.

80. Stanley Fish, *The Living Temple: George Herbert and Catechizing* (Berkeley: University of California Press, 1978); see pages 10-11.

81. Herbert, *Works,* ed. F.E. Hutchinson (Oxford: Clarendon, 1941) 256.

82. Fish, *The Living Temple,* p. 27.

83. Herbert, *Works,* p. 26.

84. Ibid.

85. John E. Booty, 'George Herbert: *The Temple* and *The Book of Common Prayer',* *Mosaic,* 12/2 (Winter 1979) 75-90.

86. *The Book of Common Prayer 1559,* p. 14.

87. Ibid., pp. 49-60.

88. Ibid., p. 253.

89. Ibid., p. 264.

90. See John E. Booty, 'Richard Hooker', *The Spirit of Anglicanism,* ed. W.J. Wolf (Wilton, Conn.: Morehouse-Barlow, 1979) 31-2, and Hooker, *Lawes* V, 67.6.

BIBLE AND EXPERIENCE
PURITAN SPIRITUALITY

NOTES

1. Among his books I would cite especially *The Holy Spirit in Puritan Faith and Experience* (Oxford, 1947), and *The Puritan Spirit* (London, 1967) which is a collection of previously published articles.

2. (New Haven and London: Yale University Press, 1976).

3. (Chicago and London, University of Chicago Press, 1980).

4. (New York, 1971).

5. (London: Macmillan, 1971).

6. (Cambridge, University of Cambridge, 1958).

7. *The Elizabethan Puritan Movement* (Los Angeles: U. of California, 1967) and *Archbishop Grindal, 1519-1593* (Los Angeles: U. of California, 1979).

8. *The Shaping of the Elizabethan Regime* (Princeton: Princeton University Press, 1968).

9. *The Cambridge Connection and the Elizabethan Settlement of 1559* (Durham, N.C.: Duke University Press, 1980).

10. 'Reflections on the Nature of English Puritanism,' *Church History* 23 (1954) 99-108.

11. 'Puritanism as a Movement of Revival', *Evangelical Quarterly* 52:1 (1980) 2-16.

12. See esp. his 'Puritan and Quaker Mysticism, *Theology* (1975) 518-531.

13. 'Origins of Puritanism', *Church History* 20 (1951) 35-57, and 'A Reappraisal of William Tyndale's Debt to Martin Luther', *Church History* 31 (1962) 24-45.

14. 'Anglican Against Puritan: Ideological Origins during the Marian Exile', *Church History* 42 (1973) 45-57.

15. While nearly every writer on Puritanism addresses this question of definition, a good orientation to the problems remains Basil Hall's article, 'Puritanism: the Problem of Definition', in *Studies in Church History II*. E. J. Cuming, ed. (London: Nelson, 1965), p. 288.

16. *The Protestant Mind of the English Reformation* (Princeton, 1961), and especially the article 'Puritanism as History and Historiography', *Past and Present* 41 (1968) 77-104 where it is proposed that we abandon the whole concept of 'Puritanism'.

17. *English Puritanism from John Hooper to John Milton,* (Durham, N.C.: Duke University Press, 1968) p. 46.

18. 'A Devotion of Rapture in English Puritanism', in R. B. Knox, ed. *Reformation, Conformity and Dissent: Essays in Honour of Geoffrey Nuttall* (London: Epworth, n.d.) p. 119.

19. *Puritanism in Tudor England*, p. 7.

20. Geoffrey Nuttall, in *The Puritan Spirit: Essays and Addresses* (London: Epworth, n.d.) p. 17.

21. As quoted in H. C. Porter, *Puritanism in Tudor England*, p. 7.

22. *The Puritan Spirit*, p. 82.

23. 'Origins of Puritanism', p. 37.

24. 'Answering the "Known Men": Bishop Reginald Pecock and Mr. Richard Hooker', *Church History* 49 (June, 1980) 133-146.

25. *Ibid.*, page 134.

26. See, e.g., R. Vander Molen, 'Anglican Against Puritan' (see n. 14).

27. From II Corinthians 6:17.

28. As quoted in *Puritanism in Tudor England*, p. 3.

29. I am indebted to Father Jean Leclercq for his suggestion that the *puritas* theme of the Cistercians is akin to the Puritan spirit.

30. In G. E. Duffield, ed., *The Work of William Tyndal* (Philadelphia: Fortress Press, 1965), p. 49 My emphasis.

31. In his 'Prologue to the Book of Genesis', *ibid*, p. 38.

32. This should not be interpreted to mean that Puritan spirituality is dour and joyless. On the contrary there is a strong emphasis upon joy, victory and gladness in one's daily 'walk' before God and man.

33. *Puritanism in Tudor England*, page 9.

34. John Brown, *The English Puritans* (Cambridge, England: The University Press, 1910) p. 1.

35. I use here the categories used by Prof. Rupp in 'A Devotion of Rapture' (see n. 18) p. 126.

36. I am, of course, aware that Tyndale was dead long before the historical event which made of Puritanism a movement distinct from Anglican.

37. In spite of many superficial similarities, the way in which the Puritan expresses this polarity and his emphases are quite different from the well-known 'Word and Spirit' emphasis of the Calvinist theologies. The strong noetic aspect of Calvinist theology is considerably muted and replaced by an experiential aspect.

38. E. Gordon Rupp, 'A devotion of Rapture', p. 120.

39. 'Reflections on the Nature of English Puritanism', p. 102.

40. *Grace Abounding to the Chief of Sinners* (London: SCM, 1955) p. 124.

41. *Ibid.*, p. 148.

42. *The Bruised Reed,* p. 349.

43. *Religion and the Rise of Capitalism* (New York: Harcourt, Brace and Co., 1937) p. 165.

44. James Maclear, 'The Birth of the Free Church Tradition', *Church History* p. 26 (June, 1957) p. 101.

45. *Ibid.*

46. John Brown, *The English Puritans,* p. 3.

47. G. B. Tatham, *The Puritans in Power.* (Cambridge, England: The University Press, 1913) p. 3.

48. Compare, however, how John Goodwin (*plēroma to pneumatikon.* 1857 edition, p. 361) relates to this doctrine. 'How far, and in what respect the apostles themselves were infallible is worthy of consideration. Certain it is that their infallibility . . . did depend upon their care and circumspection; so that . . . they might deviate and swerve from the truth . . . the apostles themselves, as infallible as they were, yet without a serious, close and conscientious minding of what they had received from the Holy Ghost, might mistake'.

49. R. Baxter, *Works.* II, p. 104.

50. The best treatment I have found of this topic is that of John Ray Knott, Jr. *Sword of the Spirit* (Chicago & London: University of Chicago Press, 1980). I am indebted to Knott for several insights.

51. *The Essence of Puritanism,* p. 83.

52. *The Work of William Tyndale,* Duffield ed., p. 36. Emphasis added.

53. *Ibid,* p. 37.

54. *Ibid.*, p. 49.

55. *Ibid.*, p. 99. Emphasis added.

56. *Ibid.*, p. 129.

57. *Ibid.*

58. *Ibid.*, p. 176.

59. See *The Works of John Jewel, Bishop of Salisbury,* Parker Society ed., (Cambridge, 1850) vol. IV, pp. 1161-1188.

60. *Plaine Mans Path-Way to Heaven* (London, 1601), p. 18. Emphasis added. It is well to note the 'plain man' stress seen even in the title of this piece.

61. *Ibid.*, p. 19.

62. Compare, e.g., Hooker's forceful position as found in the *Laws of Ecclesiastical Polity,* XI. viii. 5: His statement that 'The testimonies of God are

true, the testimonies of God are perfect, the testimonies of God are all sufficient *unto the end for which they were given*' suggests the thinking of the Established Clergy at this point. The obvious inference is that one should not
try to use the Scripture for ends other than that for which it was intended,
and that those ends must be decided by reason.

63. The Puritan view is clearly set forth in the following: 'The Scripture is
not a partial, but a perfect rule of faith and manners; neither is there anything that is constantly and everywhere to be observed in the Church of God,
which depends either upon any tradition, or upon any authority whatsoever,
and is not contained in the Scriptures'. (William Ames as quoted in H. Davies,
The Worship of the English Puritans [Glasgow: Rober Maclehose & Company Limited, 1948], p. 5) Or again, William Bradshaw in 1605 writes 'IM-
PRIMIS they hold and maintain that the word of God contained in the writings of the Prophets and Apostles, is of absolute perfection, given by Christ
the Head of the Church, to be unto the same, the sole Canon and rule of all
matters of Religion, and the worship and service of God whatsoever. And
that whatsoever done in the same service and worship cannot be justified by
the said word, is unlawful'. (Also quoted by Davies, p. 50).

PIETIST SPIRITUALITY
PRESENT RESEARCH

NOTES

1. Godfroid Michel, 'Le Pietisme allemand a-t-il existe? Histoire d'un concept fait pour la polemique', *Etudes Germaniques* 101 (1971) 45.

2. For the best English review of the movement see the studies by F. Ernst
Stoeffler, *The Rise of Evangelical Pietism* (Leiden: Brill, 1970), and *German
Pietism During the Eighteenth Century* (Leiden: Brill, 1973).

3. For a general overview see Martin Schmidt, *Pietismus* (Stuttgart: W.
Kohlhammer, 1972) 143ff.

4. On early contacts between Pietists and Wesley see J. Taylor and Kenneth
Hamilton, *History of the Moravian Church* (Bethlehem, Pa.: Moravian
Church of America, 1967) 68-71. An excellent study of Pietism directed at
contemporary evangelical readers is Dale Brown, *Understanding Pietism*
(Grand Rapids, Michigan: Eerdmans, 1978).

5. See Philipp Jakob Spener, *Pia desideria*, trans. with intro. by Theodore
G. Tappert (Philadelphia: Fortress Press, 1964). On Arndt see my introduction to Johann Arndt, *True Christianity* (New York: Paulist Press, 1979).

6. Spener, *Pia desideria*, 94.

7. *Ibid.*, 95.

8. *Ibid.*, 96.

9. Ernest Käseman, *New Testament Questions of Today*, trans. by W.J.
Montague (Philadelphia: Fortress Press, 1969) 4, 260-285.

10. Albrecht Ritschl, *Geschichte des Pietismus* (3 Bde; Bonn: Adolph
Marcus, 1880-1886).

11. See Heinrich Bullinger, *Der Widertäufferen ursprung, fürgang, secten, wäsen* . . . (Zurich, 1560) and Max Goebel, *Geschichte des Christlichen Lebens in der rheinisch-westphalischen evangelischen Kirche* (3 Bde.; Coblenz: Carl Badeker, 1852-1860).

12. The Journal is published by the Luther-Verlag in Bielefeld.

13. *Arbeiten zur Geschichte des Pietismus*, hrsg. von K. Aland, E. Peschke und M. Schmidt (Witten: Luther Verlag, 1967-   ). Eighteen volumes appeared between 1967 and 1979.

14. The series is published by Walter de Gruyter, Berlin. One bibliographic volume and six editions have appeared to the present.

15. For a bibliography of Schmidt and other important figures see Martin Greschat, hrsg., *Zur neueren Pietismusforschung* (Darmstadt: Wissenschaftliche Buchgesellschaft, 1977), 435ff. and Kurt Aland, hrsg., *Pietismus and Bibel* (Witten: Luther Verlag, 1970), 231 ff.

16. See n. 2 above.

17. See F. Ernst Stoeffler, *Continental Pietism and Early American Christianity* (Grand Rapids, Mich.: Eerdmanns, 1976) and his *Mysticism in German Devotional Literature of Colonial Pennsylvania* (Allentown, Pa.: Schlechter's, 1950).

18. Dietrich Blaufuss, *Reichstadt und Pietismus* (Neustadt a.d. Aisch: Degener, 1977).

19. On scholastic Orthodoxy see for example Isaac A. Dorner, *History of Protestant Theology*, trans. George Robson and Sophia Taylor (2 vols.; Edinburgh, 1871), Otto Ritschl, *Dogmengeschichte des Protestantismus* (3 Bde.; Göttingen, J.C. Heinrich'sche Buchhandlung und Vandenhoeck u. Ruprecht, 1908-1926), Hans Emil Weber, *Reformation, Orthodoxie und Rationalismus* (2 Bde.; Gütersloh, Gütersloher Verlagshaus, 1937-1951) and Robert D. Preuss, *The Theology of Post-Reformation Lutheranism* (St. Louis Mo: Concordia, 1970-   ). On the Proto-Pietist movement see Heinrich Heppe, *Geschichte des Pietismus und der Mystik in der Reformierten Kirche* (Leiden, 1879), Wihelm Goeters, *Die Vorbereitung des Pietismus in der Reformierten Kirche* (Leipzig u. Utrecht: J.C. Heinrich'sche Buchhandling, 1911) and Max Goebel, *Geschichte des Christlichen lebens in der rheinisch-westphälischen Kirche* (3 Bde.; Coblenz: Carl Badeker, 1852-1860).

20. See Wilhelm Koepp, 'Würtzeln und Ursprung der orthodoxen Lehre der *unio mystica*', *Zeitschrift für Theologie und Kirche* 29 (1921) 41-71, 134-171 and Paul Althaus d. A., *Forschungen zur Evangelischen Gebetsliteratur* (Gütersloh: C. Bertelsmann, 1927).

21. Werner Elert, *The Structure of Lutheranism*, trans. Walter A. Hanson (St. Louis, Missouri; Concordia, 1962, 166).

22. See Heiko Oberman, *The Harvest of Medieval Theology* (Cambridge, Massachusetts: Harvard University Press, 1963) 341-343.

23. Martin Luther, *Werke* (Weimar: Hermann Bohlau, 1883-   ) 4:265.

24. *Ibid.*, 4:519.

25. See my introduction to Arndt *True Christianity* for details.

26. Translated in *ibid*, 245ff.

27. Joh, Andreas Quenstedt, *Theologia Didactico-Polemica sive systema*

theologicum in quas sectiones didaticum et polemicum divisum . . . (Lipsiae, apud Thomam Fritsch, 1715).

28. *Ibid.*, II, 4-11.

29. See Heinrich Schmid *The Doctrinal Theology of the Evangelical Lutheran Church*, trans. Charles A. Hay and Henry E. Jacobs (Minneapolis, Minn.: Augsburg Publishing House, 1899) 480 f.

30. Quenstedt, II, 10; 1.

31. Cf. Schmid, *Doctrinal Theology*, 480, 481, 483.

32. On Arnold see my *The Role of Late Medieval Spirituality in the Work of Gottfried Arnold* (unpubl. Ph.D., University of Toronto, 1976).

33. Gottfried Arnold, *Die Erste Liebe, Das ist: Wahre Abbildung Der Ersten Christen Nach ihrem Lebendigen Glauben und Heiligen Leben* . . . Zu finden in Gottlieb Friedeburgs Buchhandlung jm Jahre, 1696 (hereafter EL).

34. Arnold, *EL*, 'Vorrede', 3-6.

35. *Ibid*, I, 1-2.

36. *Ibid.*, I, 3:9; 12:1; *VI*, 3, 11 and 4, 14.

37. See *Ibid.*, I, 1:15.

38. *Ibid.*, I, 4:12.

39. *Ibid.*, I, 5-6.

40. *Ibid.*, I, 7-18.

41. *Ibid.*, I, 13:2.

42. *Ibid.*, I, 13:10.

43. *Ibid.*, I, 20:13.

44. See Hermann A. Preuss and Edmund Smits (eds.), *The Doctrine of Man in Classical Lutheran Theology* (Minneapolis, Minn.: Augsburg, 1962) xix-xxii.

45. See my introduction to Arndt, *True Christianity*, 7n 22. Note David Hollaz, *Evangelische Gnaden=Ordnung* . . . (Philadelphia, Pa.: Conrad Zentler, 1810).

46. See my introduction to Jacob Boehme, *The Way to Christ* (New York: Paulist Press, 1978).

47. *Die Werke der Württembergischen Pietisten* . . . , bearbeitet von Gottfried Mälzer (Berlin: Walter de Gruyter, 1972).

48. See August Hermann Francke, *Schriften und Predigten* hrsg. E. Peschke (Berlin: Walter de Gruyter, 1981-   ) and cf. Philipp Jakob Spener, *Hauptschriften und Ergänzungsreihe*, hrsg. E. Beyreuter (Hildesheim: Georg Olms, 1980-   ).

49. The fullest discussion of Ephrata to date remains Julius F. Sachse, *The German Sectarians of Pennsylvania* 1708-1800 (2 vols.; Philadelphia Pa, 1899-1900). Note however Donald F. Durnbough, *The Brethren in Colonial America* (Elgin, Ill.: The Brethren Press, 1967).

50. The relevent selection is printed in *Ephrata as Seen by Contemporaries* ed. by Felix Reichmann and Eugene E. Doll (Allentown, Pa.: Schlechter's, 1953).

51. See Eugene E. Doll and Anneliese M. Funke, *The Ephrata Cloisters: An Annotated Bibliography* (Philadelphia, Pa.: Carl Schunz Memorial Foundation, 1944). The results of Hollyday's work have still not been printed.

52. See Charles M. Treher, 'Snow Hill Cloister', *Publications of the Pennsylvania German Society* 2 (1968).

53. Johann Friedrich Starck, *Tägliches Handbuch in guten und bösen Tagen* first appeared in 1728 and was reprinted regularly thereafter, see edition printed in Konstanz: Verlag von Carl Hirsch, n.d.

54. One example with which I am closely acquainted is the Schwenkfelder Library, Pennsburg, Pennslyvania. The institution still uses a rough catalogue done in the 1930s. It is this inadequate listing which is printed in the National Union Catalogue.

55. *Q.D.B.V. Locutionem Angelorum* . . . M. Godo Fredus Arnold . . . XIV Decemb. Anno 1687, Wittenbergae, Typis Christiani Fincelii. (exemplar in Nationale Forschungs– und Gedenkstätten der klassichen deutschen Literatur in Weimar, DDR).

56. See above n. 48 and Freidrich Christoph Oetinger, *Theologia ex idea vitae deducta* hrsg, Konrad Ohly (2 Bde,; Berlin: Walter de Gruyter, 1979).

57. See above n. 2 and Johannes Wallmann, *Philipp Jakob Spener und die Anfänge des Pietismus* (Tübingen: J.C.B. Mohr (Paul Siebeck), 1970), *passim.*

58. See George H. Williams, *The Radical Reformation* (Philadelphia, Pa.: The Westminster Press, 1962), 803, 810-814.

59. Robert Friedmann, *Mennonite Piety Through the Centuries* (Goshen, Ind: Mennonite Historical Society, 1949).

60. See my introduction to *The Spiritual Diary of Christopher Wiegner* (Pennsburg, Pennsylvania: Descendants of the Schwenkfelder Exiles, 1979).

61. See Wallmann, 283ff.

62. Note in particular Johann Albrecht Bengel, *Erklärte Offenbarung Johannis oder vielmehr Jesu Christi* (Frankfurt-am-Main, 1740).

63. See Goebel, III, 71-125.

64. Friedrich Christoph Oetinger, *Inquisitio in sensum communem,* mit Einleitung von Hans Georg Gadamer (Stuttgart: Friedrich Fromann Verlag, 1964).

65. See August Langen, *Die Wortschatz des deutschen Pietismus* (Tübingen: Max Niemeyer, 1954).

66. See Schmidt, 148.

67. Note *ibid.,* 158, 165 and Eberhard Busch, *Karl Barth und die Pietisten* (München: Chr. Kaiser Verlag, 1978).

68. Note in particular, Koppel S. Pinson, *Pietism as a factor in the Rise of German Nationalism* (New York, 1934; reprint, New York: Octagon Books, 1968).

Pietist Spirituality
The Medieval Sources

NOTES

1. Compare Emil Brunner, *The Philosophy of Religion from the Standpoint of Protestant Theology,* trans. A.J.D. Farrar and Bertram Lee Woolf

(London: James Clarke, 1958) 40, and Martin Schmidt, 'Ecumenical Activity on the Continent of Europe in the seventeenth and eighteenth centuries', in Ruth Rouse and Stephen Charles Neill eds., *A History of the Ecumenical Movement* (Philadelphia, Pa.: The Westminster Press, 1954) 1:99-100.

2. On Arnold see above all Erich Seeberg, *Gottfried Arnold: Die Wissenschaft und die Mystik seiner Zeit* (Meerane i.S., 1923). For more recent literature see Jurgen Büchsel, *Gottfried Arnold: Sein Verständniss von Kirche und Wiedergeburt* (Witten: Luther-Verlag, 1970) 13-24, 210ff.

3. See particularly Hermann Dörries, *Geist und Geschichte bei Gottfried Arnold* (Göttingen: Vandenhoeck und Ruprecht, 1963).

4. For full list of Arnold's works see Seeberg, 51ff.

5. See Gottfried Arnold *Die Erste Liebe* . . . (Franckfurt am Main, 1696), 'Vorbericht', LXXXI.

6. Gottfried Arnold, *Unparteiische Kirchen-und Ketzer-Historie* (Franckfurt am Main bey Thomas Fritsch, 1699-1700) I:13-15.

7. *Ibid.*, 1:13; 2:8-11.

8. On Sudermann, see my 'Medieval Spirituality and the Development of Protestant Sectarianism: A Seventeenth Century Case Study', *Mennonite Quarterly Review* 51 (1977) 31-40.

9. Gottfried Arnold, hrsg., *Auserlesene Sendschreiben Derer Alten/* . . . *gesammelt und verteutscht* . . . (Franckfurt und Leipzig: In Verlegung Theod. Philippe Calvisio/Buchhandl. Im Jahr 1700).

10. Gottfried Arnold, hrsg., *VITAE PATRUM Oder: Das Leben Der Altväter und anderer Gottseliger Personen Auffs Neue erläutert und Vermehret,* (HALLE/ in Verlegung des Waysen-Hauses/ 1700).

11. *Das Leben Der Gläubigen Oder: Beschreibung solcher Gottseligen Personen/welche in denen Letzten 200. Jahren sonderlich bekandt worden ausgefertigt von Gottfried Arnold* (Halle, 1701; Andere Auflage . . . HALLE, In Verlegung des Waysen-Hauses, 1732).

12. *HISTORIA ET DESCRIPTIO THEOLOGIAE MYSTICAE, Seu THEOSOPHIAE ARCANAE ET RECONDITAE, item veterum & Novorum MYSTICORVM,* (FRANCOFVRTI apvd Thomam Fritsch Anno MCDII); *Historie und beschreibung der mystichen Theologie/oder geheimen Gottes Gelehrtheit/wie auch derer alten und neuen MYSTICORVM* (Franckfurt bey Thomas Fritschen/ 1703).

13. On Sandaeus see Joseph de Guibert, *The Jesuits: Their Spiritual Doctrine and Practice,* trans., William J. Young (St. Louis, Mo.: The Institute of Jesuit Studies, 1972), 331. For theological information on mysticism Arnold consulted as well Sandaeus' *Pro Theologia Mystica Clavis,* (Coloniae Agrippiane Ex Officina Gualteriana Anno Societatis Iesv Seculari, M. DC. XL).

14. On Arnold and Ruusbroec see my "The Use of Ruusbroec in German Protestantism," XIth International Colloquium, Instituut voor Middeleeuwse Studies, Katholicke Universiteit Leuven, May 20, 1981.

15. *Wahre Abbildung Des Inwendigen Christenthums, Nach desen Anfang und Grund, Fortgang oder Wachsthum, und Ausgang oder Ziel in Lebendigen Glauben und Gottseligen Leben/Aus den Zeugniszen und Exempeln der gottseligen Alten zur Fortsetzung und Erläuterung Der Abbildung der Ersten*

Christen dargestellet (Frankfurt, 1709; reprint Leipzig Bey Benjamin Walthern, 1732) [Hereafter WAIC]. Note also his use of medieval authors in *Die Abwege, Oder Irrungen und Versuchungen gutwilliger und Frommer Meschen, aus Beystimmung des gottseligen Alterthums angemercket* (Franckfurt, bey Thomas Fritschen, 1708), and his edition *Thomas von Kempis Geistliche Scriften, so wol die vier Bücher Von der Nachfolge Christi, als auch dessen anderer in vier und zwantzig Büchern bestehende Betrachtunge . . . Nebst einem historischen Vorbericht und Einleitung Gottfried Arnolds . . .* (Leipzig und Stendal, 1712, 2 Aufl.; Leipzig, bey Samuel Benjamin Walthern, 1733).

16. *WAIC*, I, 1:7-8 cites Bernard, *De diligendo deos* and Harphius, *Theologia Mystica*, and quotes from Ruusbroec's *Vanden Gheesteliken Tabernakel* (hereafter: *Tabernakel*), 19 and *Brulocht*, III, 4, and Suso's *Buchlein der Ewigen Weisheit*, 9. All references to Ruusbroec when quoted are to the German translation of G.J.C. as published in 1701 and used by Arnold in his *Wahre Abbildung*. The 1701 edition follows the Surius translation in its divisions of the Ruusbroec text. The respective Surius chapter numbers are indicated in the margins to Jan van Ruusbroec, *Werken*, ed., J.B. Poukens *et al.*, (Tielt; Drukkerij-Uitgeverij Lannoo, 1944-1948). For Suso see Heinrich Seuse, *Schriften*, hrsg., Karl Bihlmeyer (Stuttgart, 1907; reprint, Frankfurt am Main: Minerva GMbH, 1961).

17. *WAIC*, I, 1:19 reference to Ruusbroec, *Spiegel*, 17, *Beghinen*, 21.

18. *WAIC*, I, 5:3 quotes from Johann Tauler, *Predigten auf alle Sonn-und Feyertage . . .* nebst einer Vorrede Herrn. D. Philipp Jacob Speners . . . (Franckfurt am Main und Leipzig/Verlegts Johann Friedrich Gleditsch/Im Jahr Cristi 1703) 1176.

19. *Formula of Concord*, I, 3 in *Concordia Triglotta* (St Louis, Mo.: Concordia, 1921), 863.

20. *WAIC*, I, 1:22-23.

21. *WAIC*, I, 6:3, 16-17 refers to the *Theologia deutsch*, 2, 3, 4, 5, 22, and 34, and quotes from the 1703 Tauler, 283, and the *Nachfolgung des armen Lebens Christi*, sections 30 and 125 as printed in the 1703 Tauler, Cf. as well *WAIC*, I, 6:5 and 24.

22. *WAIC*, I, 7:15 quotes from Ruusbroec, *Tabernakel*, 48 and the 1703 Tauler, 707.

23. *WAIC*, I, 7:20-21 quotes from Ruusbroec, *Van VII Trappen* (hereafter: *Trappen*), 3 and the 1703 Tauler, 435, 503. *WAIC*, I, 7:24, quotes from Ruusbroec, *Trappen* 19 and the 1703 Tauler, 705, 708.

24. *Formula of Concord*, Epitome II in *Concordia Triglotta*, 787.

25. *Formula of Concord*, Epitome XI in *Concordia Triglotta*, 835.

26. *Ibid.*, 785.

27. *Formula of Concord*, VI in *Concordia Triglotta*, 963.

28. *WAIC*, I, 7:1 and *WAIC*, I, 7:16-24.

29. *WAIC*, I, 11:2 quotes from the 1703 *Tauler*, 777 and the *Medulla*, 63. Cf. *WAIC*, I, 11:11.

30. *WAIC*, I, 13:14, 17, 20 quotes from the 1703 Tauler, 584, 678, Thomas à Kempis, *In Hospitali Pauperum*, 17-18 and William of St. Theirry, *Ad fratres*

de monte dei, 10. WAIC, I, 13:29 quotes from Ruusbroec, *Sloten,* 4 and WAIC, I, 14:2.

31. *WAIC,* I, 14:3, 5, quotes from the 1703 Tauler, 937.

32. *WAIC,* I, 15 quotes extensively from the 1703 Tauler, 134, 187, 220, 284, 682, 1062, 1647; the *Medulla,* 7, 14, 16, 45, 63; the *Nachfolge des armen Lebens Christi,* sections 58, 88, 115, 157; Ruusbroec, *Het Rijck der Ghelieven* 3, 9 and others. *WAIC,* I, 16, quotes from the 1703 Tauler, 45, 88, 257, 632, 939, 1346, 1407, 1507; the Medulla, 29, 59; the *Nachfolge des armen Lebens Christi,* 65, 104, 133; the *Theologia deutsch,* 5; Suso, *Buchlein der ewigen* Weisheit, 16; and Ruusbroec, *Spiegel,* 2.

33. *WAIC,* I, 17-18 quotes extensively from the 1703 Tauler, 226, 450, 473, 474, 477, 813, 897, 1089, 1428-1429; Suso, *Buchlein der ewigen Weisheit;* Ruusbroec, *Spiegel,* 1; Thomas à Kempis, *Liber de mortificatione sui,* 1; *Theologia deutsch,* 48; and the *Imitatio Christi,* III, 9.

34. *WAIC,* II, 1:11 quotes from Ruusbroec, *Het Rijcke der Ghelieven,* 4. *WAIC,* II, 1:12 quotes from the *Medulla,* 14. *WAIC,* II, 1:13-14 quotes from the 1703 Tauler, 479, 1512.

35. *WAIC,* II, 2:22 quotes from Thomas à Kempis, *Sermo ad Novitios,* II, 4.

36. *WAIC,* II 2:27 quotes from Ruusbroec, *Brulocht,* II, 6, 8ff.

37. *WAIC,* II, 5:6-7, 10-11, 13-14, 20-21 quotes from the 1703 Tauler, 187, 429; and Ruusbroec, *Spiegel,* 1.

38. *WAIC,* II, 7:6-8, 13 quotes from Ruusbroec, *Spiegel,* 18; *Brulocht,* III, 2-3; *Dat Rijcke Der Ghelieven,* 25; the *Theologia deutsch,* 53; and the 1703 Tauler, 114.

39. *WAIC,* II, 8-9.

40. *WAIC,* III, 3:3-5 quotes from Ruusbroec, *Beghinen,* 16, 23; *Spiegel,* 17.

41. *WAIC,* III, 3:10-11 quotes from Ruusbroec, *Tabernakel,* 19; and Ruusbroec, *Brulocht,* II, 59.

42. *WAIC,* III, 5:11, 14, 16, quotes from the 1703 Tauler, 464, 1513.

43. *WAIC,* III, 8:4 quotes from the 1703 Tauler, 189. *WAIC,* III, 8:5-7 quotes from Ruusbroec, *Tabernakel,* 163; *Beghinen,* 77. *WAIC,* III, 8:12-14 quotes from the 1703 Tauler, 213; Ruusbroec, *Brulocht,* II, 20. *WAIC,* III, 8:23-24 cites Ruusbroec, *Tabernakel,* 17, 156; Suso, *Buchlein der ewigen Weisheit,* 7, 20. Cf. *WAIC,* III, 8:19-20. *WAIC,* III 8:25-30 quotes from Ruusbroec, *Trappen,* 9, 12; *Sloten,* 13; the Franckfurt 1703 Tauler, 1170; *Imitatio Christi,* III, 5. WAIC, III, 9 which quotes from the 1703 Tauler, 206 974, 1673; Ruusbroec, *Brulocht,* II, 5, 19, 20, 24, 25; and others.

44. *WAIC,* III, 10:1.

45. For discussion see Leopold Naumann, *Untersuchungen zu Johann Taulers Deutschen Predigten* (Halle a.S.: Druck von Ehrhardt Karras, 1911), 49. The sermon is that printed in Ferdinand Vetter, hrsg., *Die Predigten Taulers* (Berlin, 1910; reprint, Dublin and Zurich: Weidmann, 1968), 7-12.

46. *WAIC,* II, 12:7.

47. *WAIC,* II, 12:8.

48. *WAIC,* II, 12:12. On Tauler citation see *Die Predigten Johann Taulers* hrsg., Ferdinand Vetter (Berlin, 1910), 277-278.

49. *WAIC,* I, 1:20, I, 6:25-26; and II, 12:14-15.

50. Vetter, 331. On Tauler's use of *grunt* see Claire Champollion, 'Le vocabulaire de Tauler' in *La mystique rhénane*, (Paris, 1965) 189; and note Dietrich M. Filthaut, hrsg., *Johannes Tauler: Ein deutscher Mystical* (Essen: Hans Driewer, 1961) 122ff.

51. Vetter, 80, 117, 137, 347; Cf. Vetter, 357.

52. Vetter, 20, 114, 199, 204, 239, 298, 368, 421.

53. Vetter 331. Cf. Schlüter in Filthaut, 129-133 for discussion and numerous references in Tauler on the subject.

54. Vetter, 92-93; Cf. Vetter, 97, 100, 158, 302, 323, 364-365.

55. *WAIC*, I, 6:9-10.

56. *WAIC*, I, 15:36-37.

57. *WAIC*, I, 14:9 and 15:5. WAIC, I, 12:33-34; I, 14:23; I, 15:24-27; III, 11:23; III, 12:5-7; *TE*, 59:32; 60:26, 29; 72:56; 82:24.

58. E.J. Tursley, 'Some Principles for Reconstructing a Doctrine of the Imitation of Christ', *Scottish Journal of Theology*, 25 (1972) 47. Cf. the discussion by Jürgen Moltmann, 'Geschichtstheologie und pietistisches Menschenbild bei Johann Coccejus und Theodor Undereyck', *Evangelische Theologie*, 9 (1959) 343-361.

59. *WAIC*, III, 7:8 quotes from Ruusbroec, *Tabernakel*, 19. *WAIC*, III, 7:8 quotes from Suso, *Büchlein der ewigen Weisheit*, 5 Cf. *WAIC*, III, 7:9-11.

60. Philipp Jacob Spener, *Pia desideria* trans. by Theodore G. Tappert (Philadelphia: Fortress, 1964), 39, 40, 69, 71-73, 125.

61. *Ibid.*, 75.

62. See, for example, *Des hocherleuchteten ... D Joh. Tauleri Predigten ... Nebst einer Vorrede Herrn D. Philipp Jacob Speners* ... (Franckfurt am Main und Leipzig: Johann Friedrich Gleditsch, 1703), A2-A4.

63. Note Philipp Jakob Spener, *Hauptschriften* hrsg., Paul Grünberg (Gotha: Friedrich Andreas Perthes, 1889), 233-34 and his *Theologische Bedencken* (Halle: in Verlegung des Waisenhauses, 1700-1702), I, 63, 279; II, 698; III, 164; IV, 358, 367, 502. One must of course also consider Zinzendorf's far more irenic attitude, but even he was primarily concerned with other Protestant denominations. See A.J. Lewis, *Zinzendorf, the Ecumenical Pioneer* (London: SCM, 1962).

64. Schmidt, 99-100.

CISTERCIAN PUBLICATIONS INC.

TITLES LISTING

THE CISTERCIAN FATHERS SERIES

THE CISTERCIAN STUDIES SERIES

Temporarily out of Print   †Forthcoming

* *Temporarily out of print*   † *Forthcoming*

Temporarily out of print   † *Forthcoming*

N.